Routledge Revivals

The Origins of Theosophy

Annie Besant is primarily remembered as the international president of the Theosophical Society. One of the most important aspects of her career were the years that she was a professional atheist, which has given her a place in history as a pioneer feminist. *The Origins of Theosophy* contains thirteen of Besant's pamphlets, originally published from 1883-1890, and an introduction outlining Besant's career by J. Gordon Melton. This book is ideal for students of theology.

The Origins of Theosophy

Annie Besant – The Atheist Years

Annie Besant

Edited with an Introduction by J. Gordon Melton

Routledge
Taylor & Francis Group

First published in 1990
A reprint of thirteen pamphlets from 1883-1890
by Garland Publishing

This edition first published in 2015 by Routledge
2 Park Square, Milton Park, Abingdon, Oxon, OX14 4RN
and by Routledge
711 Third Avenue, New York, NY 10017

Routledge is an imprint of the Taylor & Francis Group, an informa business

Publisher's Note
The publisher has gone to great lengths to ensure the quality of this reprint but points out that some imperfections in the original copies may be apparent.

Disclaimer
The publisher has made every effort to trace copyright holders and welcomes correspondence from those they have been unable to contact.

A Library of Congress record exists under LC control number: 89027987

ISBN 13: 978-1-138-82452-2 (hbk)
ISBN 13: 978-1-315-74012-6 (ebk)
ISBN 13: 978-1-138-82512-3 (pbk)

The Origins of Theosophy

Annie Besant—The Atheist Years

Edited with an introduction by
J. GORDON MELTON

GARLAND PUBLISHING
New York London
1990

Library of Congress Cataloging-in-Publication Data

Besant, Annie Wood, 1847–1933.
[Selections. 1990]
Annie Besant : the atheist years / edited with an introduction by J. Gordon Melton.
p. cm. — (Cults and new religions)
"Reprint of thirteen pamphlets from 1883–1890."
ISBN 0-8240-4366-9 (alk. paper)
1. Atheism. 2. Free thought.
I. Melton, J. Gordon. II. Title. III. Series.
BP585.B3A25 1990
211'.8—dc20 89-27987

Printed on acid-free, 250-year-life paper

Manufactured in the United States of America

Contents

INTRODUCTION

Freethought, the Parent of Modern Occultism

Annie Besant is primarily remembered as the international president of the Theosophical Society, but as her capable biographer Arthur H. Nethercott [1] noted, she lived many "lives"—any one of which might have been more than enough for most people. One of the most important episodes in Besant's career, her years as a professional atheist, gave her a permanent place in the history books as a pioneer feminist. She also emerged as an important exponent of atheist ideas though today that aspect of her life is largely ignored and her atheist writings largely forgotten. Theosophists, while acknowledging her atheist past consider it at best a brief relatively unimportant phase of her pilgrimage to Truth.

Though a struggling minority in a theistic culture, contemporary atheists have been content to forget one of their most articulate advocates because in the end she found atheism inadequate and left it for what she considered something better, theosophy. Twentieth century atheists are scandalized as much by their occult stepchild as they are by Christian supernaturalism, and having disowned their daughter, established the committee for the Scientific Investigation of the Paranormal through which they have turned on her with the same passion that it have traditionally vented on Christianity.

This collection of some of Besant's most important atheist works has been compiled not only to document Besant's transition from Christian to freethinker to theosophist but to illustrate the cultural transition freethought provided to the many who used it to liberate themselves from traditional religion and as the beginning point of a pilgrimage to a new faith in one of the many forms of emerging occultism. Besant, the wife of an Anglican clergyman, rejected her husband's faith and then, as these pamphlets demonstrate, turned all her oratorical skills upon the intellectual destruction of it. But Besant's freethought atheism, however much it paid lip service to a positive presentation of its worldview, in practice accepted the destructive task *contra* theism in general and Christianity in particular as its basic chore. Rather than building atheism as a viable positive philosophy offering new insight on art and culture, love and human endeavor, and social programs to alleviate suffering, most atheists limited their activity largely to attacking what they saw as the all-pervasive oppressive Christian worldview.

While Besant explored freethought, the Theosophical Society (founded in 1875) was slowly spreading through the English-speaking world from America to India to England. It found itself in full agreement with freethought's attack upon orthodox established Christianity. But where atheism limited itself, theosophy really began. Leaving behind the Christian baggage, thanks in no small part to freethought, theosophy created a new non-theistic world using Eastern and occult ideas. It provided a positive alternative filling the vacuum created by the destructive work of the freethought movement, and as freethought declined it emerged into a worldwide movement, under Annie Besant, the former freethought leader.

Later, as she matured in her theosophical endeavors, still without leaving her atheist sentiments entirely behind, Besant could even develop a new appreciation for Christianity. Though what she would describe as *Esoteric Christianity* (1901) would be largely unrecognizable by orthodox Christians, through it she nurtured the revival of a gnostic Christianity against which she had fought so hard. But theosophy was attractive to her in part because it made no intellectual demand to disown the great majority of what she had written as an atheist while providing the satisfying spiritual life completely absent in atheism. Additionally, without violating either her atheist past or the Eastern orientation of Theosophy, she even discovered a means of incorporating the powerful Christian symbols so revered in her native land. Thus, as with so many occultists, Besant's atheist years become an important bridge on which she walked from belief in unbelief straight to the acceptance of a new faith.

The atheist years of Besant also coincide with the climactic years of the freethought movement. Producing some of its greatest work in the last half of the nineteenth century, the movement would pass from the scene as its great exponents died out, or like Besant moved on to other movements. Most of the freethought emphases would be taken over by the emerging Marxist movement while the rest would go into the Occult Revival. The 1880s, for example, would be the time when clergymen and their university-educated sons, strongly affected by freethought and modern science, would create the Society for Psychical Research as a way out of their skepticism. Only a remnant of the freethought movement would be left to provide a non-Marxist atheist voice in twentieth-century rationalism and humanism.

Annie Besant (1847–1897)

Annie Besant was born in London on October 1, 1847. Her mother raised her in a pious environment whose strong influence was manifest in her choice of Frank Besant, a priest in the Church of England, as a husband. The marriage was a brief one, however. During her early married years she increasingly absorbed skeptical notions of orthodox Christianity and refused to keep her views to herself, a continual embarrassment to her husband and a source of constant tension between them. In 1873 she moved out and took the two children with her.

Now on her own, she began to write essays on her blasphemous views. These brought her into contact with Charles Bradlaugh, editor of the *National Reformer* and the most well-known atheist (freethinker) of the period. They became friends and she joined the National Secular Society which he headed. She began to lecture for him, and at her first public appearance outlined her views on the "Political Rights of Women." In 1876, they formed a partnership, the Freethought Publishing Company, and decided to attack Victorian convention by publishing Knowlton's *The Fruits of Philosophy*, which among other things advocated birth control. The trial, though the case was lost, established Besant's position as a national personality. She defended herself, and even her enemies had to admit to her skill behind the platform.

After the trial she took up the banner of atheism with a new fire and during the 1880s and into the 1890s, by which time she had become a devout theosophist, she continued to lecture on freethought themes. In the 1880s she made the acquaintance of George Bernard Shaw, who influenced her in socialist directions. Bradlaugh forced her to choose between her continued partnership with him and her interests with Shaw's Fabian Society. She chose the latter and in 1887 resigned as coeditor of the *National Reformer*, though she remained as vice-president of the National Secular Society and active as a freethought lecturer.

In 1888 she was given a copy of Helena P. Blavatsky's *The Secret Doctrine*. This massive two volume tome was HPB's magnum opus as theoretical founder/leader of theosophy. Through reading the book and meeting with Blavatsky, Besant became thoroughly converted to theosophy, and became Blavatsky's ardent disciple in the few years left to HPB's life. Following Blavatsky's death in 1891, Besant became head of the Esoteric Section, a separate fraternity made up of members of the society who were Blavatsky's personal occult students. From her introduction to theosophy in 1888, Besant had in a mere three years become one of the most powerful people in the society.

The next decade was taken up with organizational matters. She represented theosophy at the World's Parliament of Religions in Chicago in 1893. She carried on a running feud with William Q. Judge, one of the society's founders who was in charge of the American branch and who in 1895 took the overwhelming portion of the membership with him when he declared the American Section autonomous. Her charisma and oratorical skills were a great asset as she began to work with the small remnant to rebuild. She lived to see the American lodges loyal to her thrive and the American branch eventually overtake the autonomous society in membership.

Besant's freethinking background came through once she settled in India in the late 1890s. She began several reform crusades especially in the area of education for women and in political independence for India. She became president of the Indian Nationalist Congress. Though theosophy would not continue her social and political thrust after her death, her activities had a permanent affect on India.

Besant and Atheism

Besant's atheist sentiments reach into the early years of her marriage, but her atheist career really begins after she left her home and began to write articles in a freethought vein. After meeting Bradlaugh and joining the National Secular Society, and even more so after the trial in 1877, atheism was her life and her means of livelihood. She wrote for the *National Reformer*, spoke frequently, and when the occasion presented itself engaged in that significant form of entertainment, the debate. She established herself as a platform speaker and first class debater. Most of her publications through the 1880s, as illustrated in this volume, would be transcripts of her lectures and presentations at debates. By 1880, when the first of the pamphlets reprinted below appeared, she had honed her skills and mastered all of the common nineteenth-century atheist arguments against Christianity.

In encountering these lectures and debates, one is immediately thrown back into a world that is largely foreign to the late twentieth century West. It is a world, prior to the twentieth century technological revolution, in which science offers the promise of discovering Truth (not merely a large number of truths). More important than truth, science promises progress, not just technological progress, but human progress, the creation of a new world. That promise would, of course, be left behind for Europe on the battlefields of World War I and for North America in the succession of wars and economic depressions through the twentieth century. But in the 1880s, in the name of science and its handmaiden freethought, Besant can constantly challenge Christianity as a barrier to progress. She picks up this theme in the first lecture in this collection, *The Gospel of Christianity and the Gospel of Freethought* and returns to it frequently.

In the 1883 lecture, *The Gospel of Christianity and the Gospel of Freethought*, Besant begins with a comment by an Anglican bishop in which he spoke of the "Gospel of Science." She uses the comment to build a picture of Christianity as offering a "good news" in the form of a fantasy while science deals neither in good news nor bad news, merely truth. That truth will come to some as good news and some as sad news. But based upon that truth is a new gospel—freethought, which is a gospel, good news to those currently trapped in Christianity. Christianity offers deliverance from the wrath of God and sin. Besant's argument is that Christianity is a false good news. It is good news only in the sense that it offers deliverance from an evil it has first created, and the deliverance it offers is for the future, not the real life of people in the world today. As such it turns people from the present world to the afterlife and causes them to endure patiently unnecessary evils.

The Christian Creed is one of Besant's most comprehensive presentations of her problem with Christianity. She attacks her former faith on two grounds. She is offended by Christianity's alignment with the state in order to punish those who deviate in matters of belief. For non-belief Christianity promises damnation while the law offers imprisonment. It was, at the time, a matter of law should anyone publish blasphemous material, items which contain any "ludicrous matter relating to God, Jesus Christ, or the Bible, or the formularies of the Church of England . . ." But this offense is compounded by the impossibility of having confidence in a book which she finds is so full of contradictions, errors, inconsistencies and absurdities. To believe the Bible she contends is to disregard all that science has uncovered and reject any pure moral standards in the face of the barbarous events condoned by the God of the Bible. The Bible, she contends is not of divine authority, it is a rather base human product.

In *The Christian Creed*, one can gain some sense of the passion of the atheist attack upon the pre-modern approach to the Bible that dominated Christianity prior to the development of modern Biblical criticism. Twentieth century Biblical critics have stolen much of the thunder of the freethought attack both in their development of critical tools which Besant and her colleagues hardly imagined (form criticism, for example) and adding to its understanding of any "divine" nature the Scripture might possess, a radical discernment of its very human historically-conditioned authorship. In so doing the modernist critic accepted much of the attack upon the Bible initiated by hostile critics such as Besant, but blunted it by accepting the Bible as a product of its past, often a very brutal past.

The importance of *The Christian Creed*, as indeed of the other Besant pamphlets, however, comes not so much from following the logic of her argument, as well-argued as it is, but from entering into the situation of her delivery of this lecture to an audience that had not heard it all before and for whom its arguments had both practical and immediate consequences. Besant brings all of her not inconsiderable oratorical skills to bear in compiling what by themselves might seem like minor points. One by one she lifts each into the spotlight, just long enough for the listener to catch the internal contradiction, the scientific absurdity, or the moral offense she is suggesting, and catch a bit of the picture of the Bible's God she is carefully preparing with each example. Quickly going on the next point, she overwhelms the listener with the sheer number of problems. Back in the pastor's study or seminarian's class room, the problems raised by Besant could be handled to the believers' satisfaction, but in the lecture hall the attack was devastating. In the course of an hour Besant posed enough problems to keep the Bible student busy for a year in creating solutions.

Debating the Faith

The Jesus of the Gospels and the Influences of Christianity are transcriptions of two debates between Besant and a minister. In reflecting upon the debate, some prior consideration should be given to both the educational and the entertainment role of nineteenth-century religious debates. During the century, in both England and America, such debates attained their pinnacle in popularity with religious leaders and the general public. They are not to be confused with the academic debates and theological disputations; these were designed for the lay public. At best they could be highly informative, such as Besant's debates with the Rev. Hatchard. More often than not, they were merely entertaining at the expense of serious consideration of genuine religious issues being raised. An example of this type of debate is seen below in Besant's debate with the Rev. Rowe on "The Teachings of Christianity."

The debate with Hatchard raised two questions that were vital issues a century ago, but have largely lost their impact in the late-twentieth century, though they are still a matter of heated discussion in the small organized atheist/humanist community. Many religious people today are quite unaware that beyond their attack upon the divinity of Jesus, a number of atheists have also argued that in fact Jesus never existed, that he is a mythical figure. The reason for the relative obscurity of this secondary claim, of course, is the difficulty of involving people, even the learned, in the debate. Anyone can read the Bible and consider at whatever level of sophistication they are at to judge the rationality of the miracle stories, the acceptability of the Bible's teachings, or the believability of the resurrection accounts. Consideration of the historicity of Jesus, on the other hand, demands some familiarity with both the philosophical issues involved in arriving at historical judgments, as well as a number of obscure ancient texts, some of which it is claimed make supportive extra-biblical references to Jesus.

The debate over the historicity of Jesus in England, and to a lesser extent North America, was contemporaneous with the high priority given to the work among continental scholars labeled the "search for the historical Jesus." As that debate exhausted itself, and was replaced by debates on the relative importance of the historical Jesus to Christianity and the extent of our knowledge about him, the debate over his existence lost its force. Also, in the meantime, the number of documents about which an expert on this issue would have to be aware has greatly increased in the intervening decades. However, in this debate, one can see the several questions upon which this debate, which must be called a draw, hinged.

The question of whether or not Christianity has been a good or bad influence upon the world has also lost its force as a debating point again lost in the world of philosophies of history. Christianity, under attack in previous centuries for the barbarities of the inquisition, has seen them pale in significance beside the barbarities of the Nazi Holocaust, the Stalinist purges, and other recent genocidal atrocities. On the other hand, the Christian historian has been more concerned with colleagues who deny any important role to religion (Christianity included) in history than to those who assign Christianity a negative role.

The second debate included in this selection is an entertaining debate on "The Teachings of Christianity." Entertaining is the appropriate adjective. The debate is merely a fencing match, dependent upon the questions of varying definitions, proof texting of the Bible, and only indirect confrontation between the two speakers. People could attend such a debate, cheer for their side whenever it scored a point, and have a delightful hour afterward rating the two opponents and deciding who won. Such debates have largely died out, surviving in the present time only as an anachronistic form occasionally dusted off and revived for an evening by the conservative fundamentalist Christian churches and in the minuscule non-Marxist atheist groups.

Atheist Discourses

This collection also includes a number of lectures which pick up selected points for further exploration and completion of Besant's atheist perspective presented in the debates, and longer discourses such as *The Christian Creed.* For example, while traditional Christianity is obviously the major enemy of freethought, Besant lets it be known that other current theistic options are no better. In *The World and Its Gods*, for example, she catalogs a number of alternative belief systems, including Hinduism, upon which she would later draw for her theosophical perspective, and dismisses each. She also would note the one possible challenge to traditional Christianity arising in England, the new non-traditional liberal theism which attempts to transcend a particular tradition by affirming the essential truth of all religion—God and the afterlife. In *A World Without God*, Besant turns to this liberalism, the lowest common denominator religion. The object of Besant's attack is a Miss Frances Power Cobbe, a self-described theist, who in the arena with Besant is simply mismatched. Cobbe attempts to define an essential religion but supplies neither evidence nor logic to back her choices nor the opinions which flow from them. Besant simply demolishes her argument rather mercilessly.

In other lectures, Besant seems to be centering on particular problems upon which freethinkers were called upon to comment. *Life, Death and Immortality* treats the despair over the finality of death, and in *Biblical Biology* she rejects any defense of the Bible as not being intended to speak factually on scientific questions. *The Fruits of Christianity* again picks up the theme of human progress and recounts Christianity's harmful effect upon the race. In *A Burden of Labor* and *A Creature of Crown and Parliament*, Besant ventures into what would become a dominant theme of twentieth-century atheism, the separation of church and state, by which atheists would intend the withdrawal of not only any government financial and legal support of a particular institution such as the Church of England, but the removal of any approbation of religion by the state.

In her last atheist essay, *Christian Progress*, she returns to one of her favorite themes, the problem of human progress and Christianity's role in retarding it. More important than the content, however, is the timing. This essay, released in 1890, comes several years after her conversion to theosophy and provides further evidence of the compatibility she found between the freethought past and the theosophical world she was entering.

Finally, in a most important essay, *Why I Don't Believe in God*, Besant offers what can be considered a personal credo of her atheist phase. It was published just prior to her encounter with Blavatsky and theosophy. She covers seriatim the various arguments being offered in her day for the existence of God and of course finds them wanting. She opens and closes by conceding her minority status, but also affirms that the social abuse she has experienced because of her atheism carries no impact upon her intellect. Thus she can affirm:

> I do not believe in God. My mind finds no grounds on which to build up a reasonable faith. My heart revolts against the spectre of an Almighty Indifference to the pain of sentient beings. My conscience rebels against the injustice, the cruelty, the inequality, which surrounds me on every side. But I believe in man. In man's redeeming power; in man's remoulding energy; in man's approaching triumph, through knowledge, love, and work.

But within a year she found theosophy, and her credo would go the way of the world.

J. Gordon Melton

THE

GOSPEL OF CHRISTIANITY,

AND THE

GOSPEL OF FREETHOUGHT.

BY

ANNIE BESANT.

LONDON:
FREETHOUGHT PUBLISHING COMPANY,
63, FLEET STREET, E.C.
1883.

PRICE TWOPENCE.

THE GOSPEL OF CHRISTIANITY

AND THE

GOSPEL OF FREETHOUGHT.

"I WILL not inquire," once said the Bishop of Peterborough, speaking to a large audience of Christians, "I will not inquire whether this gospel be true or false; I will only ask if it be good news." His Lordship was speaking of what he was pleased to call the Gospel of Science. I am a little at a loss to know to what the Bishop alluded in this sentence; Science can scarcely be said to pretend that her work is to proclaim a *gospel* to the world; it is hers to gaze up into the illimitable skies, and to describe to the dwellers on our earth the marvellous worlds which roll through the pure ether; it is hers to peer into the illimitable depths of existence, revealed through the microscope, and to report to us her discoveries of the fairy-lands which are hidden from our rough eye-sight in the drop of water, or in the down on an insect's wing; it is hers to scan earth's surface, and to sound the depths of ocean; to read in the records of the rocks the age of our world, or to translate the language of the hidden sea-bottom into words intelligible to us; it is her glory to search after the laws which "bind Nature fast in fate," to discover facts, to proclaim them to mankind; but I never heard it claimed for Science that she pretended to be the evangelist to men of a new gospel, or that she ever waited to ask, ere declaring some freshly-discovered fact, "is it good news?" Science worships Truth alone; her steady gaze is fixed upon the Real; she never glances aside to follow expediency. Her work is to declare what *is;* she leaves to others to say what ought to be. Pure, serene, unwavering, Science walks through this world of ours; a grand, clear, dry, light—illumining all dark places; revealing, with equal lucidity, beautiful facts and ugly facts; as the rays of the sun fall alike on gorgeous palace and on filthy hovel, on fair and happy faces, and on those ploughed deep with the lines of misery and want, so does the sunlight of Science throw clear beams on the glory of Nature, and illuminate with equal brightness its stains and its dark blots. "The gospel of Science," then, is a discovery which we owe to the supernatural vision of the Bishop of Peterborough. He takes some of the saddest revelations of Science; he points out how all Nature's order is based upon destruction; he shows how the iron chain of invariable sequence is never broken for human tears or human shrieks; he dwells on the fact that in Nature the weak must perish, while the strong survive to perpetuate their race: all these truths are dilated upon by the Bishop of Peterborough, and then he turns sharply round upon his appalled and shrinking hearers, and says: "I will not ask whether this be true or false; I will only ask if it be good news."

His Lordship of Peterborough has "digged a pit, and has fallen himself into the destruction which he made for other." Science, I have said, only claims to discover and to reveal facts; good or bad, she tells them out with equal clearness. But mark you, she reveals only that which she finds. These harsh things said about Nature by Dr. Magee are *true* things; the whole fabric of Nature is built up upon a principle of death; the destruction of one creature is the salvation of another; the death of one is the life of another; the anguish of one is the pleasure of another; the torture of one is the amusement of the other. See the panther drop on the neck of the antelope; it is natural for him to do so. See the cat play with the injured mouse; it is natural to her to do so. See the vultures peck at the eyes of the dying buffalo; it is natural to them to do so. Science reveals these facts, with many another, all bearing the same signet. She points out how the earthquake spares not for the shrieks of the terrified people; how the waves smooth not at the cries of the drowning crew; how the fire leaps none the less high for the fierce moan of the burning man. But Science did not make the facts which she reveals. Science is not responsible for the revelation she unfolds. If the news told by Science is bad news, who is to blame for its badness? Answer, Bishop of Peterborough, you who believe in a Creator of the world. Suppose that I dig a mine, and fill it with gunpowder, and lay a train, and set alight the match which will kindle it. I then go away, and leave the match to burn, foreseeing that in due time my gunpowder will explode, and bury a city in ruins. A man comes along, with clear, sharp eyes, noticing all around him; he sees the burning match, but cannot reach it to put it out; he hurries to warn the people of their danger; he shows them how to escape it. Is this man to blame for the danger of explosion, because he has discovered the danger, and not rather I, who am the cause of it? Is Science, then, to blame if the facts she reveals are sad, and not rather the cause of all those facts, he who, according to the Bishop of Peterborough, is the Author of Nature, he who foresaw all, designed all, over-rules all. If Nature is so evil, God, and not Science, is the one to be blamed.

But this is only according to the Bishop of Peterborough. *We* have no slur of this kind to cast on Nature. With many evils inherent in it, the scheme around us is slowly evolving the higher from the lower; mankind are growing gradually into a nobler type; increasing knowledge is enabling us to cope with Nature's rougher moods; nowhere is truer the axiom that "knowledge is power" than when we say that knowledge *of* Nature is power *over* Nature. While the Bishop of Peterborough is forced by his arraignment of Nature to deny either the power or the goodness of the God in whom he believes, we, who believe in no designer, award neither praise nor blame to any being for the order in which we find ourselves; the universe *is*, we are part of it; we can study it, improve it, beautify it, by means of powers inherent in itself; and therefore we meet the dangers in our path with courage, and mend its imperfections by our skill.

The facts around us not being dependent for their existence either upon our knowledge or upon our ignorance, I deny altogether that Science is to blame because much of her revelation to mankind is stern and sad. But there is a foe to Christianity in the battle-field of the world; there is a gospel, which is not Christian, which is being proclaimed to mankind; there is a banner, whose folds are just floating out upon the air of England, which is blazoned with a new heraldry for humanity. It is the gospel of Freethought, the banner of Secularism. This is the gospel which I assert as against the gospel of Christianity; this is the gospel whose superiority to the Christian gospel I am prepared to maintain. On behalf of this gospel I lift from the ground the challenge-gauntlet flung down by the Bishop of Peterborough, and I say that not only is it true, but it is also good news to the world. This gospel is very much bound up with Science, and thus there may have been some confusion about it in the episcopal mind. A rumour may have penetrated to the depths of his palace, which murmured that a foe had arisen against Christianity, and was rapidly progressing, especially among those to whom Christianity had brought no glad tidings of great joy, to be found on earth. The gospel of Freethought is the daughter of Science; the good news she brings is based upon scientific facts; along the path in which she guides the feet of men she holds up the lamp of Science to show the way.

I intend now to lay before you the leading points of these two gospels, so that you may see clearly the advantages of each, and may judge between them; may see which of them has in it most hope for man, most promise for humanity.

The gospel of Christianity is good news because it reveals to us the existence of a God. It tells us of a God who is unlimited in being, but yet limited to a personal existence; unlimited in power, but yet frustrated and checkmated at every step; unlimited in goodness, yet allowing plagues and famines to desolate the world he loves, and the children he cherishes in his "Fatherly Heart;" the author of all things and perfectly holy, yet creator and ruler of a world where evil is found in all directions; a pure spirit, yet possessing face, hands, loins, feet, like a material human being.

The gospel of Freethought knows of no such being as this. Thought cannot think him out: reason cannot found his existence on any known facts; imagination cannot paint his picture, with its contradictory attributes; her colours all run into each other, and make a confused blot. A God of love? that is, a God so loving that he made a world, whose scheme is based on suffering and death; a God so loving that he formed the parents of the human race, and made the future of all mankind depend upon the eating of an apple; a God so loving that he then sent a serpent to tempt the woman whom he had predestined to fall; a God so loving that he drowned the world in his fury, because it was exactly what he had from all eternity designed that it should be; a God so loving that in Egypt he slew the little children, because the king, whose heart he had himself hardened, was hard-hearted; a God so loving that his chosen people slew men, and women, and the little ones even yet unborn, because these poor folks were living in a land coveted by the fierce

Hebrew race; a God so loving that, as he himself says, he deceived his own messengers and put a lying spirit in the mouths of the prophet: a very loving God, truly, yet this is the God of love, whose disappearance would be so terrible a loss to the hearts of his children. A God of wisdom? that is, a wise God who made his master-piece man so badly, that he fell to pieces at the first temptation; a wise God whose whole work had to be destroyed because he had made it so badly that he himself got out of patience with it; a wise God, whose every aim is thwarted both by man and Devil; a wise God, whose wise plans are such a failure, that having drowned the world once, and tried his method over again, he has again failed so dismally that he is going to burn it all up, and make another new heaven and new earth, which, judging by past experience, are as likely to fail as their predecessors. Truly, this God has shown his wisdom very signally. A God of power? that is, a strong God, whose projects are foiled, whose plans are defeated, whose will is not done; a strong God who cannot even guard his poor creatures from a Devil, who appears, if we are to judge by results, to be more widely-present and more powerful than his own Maker. Truly a very strong God. The gospel of Secularism has no God. It sees a great universe, and knows only that it is; it believes in no origin, because there is no reason for such a belief. Uncaused and self-existent Natural order rolls on; the Secularist studies it, because, being himself a part of that order, his happiness lies in conformity with it; he reverences it, as the mother who has given him birth; he recognises the limitations imposed on him by the conditions of his being, and, instead of worshipping the Unknown, he studies it as far as he can, and devotes his whole strength to that for which his faculties fit him.

But the gospel of Christianity is good news because it speaks of a Father in Heaven, and, in painting his fair picture, it forgets the terrible blots with which this same God is disfigured. It appeals to the feeling of weakness and dependence in man, and it is here that its true power lies. A Father whose tender mercies are over all his works? we will believe it when sinking ships, and destroying pestilences, and heart-rending accidents, can be proved never to have taken place. A Father who loves his children? we will believe it when his children no longer starve and pine, when the noblest of the sons of men are no longer outcasts and martyrs, when the bad are no longer princes, and the good no longer hated. A Father who hears the cry of his children? we will believe it when we find that prayer turns aside pain, and grief, and death, when the cry of the mother saves the life of her child, the pleading of the wife gives her dead husband back living to her arms. Hitherto, as has been well said, instead of finding that faith of the size of a grain of mustard-seed will move mountains, we have never yet found faith of the size of a mountain move a grain of mustard-seed. I do not deny that it is pleasant to believe in the existence of a Being who is always at hand to remedy your mistakes, and to save you from the painful consequences of your own actions. But, unfortunately for the Bishop of Peterborough's argument, the goodness or badness of news *does* very materially depend upon its truth or its falsehood. Suppose a man, through folly or through crime, has become bankrupt; it would be very good news for him to be told that on waking up the next morning he would find his fortune as large as ever. But what is the use of the good news if it be not true? This is exactly what the gospel of Christianity does: it goes to the murderer whose life is forfeited, and it says to him: "Jesus has suffered for you, and you will be rewarded with happiness in heaven if you believe in him." No matter how foul the life, Christianity offers to wipe away all past offences, and stop the consequences of all past actions. Mark you, Christians do not live up to their creed in daily life; they do not set the murderer, who is fit company for saints in heaven, free to mingle with them again on earth; they cannot restore the squandered fortune to the spendthrift, or the lost health to the profligate and the drunkard. Facts are too strong for their creed; only in an imaginary world can they promise an imaginary happiness. Friends, against these fair promises of Christianity, Freethought has nothing to offer you. Sternly just, she decrees: laws disregarded strike the transgressor. If you are intemperate in drink or food, then shaking hands, enfeebled brain, ruined constitution, shall teach you that punishment invariably follows on transgression. If you lead impure lives, abusing the good powers given you by Nature, then disease and premature old age shall tell you that natural laws cannot be trifled with without suffering. Secularism, like Nature, is here stern and immutably severe. But if these things are so, is it not well to proclaim them, so that men, knowing the invariable law, may rule their lives well, and live happily? Show me one drunkard, who has first ruined his nerves, and has then steadied his shaking hand by prayer, and I will believe that this Christian doctrine of forgiveness by a loving Father is true and good news. Good news, I admit it to be to the thief, to the outlaw, to the murderer, in the sense that it would be good news to them to be told that all laws were repealed; but good news to the world it is not. Rather most evil news; for it encourages evil by promising escape from deserved punishment; it weakens good by giving to the good and to the bad one equal happiness. But the gospel of Freethought is really good news to the world, though bad news to the evilly-disposed while they refuse to amend their ways; for it warns men to avoid wrong-doing, by pointing out the misery which invariably follows evil; it strengthens men in leading noble lives, by showing them the good results that flow therefrom; it teaches the true path to happiness, by discovering and proclaiming natural laws. Christianity injures the world by condoning evil; Secularism blesses the world by making the happiness of one depend upon the good of all.

The gospel of Christianity is good news because it reveals to us the existence of the Devil. It does not tell us where he came from, or how he became a Devil. It tells us that God is all-holy, and it teaches us that God made good angels: it hints that Satan was a very fine specimen of an angel, a leader among angels, but that, at some indefinite time, he fell and became a Devil. Milton relates the whole affair in detail, but does not inform us how a perfect angel could do wrong of his own accord. In Job we meet Satan when he is half-way through his transformation, and is still quite at home in Heaven, and in fact plots with God to tempt Job. We meet him in the Gospels, where God, in the form of Jesus, still treats him with courteous respect, and argues with him. Later, he becomes a roaring lion and a dragon. What he is like now we are not told. But, as a Secularist, I venture to plead that this is *not* good news at all. The Christian may retort that it is true nevertheless. Then I challenge him for evidence. He can only give the assertion of his gospel: without Christianity we have no proof of the existence of the Devil, and I have, therefore, a right to say that the news is made by Christianity, and is most decidedly bad. Freethought has no Devil. It studies history, and therefore it knows, what most Christians do not know, where this notion of a Devil comes from. We can trace the genealogy of the Christian Devil back a long way. We see him in Persia, co-ruler of the world with God: we meet him in every old faith; light and darkness give birth to the ideas of God and Devil; in Egypt Typhon, the principle of darkness, slays Osiris, the sun, the principle of light. The good and bad in Nature were referred, in the childhood of the world, to two hostile principles; so far as I know, only the earlier Hebrew faith was without an evil Devil. The Hebrew Satan was originally a great and severe angel of God, who tried and tested men to see what they were worth, but this work was done in conjunction with God, as we see him in Job. The Hebrew Satan did not become God's enemy until the Jews had been captive in Babylonia, where their own majestic Satan became painted black, so to speak, and made into an evil spirit. Christianity took up this mingled Devil and darkened him yet more; but it also preserved to him the co-equal power with God given to the Devil in Eastern lore. He became again the principle of evil, struggling always with, and often conquering, the principle of good. All over the world the Devil fights with God for man's soul, and generally wins it. Few there are who are to be saved in heaven, many there are who are to be lost in hell. In the end the Devil triumphs: in spite of God, in spite of the blood of Jesus, in spite of the Holy Spirit, the Devil is to reign for ever over the vast majority of mankind. We decline to think that this news about the Devil is good news. Good news to know that there is an evil spirit ever at our elbow, prompting us to sin? Good news to know that there is a Devil always watching for a chance to seize us? Good news to know that when we die, there will be a Devil waiting to try and catch us and drag us to hell? No. This is bad news of the worst kind. And where is your God of power, O Christian, that he permits himself to be thwarted and set at nought by this Devil? where is your God of love, that he allows his dear children to be enticed into sin by this Devil? Some Christians dislike the Devil so much, that they try to refine him away, and make him into an allegory. But this cannot be allowed, unless they are willing to make God into an allegory too. The two beings must stand or fall together. If there is no need for a Devil to account for the evil in the universe, then there is no need for a God to account for the good in it. If you do not personify the destructive principle in nature, neither must you personify the preservative; there is no evidence for the existence of a God, that does not also prove the existence of a Devil. You must have both, or neither. The gospel of Christianity asserts the existence of both; the gospel of Freethought denies the existence of both. And I affirm that the disproof of the Devil is good news to the world.

The gospel of Christianity is good news, because it brings "life and immortality to light." Now, before I am prepared to say that I can feel grateful for the gift of immortal life, I must know what kind of life it is that is to be bestowed upon me. On this point, at least, Christianity speaks clearly and definitely. Immortality is, this gospel tells us, divided into two kinds; there is eternal life in heaven, and there is eternal death in hell. This heavenly life has not to me, I freely confess, many attractions. I am told that I shall meet there Abraham, Isaac, Jacob, and David; but I do not care to associate with such people. Then there is the penitent thief, but I am not much attracted by him; there are shoals of the people turned out of earth, because they were not thought fit for it, and I am not anxious to make their acquaintance. The best people of history are not there; I must not hope to meet there the bearers of the great names I reverence and honour; heretics of all ages will not be there; philosophers and thinkers will not be there; patriots and reformers will not be there. I may search in vain for the faces I love on earth; not in heaven will be found the deniers of the Godhead, and those brave men who are now fighting for reforms. What then could I do in heaven? Sadly I should walk through the golden streets, and lonely and desolate I should saunter on the banks of the river of life. Then the occupations of heaven are distasteful to me—singing evermore, and playing on a golden harp. Sweet music I should weary of. My brain and heart would cry out for work. Then the city would be comfortless; it would be a cold, dazzling, hard, home. Streets of gold, gates of jewels; barbaric splendour fit to sicken anyone, who loves the cool green of the summer forest, and the soft blue of the pure evening sky. This eternal life has no charms for me; has it any attraction to anyone? Friends, does it not draw its attracting power from the fact that *it is not hell*, from the fact that it is the only alternative of eternal death. In criticising this good news of immortality, I am bound to take into account the fact that there is an immortality of pain and anguish, which this good news tells us is to be the lot of the majority of the human race. Listen to the gospel of Christianity: "Strait is the gate and narrow is the way which leadeth unto life, and few there be that find it. Wide is the gate and broad is the way that leadeth to destruction, and many there be which go in thereat." So says Jesus himself. Hear the Roman Catholic Church; hear Spurgeon; hear the English Church in the person of one of her bishops. This is the good news to the world; this is the gospel of Christianity. Good news to the world that it shall be damned for ever in hell: that it shall be tormented with fire and brimstone in the presence of the Lamb for ever and ever, and the smoke of their torment ascendeth up for ever and ever, and they have no rest day nor night. Strange minds and hearts must Christians have if they really consider this horrible gospel to be good news. I marvel sometimes where this gospel of hell-fire had its birth; in what poor human heart, wrung with passionate hatred to mankind, embittered and soured by terrible wrongs, fired with fierce longing for revenge, did this awful phantom first take shape and form? Who first imaged out this ghastly notion of a heavenly Moloch, sitting on his throne, and wreaking on men an eternal hatred, mocking the helpless agony of his victims, and in bitter irony forcing them to call him their Father and a God of love. Never let Christianity dare to call itself good news, so long as hell is part of its gospel to mankind; never let it boast of the immortality it proclaims, so long as to the majority of mankind it only proffers an immortality of anguish unspeakable. If this gospel were true—nay, if there were even any probability of its being true—then every man and woman with a human heart would make a stern resolution never again to bring a child into the world who might be doomed to an eternity of suffering; never again would they co-operate with God, so as to form a body which God might thereafter be enabled to curse with the terrible gift of an immortal soul.

The gospel of Secularism has neither heaven nor hell to offer to the world. On the subject of immortality its lips are dumb. Science tells it nothing which points to continued life after death; all analogy is against it; we have never met life apart from organisation; we cannot conceive of mind as apart from matter. Life is, to us, an attribute of matter, under certain conditions, just as brightness is an attribute of the polished steel, sharpness of the pointed iron. But Secularism bids us leave a future life alone. If there is one, we shall get it in due time; if there is not, extinction is far preferable to torture, or to personal happiness while others are being tortured. Fix your eyes upon earth, Freethought says to the Secularist; of this life you are sure: a heaven in the clouds has nothing to do with you *now;* work rather to make a heaven upon earth: do not trouble how to meet a future life; learn rather to live your present life well. It has been justly said: "For a long time men have been taught how to die; what is wanted is, that they should be taught how to live." At any rate, Secularism removes from our sky the brooding, lowering, crowds which have darkened it so long; it clears away from the tomb that terrible shadow which enshrouds it when the Christian lays there the body of some dear relative or beloved friend who has died without faith in God; it quenches the lurid flames which might otherwise affright us when we lie upon our own death-beds, if we have spent our lives in serving man instead of in serving God; it gives us that calm serenity which can quietly do its work here so long as strength holds out, and which, when death calls us, will enable us to lie down and die in peace.

The gospel of Christianity is good news because it comes to sinners with the offer of an Atonement for sin. Man, says Christianity, is lying under the heavy wrath of a justly-offended God, and then Jesus Christ, the Son of God, mercifully comes forward, and bears the punishment of sin for us by being crucified. I am not going to deal now with the subject of the Atonement doctrinally, nor to criticise the justice of its arrangements, or the ingenuity of its design. We are only concerned with it, as a prominent feature of the gospel of Christianity, as *good news* to the world. What benefit does the Atonement, supposed to be wrought by Jesus, confer on the world? "It delivers us from sin and from the wrath of God." That it delivers us from sin, I deny; that it delivers us from the wrath of God is a work of supererogation, if the gospel of Secularism is true. At any rate, it is not good news to be told that we are under the wrath of God; news it is, for we should never have found it out for ourselves; good, it most decidedly is not. The wrath of God is one of the blessings brought to light by the gospel of Christianity. An Atheist may go out into the country in a Sunday excursion-train, he may enjoy the sweet scent of the flowers, and lie at ease on the green turf; he may listen to the rustle of the breeze through the leaves over his head, and hear the melody of the blackbird and the thrush as they warble out their happiness; all around him is, say Christians, the work of God, and all around him is ministering to his pleasure. A Christian comes along, and tells him that he is under the unchanging displeasure of God, and the Atheist feels the caress of the sunbeams, and he laughs at the idea that the Worker should be angry, when the works are so full of joy-giving power. We should never have guessed at the abiding wrath of God, if it had not been for Christianity. Christianity, however, having found the wrath, also finds the peace-offering, and then rejoices over its good news.

I would also have you observe, that all that the gospel of Christianity promises you deliverance from, it first creates; all the dangers it saves you from are pits of its own digging; all the curses it shields you from are arrows which it has first shot at you from its own bow. Search and see if any good thing promised you by Christianity be anything more than deliverance from some evil invented by this so-called gospel. It first puts chains on all your limbs, and then boasts loudly that it can show you how to take them off again. But the gospel of Secularism tells you that you *are* free men; that these chains are only shadowy links, made out of the fog of superstition; it bids you show your manhood by shaking them off you, and by standing fast in that liberty wherewith your nature makes you free. I cannot bid the Bishop of Peterborough farewell—the prelate who has so kindly given me the text of my lecture—without calling your attention to the bribe he offers to the people whom he is endeavouring to retain within the Christian fold. "I will not ask," he says, "if it be true or false; I will only ask whether it be *good* news." It is not often that a Christian speaks out so clearly about his motives in being religious. "I don't care about truth or falsehood; I only want to believe that which is pleasant." I have myself heard the question asked: "Why should I seek for truth, and why should I lead a good life, if there be no immortality, in which to reap a reward?" To this question the Freethinker has one clear and short answer: "There is no reason why you should seek Truth, if to you the search has no attracting power. There is no reason why you should lead a noble life, if you find your happiness in leading a poor and a base one." Friends, no one can enjoy a happiness which is too high for his capabilities; a book may be of intensest interest, but a dog will very much prefer being given a bone. To him whose highest interest is centred in his own miserable self, to him who only cares to gain his own ends, to him who seeks only his own individual comfort, to that man Freethought can have no attraction. Such a man may indeed be made religious by a bribe of heaven; he may be led to seek for Truth, because he hopes to gain his reward hereafter by the search; but Truth disdains the service of the self-seeker; she cannot be grasped by a hand that itches for reward. If Truth is not loved for her own pure sake, if to lead a noble life, if to make men happier, if to spread brightness around us, if to leave the world better than we found it—if these aims have no attraction for us, if these thoughts do not inspire us, then we are not worthy to be Secularists, we have no right to the proud title of Freethinkers. If you want to be paid for your good lives by living for ever, in a lazy and useless fashion, in an idle heaven; if you want to be bribed into nobility of life; if, like silly children, you learn your lesson, not to gain knowledge, but to win sugar-plums, then you had better go back to your creeds and your churches: they are all you are fit for; you are not worthy to be free. But we—who, having caught a glimpse of the beauty of Truth, deem the possession of her worth more than all the world beside; who have made up our minds to do our work ungrudgingly, asking for no reward beyond the results which spring up from our labour—we will spread the gospel of Freethought among men, until the sad minor melodies of Christianity have sobbed out their last mournful notes on the dying evening-breeze, and on the fresh morning winds shall ring out the chorus of hope and joyfulness, from the glad lips of men whom the Truth has at last set free.

I could not forbear making these remarks upon a sentiment so poor, so mean, as that we were to choose our creeds for the sake of their pleasantness; but—although I have not had time to touch upon the many other points in which the gospel of Secularism is better than the gospel of Christianity—I have yet, I hope, said enough to prove that, so far as the *goodness* of the news to the world goes, the advantage is with the message we proclaim. And naturally so. For the theory of Secularism is built up only in reference to the promotion of happiness in this world: if any course does not promote human happiness, then that course is stamped by Secularism as *bad;* if any course promotes human happiness, then that course is stamped by Secularism as *good.* The gospel of Freethought is a proclamation to mankind of their true object in life, and of the means whereby to gain that object. But Christianity, on the other hand, asserts itself as a scheme which is intended to prepare men for a future life elsewhere; for the sake of that future they are to despise the present; for the sake of a crown in heaven they are to carry a cross on earth; if they would live unto God, they must die unto the world. Therefore Christianity has no right to pretend that it is a gospel to men while they are living on the earth; it cannot maintain that it promotes temporal happiness. It turns men's eyes from earth to fix them upon heaven; it bids them be careless of the temporal, while luring them to grasp at the eternal; it makes them less earnest in the present life, by bidding them brood over a life to come; it makes them endure life's wrongs and life's tyrannies with a cowardly patience, in the hope of a glory to be revealed. And therefore this gospel is *not* good for mankind. It is not good news to the poor and the oppressed, because it bribes them to be contented with their poverty, and to remain passive under their oppression; it is not good news for those who love men, because it dooms the greater part of our race to misery unending; it is not good news to the patriot and the reformer, for it tells him that his toil is wasted, being done for a world which is soon to be destroyed. Neither is the gospel of Freethought good news to everybody. But to the world the gospel of Freethought does really bring good news; glad tidings of great joy, which shall be to all nations. It sweeps away all the terrors of the supernatural; it bids men look on earth as their fair heritage, capable of being beautified and cultured, through knowledge and skill and love. It brings tidings of peace, for it educates and refines, and teaches gentleness and brotherhood to all alike. And it brings tidings of freedom; tidings of freedom from political tyranny; tidings of freedom from priestly superstitions; tidings of freedom for heart and for brain; tidings that man shall no longer be a slave, either to a Church or to a King.

London: Printed by ANNIE BESANT and CHARLES BRADLAUGH, 63, Fleet Street, E.C. 1883.

THE

CHRISTIAN CREED;

OR,

What it is Blasphemy to deny.

BY

ANNIE BESANT.

LONDON:
FREETHOUGHT PUBLISHING COMPANY,
63, FLEET STREET, E.C.

1883.

LONDON:
PRINTED BY ANNIE BESANT AND CHARLES BRADLAUGH,
63, FLEET STREET, E.C

THE CHRISTIAN CREED;

Or, What it is Blasphemy to deny.

A STRUGGLE has begun, which promises to be one of the fiercest that this century has seen, between the bigots and persecutors on the one hand and the supporters of free speech on the other.

It appears, then, worth while to look closely into this Christian creed, which claims the right to imprison and torture men of pure life for non-belief in its tenets. Christianity threatens us with persecution here and damnation hereafter if we do not believe its doctrines. "He that believeth not shall be damned," says Jesus. "He that believeth not shall be imprisoned and pick oakum," says Mr. Justice North. The threat of damnation would trouble us little if it stood alone—we could put off consideration of that until we arrived in the other world; but the threat of imprisonment here is unpleasant. If we are to burn for ever hereafter, the Christians might really allow us to enjoy ourselves here; is their malice (like their hell) such a bottomless pit that an eternity of torture is not enough to fill it up?

Let us see what we must believe on peril of damnation and Newgate. (1) We must believe the "Holy Scriptures of the Old and New Testaments to be of divine authority;" (2) we must believe each "one of the persons in the Holy Trinity to be God," while (3) we also believe that there are not "more gods than one;" (4) we must believe the "Christian religion to be true;" we are strictly forbidden to publish any "ludicrous matter relating to God, Jesus Christ, or the Bible, or the formularies of the Church of England as by law established," and are warned that we

A 2

shall not be saved by our remarks being "intended in good faith as an argument against any doctrine or opinion."

(1) We must believe the Holy Scriptures of the Old and New Testament to be of Divine Authority.

This first demand on our faith is a very large one, and can only be met by refusing to read any scientific book, to look at any geological or antiquarian collections, to study any kind of natural knowledge; we must erase from our memories all the facts we have learned about the world; we must reject purity and decency of morals; we must revert to a condition of barbarous ignorance and barbarous conduct before we can believe very many parts of the Holy Scriptures are of divine authority. Still, as we are to be imprisoned and damned for not believing this, we must try, and we had better examine a little more exactly what we are to believe on divine authority. Only some of our imposed feats of *leger-de-foi* will be examined. Those who can accomplish these will not bungle over the rest.

It is of divine authority that god made "a firmament in the midst of the waters" and divided the waters, putting some above it and some below, and this firmament is "heaven" (Gen. i., 6—8). This heaven has windows in it which let the rain through (Gen. vii., 11), and when these windows are closed the rain stops (Gen. viii., 2). It has doors, through which the manna was rained down on the Israelites (Ps. lxxviii., 23, 24). This "sky" is very "strong," as is indeed necessary remembering all it has to support above it, and resembles "a molten looking-glass" (Job. xxxvii., 18). Another reason why it should be very strong is that god has "set" in it the sun, moon and stars. Some of the stars are large and solid, and require a very strong setting.

My unbelieving reader, you may have some difficulty in crediting all this. You may argue that the sky is not strong at all, but is only a vast space, and that to apply the word strong to space shews gross ignorance. Divine authority says the sky *is* strong, and if you persist in believing facts instead of the Bible, you will at least find Newgate strong and its space limited. You may argue that the stars are at very various distances, and cannot all be set in one arching roof resembling a molten looking-glass; that when it rains, the rain is due to condensation of watery vapor within our atmosphere, at a distance of at the most very few miles, and not to the opening of any windows at a distance of many billions of miles; that the firmament must be at least 5,480,490,000,000 miles away, as the stars are set in it, and the nearest fixed star is at that distance, while the furthest is beyond calculation. All these contentions of yours are facts, I admit, but they fly in the teeth of the fictions which are of divine authority; and as Mr. Justice North is armed with full power to vindicate the divine authority, you had better, if you want to keep out of gaol, give up the facts and pretend to believe in the fictions.

It is of divine authority that god made grass and herb and fruit tree on the "third day of creation," the day before he created the sun, two days before he made fishes and birds, and three days before he made animals. In the face of this it is a mere trifle, my dear sceptical reader, that no herb could yield seed, no fruit tree could yield fruit, without the aid of the sun. It is quite true that a plant without the sun-rays can form no chlorophyll; that without chlorophyll no starch, no reparation nor growth of tissues can proceed. What are these mere botanical facts beside the divine authority of the Holy Scriptures? It is also true that in the study of fossils no traces of all these grasses, herbs, and fruit trees are found precedent to all animal life. That the earliest living thing which has left a trace was an animal, not a plant. That fishes precede fruit trees in the fossilised history of the globe, although fruit trees precede fishes in the divinely authoritative fable. These geological facts must follow the botanical, my heretic, and you must be content to take the Holy Scriptures on faith, for they are not even tales founded on fact.

It is of divine authority that sun, moon, and stars were created on the fourth day, after the world had been in existence for three. It is true that to talk of a member of a solar system like our earth as existing three days before the central sun came into being is to talk nonsense. But that is of no importance if the nonsense is of divine authority. It is also true that the light travelling from part of the Milky Way at the rate of 186,000 miles per second would take 9,000 years (Müdler) to reach our earth, so that if the Holy Scriptures are of divine authority we should be unable to hese stars, which we nevertheless do see. Who would rashly put the testimony of everybody's eyes against the authority of this old book written in an unknown tongue, by an unknown author, at an unknown date? If the stars are there, they ought not to be, and if we can see them we ought not to be able to do so. I am not sure that they are not committing a silent and perpetual blasphemy by their very existence; but then Mr. Justice North cannot reach them to put them out, odious as is the outrage they commit on the feelings of the Christian public, and I doubt if the sentence of damnation threatened by Jesus would run in that distant spot.

It is of divine authority that on the 6th day of creation, just 5,887 years ago, god created man, male and female. It is true that man has left his bones in the ground as a record of his existence hundreds of thousands of years ago, although he has only existed during 5,887 years. But that was a thoughtless and irreverent action on his part, which cannot be allowed to have any weight as compared with the divine authority of the Holy Scriptures. Men should not leave their bones about in caves and drifts as arguments for the wicked unbeliever and puzzles for the faithful soul.

It is of divine authority that everything was once created in two different ways, perfectly incompatible the one with the other, and both equally true. The two stories of the creation are mutually exclusive; but, as they are both of divine authority, both must be believed, on peril of prison here and of damnation hereafter. It is blasphemy to deny that the world was covered with water, so that god was obliged to gather it away into one place to let the land appear, which forthwith brought forth from its moist surface herb and grass and tree (Gen. i., 12), and that the world was at the same time so dry that god could not set in it the herb and plant which he had previously made (Gen. ii., 5). It is blasphemy to deny that the vegetation was brought forth by the earth itself at the mere command of god: "Let the earth bring forth grass," etc. (Gen. i., 11). It is also blasphemy to deny that "the Lord God made . . . every plant of the field before it was in the earth, and every herb of the field before it grew," and that the reason for this creation before planting was that "the Lord God had not caused it to rain upon the earth, and there was not a man to till the ground" (Gen. ii., 5).

It is blasphemy to deny that god made man, the last of his works, after the earth was clothed with vegetation, after the seas were filled with life, and after fowl were flying in the air, and beasts and cattle and creeping things were roaming over the earth (Gen i., 11, 12, 20—27). It is also blasphemy to deny that god made man, the first of his works, before any vegetation was growing on the earth, before a single fowl of the air or a single beast of the field was made (Gen ii., 5, 7, 8, 9, 19).

It is blasphemy to deny that god commanded the "waters" to "bring forth abundantly the moving creature that hath life, and fowl that may fly above the earth" (Gen. i., 20). It is also blasphemy to deny that "out of the ground the Lord God formed . . . every fowl of the air" (Gen. ii., 19). If wicked sceptics say that the fowl cannot have been brought forth by the waters if "every fowl" was formed out of the ground, the only answer is that both these contradictory statements are of divine authority, and "he that believeth not shall be damned." Convincing, is it not?

It is blasphemy to deny that man was created with woman, in the likeness of god (Gen. i., 27, and v., 1, 2), and came into a world replete with life, with fowl and every living thing, over which god gave him dominion (Gen. i., 28). It is also blasphemy to deny that man was created without woman, and came into a world where there was no life, and that god, pitying his loneliness, formed all living things in the attempt to make a help meet for the man, and that failing in this attempt he lastly made a woman, not with man but long afterwards (the making and naming of all animals and birds intervening), out of one of the man's ribs which he detached for that purpose from his skeleton while the man was asleep (Gen. ii., 7, 18, 19—22).

It is blasphemy to deny that god gave man for food "every tree in the which is the fruit of a tree" (Gen. i., 29), while it is equally blasphemy to deny that the "Lord God" withheld from him as food one of the trees (Gen. ii., 17).

It is blasphemy to deny that god, who is "the truth," said that Adam should die "in the day that" he eat the fruit of the tree of knowledge (Gen. ii., 7), and it is blasphemy to deny that so far from dying in that day, "all the days that Adam lived were 930 years," and that "he begat sons and daughters" (Gen. iv., 5, 4) long after the day on which, unless we blaspheme and make god a liar (1 John v., 10), we must believe that he died.

It is blasphemy to deny the fable of the Fall. It is of divine authority that a talking snake persuaded Eve to eat the fruit of the forbidden tree, and that by eating this fruit man and woman found out that they were naked, a sufficiently obvious fact of which they appear to have been ignorant. The first result of eating the forbidden fruit was a regard for decency, and they made some somewhat inadequate clothes out of fig leaves, sewing them together. There is no divine authority as to the implements used, nor as to the discovery of the needles and thread which seem necessary for the sewing. God who is "a spirit" (John iv., 24) and who is "without body" and "parts" (1 Art. of the Church established by law) "walked in the garden" (Gen. iii., 8) soon afterwards; it is blasphemy to deny that god walked, and blasphemy to assert that he has legs. The method of walking without legs is not revealed to us on divine authority, so we must believe (literally) without understanding.

It is blasphemy to deny that "the eyes of the Lord are in every place;" it is also blasphemy to assert that the eyes of the Lord were in the special place wherein Adam and his wife "hid themselves from the presence of the Lord God amongst the trees" (Gen. iii., 8). The only way to reconcile these contradictions is to believe that Adam and his wife and the trees behind which they hid themselves were nowhere, and to believe this comes perilously near the blasphemy of denying the whole story.

It is blasphemy to deny that god cursed the serpent—who had unfortunately lost the power of speech just at the time at which he most required it—for being the helpless tool of Satan, and condemned him to go on his belly and to eat dust. Divine authority does not say how snakes went about before this literal fall, whether on their heads or their tails, so that the method of their locomotion is not of faith.

It is blasphemy to deny that god made coats of skins for Adam and Eve, although coat-making seems rather a curious employment for a deity, and scarcely as dignified as world-making. We are not told what became of the animals whom god deprived of their skins for this purpose; nor whether he killed them first. If he did, then death first entered into the world by god's immediate act. As it is blasphemy to deny that death entered into the world by sin (Rom. v., 12), it is difficult to avoid identifying god with sin, and this, again, is, I fear me, blasphemy.

If in any other old eastern book we read about trees the eating of the fruit of which gave knowledge, serpents which talked, gods who walked in gardens and who made coats, we should at once understand that we were reading old myths, and should never dream of regarding them as a record of historical facts. If we apply the same reasoning to the Bible, Justice North will send us to pick oakum here, and we shall be burned for ever hereafter.

It is blasphemy not to believe that "Cain went out from the presence of the Lord" (Gen. iv., 16)—whom it is blasphemy to deny is everywhere present—and that god put a mark on him lest any one—there being only in existence his own family—"finding him should kill him" (Gen. iv., 15). It is blasphemy not to believe that having a wife, who was also his sister, and who bare him a son, he "builded a city" (Gen. iv., 17) for himself, his wife and child. How many houses there were in the city, and whether each of the three inhabitants lived in a separate house, or the trio moved from house to house, so as to inhabit "the city," these things are not revealed by divine authority.

It is blasphemy not to believe that Adam lived 930 years, Cainan 910 years, Methuselah 969 years; and that the rest of the antediluvian patriarchs lived to approximate ages. It is useless to allege that such preposterous terms of life are contrary to all experience. "He that believeth not shall be damned."

It is blasphemy to deny that all the human race are descended from one man, Adam, created 5,887 years ago. It is true that there was existing in Egypt a settled government more than 11,000 years ago, and as a settled government implies centuries upon centuries of political evolution, it is hard to reconcile this fact with the declaration made on divine authority that man has only existed for about half this period. Egyptian antiquities are not safe subjects of study for the true believer, and a nation which has blasphemy laws on its statute books should shut up its museums and burn its collections of Egyptian treasures, for each room stored with these objects is a training school for blasphemers and a standing menace to the faith of the young. Justice North should also ask that the delta of the Mississipi should be blown up with dynamite to the depth of at least a thousand feet, for that blasphemous ground has given up human bones, says the blasphemer Gliddon, which formed parts of living men 57,000 years ago.

It is of divine authority that "the strength of Israel will not lie nor repent, for he is not a man that he should repent" (1 Sam. xv., 29). It is of equally divine authority that "it repented the Lord that he had made man on the earth, and it grieved him at his heart" (Gen. vi., 6). It is blasphemy to deny that god knows all things before they take place; that before he created man he knew what man would do, and slew a lamb from the foundation of the world (Rev. xiii., 8) to atone for the sins not then committed, but which man would commit in due time; that at this same period the book of life was written containing the names of all those who were to be saved (Rev. xvii., 8); that no sin occurs that god does not himself do, (Is. xlv., 7; Amos iii., 6), so that he need not have any difficulty in avoiding sin if he objects to it. Since it is blasphemy to deny any of these propositions, it is a great trial to faith to believe that god repented when he saw happen the facts he fore-ordained, and grieved over the wickedness which he caused; yet hard as this is, you will be damned if you do not believe it, so you had better try to do so.

It is blasphemy to deny that god, "whose tender mercy is over all his works" (Prayer-book), said that he would destroy "both man and beast, and the creeping things and the fowls of the air" (Gen. vi., 7). We are not told what sins had been committed by the beasts and fowls and creeping things, so that god exclaimed: "it repenteth me that I have made them." If the Bible were a mere human book, and "the Lord" were a mere ordinary man, I should say that he was behaving like a naughty, passionate child, who has lost his temper because the paper animals he has cut out very badly will not stand properly, and who tears them up in a rage. But as it is blasphemy to say this, and blasphemy to deny that god did act exactly in the fashion that would be naughty if he were a child, I can only suppose that the conduct for which a child would be put in the corner is admirable when displayed by a god.

Out of all the wicked men there was one man, Noah, who found "grace in the eyes of the Lord" (Gen. vi., 8). Noah was not what Atheists would regard as a very good man, so far as his conduct is recorded in Holy Scripture. In fact, we are not told of any one good action that he committed. He was a very selfish man, for he saved himself and his family in the ark, and left all his poor fellow-creatures to drown; he drank so much wine that he misbehaved himself shamefully before his children (Gen. ix., 21), and in any respectable society would have had a sack thrown over him, and would have been carried on a stretcher to the nearest police station; he cursed and swore at his poor grandson because his son, the young man's father, had told his brethren of the condition to which Noah had reduced himself (Gen. ix., 25). Yet, in spite of all this disgusting misbehavior, it is blasphemy to deny that "Noah found grace in the eyes of the Lord."

It is blasphemy to deny that in a vessel 300 cubits long, 50 cubits broad, and 30 cubits high, divided into three floors, with only one window in it, 1 cubit square, for purposes of light and ventilation, and this window kept shut till nearly the end of the time (compare Gen. viii., 6), eight persons with pairs or sevens "of every living thing of all flesh," lived for one year and seventeen days. It is blasphemy to deny that into this floating Black Hole went "of every living thing of all flesh, two of every sort" (Gen. vi., 19), and although only two of every sort went in, yet of some sorts "sevens" went in, "the male and his female" (Gen. vii., 2), so that two and fourteen signify the same number when the multiplication table is of faith. What the number of this numerous live cargo of fowls, of cattle, and of every creeping thing (Gen. vi., 20) must have been, may be faintly imagined by the fact that there are known 6,200 species of the "fowls of the air" alone. As the fowls were to be taken "by sevens," there must have been an aviary in the ark containing 86,800 birds, and some of these, such as the eagles, the ostriches, and the condors would require considerable room. Of Mammalia some 1,600 species are known, and elephants, hippopotami, rhinoceroses, buffaloes, giraffes—to take but a few instances—are fairly large, and one might imagine—were it not blasphemy to think so—that lions, tigers, pumas, leopards, wolves, etc., would not only be difficult to manage among the sevens of sheep, goats, and oxen, but would also suffer from the want of exercise necessitated by their caged condition. As the ark must have been packed quite closely in every division, from floor to ceiling, it is difficult to understand how the creatures survived their voyage, while it is blasphemy to deny that every one of them in due time "went forth out of the ark" (Gen. viii., 19).

In addition to all the living creatures, Noah took with him into the ark "of all food that is eaten" (Gen. vi., 21). As there could be no room for Noah and his family to walk about distributing the food (and it would have been scarcely safe to have left it to natural selection), we must suppose that layers of animals and layers of food were packed alternately all through, and even this arrangement must have given rise to some awkward complications if, in order to save space, a pair of caterpillars were dropped in among the cabbages packed round the noses of a pair of guinea-pigs. One might almost imagine that the going forth from the ark must have been a lively ante-type of the general resurrection of the dead.

But yet again, in my efforts to realise this beautiful and divinely inspired history, I am almost afraid that I am being beguiled into blasphemy. "Lord, I (do not) believe. Help thou mine unbelief."

It is blasphemy to deny that 4,232 years ago a universal flood took place, covering "all the high hills that were under the whole heaven" (Gen. vii., 19); the manner in which this was done is partly explained by Peter, who tells us that at that time the earth was "standing out of the water and in the water: whereby the world that then was, being overflowed with water, perished" (2 Pet. iii., 5, 6). This world—half in, half out of the water—is not any world known to history nor to science; there is not a shadow of proof of its existence, except that of divine authority; such a world has nothing in common with our own globe, a planet circling round the sun; the solar system, as we know it, would have been disorganised by the sudden increase in mass of one of its members; our globe has most certainly not been "overflowed with water" during the last 5,000 years, for the cones built up of scoriæ from Mount Etna have been undisturbed for at least 12,000 years. If you believe the testimony of these hills, you must believe that divine authority has blundered over the deluge; but then, if you think this you will be damned, and if you say it Justice North will send you to pick oakum.

It is of divine authority that the ark came to land upon the mountains of Ararat (Gen. viii., 4) after its long and stormy voyage. The humming-birds, the tropical butterflies, the monkeys and the animals of the equatorial zone must have found it rather chilly during their seven-months' stay in the region of perpetual snow, especially as there can have been no facilities for hot-water pipes in the ark. All the living things, tropical or polar, must have also suffered much from the difficulty of breathing on that exalted spot, as the waters went down and the higher atmosphere regained its normal rarity. But what are little difficulties of this sort to the true believer, especially when into the scale of belief are thrown the smile of god and the approval of Mr. Justice North?

It is of divine authority that Noah sent out of the ark a dove, which returned to him finding "no rest for the sole of her foot," "for the waters were on the face of the whole earth" (Gen. viii., 9); yet seven days later the same dove returned from a second excursion with "an olive leaf pluckt off," "in her mouth" (v., 11). It is, therefore, blasphemy to deny that an olive tree stood firm beneath the crushing weight of the tons of water which covered every high hill, and was so little injured by its submersion of eleven months that it promptly budded out as the water left uncovered its topmost boughs.

It is of divine authority that "every beast, every creeping thing, and every fowl, and whatsoever creepeth upon the earth after their kinds, went forth out of the ark" (Gen. viii., 19), and that Noah, lest his god should not have had his appetite for slaughter satiated by the putrifying masses of the drowned dead, scattered over the face of the whole earth, took "of every clean beast and of every clean fowl" (v. 20), and offered up his puny sacrifice by fire from the few living things left from the huge sacrifice by water. It is blasphemy to deny that as the fumes of the roasting animals went up "the Lord smelled a sweet savor" (v. 21), and gratefully declared: "neither will I again smite any more every thing living, as I have done" (v. 21). So that god appears to have made man, then to have repented that he made him, then to have destroyed him, and then to have been half sorry once more, declaring that he would not do it again. And this is the god in "whom is no variableness, neither shadow of turning" (James i., 17). It certainly required a revelation to tell us so.

It is of divine authority that the "fear" and "dread" of man is on every "beast of the earth, and upon every fowl of the air, upon all that moveth upon the earth, and upon all the fishes of the sea" (Gen. ix., 2). This fear is not very evident in the tiger as he tears a man in pieces, in the vulture who picks out the eyes of the dying traveller, in the shark who snaps in twain the swimming sailor; yet it is consoling to know that they are all trembling with dread of their prey as they swallow the toothsome morsel. The "covenant which is between me and you and every living creature of all flesh" (Gen. ix., 15) is rather funny; if it were not blasphemy to deny it I should scarcely have conceived of god entering into a covenant with, say, a blackbeetle. The covenant is not of much use to individuals apparently, though entered into with "every" one of them, for though god promises that he will not again drown them all *en masse*, he gives no pledge as to drowning in detail, and this is quite as unpleasant to the victims.

It is blasphemy to deny that 4,130 years ago "the whole earth was of one language and of one speech" (Gen. xi., 1), and the whole science of philology is therefore a delusion and a snare. As "they"—the whole earth—"journeyed from the east," they "found a plain," and made up their minds to build "a city and a tower whose top may reach unto heaven" (verses 2 and 4). It is blasphemy to deny that god—who at that time appears to have known little about the laws of gravitation or the difficulty of breathing, say, five miles up—thought they might succeed, and, being omnipresent, he changed his place, and "came down to see the city and the tower which the children of men builded." In order to prevent the appearance of the top of the tower in heaven—heaven being above the firmament, the firmament having the stars set in it, and the nearest fixed star being 5,480,490,000,000 miles away, so that if they had directed their tower towards this star, and had built at the rate of ten miles a day, it would have taken them more than 1,501,504,109 years to reach heaven, that is, they would have had to build for 1,501,599,979 years onwards from the present time—god being afraid that they would storm his realm, took the trouble to confound their language, so that they might not understand each other's speech. When we read of the Titans trying to storm heaven, we know that the story is a myth; but the same fable is "Bible truth" in Genesis, and it is blasphemy to deny it, foolish as it is.

It is blasphemy to deny that when Terah was 70 years of age he begat Abram (Gen. xi., 26), and that he died when he was 205 years of age (verse 32); it is blasphemy to deny that Abram was 75 years old when he departed out of Haran and went into Canaan (Gen. xii., 4, 5); it is blasphemy to deny that Abram stayed in Haran until after his father's death (Acts vii., 4); that is, it is blasphemy to deny that the 135 years of Terah's life are of exactly the same length as the 75 years of Abram's life. Anyone who believes not that 135=75 will be damned. Moral, parents should not allow their children to learn arithmetic, for by so doing they imperil their immortal souls, and risk their committal to gaol by the tender mercies of Mr. Justice North.

Sarai, about whose age there is some doubt, in consequence of the great length of her husband's years, was a very fair woman; reckoning by Terah's age, she must have been at this time at least 160 years old (supposing that she married at 15), but she seems to have been only 90 years of age at least 25 years later (Gen. xvii., 17). However, whether she was a fair woman of 160 summers, or a gay young thing of only 65, she proved to be indeed a treasure to her husband. For it is of divine authority that faithful Abraham pretended that his wife was only his sister, and allowed King Pharaoh to take her and to pay him for her "sheep, and oxen, and he-asses, and menservants, and maidservants, and she-asses, and camels" (Gen. xii., 16); it is blasphemy to deny that god plagued poor innocent "Pharaoh and his house with great plagues" because they were deceived by his friend's shameless venality and lying, and that when

Pharaoh discovered the fraud, Abram took himself off with his wife and all he had gained by her sale, being, as the sacred narrative naively remarks, " very rich " (Gen. xiii., 2) after this transaction.

It is blasphemy to deny that " he [god] is faithful that promised " (Heb. x., 23); it is also blasphemy to deny that he [god] broke his promises. For he promised Abram, over and over again, that he would give to him as well as to his seed the land of Canaan (Gen. xiii., 15; xv., 7, 8; xvii., 8, etc.); yet we find that Abram was obliged to buy a sepulchre for his wife's corpse, and never inherited the land at all. Even as far as his seed was concerned, god broke the " everlasting covenant " (Gen. xvii., 9) he made, to give to " thee and to thy seed after thee, the land wherein thou art a stranger, even the land of Canaan for an everlasting possession " (Gen. v., 8), for the Jews only possessed part of this land for a short time, instead of for ever, and as defined by god, " this land, from the river of Egypt unto the great river, the river Euphrates " (Gen. xv., 18), they never had it at all. It is comforting to notice that this promise-breaking god is the same who in the person of his son declared: " he that believeth not shall be damned;" for as he did not keep his word in the one case perhaps he will not do so in the other.

One day, as Abram was returning from the slaughter of some of his enemies, a certain Melchizedek, named with charming appropriateness King of Peace (Heb. vii., 2), went out to meet him, and blessed him. Nothing is said in Genesis to make us regard Melchizedek as the extraordinary being that he really was; for it is blasphemy to say that Melchizedek was ever born, that he had any ancestors, that he ever died (Heb. vii., 3); like Topsy, "'spects he growed"; where he is now nobody knows; he would be a most useful " Christian antiquity," but he is not producible. On the world's stage he made but this one appearance, "positively for the first and last time." Melchizedek is a type of Jesus Christ. Jesus was born; Melchizedek was not. Jesus had a mother; Melchizedek had none. Jesus had his descent from David; Melchizedek was without descent. Jesus died; Melchizedek had no end of life. The correspondence between them is really striking. The only similarity is that they were both without any acknowledged father, and this peculiarity they share with many pagan heroes and with some less important folk.

It is blasphemy to deny that Abram, the "friend of God," took to himself his wife's maid, Hagar, and that when this poor slave was about to bear him a child he chivalrously handed her over to her jealous mistress, Sarai, saying: "Behold, thy maid is in her hand; do to her as it pleaseth thee" (Gen xvi., 6). An ordinary man, under such circumstances, would have had some tender, pitiful feeling towards the mother of his unborn child; but Abram was a saint of God, and was above all weak sentiment of that kind, so he stood quietly by while Sarai ill-treated the woman who had lain in his arms, and let her flee away into the wilderness unhelped and unpitied. God's angel drove poor Hagar back to her bondage, and after her return her son was born. At this time Abram was 86 years of age; fourteen years later Sarah had a son, Isaac, and some time after she insisted on turning out poor Ishmael, with his mother, Hagar. A sweet, womanly creature was Sarah. Abraham made no objection, but "rose up early in the morning" to send off his first-born son and his mother, and was generous enough to take "bread and a bottle of water," and to make this splendid present to Hagar "putting it on her shoulder, and the child, and sent her away." "The child" was now about fifteen years of age, and would have been a little heavy for poor Hagar to carry if he had been an ordinary well-grown boy; he was, however, curiously small for his age, for we learn that when "the water was spent in the bottle" "she cast the child under one of the shrubs" (Gen. xxi., 15). It is blasphemy to deny that Hagar carried this big baby, and threw him about like a toy.

It is blasphemy to deny that "the Lord" appeared to Abraham in the plains of Mamre, and that he, with two others, eat dressed calf, butter and milk (Gen. xviii., 1—8). It is blasphemy to say that god has parts (Art. I.), but it is difficult to understand how he eat without teeth, and swallowed without a throat; besides, what became of the eaten meat if there was no stomach to receive it? Truly, the gate is narrow which leadeth unto life, and narrow must be the brains that go in therethrough.

It is blasphemy to deny that god, who knows everything, did not know what was going on in Sodom and Gomorrah.

B

He said: "Because the cry of Sodom and Gomorrah is great, and because their sin is very grievous, I will go down now, and see whether they have done altogether according to the cry of it, which is come unto me; and if not, I will know" (Gen. xviii., 20, 21). Much faith is necessary to believe that god knew and that he did not know all at once, but "he that believeth not shall be damned."

It is blasphemy to deny that the same god who did not punish Lot and his daughters for incest, punished Lot's poor wife because she committed the terrible crime of looking back towards her burning home. She was turned into a "pillar of salt" (Gen. xix., 26), and Jesus bids us remember her (Luke xvii., 32), but does not say why we should do so. If god had forgotten her and had turned the two daughters into salt, the family history would have been less scandalous than it is.

It is blasphemy to deny that god "rained upon Sodom and Gomorrah brimstone and fire from the Lord out of heaven" (Gen. xix., 24). Heaven must be a pleasant place if it contains stores of brimstone and fire which can be rained down in this fashion. Action of this kind is supposed to be wicked when done by man, but a divine O'Donovan Rossa is apparently held up for our admiration. I have sometimes wondered whether this brimstone may not possibly have come from the lake of brimstone and fire connected with the bottomless pit (Rev. xx., 10); if so, it is very probable that as the earth turned round and Sodom and Gomorrah came opposite the bottomless pit, so that it was above those "towns," god lifted the lid and let out some of the contents. This view should commend itself to the religious, as it cannot be pleasant for them to look forward to spending eternity in the close neighborhood of a celestial manufactory of dynamite.

It is blasphemy to deny that "just Lot" (2 Pet. ii., 7) offered his two virgin daughters to satiate the lust of the crowd surrounding his house: "let me, I pray you," said this good father, "bring them out unto you, and do ye to them as is good in your eyes." This generous offer, which would be vile in any one but a saint, throws much light on his later relations with these young women. The frightful crime related in Gen. xix., 30—36, seems to have been much approved of by god; for we learn in Deut. ii., 9 and

19, that the Moabites and Ammonites were not to be molested, for their lands were given "unto the children of Lot for a possession," and the reference Bible refers us back on this to the beautiful story in Genesis. Little English girls are given this story to read, and it would be blasphemous to teach them that Lot and his daughters were criminals of the filthiest type. The holy book of god says that Lot was a "just" man, and there is not a word of disapproval of his vice. If it were not that all good little girls must read the Bible, it would be far better that they should not know that such crimes are committed at all. Children's thoughts should never be turned towards sexual matters in any fashion, and they do not so turn of themselves, and it would be one of the worst mischiefs done by the Bible—if it were not the book of god—that it destroys this natural healthy indifference in children's minds. It is not wonderful that such frightful tales of family immorality are but too often told at the assizes, or that poor ignorant people, believing with blind faith in the Bible, repeat the crime of Lot and his daughters, and are startled when our human laws punish peremptorily the crime which in the Bible is blessed of god.

It is blasphemy to deny that god plagued the innocent household of Abimelech, the king of Gerar, because Abimelech had been deceived by the lie of Abraham, god's friend. From the story as related in Genesis xx. we learn that Abimelech took Sarah—then over ninety years of age—believing her to be Abraham's sister; next, that finding out the trick played on him, he gave her back to her base husband, rebuking him in "that thou hast brought on me and on my kingdom a great sin;" next, that Sarah was Abraham's half-sister, although she was also his wife, and that such marriage unions between children of the same father by different mothers are pleasing to god; next, that Abraham accepted "sheep and oxen and men-servants and women-servants" from Abimelech with his restored wife, as well as "a thousand pieces of silver," ironically bestowed on him as her "brother;" and, finally, we learn that it is blasphemy to deny that just the same sequence of events happened twice over to Abraham, and also happened to Isaac his son (Gen. xxvi., 7—11), who inherited the family untruthfulness and the family cowardice with the family property.

It is blasphemy for a man to say "when he is tempted,

B 2

I am tempted of god; for god cannot be tempted with evil, neither tempteth he any man" (James i., 13). Yet it is blasphemy to deny that "after these things god did tempt Abraham (Gen. xxii., 1). If anybody is infidel enough to ask how a god that tempts no one could have tempted Abraham, the best answer is: "He that believeth not shall be damned." Perhaps Abraham was no one, and in that case both statements would be true.

Everyone knows the beautiful story of Abraham and the sacrifice of Isaac. How this noble father led his child to the slaughter; how Isaac meekly submitted; how the farce went on till the lad was bound and laid on the altar, and how god then stopped the murder, and blessed the intending murderer for his willingness to commit the crime. If anyone now tries to emulate Abraham's faith, he is treated as a dangerous lunatic; but it is blasphemy to deny that that which would be murder now was virtue then.

It is blasphemy to deny that Isaac was born when his father and mother were too old for his birth to be natural (Gen. xvii., 17); in fact, Abraham was "as good as dead" and Sarah "was past age" (Heb. xi., 11, 12), and we are told that when "he was about an hundred years old" "his own body" was "now dead" (Rom. iv., 19). Although it is blasphemy to assert that he was *not* too old at 100 to become the father of one son, it is also blasphemy to assert that he *was* too old more than 37 years later to become the father of six sons (Gen. xxv., 2). We are bound to believe that Abraham was naturally capable of becoming a father when he was 86 years of age, and when he was over 137 years of age, but that it was only by a miracle that he was capable of becoming a father when he was 100 years of age. Truly there are in the Bible "some things hard to be understood" (2 Pet. iii., 16).

It is blasphemy to deny that before Esau and Jacob were born god chose one as his favorite, and declared: "Jacob have I loved, but Esau have I hated" (Rom. ix., 13). If anyone should carpingly allege that it was wrong to hate poor unborn Esau before he had committed "any good or evil" (Rom. ix., 11), the right answer is that "god's ways are not as our ways," and that which would be wickedness in man is righteousness in god. God loved Jacob. Jacob would not give his starving brother food until he had bargained for his birthright in return (Gen. xxv., 29—34); but god loved Jacob. Jacob cheated his blind father, pretending to be his brother, and deceived the old man's sense of touch, the sense of vision having failed (Gen. xxvii., 11, 12, 15, 16, 22, 23); but god loved Jacob. Jacob was a hypocrite, and when he took a kid dressed to imitate vension to his father, pretended that he had found it quickly "because the Lord thy god brought it to me" (v. 20); but god loved Jacob. Jacob was a liar, declaring that he was his brother Esau (v. 19, 24); but god loved Jacob. Jacob was a coward, and ran away from his defrauded brother; but god loved Jacob. Jacob hated his wife (Gen. xxix., 31); yet god loved Jacob. Jacob swindled his hospitable uncle Laban out of his flocks and herds (Gen. xxx., 31-43); yet god loved Jacob. Jacob ran away from his uncle with his ill-gotten gains, like a thief in the night (Gen. xxxi, 20); yet god loved Jacob. Jacob was once more a coward, afraid of the brother he had wronged, and sent on some of his people to get killed that he might escape (Gen. xxxii., 7, 8); yet god loved Jacob. It is instructive to know the kind of men that god loves, and to know that god loves a bargaining, cheating, hypocritical, lying, swindling coward. As to poor Esau, on whom fell the awful hate of god before he was born, he seems to have been a brave, loving, generous-hearted man. The kindly words of the man god hated, as he refused his cringing brother's present: "I have enough, my brother; keep that thou hast unto thyself" (Gen. xxxiii., 9), contrast forcibly with the mean, despicable conduct of the man god loved. It is blasphemy to deny that god abetted pious Jacob's frauds, for we learn that "god hath taken away the cattle of your father, and given them to me" (Gen. xxxi., 9), and that in suggesting the method of fraud god reminded him of the share due to himself by the vow he had made (Gen. xxxi., 13), the said vow being that "of all that thou shalt give me I will surely give the tenth to thee" (Gen. xxviii., 22).

It is blasphemy to deny that the foul stories of Tamar and Onan, of Tamar and Judah, and of the births of Pharez and Zarah—the children of Judah and his daughter-in-law—with all the details of the several events (Gen. xxxviii.), are of divine authority. If any one but god had told the stories they would be indecent, and the teller would be liable to prosecution under Lord Campbell's act. Out of the filthiest literature the story told in verses 27—30 could not be paralleled, and I doubt if Holywell Street has anything fouler on its book-shelves. Yet little innocent girls are given the book containing these perfectly useless and indescribable nastinesses; and if decent people venture to criticise the book, avoiding the parts of it only fit for pious hands, they are liable to be sent to gaol, and the judge accuses them of undermining morality! The sooner the morality built on Judah, Tamar, and the stories of Onan and Pharez, is undermined the better for decent society.

The story of Joseph and Potiphar's wife is told in the next chapter (Gen. xxxix.), and I have heard a clergyman read this story out in church without the smallest hesitation to listening men, women, and children. Christianity blunts the very commonest feelings of human decency in the minds of its followers; and the clergy, who deprave the minds of the young by circulating the Holy Book, have the insolence to accuse unbelievers in its divinity of undermining morality!

It is blasphemy to deny that god blessed the Egyptian midwives for telling a deliberate lie (Ex. i., 19, 20). It is also blasphemy to deny that "Lying lips are an abomination to the Lord" (Prov. xii., 22). The only deduction we can draw from these two facts, both given on divine authority, is that god blesses that which is an abomination to him. Once again we must say piously: "His ways are not as our ways."

With the second chapter of Exodus begins the story of Moses, "the man of god." Like most of the Bible saints, Moses was a great sinner from the point of view of ordinary morality. He began his public career with a murder. "And it came to pass in those days, when Moses was grown, that he went out unto his brethren and looked on their burdens; and he spied an Egyptian smiting an Hebrew, one of his brethren. And he looked this way and that way, and when he saw that there was no man, he slew the Egyptian and hid him in the sand" (Ex. ii., 11, 12). The careful looking "this way and that way" before he interferes shows the care for his own person that characterises Moses. A man might have been moved by honest indignation to smite an oppressor. The careful looking round and the hiding of the body do not impress us with a sense of the heroic.

After this adventure Moses ran away from Egypt and dwelt in Midian, and while looking after his father-in-law's flock, he saw a remarkable sight, a bush burning, but not consumed. It is blasphemy to deny that god was in the "midst of the bush" (Ex. iii., 4), and it is blasphemy to suggest, what is nevertheless true, that this legend of a god in the midst of a bush is a trace of the old tree-worship so common in Eastern lands, a worship constantly referred to later in the Hebrew scriptures under the name of "the grove." This god who spoke to Moses was one of the gods of the grove. It is very unfortunate that the truth should be so blasphemous.

It is blasphemy to deny that god said: "Thou shalt not steal" (Ex. xx., 15), and also blasphemy to deny that he commanded the Israelites to rob the Egyptians (Ex. iii., 21, 22). Little discrepancies of this sort must not be allowed to trouble the true believer. Moses did not believe what god said, and in later times he that believeth not shall be damned. But in those days god treated sceptics more mercifully, and instead of damning Moses god performed two miracles to convince him. What a pity that Mr. Foote did not live in the days of Moses; if his walking-stick had turned into a snake, and then when he had caught hold of the snake's tail it had turned back into a walking-stick, perhaps he might have become a believer. It puzzles me a little, however, why the performance of useless and childish miracles of this sort should be admitted as proving anything. If I go to Maskelyne and Cooke's I see much more wonderful transformations than those performed on Mount Horeb, but I do not, therefore, feel inclined to worship Mr. Maskelyne or to take Mr. Cooke as my guide and mentor. Miracles are hopelessly irrelevant; if they were all true they would prove nothing beyond the dexterity of the miracle-worker.

It is blasphemy to deny that the rod changed into a serpent; yet who can believe this who tries to realise what the words mean? a piece of wood, of vegetable tissue, is suddenly transformed into a snake, into bones and muscle, and nerve and blood, and skin! We are here in the region of fairy-tale, not of history. We may also note that when this wonderful transformation-scene was repeated before Pharoah, the Egyptian jugglers proved themselves to be quite as skilful at snake-making as were Moses and Aaron. The scene ended, however, with a grand effect: for "Aaron's rod swallowed all their rods" (Ex. vii., 12). The sacred narrative does not state the result on the triumphant stick, nor whether it showed the thickness of all the rods combined, when it turned back again into a stick.

Moses appears to have shared my doubts as to the point of the miracles, for he persisted that he did not want to go, until god, who is without passions (Art. I.) got very angry (Ex. ix., 14). At last, he agreed to go, and god informed him as to Pharoah: "I will harden his heart, that he shall not let the people go" (Ex. ix., 21). This unhappy Pharaoh was "raised up" by god in order that god's power might be manifested in tormenting him and his miserable people; over and over again, god "hardened his heart," and Paul, instead of being ashamed of this awful conduct actually justifies it (see p. 25). If any human being forced a helpless creature into crime, and then punished him for committing it, no words of abhorrence could be found too strong to express the loathing which would fill every just and righteous heart in contemplating such conduct. Yet it is blasphemy to deny that the "heavenly Father" behaved in this fashion towards Pharaoh.

The odd little interlude which takes up vv. 24, 25, 26 of the same chapter has been a sore trouble to commentators. Why "the Lord" tried to kill somebody, who it was he tried to kill, where "the inn" was by which he met him, what the mutilation of her son by Zipporah had to do with the quarrel, all these things have been discussed and re-discussed *ad nauseam.* Students of ancient religions will find that nature-worship throws some light on the matter, but it is blasphemous light, and must be carefully avoided by all true believers who are anxious about the salvation of their souls.

It is blasphemy to say that god was known to Abraham "by my name Jehovah" (Ex. vi., 8); it is also blasphemy to deny that Abraham knew him as Jehovah and "called the name of the place Jehovah-jireh" (Gen. xxii., 14).

It is blasphemy to deny that Moses turned all the water in Egypt, the water in streams, rivers, ponds, pools, as well as all in vessels; after *all* the water had been thus turned into blood, the Egyptian magicians turned the rest into blood (Ex. vii., 19, 20, 22). This is a very remarkable miracle, showing great skill on the part of the Egyptians.

It is blasphemy to deny the historical truth and perfect accuracy of the Biblical account of the miracles wrought by the hand of the Lord in the land of Egypt. It is very hard work to believe, but we must try, for it is clear that if we go to gaol for denying them, we shall not get out "till we have paid the uttermost farthing" demanded by law.

First, we must believe that "the Lord" kept on sending messages to Pharaoh, commanding him to let the people go, while at the same time "the Lord hardened Pharaoh's heart, so that he would not let the children of Israel go" (Ex. x., 20). It is blasphemy to deny that god behaved in this horribly wicked manner, compelling Pharaoh to refuse, and then plaguing him and his people for the refusal; we deserve damnation if we do not agree with Paul, when he writes: "It is not of him that willeth, nor of him that runneth, but of God that showeth mercy. For the Scripture saith unto Pharaoh, Even for this same purpose have I raised thee up, that I might show my power in thee, and that my name might be declared throughout all the earth. Therefore hath he mercy on whom he will have mercy, and whom he will he hardeneth. Thou will say then unto me, Why doth he yet find fault, for who hath resisted his will? Nay but, O man, who art thou that repliest against God? Shall the thing formed say to him that formed it: Why hast thou made me thus?" (Rom. ix., 16—20.) Yes, most certainly it should so say, if it be a living sentient thing, capable of enjoyment and of agony. No god has the right to create sentient beings, to harden them, and then to find fault with them and torture them for being hardened. The challenge, "Why doth he yet find fault?" is a very proper one, and Paul cannot answer it, so he falls back on god's power to do as he chooses; but the exercise of the power would be a crime, and if it be blasphemy to say that such unutterable wickedness is criminal, then I will blaspheme as long as I live, rather than turn flattering courtier to a monarch more cruel than Caligula, a despot more tyrannical than any Eastern potentate known to history.

After the duel about the water between Moses and the Egyptian magicians—in which the magicians certainly shewed the greater power and dexterity—Moses and Aaron covered the land of Egypt with frogs (Ex. viii., 6), and again the magicians proved quite as capable. Exit frogs. Enter lice. This was too much for the magicians; "all the dust of the land became lice" (viii., 17)—note this proof of spontaneous generation—so the material was lacking to the magicians, but as they had done so well in turning the water into blood after it had all become blood already, it is disappointing to find that they broke down at this critical period. Perhaps they were tired.

Exit lice. Enter flies. That was a very horrid plague. Blue-bottles everywhere. They filled the cream-jugs, they covered the joints, they fell into the jam, they stuck in the treacle. Fly-papers went up 100 per cent, and several gentlemen in the profession made fortunes during the rush. "A greater than" these, however, came to the rescue: "the Lord" himself "removed the swarms of flies," and joyful to relate, "there remained not one" (viii., 31). I should like to have spent the remainder of that summer in Egypt. As day after day went on, and not a solitary buzz was heard, how joyfully must the maids and matrons of Egypt have chanted in thankful chorus: "Fly not yet!"

Pharaoh's heart remaining petrified, an attack was made on the flocks and herds. "A very grievous murrain" was sent "upon thy cattle which is in the field, upon the horses, upon the asses, upon the camels, upon the oxen, and upon the sheep" (Ex. ix., 3). And they *all* died. Between the dead frogs and the dead cattle Egypt must have been . . . . well, let us say fragrant. While they were all lying there dead, god sent boils on them; the object of this is not clear, and it is a little difficult to understand how the boils flourished on cold corpses; still the Scriptures cannot lie, and thus it is written. With that appropriateness which shews real genius, Moses, at the Lord's command, sprinkled "handfuls of ashes of the furnace," and in "these ashes glowed their former fires," and they caused "a boil."

The next miracle is a very remarkable one. Forgetting that all the beasts were dead and boiled, the Lord said: "Send therefore now and gather thy cattle and all that thou hast in the field; for upon every man and beast which shall be found in the field and shall not be brought home, the hail shall come down upon them and they shall die" (ix., 19). Some made their dead "cattle flee into the houses," thus showing a skill and a miracle-working power which must have made Moses very jealous; others left theirs in the field, probably thinking that the boil-covered carcases were not worth the trouble of carriage. Down came the hail, and smote "all that was in the field, both man and beast" (ix., 25). Here indeed was an exemplification, so far as the cattle were concerned, of the second death.

Next came the locusts, to "eat the residue of that which is escaped, which remaineth unto you from the hail" (x., 5). As the hail "smote *every* herb of the field and brake *every* tree of the field" (ix., 25), there cannot have been much left for the locusts; however, they made a clean sweep of all the vegetable life in Egypt, "and there remained not any green thing in the trees or in the herbs of the fields" (x., 15). On the whole it was by a merciful dispensation of Providence that the cattle were all dead, and were not left to starve. As all the animals were dead and there were no plants left, the Lord had nearly come to the end of his plagues; so he sent "darkness which may be felt" for three days, while trying to invent some more. None of the Egyptians, we are told, rose "from his place for three days;" why nobody struck a light we are not told; now-a-days we often have plagues of darkness in London from the fogs, but we make shift with gas and the electric light until the sunlight returns.

The last miracle in Egypt was a very wonderful one; it was the killing for the third time of some—the first-born—cattle. The first-born of men were also slain; but that was only for the first time, and all men are mortal. This was too much for the Egyptians, and they rose up to drive out the Israelites, the latter picking up, as they went, "jewels of silver, jewels of gold, and raiment" (xii. 35), and so robbing their unlucky hosts of the little property they had left.

But poor Pharaoh was not yet safe: "The Lord hardened the heart of Pharaoh king of Egypt, and he pursued after the children of Israel" (xiv. 8). He yoked into his chariots the twice-slain horses, and mounted his men on others of these re-revivified quadrupeds, and galloped after the flying robbers. God, to deliver his people, divided the sea before them, piling up the waters on each side as a wall. Down along this curious and unique path plunged the men and the horses, the latter probably thinking that one death, more or less, couldn't hurt them. A new difficulty arose. God pulled off their chariot-wheels, and so delayed them; and then suddenly down came the water-walls, and the poor Egyptians were all drowned. Like the flies and the locusts, "there remained not so much as one of them" (xiv. 28). The horses also were drowned, and let us hope they did not come to life again.

Thus endeth the story of the miracles of Egypt, which story is part of the Christian creed as defined by law, and which it is blasphemy to deny.

After the Lord had thrown "the horse and his rider" into the sea, the children of Israel went on into the wilderness, and found no water for three days. At the end of that time they found some "bitter" water, but the Lord showed Moses a tree which made the water sweet. Genus and species not revealed to us. It is very odd that, when the Bible mentions anything that might be practically useful, it never gives such particulars as would enable us to repeat the experiment.

The next trial to our faith is the story of the manna. The people might well ask: "What is this?" It was so expansible and contractile that, when they measured it, having "gathered some more, some less," if a man gathered much he had "nothing over, and he that gathered little had no lack" (Ex. xvi., 17, 18). This curious result of measuring it "with an omer" is, however, susceptible of explanation, for we read, in Ex. xvi., 36, that "an omer is the tenth part of an ephah," whereas, in Ezech. xlv., the ephah contains "the tenth part of an homer." Perhaps in measuring some of the Jews dropped their h's. The variable expansion of the manna is not its only peculiarity. Manna gathered on Thursday "bred worms and stank" if kept till Friday; manna gathered on Friday "did not stink, neither was there any worm therein" on Saturday (xvi., 20 and 24).

The bread difficulty disposed of, the water difficulty again came to the front, but Moses smote a rock, and water came out of it (Ex. xvii., 6). Later, under very similar circumstances, Moses smote another rock with the like result (Numb. xx., 11.), and the Lord was very angry with him, and refused to let him enter "the promised land." It is curious that in both these cases the place was called Meribah, because of the complaints of the Israelites; but it would be blasphemy to say that two traditions of one incident have been inserted in the text.

Soon after this a wonderful battle took place, in which Israel fought against Amalek, and "it came to pass when Moses held up his hand that Israel prevailed, and when he let down his hand Amalek prevailed" (Ex. xvii., 11). The relation of cause and effect is not clear, but it is satisfactory to know that Moses' hands were held up by main force until evening stopped the slaughter.

It is blasphemy to say that there are more gods than one (Statute of Will. III.), yet it is blasphemy to deny that "the Lord is greater than all gods" (Ex. xviii., 11). It is hard to understand how the Lord can be greater than gods which do not exist; nevertheless "he that believeth not shall be damned."

Chapters xix. and xx. of Exodus can only be believed by those who have not risen above the most anthropomorphic conception of their god. God is everywhere, yet Moses went backwards and forwards between the people and god (xix., 3—9). God is everywhere, yet Moses "brought forth the people out of the camp to meet with God" (v., 17), and "the Lord descended upon" a particular mountain (v. 18), and "came down upon Mount Sinai, on the top of the mount" (v. 20). God is invisible, one "whom no man hath seen nor can see" (1 Tim. vi., 16), whom "no man hath seen at any time" (John i., 18); yet he was afraid lest the people should "break through unto the Lord to gaze" (Ex. xix., 21), and up the mount went "Moses, and Aaron, and Nadab, and Abihu, and seventy of the elders of Israel; and they saw the God of Israel" (Ex. xxiv., 9, 10). God dwells "in the light which no man can approach unto" (1 Tim. vi., 16), and "God is light and in him is no dark-

But poor Pharaoh was not yet safe: "The Lord hardened the heart of Pharaoh king of Egypt, and he pursued after the children of Israel" (xiv. 8). He yoked into his chariots the twice-slain horses, and mounted his men on others of these re-revivified quadrupeds, and galloped after the flying robbers. God, to deliver his people, divided the sea before them, piling up the waters on each side as a wall. Down along this curious and unique path plunged the men and the horses, the latter probably thinking that one death, more or less, couldn't hurt them. A new difficulty arose. God pulled off their chariot-wheels, and so delayed them; and then suddenly down came the water-walls, and the poor Egyptians were all drowned. Like the flies and the locusts, "there remained not so much as one of them" (xiv. 28). The horses also were drowned, and let us hope they did not come to life again.

Thus endeth the story of the miracles of Egypt, which story is part of the Christian creed as defined by law, and which it is blasphemy to deny.

After the Lord had thrown "the horse and his rider" into the sea, the children of Israel went on into the wilderness, and found no water for three days. At the end of that time they found some "bitter" water, but the Lord showed Moses a tree which made the water sweet. Genus and species not revealed to us. It is very odd that, when the Bible mentions anything that might be practically useful, it never gives such particulars as would enable us to repeat the experiment.

The next trial to our faith is the story of the manna. The people might well ask: "What is this?" It was so expansible and contractile that, when they measured it, having "gathered some more, some less," if a man gathered much he had "nothing over, and he that gathered little had no lack" (Ex. xvi., 17, 18). This curious result of measuring it "with an omer" is, however, susceptible of explanation, for we read, in Ex. xvi., 36, that "an omer is the tenth part of an ephah," whereas, in Ezech. xlv., the ephah contains "the tenth part of an homer." Perhaps in measuring some of the Jews dropped their h's. The variable expansion of the manna is not its only peculiarity. Manna gathered on Thursday "bred worms and stank" if kept till Friday; manna gathered on Friday "did not stink, neither was there any worm therein" on Saturday (xvi., 20 and 24).

The bread difficulty disposed of, the water difficulty again came to the front, but Moses smote a rock, and water came out of it (Ex. xvii., 6). Later, under very similar circumstances, Moses smote another rock with the like result (Numb. xx., 11.), and the Lord was very angry with him, and refused to let him enter "the promised land." It is curious that in both these cases the place was called Meribah, because of the complaints of the Israelites; but it would be blasphemy to say that two traditions of one incident have been inserted in the text.

Soon after this a wonderful battle took place, in which Israel fought against Amalek, and "it came to pass when Moses held up his hand that Israel prevailed, and when he let down his hand Amalek prevailed" (Ex. xvii., 11). The relation of cause and effect is not clear, but it is satisfactory to know that Moses' hands were held up by main force until evening stopped the slaughter.

It is blasphemy to say that there are more gods than one (Statute of Will. III.), yet it is blasphemy to deny that "the Lord is greater than all gods" (Ex. xviii., 11). It is hard to understand how the Lord can be greater than gods which do not exist; nevertheless "he that believeth not shall be damned."

Chapters xix. and xx. of Exodus can only be believed by those who have not risen above the most anthropomorphic conception of their god. God is everywhere, yet Moses went backwards and forwards between the people and god (xix., 3—9). God is everywhere, yet Moses "brought forth the people out of the camp to meet with God" (v., 17), and "the Lord descended upon" a particular mountain (v. 18), and "came down upon Mount Sinai, on the top of the mount" (v. 20). God is invisible, one "whom no man hath seen nor can see" (1 Tim. vi., 16), whom "no man hath seen at any time" (John i., 18); yet he was afraid lest the people should "break through unto the Lord to gaze" (Ex. xix., 21), and up the mount went "Moses, and Aaron, and Nadab, and Abihu, and seventy of the elders of Israel; and they saw the God of Israel" (Ex. xxiv., 9, 10). God dwells "in the light which no man can approach unto" (1 Tim. vi., 16), and "God is light and in him is no darkness at all" (1 John i., 5); yet "Moses drew near unto the thick darkness where God was" (Ex. xx., 21). It is blasphemy to deny that all these contradictions are true.

It is blasphemy to deny that god, on Mount Sinai, gave commands among which we find the following revolting and immoral ones: If the owner of a Hebrew slave give the slave a wife, and the slave goes out at the end of seven years, "the wife and her children shall be her master's; he shall go out by himself" (Ex. xxi., 4). The wife is like any other female animal; she and her young belong to her master, and she may be used to increase his stock. If the husband and father clings to his family, god mercifully allows him to buy the right to live with them with the price of his freedom. A man may sell his daughter to be a concubine, and if her purchaser starve her, or let her go naked, or does not perform his marital duty, she may leave him (vv. 7—11). A man may beat his man or woman slave to death, provided that he or she lives "a day or two" after the flogging, for "he is his money" (vv. 20, 21), and the loss of his valuable chattel is punishment sufficient. If an ox gore a man, the ox is to be stoned (v. 28), a form of vivisection which Lord Coleridge can scarcely approve; but, as Paul says: "Doth god take care for oxen?" (1 Cor. ix., 9). If the ox gore a slave, the owner of the slave is to be paid for the value of his property (v. 32). If a thief be unable to restore the double or fourfold value, as the case may be, of that which he has stolen, "then he shall be sold for his theft" (xxii., 3). A witch is to be murdered (v. 20). An idolater is to be murdered (v. 20). "The first-born of thy sons shalt thou give unto me. Likewise shalt thou do with thine oxen and with thy sheep" (vv. 29, 30). Is it credible that by the law of England it should be blasphemy to deny that these horrible commands are "of divine authority"?

And as though to show that this book is of purely human origin, with the mingled good and evil inseparable from all early efforts at legislation, we read, after the foregoing horrors the following noble and generous teaching:

"Thou shalt not raise a false report: put not thine hand with the wicked to be an unrighteous witness. Thou shalt not follow a multitude to do evil; neither shalt thou speak in a cause to decline after many to wrest judgment. Neither shalt thou countenance a poor man in his cause.

If thou meet thine enemy's ox or his ass going astray, thou shalt surely bring it back to him again. If thou see the ass of him that hateth thee lying under his burden, and wouldest forbear to help him, thou shalt surely help with him. Thou shalt not wrest the judgment of thy poor in in his cause. Keep thee far from a false matter; and the innocent and righteous slay thou not: for I will not justify the wicked. And thou shalt take no gift: for the gift blindeth the wise, and perverteth the words of the righteous. Also thou shalt not oppress a stranger: for ye know the heart of a stranger, seeing ye were strangers in the land of Egypt." (xxiii., 1—9.)

Here we see the pen of some lofty and tender lawgiver, who has nothing in common with the savage chief who "breathed out threatenings and slaughter."

It is blasphemy to deny that the Lord on Mount Sinai gave a number of frivolous commands, about a candlestick (Ex. xxv., 31—39) with its snuff-dishes, and curtains, and hangings, and dresses, with their trimmings of "a golden bell and a pomegranate, a golden bell and a pomegranate, upon the hem," and "holy ointment," and "perfume," etc., etc. (Ex. xxv.—xxx.). After the making of stars and suns it seems but poor work to give directions about "loops," and "taches," and a "curious girdle," fitter employment for a cabinet maker and a tailor than for a god with "thunders and lightnings, and a thick cloud upon the mount, and the voice of the trumpet exceeding loud."

While Moses and the Lord were discoursing on upholstery the people were getting into trouble down below, and god, who is "without passions," (Art. 1) felt his wrath "wax hot against them" (Ex. xxxii., 10). Moses did not ask for forgiveness on the ground of god's goodness, but he appealed to his vanity, and reminded him that the Egyptians would crow over him if he destroyed his own people (xxxii., 12.) Thereupon god, who is not a man "that he should repent" (Numb. xxiii., 19), "repented of the evil which he thought to do" (Ex. xxxii., 14). God who is "without body" (Art. 1) had written two tables with his "finger" (Ex. xxxi., 18), and these tables "were the work of god, and the writing was the writing of god" (xxxii, 16). So careless was Moses of this unique specimen that he lost his temper and broke it in pieces, and then, arriving at the camp, he sent the sons of Levi throug the camp, bidding them "slay every man his brother, an every man his companion, and every man his neighbor, and when 3,000 men had fallen he bade the murderers "Consecrate yourselves to-day to the Lord, even every man upon his son and upon his brother, that he may bestow a blessing upon you" (vv., 27—29). Yet it is blasphemy to deny that this great wickedness was god-inspired.

It is blasphemy to deny that "the Lord spake unto Moses face to face" (Ex. xxxiii., 11); also it is blasphemy to deny that god told Moses: "Thou canst not see my face, fo there shall no man see me and live" (v. 20, compare with ch. xxiv., 10, 11). And while it is blasphemy to deny tha god is "without parts" (Art 1), it is equally blasphemy to deny that he has "back parts" (Ex. xxxiii., 23). Either the Prayer Book or the Bible clearly needs revision; meanwhile it is blasphemy to deny either.

It is interesting to observe the fashion in which Christians pick and choose among the commandments given "by divine authority" while they imprison heretics for attacking those of which they, in their turn, disapprove. Thus we have (Ex. xxxv., 2, 3): "Six days shall work be done, but on the seventh day there shall be to you a holy day, a sabbath of rest to the Lord; whosoever doeth work therein shall be put to death. Ye shall kindle no fire throughout your habitations upon the sabbath day." The Sabbatarians quote verse 2 as a reason for shutting up all museums and art galleries on "the Lord's day," and they abuse as rebels against the law of god all the liberal-minded of their own creed. But they quietly ignore verse 3, because that would cause discomfort to themselves, and the very peers who, in the House of Lords, vote to shut working men out of an education go home to sit over their comfortable fires, and to wander through their own galleries warmed by a fir kindled against their god's direct command. Wonderful, indeed, are the ways of religious men!

The book of Leviticus is "of divine authority." It i blasphemy to deny that a bullock, flayed and cut into pieces and burned, makes a sweet smell to god (Lev. i., 5—9) Tastes differ. Also burning a goat, with "the fat tha covereth the inwards, and all the fat that is upon the inwards, and the two kidneys, and the fat that is upon them which is by the flanks" (iii., 14, 15), makes a sweet savor as it frizzles and drips. The tabernacle of the congregation must have smelt like the kitchen of a dirty cook. Yet it is blasphemy to deny that god enjoyed it. "All the fat is the Lord's" (16). Not a morsel of fat might the Israelite eat (17). Personally, I should have been quite willing to give all the fat to the Lord, but some of the people probably felt envious.

It would be wearisome to recite all the extraordinary commands given by god in this "third book of Moses." Christians disregard them, on the pretence that the ceremonial law is not binding on them, yet it is blasphemy to deny that "whosoever shall break one of these least commandments, and shall teach men so, he shall be called the least in the kingdom of heaven" (Matt. v., 19).

It is blasphemy to deny that the hare chews the cud (xi., 6); as a matter of mere fact it does nothing of the kind. It is blasphemy to deny that the locust, the beetle, and the grasshopper have more than four feet (xi., 21—23): as a matter of fact they each have six. It is very awkward when fact and faith clash in this numerical fashion.

It is blasphemy to deny that god concerns himself with the way a man cuts his beard; "neither shalt thou," says he, "mar the corners of thy beard" (xix., 27). Is it conceivable that the creator of the universe should trouble himself with such barber's work as this? If such a being existed would it not rather be blasphemy to ascribe such directions to him?

It is blasphemy to deny that Jahveh, like other gods of his time, commanded human sacrifice. He says: "No devoted thing that a man shall devote unto the Lord of all that he hath, both *of man* and beast, and of the field of his possession, shall be sold or redeemed; every devoted thing is most holy unto the Lord. None devoted which shall be devoted *of men* shall be redeemed, but *shall surely be put to death*" (xxvii., 28, 29). This abomination is commanded by divine authority, and he is in danger of gaol and damnation who shall honestly repudiate the detestable thing.

It is blasphemy to deny that Jahveh ordained the disgusting trial of a wife suspected of infidelity which is related in Numbers v., 12—31. If the "spirit of jealousy" come

C

on a man, he is to bring his wife to the priest. "And the priest shall take holy water in an earthern vessel; and of the dust that is in the floor of the tabernacle the priest shall take, and put it into the water;" this delectable but dirty drink is to be swallowed by the woman, after a charm has been repeated by the priest, as "an oath of cursing," and if the woman has been unfaithful the water will have very unpleasant physical results, while if the suspicion of her husband be false "she shall be free." This prompt way of settling matters would obviate all the expenses and formalities of a divorce court, and if the arrangement could be extended to include unfaithful husbands, this Christian country would be saved much cost. But though the Christians punish other people for unbelief they are thorough infidels themselves in all practical matters. They would far rather trust Sir James Hannen than dirty holy water, when they suspect conjugal infidelity.

It is blasphemy to deny that Jahveh was so passionate (God is without passions, Art. I.), and so vain that he could only be restrained from smiting his people by the appeal of Moses to his vanity: "Then the Egyptians shall hear it .... and they will tell it to the inhabitants of this land .... the nations which have heard the fame of thee will speak, saying: Because the Lord was not able to bring this people into the land which he sware unto them, therefore he hath slain them in the wilderness" (Numbers xiv., 12—16). This suggestion, most ingeniously introduced by Moses — who "managed" Jahveh with admirable tact — proved successful, and "the Lord said, I have pardoned according to thy word" (v. 20). Yet it is blasphemy to say that god changes his purpose.

Furthermore, although it is blasphemy to deny that "he is faithful that promised" (Heb. x., 23), yet we must believe that Jahveh declared to the Israelites, "ye shall know my breach of promise" (Numbers xiv., 34).

It is blasphemy to deny that Jahveh commanded that a man who "gathered sticks upon the sabbath day" (xv., 32—36) should be stoned to death. Yet is it equally blasphemy to deny that Jesus, the representative and first-begotten of Jahveh, condemned the Pharisees who declared that his disciples did "that which is not lawful to do upon the sabbath day" (Matt. xii., 2), when they gathered corn.

The poor Pharisees tried to obey the law as given by Jahveh; their reward was to be condemned by his son. Yet it is blasphemy to deny that "I and my Father are one" (John x., 30).

It is blasphemy to deny that Jahveh commanded the Israelites to "make them fringes in the borders of their garments throughout their generations, and that they put upon the fringe of the borders a riband of blue: and it shall be unto you for a fringe" (Numbers xv., 38, 39). It is hard to believe, though it is blasphemy to deny, that the "Eternal Spirit" troubled himself about "a fringe."

It is blasphemy to deny that there is a "pit," within the earth, into which people may fall alive, when the earth opens her mouth and swallows them up; further, that Korah, Dathan and Abiram, their wives, their sons and their little children, were so swallowed up, and "went down alive into the pit, and the earth closed upon them" (Numb. xvi., 27—33).

It is blasphemy to deny that a plague so fierce that it slew 14,700 people in a few hours could be stopped by a man with a censer full of incense who "stood between the dead and the living" (xvi., 46—49). One can only suppose that the plague advanced steadily across the camp, like a fog, killing every person it covered. Thus only could a man stand between the living and the dead. Yet no such advancing destruction is known to history.

It is blasphemy to deny that a dry old rod belonging to Aaron blossomed miraculously when eleven other dry old rods behaved in the normal fashion (xvii., 2—9). And not only did Aaron's rod bud and blossom, but it also yielded almonds, and this all in the course of one night. It is blasphemy to suggest that Moses, Aaron's brother, who took the rods and who hid them "before the Lord in the tabernacle of witness," quietly substituted a blooming and fruiting branch in the place of his brother's rod, and yet this would be the explanation which would be at once suggested if a similar trick were played now-a-days. But in those easy-going and credulous times very little skill was needed to impose upon a crowd ready to be deceived.

It is interesting to note, in passing, the admirable provision made by Jahveh—through the mouth of his servant, Moses—for Aaron and his family. "All the best of the oil, and

c 2

all the best of the wine, and of the wheat, the first fruits them which they shall offer unto the Lord, them have given thee. And whatsoever is first ripe in the land, whi they shall bring unto the Lord, shall be thine" (Num xviii., 12, 13). This claim on the part of the priesthood h never been regarded as part of that ceremonial law whic has been "done away in Christ."

The story of Balaam is one of the tests to which tru faith must be submitted. We learn in this that when Bala sent to ask Balaam to go to him that he might curse Israe god at first commanded him not to go (Numbers xxii., 12 but a little later commanded him to go (20). God, as w know, never changes. When Balaam obeyed god's com mand and went, "god's anger was kindled against him be cause he went" (22), that is because Balaam did what go told him to do, and "the angel of the Lord stood in the wa for an adversary against him." Balaam was riding on donkey, and the donkey saw the angel, though no one els did, "and the ass turned aside out of the way." Again th angel placed himself in front of the donkey, and the donke squeezed past him, crushing Balaam's foot against the wal For the third time the angel confronted the donkey, and on this occasion in a narrow place, "where there was no wa to turn either to the right hand or to the left." Then th donkey tumbled down. Balaam was, not unnaturally, dis turbed at his donkey's extraordinary behavior, and he ha struck her each time that she had, as he thought, misbe haved. And now occurred a wonderful thing. "The Lor opened the mouth of the ass, and she said unto Balaam What have I done unto thee, that thou hast smitten m these three times? And Balaam said unto the ass, Be cause thou hast mocked me: I would there were a sword i my hand, for now would I kill thee. And the ass said un Balaam, Am not I thine ass, upon which thou hast ridde ever since I was thine unto this day? was I ever wont to d so unto thee? And he said, Nay." Sensible persons a expected to believe this absurd story of a conversation be tween a man and a donkey. Peter speaks of it without an expression of doubt, saying: "the dumb ass, speaking wit man's voice, forbad the madness of the prophet" (2 Pete ii., 16). It is blasphemy to deny it; it is madness to be lieve it. Balaam's ass stands on a level with Mahomet's and only the credulous and superstitious can yield credence to the stories of either.

It is not worth while to delay over Balaam's rhapsodies, except to note their extreme inaccuracy. "God is not a man that he should lie" (Numbers xxiii., 19); yet "I, the Lord, have deceived that prophet" (Ezech. xiv., 9). "Nor the son of man that he should repent" (Numbers xxiii., 19); yet "it repented the Lord that he had made man" (Gen. vi., 6). "He hath not beheld iniquity in Jacob, neither hath he seen perverseness in Israel" (Numbers xxiii., 21); yet, "I have seen this people, and behold it is a stiff-necked people;" "how long will this people provoke me?" (Exodus xxxii., 9, and Numbers xiv., 11). This declaration is the more startling when we find Moses—whose acquaintance with the people was more intimate than that of Balaam—saying: "Remember, and forget not, how thou provokedst the Lord thy God to wrath in the wilderness; from the day that thou didst depart out of the land of Egypt, until ye came unto this place, ye have been rebellious against the Lord. . . . . Ye have been rebellious against the Lord from the day that I knew you" (Deut. ix., 7 and 24). It is needless to accumulate these contradictory statements, all of which we are commanded to believe on peril of damnation.

Immediately after Balaam's declaration of Israel's holiness, we read how the people reverted to idolatry, and how "the anger of the Lord was kindled against them" (Numbers xxv., 3). Some more murders were committed to pacify Jahveh, and he himself slew 24,000 by a plague.

In Numbers xxxi. we have one of the most horrible stories related even in the Bible, the story of the slaughter of the Midianites. Jahveh sent his tribes against this unhappy race, and, after their usual wicked fashion, they "slew all the males." Moved, however, by an unwonted touch of pity, they "took all the women of Midian captives, and their little ones," and brought them alive back to their camp. Moses, Jahveh's friend, "was wroth with the officers of the host" for their unworthy humanity, and shrieked out in his rage: "Have ye saved all the women alive?" And then he commanded them to "kill every male among the little ones, and kill every woman" that had been married, "but all the women children that" were virgins "keep alive for yourselves." This bloodthirsty and loathsome command is of "divine authority." It is blasphemy to deny that it was god-given. Yet what of the blasphemy that ascribes an order so fiendish to "the God of the spirits of all flesh?" These baby boys and prattling children, kill every one; these mothers and matrons of Midian, murder them one after another. Such is the command of Jahveh, who said: "Thou shalt not kill." And these fair and pure maidens, these helpless women-children, whose natural guardians ye have slain, keep these for the satisfactions of your passions. Such is the command of Jahveh, who said: "Thou shalt not commit adultery."

Some of these fair girls were claimed as "the Lord's tribute," 352 in all. These were handed over to the Levites, and small doubt can be felt as to their fate.

To add a touch of the comic to this tragic scene, we learn that after all the fighting and the slaughter, not one solitary Israelite was missing, while the Midianitish nation, of which not a male was left alive, turns up again later as merrily as though it had never been destroyed, and "prevailed against Israel, and because of the Midianites the children of Israel made them the dens which are in the mountains, and caves, and strongholds" (Judges vi., 2).

The book of Deuteronomy is awkward for the true believer, because it is a recital of the story related in the preceding book, and constantly contradicts the previous narrative. Thus Moses commands Israel to make no likeness or similitude of Jahveh on the ground that when he spake to them "out of the midst of the fire," "ye heard the voice of the words but saw no similitude" (Deut. iv., 12); yet turning back we read that seventy-four of them "saw the god of Israel, and there was under his feet as it were a paved work of a sapphire stone, and as it were the body of heaven in his clearness. And upon the nobles of the children of Israel he laid not his hand: also they saw God" (Ex. xxiv., 10, 11). It can scarcely be pretended that when they saw a visible being with "feet" and a "hand," they "saw no similitude."

In Deut. v., 15, the reason for keeping holy the sabbath day is different from the reason given in Ex. xx., 11. Both of these are given as the very words of Jahveh, spoken from "Horeb" or "Sinai." One of the versions must be inaccurate, yet it is blasphemy to deny either. In Deut. v., 22, Moses says that after the ten commandments "he added no more." In Exodus he added a large number of other commands (see xx.—xxiii.).

We learn in Deut. viii., 4, that during the forty years wasted in the wilderness "thy raiment waxed not old upon thee." This was very satisfactory for the adults, but what happened to the growing children? The raiment of a week-old baby can scarcely have been suitable to the man of forty; did the clothes grow with the body, and as the numbers of the people increased very much during the forty years, were new clothes born as well as new babies? If such questions are regarded as blasphemous, I can only answer that they are suggested by Moses' assertion of the remarkable durability of the raiment, and raiment that did not become old might surely also grow and reproduce itself. Once begin miracle-working on old clothes, and none can say how far it may go.

It is blasphemy to assert that it is wrong to swear, for the Bible commands: "Thou shalt fear the Lord thy God . . . . and swear by his name" (Deut. x., 20). It is blasphemy to assert that it is right to swear, for the Bible commands: "Swear not at all" (Matt. v., 34).

Deuteronomy xiii., from the first verse to the last, is a disgrace to the book in which it is contained, and a scandal to the community which permits it to be circulated as of divine authority. Yet it is blasphemy to attack it and to show its horrible atrocity. If a prophet or dreamer arise and try to turn away the Hebrews from Jahveh, then they are told: "The Lord your God proveth you, to know whether ye love the Lord your God" (v. 3). Yet, although it is Jahveh's own doing, that unfortunate "prophet, or that dreamer of dreams, shall be put to death" (v. 5). The same fate is to befall "thy brother, the son of thy mother, or thy son, or thy daughter, or the wife of thy bosom, or thy friend, which is as thine own soul" (v. 6), if such try to turn any away from Jahveh's worship; with a refinement of cruelty, devilish in its wickedness, "thine hand shall be first upon him to put him to death" (v. 9). The wife, passionately loved, is to see her husband, in whose bosom she has lain, raise his hand against her, foremost of a howling mob, greedy for her blood. The daughter is to clasp her father's knees in vain; he must strike her down as she clings to him in her agony. The trusting and trusted friend is to be betrayed to the slaughterers, and the hand most closely grasped in love is to be the first to catch up the heavy stone and to beat out the faithful life. And it is blasphemy to cry out against this horror, but not blasphemy to ascribe its invention to the god "whose tender mercy is over all his works."

The murder commenced in the family circle is to be continued in the national policy. If a city of the Hebrews reject Jahveh, "thou shalt surely smite the inhabitants of that city with the edge of the sword, destroying it utterly, and all that is therein, and the cattle thereof, with the edge of the sword" (v. 15); nothing is to escape, a burning bloodstained ruin is to be left "for the Lord thy God" (v. 16), and then Jahveh will bless his brutal servants, who have done "that which is right in the eyes of the Lord thy God" (v. 18). This command is of divine authority, and has been largely obeyed in Christendom, but people have fortunately become too civilised to carry it out now.

In Deut. xiv., some of the natural history blunders of Lev. xi. are repeated. It is confusing, however, after reading in Lev. xi., 21—23, "these may ye eat, of every flying creeping thing," etc., to find in Deut. xiv., 19, "Every creeping thing that flieth is unclean unto you; they shall not be eaten." So that the Israelites are deprived of those remarkable four-legged locusts, beetles and grasshoppers which "have legs above their feet." (Do other animals carry their feet above their legs?) It is delightful to find Moses speaking of a bat as a bird; clearly in those days the schoolmaster was not abroad, but it is hard that we should be compelled to choose between the blasphemy of speaking of the bat as a mammal, and the falsehood of treating it as a bird. A beautiful touch of generosity is to be found in v. 21: "Ye shall not eat of anything that dieth of itself; thou shalt give it unto the stranger that is in thy gates, that he may eat it; or thou mayest sell it unto an alien."

The general law of warfare laid down in Deut. xx., 10—15, is brutal in the extreme. If any foreign city ventures to defend itself against Hebrew aggression, and closes its gates against the invader, then it is to be besieged, and "when the Lord thy God hath delivered it into thine hands, thou shalt smite every male thereof with the edge of the sword." A yet worse fate is to be dealt out to the cities of Palestine, for in these "thou shalt save alive nothing that breatheth" (v. 16). Of course such method of war has nothing surprising, when we consider the cruelty and barbarism of the Eastern nations of which the Hebrews were one, but it *is* surprising that in the nineteenth century the bloody customs of a savage tribe should be set forth as founded on "divine authority."

If possible, still viler is the treatment of captive women; when thou "seest among the captives a beautiful woman, and hast a desire unto her that thou wouldst have her to thy wife; then thou shalt bring her home to thine house . . . . and after that thou shalt . . . . be her husband, and she shall be thy wife. And it shall be if thou have no delight in her," thy passions being satisfied, "then thou shalt let her go whither she will" (Deut. xxi., 11—14). No wonder that prostitution is rife in every Christian city, when this command is placed before young men's eyes as "of divine authority." Similar low views are taken in Deut. xxiv., 1. While this degrading teaching is that of Jahveh, Manu, a mere man, with no "divine authority," but with only a human heart, taught his followers to treat every aged woman as their mother, every young woman as their sister.

It is rather odd to note in passing that he is declared to be cursed who marries "his sister, the daughter of his father, or the daughter of his mother" (Deut. xxvii., 22), when we remember that Abraham said of his wife Sarah: "Indeed she is my sister; she is the daughter of my father, but not the daughter of my mother; and she became my wife" (Gen. xx., 12). Thus Abraham, who is so highly blessed in one part of god's word, is cursed in another.

The book of Joshua is taken up with the bloody wars of the Israelites; it is a mere record of savage butchery; every page reeks with slaughter. "They utterly destroyed all that was in the city, both man and woman, young and old, and ox, and sheep, and ass, with the edge of the sword" (Josh. vi., 21). This, repeated *ad nauseam*, is the book of Joshua. The tale is varied now and then with the record of absurd miracles, as that of the falling down of the walls of Jericho, or the standing still of the sun and moon at the command of Joshua. From its ferocity and absurdity, the book is beneath contempt, yet it is of "divine authority."

In the Book of Judges we have the record of a number of utterly unimportant victories and defeats in the history of the Hebrew nation. Why should these be accepted as "of divine authority" any more than any corresponding history of some other equally obscure and barbarous people?

Over the barbarous stories of Ehud stabbing Eglon, with its disgusting details (iii., 21, 22); of Jael murdering her guest, in defiance of all desert laws of hospitality, and receiving for her treachery the blessing of the Lord, a blessing shared only with Mary, the mother of Jesus (v. 24, compare Luke i., 28); of Gideon and of Abimelech, with the evil spirit sent by god (Judges ix., 23); of Jephthah and his vow and his sacrifice of his daughter (xi., 29—39), as Agamemnon sacrificed Iphigenia; of Samson with his absurd and brutal conduct (xiv., 19; xv., 4, 5; and 14—19, etc.); of the Levite and his concubine, and the foul details thereon (xix.)—what can any say of these save that such coarse and brutal stories belong to the childhood of every nation, and that while other peoples look back on their savage history as a thing that is past, these Hebrew stories are preserved in perennial freshness, and are placed as a burden on the consciences of the civilised nations of Europe, and, to our shame, are defended from criticism by the brutal laws of blasphemy invented in savage times and sanctioned in England to-day.

The books of Samuel, Kings, Chronicles, Ezra and Nehemiah are interesting for the light they throw on the growth of the Israelitish people, but regarded as of divine authority, they give manifold occasion "for the enemies of the Lord to blaspheme."

Thus we read how the "ark of God" was carried to battle, and how the Philistines were afraid, and asked: "Who shall deliver us out of the hand of these mighty Gods?" But they wisely determined to try and save themselves, and bade each other: "Quit yourselves like men, and fight." So they overcame Israel and his "mighty Gods," and took the ark itself captive (chap. iv.). Jahveh, however, if he could not fight the Philistines, was strong enough to fight their gods, and when he was offered the hospitality of Dagon's temple, and was left quiet for the night, he knocked poor Dagon down. The Philistines put Dagon up again, and this so annoyed Jahveh that on the following night he knocked Dagon down again, and cut off his head and "the palms of his hands" on the threshold. After that Jahveh performed a miniature edition of the plagues of Egypt in the various towns to which his ark was carried, until some clever priests hit upon the idea of putting the ark on a cart and harnessing in two milch kine, and letting them go wherever they pleased. Off marched the kine to Bethshemesh, and there they met the fate of all the unlucky creatures that did Jahveh any service, for the men of Bethshemesh took them and offered them as "a burnt offering to the Lord." Then Jahveh broke out on the poor men of Bethshemesh, and killed 50,070 of them, because they (all of them ?) had peeped into the ark (chaps. v., vi.). And it is actually blasphemy to deny any detail of this absurd story.

1 Samuel xv. is a chapter that many a pious soul must wish blotted out from the Old Testament. Samuel, as bloodthirsty as Moses, gave in "the Lord's" name the horrible command: "Go and smite Amalek, and utterly destroy all that they have, and spare them not; but slay both man and woman, infant and suckling, ox and sheep, camel and ass" (v. 3). This fiendish command was not wholly obeyed, for Saul saved the king, and the best of the sheep and of the other animals. Thereupon Samuel came down and cursed Saul vigorously, and then committed the absurdity of telling Saul that the "Strength of Israel," whose change of purpose he had just announced, and who "repented that he had made Saul king" (v. 35), was "not a man that he should repent" (v. 29). After this manifest untruth, he murdered poor Agag, hewing him "in pieces before the Lord" (v. 33). Yet it is blasphemy to deny that this tissue of bloodshed and lying is inspired by "the spirit of truth."

After this the contradictions about the connexion of Saul and David are of small moment. In chap. xvi., 18—23, David is brought to play the harp to Saul, and he is described as "a mighty valiant man and a man of war," and he became Saul's armor-bearer as well as musician. In the next chapter David leaves him (v. 15) and goes back to feed his father's sheep, when a war breaks out; a curious proceeding for a "mighty valiant man." Six weeks later David carries some food to his brethren in the camp, and hearing the Philistine giant Goliath utter a challenge, he offers to go and fight him. Saul points out to the man who six weeks before was "mighty valiant" and "a man of war," that he could not fight the Philistine, for he was "but a youth," while Goliath was "a man of war from his youth." David then relates the story of a struggle he had with a curious composite animal, a "lion and a bear," who stole a lamb, and "I went out after him and smote him, and delivered it out of his mouth, and when he arose against me I caught him by the beard and slew him." Saul then put his armor on him, but the former armor-bearer and man of war had forgotten how to use armor, and refused to wear it. He then killed the Philistine, and Saul, in whose court he had lived six weeks before, and who "loved him greatly" (xvi., 21), asked one of his captains who he was, and bade him "inquire whose son the stripling is" (xvii., 55, 56). We can only understand the king's loss of memory when we think how much changed David was; the "man of war" had become a "stripling," the "mighty valiant man," the armor-bearer, had changed into a "youth" who could not wear armor. No wonder poor Saul was puzzled, and if he could not understand it when he was on the spot, how cruel to threaten us with imprisonment and damnation if we blunder about it 3,000 years afterwards. Almost immediately after David is playing away on his harp "as at other times" (xviii., 10).

The bloodthirsty, treacherous, profligate character of David is so well known that I will not deal with it here, further than to call attention to the fact that this deep-dyed criminal was the man "after God's own heart," the man who "did that which was right in the eyes of the Lord, and turned not aside from anything that he commanded him all the days of his life, save only in the matter of Uriah the Hittite" (1 Kings xv., 5).

There is one grave difficulty of identity that meets us here which we must not overlook. In 1 Sam. xxiv., 1, we read: "The anger of the Lord was kindled against Israel, and he moved David against them to say: go number Israel and Judah." In 1 Chron. xxi., 1, we read: "And

Satan stood up against Israel, and provoked David to number Israel." Are "God" and "Satan" convertible terms? It is clearly blasphemy to say that they are not, since the above verses prove that they are, yet I fancy it must be blasphemy to say that they are.

The barbaric magnificence of the temple built by Solomon is fully described in 1 Kings vi.—viii., and we are bound to believe that Solomon offered up 22,000 oxen and 120,000 sheep! It would scarcely have been possible for him to have killed more than one animal in five minutes, for each corpse would have to be dragged away to make room for the next, and this is supposing that others prepared the dead animals for sacrifice. Yet at this rapid rate, without stopping for food or rest or sleep, it would have taken Solomon 11.833 hours and 15 minutes to complete his task, or 493 days. As he must have stopped for food and sleep we may double this time, and a pleasant 2¾ years poor Solomon must have passed.

Numberless contradictions may be found in these historical books, but I pass over them all at present, as well as over the succeeding books until we come to the prophets, for to these I must devote the remainder of the space allotted to this part of my subject. We may note in passing the ludicrous absurdity of the headings, "reciprocal love of Christ and his Church," etc., put by commentators over the sensual and suggestive descriptions of male and female beauty in the amorous "Song of Solomon."

Isaiah is by far the finest and least objectionable of the seventeen prophets whose supposed productions form the latter part of the Old Testament. A distinctly higher moral tone appears in the writings called by his name, and this is especially noticeable in the "second Isaiah," who wrote after the Babylonish captivity. There is also much fine imagery and poetic feeling, and a distinct effort to raise the people above the brutal savagery of animal sacrifice to the recognition that justice and right-doing are more acceptable to Jahveh than dead animals. Jahveh himself has wonderfully altered, and though there are many traces of the savage Mosaic deity, the prevailing thought is of the "High and lofty One that inhabiteth eternity, whose Name is Holy" (Is. lvii., 15).

It seems strange, after reading some of the more beautiful passages, to suddenly come upon such a passage as that in chapter xxxiv., 6—8. Yet all are equally inspired, and must be equally accepted as divine. It is hard to imagine that the coarse indecency of chapter xxxvi., 12, is dictated by "a God of purity." Nor is it easy to see what good Isaiah did by walking about "naked and barefoot" (chap. xx., 2, 3). The completeness of the nakedness is not left in doubt (v. 4). In any civilised community Isaiah would have been taken up by the police. A fresh difficulty is thrown in the believer's way by the statement: "The grave cannot praise thee; death cannot celebrate thee; they that go down into the pit cannot hope for thy truth" (chap. xxxviii., 18). It is therefore blasphemy to say that there is any "hope" for the dead. Yet it is equally blasphemy to deny that the dead have hope of resurrection.

Jeremiah is a most melancholy prophet. He wails from beginning to end; he is often childish, is rarely indecent, and although it may be blasphemy to say so, he and his "Lamentations" are really not worth reading.

Ezekiel is both childish and obscene in the grossest sense. I can fancy how Sir W. V. Harcourt would characterise Ezekiel if he were not protected by law. In the first chapter we are introduced to a wonderful chariot, borne by four living creatures, each of whom had four wings and four faces, and four sides, and they had a "likeness" which was separate from them, for "it went up and down among the living creatures" (chap. i., 13); and the chariot had four wheels, or perhaps eight, for there was "as it were a wheel in the middle of a wheel" (v. 16); these wheels "went upon their four sides" (v. 17), which must have been very awkward, and they were full of eyes—what do wheels do with eyes?—and were "so high that they were dreadful" (v. 18); on the top of this conglomeration of four-faced creatures and eyed wheels was a firmament, and on the firmament a throne, and on the throne a man, amber-colored, and fire enwrapped, and the man was "the Lord." And it is blasphemy to deny the truth of this unintelligible jargon of absurdities. Then this man converses with Ezekiel, and "a hand"—apparently minus an arm and a body—brings a book (chap. ii., 9), and Ezekiel eats this "roll" (chap. iii., 1—3), a very indigestible one, I should fancy. Then Ezekiel takes a tile, and sketches a town on it, and pretends to besiege the tile, and sticks up an iron pan which he makes believe is an iron wall, and then he lies before it, making a fort and a mount, and bringing battering rams to bear on his old brickbat (chap. iv., 1—4). And it is blasphemy not to believe that this midsummer madness was god-inspired. The remainder of his conduct (vv. 9—15) is too disgusting to mention, and as we are not protected, to print it would bring us under Lord Campbell's Act. The same remark applies to the unutterable nastiness of chaps. xvi. and xxiii. And this is in a book put into the hands of little boys and girls, without one protest from the Home Secretary. After all this we are not surprised to read "the spirit" lifted Ezekiel up in the air, "the form of a hand" taking him "by a lock of mine head" (chap. viii., 3). When we read that Gabriel lifted Mahomet in this manner, we say it is an impudent fraud; when we read it of Ezekiel it is "the very truth of God."

The book of Daniel has been so utterly destroyed by criticism that it would be wasted time to dwell upon it. Yet this book is kept as one of the "prophets," although it has been proved to demonstration that the pretended prophecies were written after the event.

The "minor prophets" deserve a pamphlet to themselves, so full of absurdities are they. Hosea, judging by chap. i., 2, 3, and iv., 1, 2, must have been a man of very indifferent character. His writings have the two characteristics of the minor prophets, indecency and maniacal raving; sexual vice is played upon in a manner that is wearisomely disgusting (see v., 1—13; iv., 12—14; v., 3, 4; vi., 10, etc., etc.). Amos tells us how "the Lord stood upon a wall made by a plumbline, with a plumbline in his hand. And the Lord said unto me, Amos, what seest thou? And I said, a plumbline" (chap. vii., 7, 8). Amos was always seeing queer things, and "the Lord" was always asking him what he saw! He saw some grasshoppers (vii., 1, 2), and a basket of summer fruit (viii., 1), and the "Lord standing upon the altar" (ix., 1). Jonah's adventures are famous, and it is blasphemy to deny that throwing Jonah into the sea stilled the waves, that a great fish swallowed him, that the fish was a whale (Matt. xii., 40), that he lived in the whale's stomach for three days and three nights, said his prayers there, and was thrown up safe and sound after living for seventy-two hours inside an animal! Zechariah is as bad for vision-seeing as Amos. He sees red, speckled and white horses among myrtle trees (i., 8), and then four horns (v. 18); a friendly angel talks with him (v. 9), and explains matters in a fashion that makes them more confused. Then there is a "man with a measuring line" (ii., 1), and Joshua the high priest "in filthy garments," whom they undressed and dressed up again (iii., 1—5). And there are a candlestick, and two olive-trees, and some pipes which "empty the golden oil," and which are the "two anointed ones" (iv.). Next comes "a flying roll," and then can anyone make sense of the following: "Then the angel that talked with me went forth, and said unto me, Lift up now thine eyes, and see what is this that goeth forth. And I said, what is it? And he said, this is an ephah that goeth forth. He said moreover, this is their resemblance through all the earth. And, behold, there was lifted up a talent of lead, and this is a woman that sitteth in the midst of the ephah. And he said, This is wickedness. And he cast it into the midst of the ephah; and he cast the weight of lead upon the mouth thereof. Then lifted I up mine eyes, and looked, and behold there came out two women, and the wind was in their wings; for they had wings like the wings of a stork: and they lifted up the ephah between the earth and the heaven. Then said I to the angel that talked with me, whither do these bear the ephah? And he said unto me, to build it an house in the land of Shinar: and it shall be established, and set there upon her own base." (Zech. v., 5—11.) Yet if we do not believe this we shall be dammed.

I might heap together yet more of these absurdities, but to what end? Who but a lunatic could have written such incoherent matter? Yet this Old Testament, containing error, folly, absurdity and immorality is by English statute law declared to be of divine authority, a blasphemy—if there were anyone to be blasphemed—blacker and more insolent than any word ever written or penned by the most hotheaded Freethinker.

END OF PART I.

THE

CHRISTIAN CREED;

OR,

What it is Blasphemy to deny.

PART II.

BY

ANNIE BESANT.

LONDON:
FREETHOUGHT PUBLISHING COMPANY,
63, FLEET STREET, E.C.

1884.

LONDON
PRINTED BY ANNIE BESANT AND CHARLES BRADLAUGH
63, FLEET STREET, E.C.

THE CHRISTIAN CREED;

Or, What it is Blasphemy to deny.

In Part I. of "The Christian Creed" I exposed some of the "errors, inconsistencies and absurdities" contained in that part of "God's Holy Word" known as the Old Testament. I propose now to perform a similar task for that part of the same book which is known as the New Testament. I say "the same book," because it is as one book that "the Bible" is imposed upon us, and it is claimed that it has one author, the "Holy Ghost." The various writers thereof are mere tools in his hand, and can no more be regarded as the authors of the treatises that bear their names than can the pens wherewith an ordinary author writes the chapters of his book. As a matter of fact, however, the Bible is not one book at all, it is merely a number of treatises bound up in one volume, and its contents have varied from time to time. Some treatises once forming part of it have been dropped out; others have been included; and there is by no means a universal agreement as to what the Holy Ghost wrote and what was the work of some inferior penman. The version of the Holy Scriptures accepted in the church as by law established is the book which in this happy land it is blasphemy to deny, blasphemy to ridicule. And it is this same version of the Holy Scriptures which it is the duty of honest people to attack and to expose.

Matthew begins his account of the events of the life of Jesus of Nazareth by giving us "the book of the generation of Jesus Christ, the son of David, the son of Abraham." Of the first six verses we need only remark that were it not blasphemy to object to it we might be disposed to cavil at the female characters chosen by God incarnate for his ancestresses. Four women only are mentioned in this list: Tamar, the daughter-in-law of Judah, bore to her father-in-law a son, Phares; Rachab, the mother of Boaz, was a common harlot; Ruth, the wife of Boaz, was a young lady who "when Boaz had eaten and drunk, and his heart was merry" "came softly and uncovered his feet and laid her down" there all night, holding a conversation with him at midnight and departing before daylight, so that it might "not be known that a woman came into the floor" (Ruth iii., 7—14); the mother of Solomon was Bathsheba, the accomplice of David in his treachery towards and murder of Uriah, her husband. Christians allege that God incarnate could only be born of a pure and spotless virgin; it seems to me that he need scarcely have been so particular about his mother considering how indifferent he was with regard to his other female relations.

There are various contradictions of the genealogy given in Matthew in the parallel genealogies given in Chronicles and in Luke, contradictions which it is impossible to believe, but which it is blasphemy to deny. Thus we must believe and confess that Salathiel begat Zerubbabel (Matt. i., 12), while we must not deny that Zerubbabel was the son of Pedaiah, the brother of Salathiel, and therefore was the nephew of his own father (1 Chron. iii., 17, 19). We must gladly recognise that Zerubbabel begat Abiud (Matt. i., 13), and that Rhesa was his son (Luke iii., 27), while we believe with joy that Zerubbabel had only five sons, among whom Abiud and Rhesa are not to be found (1 Chron. iii., 19, 20). So also must we say that "Matthan begat Jacob, and Jacob begat Joseph the husband of Mary, of whom was born Jesus, who is called Christ" (Matt. i., 15, 16), while we equally acknowledge that Jesus was supposed to be "the son of Joseph, which was the son of Heli, which was the son of Matthat" (Luke iii., 23, 24). We must not stagger through unbelief when we find that Jesus had no father, that his reputed father had two fathers, but only one grandfather on the bi-paternal side. It is blasphemy to deny any one of these complicated and uncommon family relationships, and the denial of one or of all of them may land us in Holloway gaol.

Mary, the mother of Jesus, was espoused to Joseph, and previous to the marriage "was found with child of the Holy Ghost" (Matt. i., 18). Joseph was naturally displeased at his wife's infidelity, but being a merciful man "was minded to put her away privily," and was only prevented from so doing by a dream. We learn from Luke that Mary had been visited by "the angel Gabriel" (i., 26), and that Gabriel had announced to her that "the Holy Ghost shall come upon thee, and the power of the Highest shall overshadow thee: therefore that holy thing which shall be born of thee shall be called the son of God" (verse 35). Mary, therefore, knew all about her own condition, and it seems a marvellous thing that she should not have defended herself when Joseph accused her, but should have left it to a dream to vindicate her honor to her husband. It would be blasphemy to suggest that in Matthew there is incorporated a tradition differing from that followed by Luke, and that for this very simple reason we find the machinery different in the two stories; in Matthew dreams play a prominent part (i., 20; ii., 12, 13, 19, 22), whereas in Luke angels appear to people who are wide awake (i., 11, 26; ii., 9).

Blasphemous also would it be to think—or at least to say—that this whole story of the birth of Jesus of a virgin is the counterpart of the numerous stories familiar to every student of mythology, in which a God weds a maiden, and a demi-God is born of the union. The Holy Ghost is a dove, Zeus is a swan, and so on. The actors and the plot are always the same, though bearing varied names and attired in varied dresses. Further, it is very difficult to read the account of Gabriel's visit to Mary, and not compare it mentally with the accounts we read of the priests who received young maidens into the temples of the Gods they served. In each case the servant of the God assures the maiden that she will be visited by the Deity in person; where the Pagan God is concerned, everyone admits that the priests were not only the messengers, but were also the representatives of the God; where the Christian God is concerned, it is blasphemy to suggest that the part played by the priests in the one case was played by "Gabriel" in the other. Children born under such circumstances were always Sons of God.

Matthew and Luke agree that Jesus was born at Bethlehem, but with this exception—and that of the names of his reputed father and mother—the stories are contradictory from beginning to end. Yet we must believe both, for "he that believeth not shall be damned" (Mark xvi., 16). Let us try.

According to Matthew, Joseph and Mary only went to "a city called Nazareth" because they were afraid of Archelaus, and because there was a prophecy to be fulfilled (Matt. ii., 21—23). According to Luke, Joseph and Mary both belonged to Nazareth, and only went to Bethlehem on business, returning thither as a matter of course (Luke i., 26, 27; ii., 4, 5, 39). The whole second chapter of Matthew has nothing in common with the account in Luke; the following is Matthew's story as therein given: When Jesus was born some wise men from the East arrived in Jerusalem, having been guided thither by a star; they interviewed Herod the king, and all Jerusalem was troubled and astir; after worshipping the child at Bethlehem they departed homewards, and Joseph, Mary and the child fled into Egypt from the wrath of Herod; Herod sent out and slew all the infants in Bethlehem and the neighborhood from two years old and under, and there was a terrible mourning in the land; on Herod's death, Joseph, Mary and the child returned, and fearing Archelaus avoided Judæa, and went northwards into Galilee. According to Luke ii., Jesus was visited by shepherds, who "made known abroad the saying which was told them concerning this child," and though the people "wondered at those things which were told them by the shepherds," no trouble and no hostility were shown; Jesus was taken up to Jerusalem (where Herod was raging, according to Matthew), and was presented to the Lord, according to the law, in the temple; there he was blessed by Simeon, and Anna, the prophetess, "spake of him to all them that looked for redemption in Jerusalem," and yet all Jerusalem, which had been so troubled according to Matthew, did nothing at all. Herod, who so desired to find him and slay him, allowed him to be publicly presented in the temple and did not touch him; there was no flight into Egypt; on the contrary, "when they had performed all things according to the law of the Lord, they returned into Galilee, to their own city, Nazareth." These two stories are mutually exclusive. If Jesus remained in Bethlehem for forty days (Luke ii., 22), was then carried to Jerusalem, and when the legal ceremony of purification was accomplished was taken into

Galilee, he cannot have fled down into Egypt and have gone later into Galilee to escape Archelaus. Yet it is blasphemy to deny either of these incompatible stories, and so thoughtless and so cowardly are the majority that they pretend to believe them both at the same time!

A word must be said on the absurd pretence of Matthew that the reason for the choice of Nazareth by Joseph as his place of residence was "that it might be fulfilled which was spoken by the prophets, He shall be called a Nazarene" (ii., 23). Everyone knows that there is no such prophecy in any prophet in the Bible, yet, in order to maintain the delusion, a reference Bible gives a collection of references as though to the alleged prophecies. They are worth examining. Number one is Num. vi., 13: "And this is the law of the Nazarite, when the days of his separation are fulfilled: he shall be brought into the door of the tabernacle of the congregation;" and then follow various directions as to sacrifices and shaving. What has this to do with Jesus? A Nazarite and a Nazarene had no connexion with each other, and we can only suppose as to this that the Holy Ghost amused himself by making a pun on the similarity of the names. Further, Jesus was never brought to the door of the tabernacle at all, for one simple and sufficient reason, if for no other, that the tabernacle and its door had disappeared long before Jesus was born. Number two is Judges xiii., 5: "For, lo, thou shalt conceive and bear a son; and no razor shall come on his head: for the child shall be a Nazarite unto God from the womb; and he shall begin to deliver Israel out of the hand of the Philistines." Nothing there about Jesus being called a Nazarene. Number three is 1 Sam. i., 11: "And she vowed a vow, and said, O Lord of hosts, if thou wilt indeed look on the affliction of thine handmaid, and remember me, and not forget thine handmaid, but wilt give unto thine handmaid a man child, then I will give him unto the Lord all the days of his life, and there shall no razor come upon his head." Connexion with Jesus equally wanting. Number four is Amos ii., 10—12: "Also I brought you up from the land of Egypt, and led you forty years through the wilderness, to possess the land of the Amorite. And I raised up of your sons for prophets, and of your young men for Nazarites. Is it not even thus, O ye children of Israel, saith the Lord. But ye gave the

Nazarites wine to drink; and commanded the prophets, saying, prophesy not."

Now what reference is there to Jesus in any one of these verses, and yet they are the nearest approach to that "which was spoken by the prophets, He shall be called a Nazarene!" And the law has the insolence to impose on us this folly for our belief, and to menace us with prison if we dare to be honest and reject. But better a thousand times the gaol than the blasphemy against truth which is implied in its acceptance.

The story of John the Baptist and of the relations existing between him and Jesus is one which it is very difficult to relate without falling into blasphemy, for the accounts given in the four gospels contradict each other in most remarkable fashion. Let us try to piece them together into a connected if self-contradictory account.

In Matthew, Mark and John, the Baptist appears suddenly full grown on the scene; Luke stands alone in telling us of his birth. As there is only one story we have here no contradiction; and we learn that Zacharias, his father, and Elisabeth, his mother, had had no children, "because that Elisabeth was barren and they both were now well stricken in years" (i., 7). They were Levites, Zacharias being a priest and Elisabeth "of the daughters of Aaron" (v. 5), and while Zacharias was burning incense the angel Gabriel appeared to him and announced the approaching birth of a son, to be named John, and further struck him dumb because he asked a very simple question. Gabriel was much more considerate to Mary when she showed a similar curiosity (compare verses 18 and 34).

Elisabeth was Mary's cousin and was visited by the latter, but the account of their meeting possesses a delicacy so thoroughly scriptural that I must refer my readers to the Gospel for it (verses 41—44). If anyone but the Holy Ghost had written these verses they would be called very coarse, but to the Holy Ghost great license is permitted on account of his high rank and antiquity.

John remained "in the deserts till the day of his showing unto Israel" (verse 80), and there the word of the Lord came unto him, and "he came into all the country about Jordan, preaching the baptism of repentance for the remission of sins" (iii., 2, 3). He appears to have been one of the wild monks common in the East, living on what rough food he could find in the desert, and clothed in a skin (Matt. iii., 4). His preaching, according to Luke, was practical and sensible (iii., 10—14), and following the custom of his nation he baptised those who professed themselves ready to lead a righteous life.

Among others Jesus came to the baptism, and John at first refused to baptise him on the ground of Jesus' superiority (Matt. iii., 13—15), although he did not know who he was until after the baptism and the descent of the Holy Ghost (John i., 33). In a mere human book this would be a contradiction, but in works written by the Holy Ghost there is nothing strange in a man recognising another before an event, although he did not know him until after the same event. It is blasphemy to deny that John knew Jesus before he baptised him, and that he did not know him until afterwards. The way that leadeth unto life may be difficult because of its narrowness, but it is far more difficult when it divides into two paths leading in opposite directions, and we have to walk down both at the same time.

A yet more complex feat is put before us with regard to the words spoken when the Holy Ghost "descended in a bodily shape like a dove" (Luke iii., 22), and sat on Jesus; a "voice from heaven" said: "This is my beloved Son, in whom I am well pleased" (Matt. iii., 17); or, "Thou art my beloved Son, in whom I am well pleased" (Mark i., 11); or, "Thou art my beloved Son, in thee I am well pleased" (Luke iii., 22). To avoid the sin and peril of blasphemy we must believe that the voice said each of these three different phrases; the Holy Ghost was so close by that he must have heard distinctly what was said, and yet he has given us three versions. There are four ways open to us: I. To believe Matthew; II. To believe Mark; III. To believe Luke; IV. To believe none of them. The only way to avoid damnation is to take the first three all together, all at the same time. This I cannot do, and I select the fourth, there being no reason for preferring any one of the three above the others. Will it not be a little unfair if God damns me because he has given me a brain which is not able to believe three contradictory propositions all at the same time?

The unregenerated sceptic has many qualms and difficulties in connexion with this story of the baptism of Jesus.

There s only one God; yet Jesus—one God—is being baptised; the Holy Ghost—one God—is in the shape of a dove lighting on Jesus; the voice of the Father—one God—proclaims Jesus as his beloved son. The separation seems complete, voice, man, dove; yet they are all one God, and God alighting on himself and proclaiming himself his own son is the picture presented for our worship. Again, where is "heaven" from which the voice "came"? The nearest fixed star is distant 21,996,360,000,000 miles. Is heaven on the other side of this star? If yes, the voice must have been a strong one.

Yet again, since the Holy Ghost is God and God is everywhere, whence did the Holy Ghost descend? If he is present everywhere, he cannot move from place to place like a person who is localised, he cannot descend to a spot where he was not before. Everywhere at every moment of time, he cannot move from one place and alight on another. Blasphemy again! But blasphemy is inseparable from thought on the Bible.

To return to the story of Jesus in connexion with John: after his baptism Jesus went away into the wilderness according to Matthew, Mark and Luke, and, according to Matthew and Mark, he did not return into Galilee until after John was cast in prison (Matt. iv., 12; Mark i., 14); it was only after that event that "Jesus began to preach" (Matt. iv., 17). But according to John, Jesus, instead of going into the wilderness gained three disciples on the day after his baptism; on the second day he went into Galilee, and on the third worked his first miracle (John i. and ii.). He then went to Capernaum, visited Jerusalem, taught so that he had disciples (John ii., 17), worked miracles (verse 23), and baptised (iii., 22), and all this before John was cast into prison (iii., 23, 24). It needs much faith to believe simultaneously that Jesus only *began* to teach after the Baptist's imprisonment, although he had taught long before it. Yet this faith is necessary for those who would avoid gaol here and hell hereafter.

The story of the temptation is another of the facts which are difficult to swallow. God the Spirit led God the Son to be tempted, yet we are distinctly told that "God cannot be tempted with evil, neither tempteth he any man" (James i., 13). If this be true Jesus was not tempted of the devil, for Jesus is God, and the devil is evil. But it is blasphemy to allege that Jesus was not tempted of the devil. Jesus was "led up of the Spirit .... to be tempted" (Matt. iv., 1), but James said: "Every man is tempted when he is drawn away of his own lust and enticed" (i., 14). According to this the Spirit was Jesus' own lust, and it was not God who led him "to be tempted" (Matt. iv., 1), for "neither tempteth he any man."

The temptations were curious. First, "the tempter" invited him to turn stones into bread; Jesus declined to do so, as would most of us if we underwent a similar temptation. Next the devil picked him up and put him on a pinnacle of the temple, and suggested that he should throw himself down; this tempting proposal was declined by Jesus, as again I think it would have been by most people outside a lunatic asylum. The third time the devil took him up an "exceeding high mountain"—very exceedingly high it must have been to enable them to see all round the world; I will believe the whole Gospel to-morrow if that mountain can be rediscovered—and offered him all the kingdoms of the world. Now, there was something like a temptation, but if Jesus were God the whole universe was his, and a few paltry kingdoms which were already his own could not have seemed much of a bribe with which to induce him to worship his own creature.

According to Luke the second and third temptations, as given above from Matthew, were reversed, and the world was seen "in a moment of time" (iv., 5). If, however, we believe in the high mountain from which we can survey a globe, we shall not stumble over the moment of time which sufficed for the survey. Big miracles are as easy—or as difficult—to believe as are little ones.

It must have startled the folk at Jerusalem when they saw Jesus and the devil flying through the air and alighting on the temple. We are very unfairly dealt with, we unbelievers of these latter days. If the devil would pick up Mr. Spurgeon or the Archbishop of Canterbury, or even General Booth, and set him on the cross of St. Paul's, it would convert many to belief in his Satanic Majesty. The Jews had so many miracles that they regarded them with indifference, while not even a little one is vouchsafed to us. I don't think it is fair.

The calling of Simon Peter, Andrew, James and John took place in various fashions. Immediately after the baptism of Jesus, two of John the Baptist's disciples left their master and followed Jesus, and one of these was Andrew; he at once brought Simon Peter his brother to Jesus, and they followed Jesus from Bethabara beyond Jordan into Galilee (John i., 28, 35—42), and thence, after visiting Capernaum, to Jerusalem (ii., 12, 13). There is nothing in this account to lead us to suppose that Andrew and Simon Peter were fishermen of Galilee. It is, however, as fishermen that Jesus became acquainted with them, and that not until after John the Baptist's imprisonment. For we read that after that event Jesus began to preach, and "walking by the sea of Galilee, saw two brethren, Simon called Peter and Andrew his brother, casting a net into the sea; for they were fishers. And he saith unto them, Follow me and I will make you fishers of men" (Matt. iv., 18, 19). If this account be true, Simon Peter and Andrew must have deserted their master, after following him from Bethabara to Galilee, from Galilee to Jerusalem, from Jerusalem back again to Galilee (see John i., ii., iii., iv.), and after all this Jesus met them as though nothing had happened, and bade them follow him. Yet a third account of the calling of these famous apostles is given in Luke. According to this, Jesus did not find Andrew and Simon Peter "casting a net into the sea," but being pressed on by the crowd, he entered a ship "standing by the lake" which was left by the fishermen who "were washing their nets" (v. 2). The ship belonged to Simon, who pushed it out from the shore for the convenience of Jesus, and when the preaching was over he launched "out into the deep" and let down his net at the command of Jesus. An enormous catch was made, and "when Simon Peter saw it he fell down at Jesus' knees, saying, Depart from me; for I am a sinful man, O Lord. . . . . And Jesus said unto Simon, Fear not; from henceforth thou shalt catch men" (v., 4—10). If the accounts in Matthew and Luke were not written by the Holy Ghost I should call them inconsistent with each other. (I have omitted the account in Mark, which resembles that in Matthew.) Equally inconsistent are the notices of the calling of James and John, the sons of Zebedee. According to Matthew and Mark they were mending their nets, "and straightway he called them: and they left their father Zebedee in the ship with the hired servants and went after him" (Mark i., 19, 20; see also Matt. iv., 21, 22). Zebedee's views of this sudden desertion are not written for our learning. According to Luke, James and John went to help Simon with his great draught of fishes, and on reaching the land "forsook all and followed him" (v. 10, 11). So they were called on sea and on land, mending their nets with their father and catching fish with Peter, and "he that believeth not" both accounts "shall be damned."

There are some very instructive inconsistencies between the reports of the "sermon on the mount" given by Matthew and by Luke, or rather by the Holy Ghost, using Matthew and Luke as his instruments. Of the two, Luke is clearly the older; Matthew has been toned down to meet the views of Christians as they rose in social position; Luke says out straight and clear: "Blessed be ye poor: for yours is the kingdom of God. Blessed are ye that hunger now: for ye shall be filled. Blessed are ye that weep now: for ye shall laugh. . . . But woe unto you that are rich! for ye have received your consolation. Woe unto you that are full! for ye shall hunger. Woe unto you that laugh now! for ye shall mourn and weep" (vi., 20, 21, 24, 25). It is the raving of a fanatic and ascetic, hating all the joy and mirth of life. In Matthew it is discreetly toned down, and the curses levelled at the rich are omitted, and a gloss is put on the states that are pronounced blessed: "Blessed are the poor *in spirit*: for theirs is the kingdom of heaven. Blessed are they that mourn: for they shall be comforted. . . . Blessed are they which do hunger and thirst *after righteousness*: for they shall be filled" (v., 3, 4, 6). The absurdity of the gloss is seen if it is read into the corresponding curse: "Woe unto you that are full *of righteousness*: for ye shall hunger," and yet if the blessing is not on bodily hunger but on hunger after righteousness, the corresponding curse cannot be on bodily repletion but on fullness of righteousness.

Even the prayer given by Jesus to his disciples and known as "the Lord's prayer" exists in two versions, one of which must be inaccurate. Matthew has: "Our Father which art in heaven, hallowed be thy name. Thy kingdom come. Thy will be done in earth, as it is in heaven. Give us this day our daily bread. And forgive us our debts, as we forgive our debtors. And lead us not into temptation, but deliver us from evil. For thine is the kingdom, and the power, and the glory, for ever. Amen." (vi., 9, 11). Luke has: "Our Father which art in heaven, hallowed be thy name. Thy kingdom come. Thy will be done, as in heaven, so in earth. Give us day by day our daily bread. And forgive us our sins; for we also forgive every one that is indebted to us. And lead us not into temptation, but deliver us from evil" (xi., 2, 3, 4)—and there it stops abruptly. The Holy Ghost is evidently a very careless reporter.

It is odd, too, that God should have been forestalled in the invention of this prayer by one of his own creatures; a work ought, in common honesty, to be known by the name of the composer and not of the copyist, and this prayer might be as truly called "Matthew's prayer," as "the Lord's prayer," for both Jesus and Matthew copied it from an older source, and but slightly changed it. Readers can judge for themselves: "Our Father, which art in heaven, be gracious to us. O Lord our God, hallowed be thy name, and let the remembrance of thee be glorified in heaven above, and upon earth here below. Let thy kingdom reign over us, now and for ever. The holy men of old said, remit and forgive unto all men whatsoever they have done unto us. And lead us not into temptation, but deliver us from the evil thing. For thine is the kingdom, and thou shalt reign in glory for ever, and for evermore."

We must also remark that the so-called "Sermon on the Mount," as given in Matthew, appears to be a collection of sayings spoken at various times and places, and put together and edited by the transcriber. Such proceedings are all very well in fiction, but cast considerable doubt on a narrative that pretends to be historical.

The incident which ended in the destruction of the herd of swine deserves a word of notice: two men (Matt. viii., 28), or one man (Mark v., 2, and Luke viii., 27), possessed with devils and, according to Mark and Luke, wearing no clothes, came "out of the tombs, exceeding fierce"; this individual, or these individuals, was or were "night and day" "crying and cutting himself with stones." He or they cried out to Jesus, and asked what they had to do with him, and after some conversation between Jesus and the devils inside the possessed, it was arranged that the devils might, on leaving their human dwelling, take lodgings in a neighboring herd of swine. The swine did not approve of their new tenants, and the whole two thousand of them ran down a steep place into the sea and committed suicide. It is a little difficult to see what the devils gained by this brief pig-incarnation. They clearly went "into the deep" with great promptitude, and this was just the thing which they desired to avoid (Luke viii., 31). Only the Holy Ghost can explain this curious demoniac action, but most folk will agree with the feeling of the poor Gadarenes, robbed of their two thousand pigs, when they "came out to meet Jesus, and when they saw him, they besought him that he would depart out of their coasts."

It is not worth while to delay over the many accounts of miracles performed by Jesus; thaumaturgic feats by his hero are the stock-in-trade of every religious biographer, and it is not to be supposed that "God incarnate" should be less successful in his miracle-working than his predecessors and rivals. Besides, miracles can at the most prove nothing except themselves; supposing that a man came to me and worked a miracle, and then demanded that I should murder the Queen; his working the miracle—*i.e.*, his doing something unusual, something I could not do—would prove that he understood and used some force which I did not understand and could not use, but it would do no more; it would not give him any authority over me, nor would it make murder right. Granted a man who does an act we cannot explain; he may be a conjurer, deceiving our senses; he may be a scientist utilising a force newly discovered by himself and unknown to all others. His proceedings may be very interesting, but they give no authority in morals. Let us suppose even the extremest case, that a man is able to revivify the dead; he would have the world at his feet; we would pour out our gold to persuade him to use his power on the corpse of our beloved; nay, we might even commit a crime if he made the committal of the crime the condition of the exercise of his power; but all this would not make his opinion on anything save the revivifying of the dead more valuable than the opinion of anybody else. Even a proven miracle—and such a thing has never been—would become worthless when considered in this light of calm reason and judgment.

It is worthy remark that this view of the value of miracles is strongly inculcated in the Old Testament: "If there arise among you a prophet, or a dreamer of dreams, and giveth thee a sign or a wonder, and the sign or the wonder come to pass, whereof he spake unto thee, saying, Let us go after other gods, which thou hast not known, and let us serve them; thou shalt not hearken unto the words of that prophet, or that dreamer of dreams: for the Lord your God proveth you" (Deut. xiii., 1—3). The Jews followed the command of their law, and refused to allow that the doctrines of Jesus were proved by his miracles; strictly following their law "the Pharisees said, he casteth out devils through the prince of the devils" (Matt. ix., 34), and would have none of him. If Jesus were God, and if God gave the Mosaic law, his rejection was a charming instance of "the engineer hoist with his own petard." But one would have thought that God would have been more careful.

An admirable legend touching this deep-seated—and most philosophic—view of the worthlessness of miracles, held by the Jews, is quoted by Mr. Yorke in his valuable "Notes on Evolution and Christianity;" it runs as follows:

"In one of the celebrated academies where all the sages of Israel were assembled, there arose an important discussion between Rabbi Eliezer, one of the glories of the synagogue, and his colleagues, as to the interpretation of certain doctrinal matters referring to things clean and unclean. All the arguments advanced by Rabbi Eliezer in support of his opinions had been unanimously opposed and rejected by the other doctors. 'Well,' indignantly exclaimed the illustrious Rabbi, 'let this banana part from its roots, and plant itself on the opposite side.' At these words, the tree detached itself from its roots, and planted itself on the opposite side. 'What does that prove?' cried the doctors with one voice; 'and what connexion has the value of this banana with the question which occupies us?' 'Well,' again exclaims Rabbi Eliezer, 'may the rivulet that flows near us demonstrate the truth of my opinion;' and suddenly, oh miracle! the waters of the brook reascended to their source. 'Well,' once more replied the doctors, 'whether the waters flow in one direction or another, what connexion is there between this circumstance and the subject of our controversy?' 'Well,' impatiently said Rabbi Eliezer, 'may the walls of this room serve me as proof and testimony;' and the pillars supporting the edifice bow, obedient to the voice of their master, and the walls crack and threaten to overwhelm them. Then Rabbi Schoschonah, one of the most renowned sages of the age, exclaimed: 'O walls! O walls! when sages discuss the interpretation of the law, what have you to do with their arguments?' And the walls stopped as they were falling, and remained leaning suspended over the heads of the doctors. 'May God himself pronounce supreme judgment,' cried Rabbi Eliezer; and from the heavenly heights the daughter of the voice was heard saying: 'No longer call in question the doctrine of Rabbi Eliezer: reason is on his side.'

"But Rabbi Schoschonah protested: 'Neither reason, nor the law,' he cried, 'is now in the depths of the heavens; neither miracles nor mysterious voices have, in our eyes, the power to demonstrate the truth. To human reason, to the decision of the majority of the sages of Israel, is committed the interpretation of thy law, O Lord! Henceforth these alone are the only powers that can prevail.' Notwithstanding the miracles that were performed, notwithstanding the intervention of the Divine voice, the opinion of Rabbi Eliezer was condemned by the doctors, his contemporaries. And (adds the Talmud) Rabbi Nathan, having met the prophet Elijah, asked him what had been said in heaven respecting the debate, and received the following answer: 'The Eternal smiled, and replied: "My sons are the strongest, my sons have triumphed!"'"

Allow for the superstitious belief in "the Eternal" as a person, and the legend is most instructive. And truly the very expression "the Eternal" is a rebuke to the anthropomorphism of the god-idea, for to the scientific thinker the steadfast changelessness of nature is verily "the Eternal," and while our ignorance forbids us to say "as ever shall be," our knowledge justifies us in saying of much, "as it was" and "as it is."

Remembering that the Holy Ghost is the real author of the New Testament, it is a little puzzling to discover that he was not sure about the names of the "twelve apostles": Simon Peter, Andrew, James, John (sons of Zebedee), Philip, Bartholomew, Thomas, Matthew, James (son of Alpheus), and Judas Iscariot are named by Matthew, Mark and Luke (Matt. x., 2—4; Mark iii., 16—19; Luke vi., 14—16). Then there is a "Simon, the Canaanite" (Matt. x., 4; Mark iii., 18), whom we may accept, I suppose, as the "Simon called Zelotes," of Luke vi., 15. But there is a "Lebbæus, whose surname was Thaddæus" (Matt. x., 3), who also appears in Mark iii., 18, as Thaddæus, but who has utterly vanished in Luke, his place being taken by "Judas, the brother of James"—which James? the son of Zebedee or the son of Alphæus?—a Judas unknown to Matthew or to Mark. As these twelve are to "sit upon twelve thrones, judging the twelve tribes of Israel" (Matt. xix., 28), there seems likely to be a quarrel over one throne, and Judas Iscariot, safely seated on the undoubted throne promised to him by Jesus, will, I should fancy, feel intensely amused over the tussle going on between "Lebbæus whose surname was Thaddæus" and his own namesake "Judas, not Iscariot," for the one seat left for the twain. There will apparently be a game of "Post" on the morning of the Resurrection, in which a third claimant, Matthias (see Acts i., 15—26), may possibly take part.

The spirit inculcated by Jesus in his apostles is worthy notice. He says to them: "Whosoever shall not receive you nor hear your words, when ye depart out of that house or city, shake off the dust of your feet. Verily I say unto you, it shall be more tolerable for the land of Sodom and Gomorrah in the day of judgment, than for that city" (Matt. x., 14, 15). Here is the very essence of the Gospel: Show childish rudeness and petulance when people disagree with your opinions, and comfort yourselves with remembering that hereafter you shall gloat over the agonies of those who have ventured to differ from you; you are weak and helpless now, but hereafter your malice shall be sated with the torments of those who here have refused to submit to you. As the very echo of these words of Jesus come the brutal rejoicings of Tertullian, possible only to the petrified heart of the Christian, over "kings groaning in that darkness; persecutors liquefying in flames; wise men glowing red in the conflagration." Here is the very essence of the spirit of Jesus, of the spirit that built the Inquisition, and that drenched the world in blood.

This same tenth chapter of Matthew brings us face to face in its twenty-third verse, with a puzzle which has grieved many a Christian heart: "Verily I say unto you, Ye shall not have gone over the cities of Israel, till the Son of Man be come." Here is but one of the many passages in the New Testament, which announce the return of Jesus within the life-time of the generation to which he himself belonged. Take the following declarations; so-called prophecies, far less plain and explicit, have been claimed as fulfilled, in order to endorse the claims of the Bible; in the whole range of the "Holy Scriptures" there is no set of prophecies as plain, distinct, and explicit as are these; yet because history proves their falsity, the Christian world tries to explain away their obvious meaning, so that it may feebly cling to its belief in the foreknowledge and veracity of one proved to have been in error by the inexorable logic of facts.

"Ye shall not have gone over the cities of Israel till the Son of Man be come" (Matt. x., 23).

"The Son of Man shall come in the glory of his Father, with his angels; and then shall he reward every man according to his works. Verily I say unto you, There be some standing here, which shall not taste of death, till they see the Son of Man coming in his kingdom" (Matt. xvi., 27, 28).

"Verily I say unto you, This generation shall not pass till all these things be fulfilled" (Matt. xxiv., 34, and see *Ibid*, 14—44).

"Whosoever therefore shall be ashamed of me and of my words in this adulterous and sinful generation, of him also shall the Son of Man be ashamed, when he cometh in the glory of his Father, with the holy angels. And he said unto them, Verily I say unto you, that there be some of them that stand here, which shall not taste of death, till they have seen the kingdom of God come with power" (Mark viii., 38, and ix., 1).

"Verily I say unto you, That this generation shall not pass, till all these things be done" (Mark xiii., 30, and see *Ibid*, 19—37).

"For whosoever shall be ashamed of me and of my words, of him shall the Son of Man be ashamed when he shall come in his own glory, and in his Father's, and of the holy angels. But I tell you of a truth, there be some standing here, which shall not taste of death, till they see the kingdom of God" (Luke ix., 26, 27).

"Verily I say unto you, This generation shall not pass away till all be fulfilled" (Luke xxi., 32, and see *Ibid* 25—36).

"We shall not all sleep, but we shall all be changed . . . . the trumpet shall sound, and the dead shall be raised incorruptible, and we shall be changed" (1 Cor. xv., 51, 52).

"We look for the Savior, the Lord Jesus Christ; who shall change our vile body" (Phil. iii., 20, 21).

"We which are alive and remain unto the coming of the Lord . . . . the dead in Christ shall rise first; then we which are alive and remain, shall be caught up" (1 Thess. iv., 15, 16, 17).

Thus, over and over again, the pledge was given; the early Christians believed it, and looked for the coming of their Lord; but the centuries have rolled on, and no trumpet-call has broken through the silence of the heavens, no coming of the Son of Man has lightened from the east unto the west. "There be some standing here which shall not taste of death till they see the Son of Man coming in his kingdom." He has not yet come in his kingdom; if his words be true, there are some now living who heard him speak those words; let the Christians produce one of those living in the first century who has not "tasted of death," and I will believe. It may be blasphemy to say that Jesus made a palpable mistake and deceived both himself and his followers, but it is true if the Bible record be trustworthy. It is not our fault that he did not fulfil his promise; it is not our fault that history has proved him self-deluder; the facts are there, and if facts are blasphemy, so much the worse for the superstition that demands that reason shall be sacrificed, if earthly comfort and "eternal safety" are to be secured.

There is, however, a prophecy of Jesus in this tenth chapter of Matthew that has been fully and terribly fulfilled. "Think not that I am come to send peace on earth: I came not to send peace but a sword. For I am come to set a man at variance against his father, and the daughter against her mother, and the daughter in law against her mother in law. And a man's foes shall be they of his own household" (verses 34—36). Truly a sword has Jesus sent through earth; from the moment that his religion seized temporal power under Constantine until the power of Reason made murder of heresy impossible, it has drenched the earth with blood. It has burned, and tortured, and rent, and wounded; it has held high carnival amid the corpses of unbelievers, and rioted amid the ruins of the homes it has laid desolate. Follow its destroying course as it "converts Europe"; watch it in its power in Spain, in Italy, in France; traverse the Atlantic to America, and see it tear down the gracious civilisation of Peru, and scourge the gentle natives through the silver mines of the New World; count, if you can, the millions it has murdered; measure the blood which has been shed by the sword which Jesus came to send. The sword has been sharp, and long, and far-reaching; but now, Oh thanks be to man's brain and to man's heart for it, now its edge is blunted, it can only wound where once it slew, and soon it shall be broken in the hands that wield it, and the peace shall come on earth which the Galilean did not bring.

The last verses of this tenth chapter of Matthew throw light on the second great reason for the success of Christianity; if by persecution it has appealed to human fear, by bribery it has appealed to human cupidity. "He that receiveth a prophet in the name of a prophet shall receive a prophet's reward; and he that receiveth a righteous man in the name of a righteous man shall receive a righteous man's reward. And whosoever shall give to drink unto one of these little ones a cup of cold water only in the name of a disciple, verily I say unto you, he shall in no wise lose his reward" (verses 41, 42). This idea of "reward" is the great argument still used for enforcing the Christian creed, and it constantly appears in the Bible. "Thy Father, which seeth in secret, himself shall reward thee openly" (Matt. vi., 4). "Then answered Peter, and said unto him, behold we have forsaken all, and followed thee; *what shall we have* therefore? And Jesus said unto them, Verily I say unto you, That ye which have followed me, in the regeneration, when the Son of Man shall sit in the throne of his glory, ye also shall sit upon twelve thrones, judging the twelve tribes of Israel. And everyone that hath forsaken houses, or brethren, or sisters, or father, or mother, or wife, or children, or lands, for my name's sake, shall receive an hundredfold, and shall inherit everlasting life" (xix., 29, 30). There is here no devotion to a great cause, no self-sacrifice for a great principle, but a mere sordid calculation of increased personal gain to reward a temporary loss. "What shall it profit?" The spirit alleged to be that of the Jew (my own personal experience has not borne out the tradition), of always calculating personal profit, is essentially that of Christianity.

It is blasphemy to disbelieve Jesus when he says: "I am meek and lowly in heart" (Matt. xi., 29), but we search in vain for signs of the meekness and lowliness. Just before making this unfounded declaration he had been cursing the cities which did not bow down to him (verses 21—24), and had been, with the rude self-conceit of the fanatic, rejoicing over ignorance as a virtue, and declaring that no one knew him save God, and that none knew God save he himself and those to whom he vouchsafed the knowledge. Was Jesus meek and lowly, or even commonly well-mannered, when he said: "O generation of vipers! how can ye, being evil, speak good things" (Matt. xii., 34)? Or when in answer to the courteous Pharisees, "Master, we would see a sign from thee," he cried: "An evil and adulterous generation seeketh after a sign" (verse 38, 39)? [On another occasion he inconsistently tells them: "If I do not the works of my Father, believe me not. But if I do, though ye believe not me, believe the works" (John x., 37, 38). They are to believe the works, but if they ask to see one, they are "evil and adulterous"!] Or when the scribes and Pharisees, having gently asked him why his disciples broke the religious customs of their nation, he replied: "Ye hypocrites" (Matt. xv., 7)? Or when he said to the weeping mother: "It is not meet to take the children's bread, and to cast it to dogs" (verse 26)? Or when he repeated the insult to enquiring Pharisees and Sadducees (xvi., 1—4)? Or when he turned to his disciple and said: "Get thee behind me, Satan; thou art an offence unto me" (xvi., 23)? Or when he answered the kneeling father who craved his help: "O faithless and perverse generation! how long shall I be with you? how long shall I suffer you" (verse 17)? Or when he cursed the Pharisees and scribes: "Woe unto you, scribes and Pharisees, hypocrites! for ye compass sea and land to make one proselyte, and when he is made ye make him twofold more the child of hell than yourselves. Woe unto you, ye blind guides. . . . . ye fools and blind! ["Whosoever shall say, Thou fool, shall be in danger of hell fire:" Matt. v., 22.] . . . . Thou blind Pharisee! . . . . Ye serpents, ye generation of vipers! how shall ye escape the damnation of hell" (xxiii., 15, 16, 17, 26, 33, and indeed from 13—33)? All these treasures of meekness and lowliness are selected from one gospel! We might recall many others, as his polite remark to the Pharisee who "besought him to dine with him," and to whom, after accepting his hospitality, he said: "Now do ye Pharisees make clean the outside of the cup and the platter; but your inward part is full of ravening and wickedness. Ye fools!" and then he proceeded to a violent diatribe against his host and his host's friends (Luke xi., 38—52); or as his message to Herod: "Go ye, and tell that fox" (xiii., 32); or as his remark to his apostles: "Have not I chosen you twelve, and one of you is a devil" (John vi., 70); or as his insult to the Jews: "Ye are of your father the devil, and the lusts of your father ye will do" (viii., 44); or as his insolent brag: "All that ever came before me are thieves and robbers" (x., 8). Such are the proofs, and they might be added to, of the meekness and lowliness of Christ; yet we are threatened as blasphemers if we do not acknowledge that he was meek and lowly, and as blasphemers if we cavil at the self-assertive and vulgar abuse which he levelled at his foes.

It is blasphemy to allege that Jesus was imperfect, but if anyone else had treated his mother in the way in which Jesus treated Mary, he would be regarded as lacking in all good feeling and in the commonest respect. The incident related in Matt. xii. 46—50 is but one of several cases, and we may as well take them all together, so that we may learn how the "perfect God and perfect Man" set an example of sonhood.

As a small boy of twelve, Jesus deserted his parents and remained behind in Jerusalem; after an agonised search of three days, Joseph and Mary found him in the temple, and in answer to his mother's gentle reproach: "Son, why hast thou thus dealt with us? behold thy father and I have sought thee sorrowing," the lad said rudely: "How is it that ye sought me? wist ye not that I must be about my Father's business?" (Luke ii., 45—50) (It is worthy of notice in passing that Mary appears to have forgotten all about her son's miraculous birth, and says quite simply, "thy father and I," as though Jesus were the son of her husband Joseph!)

At the opening of his ministry, Jesus fulfils the promise of his boyhood; on the occasion of the marriage feast at Cana of Galilee, "when they wanted wine, the mother of Jesus saith unto him, They have no wine. Jesus saith unto her, Woman, what have I to do with thee? mine hour is not yet come" (John ii., 3, 4). He then immediately showed that he had been inaccurate as well as discourteous, by proceeding to supply the deficiency to which she had called his attention.

We then come to the story in Matthew: "While he yet talked to the people, behold, his mother and his brethren stood without, desiring to speak with him. Then one said unto him, Behold, thy mother and thy brethren stand without, desiring to speak with thee. But he answered and said unto him that told him, Who is my mother? and who are my brethren? And he stretched forth his hand toward his disciples, and said, Behold my mother, and my brethren! For whosoever shall do the will of my Father which is in heaven, the same is my brother, and sister, and mother." If Mary, during the infancy of Jesus, had shown the same indifference to him that later he showed to her, he would not have grown into manhood to insult her. We are asked to believe that Jesus, as God, commanded: "Honor thy . . . . mother" (Ex. xx., 12), and as man, insulted his own. But Jesus showed this contempt for family relations in the case of others, and was, indeed, blasphemous as the statement may be, one of those fanatical enthusiasts who trample on all love and on all sweet human ties in their mania for some overpowering superstition. "He that loveth father and mother more than me is not worthy of me: and he that loveth son or daughter more than me is not worthy of me" (Matt. x., 37). "If any man come to me, and hate not his father, and mother, and wife, and children, and brethren, and sisters, yea, and his own life also, he cannot be my disciple" (Luke xiv., 26). (Note the putting of "his own life" as dearer than the closest relatives.) "He said unto another, Follow me. But he said, Lord, suffer me first to go and bury my father. Jesus said unto him, Let the dead bury their dead; but go thou and preach the kingdom of God" (Luke xiii., 59, 60). Leave your father's corpse to chance, and go preach! "Another also said, Lord, I will follow thee; but let me first go bid them farewell which are at home at my house. And Jesus said unto him, No man, having put his hand to the plough, and looking back, is fit for the kingdom of God" (verses 61, 62). And no man, careless of every tie of human love and duty, is fit for the commonwealth of Man. With such maxims as these, no wonder that the Christians were looked upon in countries where the social bond was strong, as "the enemies of the human race."

It is blasphemy to say that Jesus was not good, but what view can we take of a man who said to his disciples: "Unto you it is given to know the mystery of the kingdom of God; but unto them that are without, all these things are done in parables: that seeing they may see, and not perceive; and hearing they may hear, and not understand; lest at any time they should be converted, and their sins should be forgiven them" (Mark iv., 11, 12). Here is one "come to be the Savior of the world," and he wraps up his message in incomprehensible language, lest those he professes to have come to save should be converted and have their sins forgiven. It is of a piece with his cruel declaration: "I pray for them; I pray not for the world, but for them which thou hast given me" (John xvii., 9).

In these words of Jesus "to you it is given," and "them which thou hast given me," lies the horrible doctrine of predestination either to immortal happiness or to immortal woe. Over and over again he preaches the same doctrine: "No man can come to me, except the Father which hath sent me draw him" (John vi., 44). "All that the Father giveth me shall come to me" (verse 37). "Without me ye can do nothing" (John xv., 5). Yet, spite of this, he threatens eternal torture for those whom the Father has not drawn, whom the Father has not given. Elsewhere we are told that the Father's choice is pre-natal; "the children being not yet born, neither having done any good or evil, that the purpose of God, according to election, might stand, not of works, but of him that calleth" (Rom. ix., 11). "Whom he did foreknow, he also did predestinate .... Moreover, whom he did predestinate, them he also called" (Rom. viii., 29, 30). "God shall send them strong delusion, that they should believe a lie; that they all might be damned" (2 Thess. ii., 11, 12). Thought grows dizzy before the horror of an almighty Creator, who foredooms his hapless creatures to damnation, sends them delusions to ensure it, and who becomes incarnate that the vast majority may seeing "see and not perceive, and hearing they may hear and not understand, lest at any time they should be converted, and their sins should be forgiven them." It is a nightmare which leaves us shuddering, even when we open our eyes to the wholesome light of day.

Besides, this vile teaching paralyses all human effort. If God has foreknown me before my birth, he will save me; if he has not, he will damn me. The whole affair is entirely outside my control; I am a mere puppet, dancing at the end of a wire as my strings are pulled by God. The 17th article of the Church of England teaches the doctrine with delightful clearness: "Predestination to life is the everlasting purpose of God, whereby (before the foundations of the world were laid) he hath constantly decreed by his counsel secret to us, to deliver from curse and damnation those whom he hath chosen in Christ out of mankind, and to bring them by Christ to everlasting salvation, as vessels made to honor. Wherefore, they which be endued with so excellent a benefit of God be called according to God's purpose by his Spirit working in due season; they through Grace obey the calling; they be justified freely; they be made sons of God by adoption: they walk religiously in good works, and at length, by God's mercy, they attain to everlasting felicity."

This is charming, indeed, for the folk predestinated to salvation, but what of those who are equally predestinated, unluckily for them, to damnation? The difficulty is recognised, but not met, by the article. "As the godly consideration of Predestination, and our election in Christ, is full of sweet, pleasant and unspeakable comfort to godly persons, and such as feel in themselves the working of the Spirit of Christ, mortifying the works of the flesh, and their earthly members, and drawing up their mind to high and heavenly things, as well because it doth greatly establish and confirm their faith of eternal salvation to be enjoyed through Christ, as because it doth fervently kindle their love toward God. So, for curious and carnal persons, lacking the Spirit of Christ, to have continually before their eyes the sentence of God's Predestination, is a most dangerous downfall, whereby the Devil doth thrust them either into desperation or into wretchlessness of most unclean living, no less perilous than desperation." It seems to me that it is "God," not "the Devil," who thrusts them into desperation, and if they are predestinated to be damned the question of peril hardly comes in. Being myself a "curious and carnal person" I fail to see why anyone's love should be fervently kindled towards God by knowing that he was to be saved while his brethren were damned.

It would kindle my hatred to know he was torturing my friends, although he had, from caprice, saved me. No honest person would care to be saved by a tyrant's whim.

In Matt. xiv. we have two absurd stories, which it is blasphemy to deny. One is that Jesus fed "five thousand men, beside women and children" to repletion with five loaves and two fishes, and had twelve baskets full of fragments at the end! The other that he walked on the sea of Galilee, and that Peter did the same till he grew afraid, whereupon he began to sink; it would want much faith to enable anyone to walk *on* the water, but the writer is accurate in ascribing sinking to fear in an ordinary way; many people who have been drowned would have escaped if they had remained lying quietly down instead of kicking. In chapter xv. there is a repetition of the miraculous feeding, only on this occasion "four thousand men, beside women and children" were fed off seven loaves and "a few little fishes" (verses 34—38). It seems rather odd that when on this second occasion Jesus said that he would not send away the multitude fasting, the disciples should have replied: "Whence should we have so much bread in the wilderness, as to fill so great a multitude?" Their memories must have been very short, since he had fed a larger multitude with a smaller supply of food, so brief a time before. One would have expected them to have trusted their Master, but they were as chary of belief, apparently, as are modern sceptics. It seems unfair that they should have had such reiterated proofs given to them, while we are not allowed one, not even a little one. To them with so much evidence only the gentle reproach: "O ye of little faith, wherefore did ye doubt?" To us with none: "He that believeth not shall be damned."

It is blasphemy to laugh at the funny money-carrying fish caught by Peter (Matt. xvii., 27); plenty of fishermen would be glad to catch such fish now-a-days; but in this, as in other things, the people who lived in the first century were much better off than we who live in the nineteenth.

It is blasphemy to protest against the horrible doctrine of self-mutilation taught by Jesus (Matt. xix., 10—12), but it is blasphemy against human nature to accept it. To these odious and (in the bad sense) unnatural words have been due the monasteries and nunneries which have marred Christendom with fungoid growth, and in the earlier days, when Christians really believed in Christ, many a man literally obeyed the terrible suggestion of Jesus, and degraded himself and ruined his whole life "for the kingdom of heaven's sake." The brutal asceticism, born of Eastern superstition and fanaticism, spread over Western lands, and even in those countries in which Free Thought has partially undone the harm wrought by Jesus, there are still left traces of his anti-human and anti-social theories, while among Roman Catholics the virginal life is still regarded as higher and purer than the married.

The usual contradictions between the gospels meet us in the accounts given in Matthew, Mark and Luke of the healing of the blind man or men near Jericho. Matthew tells us that as Jesus and his disciples left Jericho, two blind men cried to Jesus, and on Jesus asking: "What will ye that I shall do unto you? They say unto him, Lord, that our eyes may be opened," and Jesus healed them (Matt. xx., 29—34). According to Mark the miracle was worked as Jesus left Jericho, but there was only one blind man, Bartimæus, the son of Timæus, to whom Jesus addressed the question as given in Matthew (substituting "thou" for "ye") and from whom he received the same answer (Mark x., 46—52). Luke agrees with Mark that there was only one blind man, but he places the miracle before Jesus enters Jericho and not after he leaves it, the same question and answer passing between them (Luke xviii., 35—43). So that if we would avoid the sin and the peril of blasphemy we must believe that as Jesus went into Jericho he healed one blind man, and as he went out one and two, and that on each of the three several occasions he and the blind man and blind men made exactly the same remarks.

All the four gospels mention the triumphal entry of Jesus into Jerusalem, though they differ in details much. According to Matthew Jesus was travelling from Jericho and had reached Bethphage, when he sent for an ass and a colt, and the disciples "brought the ass and the colt, and put on them their clothes and set him thereon" (xxi., 1—7). Mark does not make his hero perform this remarkable equestrian feat of riding on two animals at the same time, but is satisfied to make him ride an unbroken colt (x., 2), showing very skilful horsemanship, though not the circus-like dexterity ascribed to him by Matthew. According to

John, Jesus did not come from Jericho, but had been staying at Ephraim, whence he went to Bethany a week before the passover; from Bethany he went to Jerusalem, sitting on a young ass. In Matthew the people of Jerusalem do not know him, and ask: "Who is this?" receiving for answer from those who surrounded him: "This is Jesus, the prophet of Nazareth in Galilee" (xxi., 10, 11). In John, the people of Jerusalem know him quite well, and go out to meet Jesus, because "they heard that he had done this miracle," *i.e.*, the raising of Lazarus, a miracle of which the synoptics know nothing.

According to the synoptics, again, Jesus, after entering the city, went to the temple, and cast out the money-changers and the traders; according to John, this miracle took place at the beginning, not at the close of his ministry, and the answer therein given by Jesus is perfectly meaningless so long before his death.

It is blasphemy not to believe that Jesus, being hungry, went towards a fig-tree, "if haply he might find anything thereon" (Mark xi., 13); that as "the time of figs was not yet" (verse 13) he found nothing, and thereupon cursed the unlucky tree; that in consequence "in the morning, as they passed by, they saw the fig-tree dried up from the roots" (verse 20). It is blasphemy to deny that Jesus acted like a naughty boy, who is angry because he cannot have impossibilities, and cursed a tree because it did not bear fruit at the wrong season of the year. I could have understood it if Christians had accused the writer of the story of blasphemy, because he has represented their god as behaving in so ludicrous and so contemptible a fashion, but it is hard to see how we blaspheme in not giving credence to the story.

The contradictions in the gospel reach their highest point in the accounts given of the last days of Jesus and of his resurrection from the dead. Yet it is blasphemy to deny any one of the stories, although they are mutually exclusive. The story of the two last days only varies triflingly in Matthew, Mark and Luke, but John is in flagrant contradiction with them throughout. According to the three, Jesus eats the passover before he is betrayed (Matt. xxvi., 17-21; Mark xiv., 12-18; Luke xxii., 7-16); according to John the passover is not eaten until after his crucifixion (xviii. 28). John therefore omits all account of the passover eaten with the disciples, all account of the institution of the "sacrament," and he equally omits any mention of the agony in Gethsemane. In John's gospel Jesus is represented in a more dignified light than in the three; in the latter he shrinks from the coming hour of death, and prays that "if it be possible" the cup may pass away; in the fourth gospel his prayer meets death open-eyed and willingly: "Father, the hour is come" (xvii., 1), and instead of being betrayed with a kiss (Matt. xxvi., 48-50; Mark xiv., 43-45; Luke xxii., 47, 48), he goes forward boldly to meet his foes, declares that he is Jesus of Nazareth, and before him those who had come to arrest him "went backward and fell to the ground" (xviii., 4-9).

According to the three, the captive is led to Caiaphas (Matt. xxvi., 57; Mark xiv., 53; Luke xxii., 54); according to the fourth, to Annas first (xviii. 13). According to Matthew and Mark, Peter is challenged by two women and "they that stood by" (Matt. xxvi, 69, 71, 73; Mark xiv., 66, 69, 70); according to Luke by one woman and two men (xxvi., 56, 58, 60); according to John by one woman, "they" and a man (xviii., 17, 25, 26). According to Matthew, Luke and John, the cock crew once after the three denials were ended; according to Mark the cock crew after the first denial, and crew for the second time after the third. According to Matthew, Judas cast down in the temple the money paid for the betrayal of Jesus, and "departed and went and hanged himself," and the chief priests took the money and bought with it a field "to bury strangers in" (xxvii., 5-7); according to Acts, Judas, instead of throwing away the money, "purchased a field with the reward of iniquity," and, instead of hanging himself, "falling headlong, he burst asunder in the midst, and all his bowels gushed out" (i., 18). According to Matthew, Mark and Luke, Jesus was crucified some time before noon—Mark specifies "the third hour" (xv., 25) 9 A.M.—and there was darkness from the sixth to the ninth hour (Matt. xxvii., 45; Mark xv., 23; Luke xxiii., 44), that is, from 12 to 3 p.m. According to John, Jesus was shown to the Jews by Pilate at "the sixth hour" (xix., 14), so that he was standing before the judgment seat in daylight at the very same moment that he was hanging on the cross in the darkness. According to Matthew both the thieves mocked him (xxvii., 44); according to Luke one of them rebuked his fellow-thief and prayed to Jesus (xxiii., 39-43). According to Matthew and Mark the last intelligible words of Jesus were: "My God, my God, why hast thou forsaken me?" (Matt. xxvii., 46, 50; Mark xv., 34, 37) the last cry was wordless; according to Luke, after that cry "with a loud voice" he said: "Father, into thy hands I commend my spirit," and died (xxiii., 46); according to John, "he said, It is finished; and he bowed his head and gave up the ghost" (xix., 30). And it is this tissue of contradictions for which our credence is demanded. If we do not believe every one of these mutually exclusive details, we may be sent to gaol here and will certainly be damned hereafter.

Jesus being dead, we might hope that the contradictions in his fourfold biography would come to an end, but after his death the difficulties are, on the contrary, increased, for two other "authentic accounts" chime in and make a sixfold discord.

Before we analyse the confused story of the resurrection, we must pause for a moment on some curious incidents accompanying the death of Jesus. According to Matthew "the earth did quake, and the rocks rent; and the graves were opened; and many bodies of the saints which slept arose, and came out of the graves after his resurrection, and went into the holy city and appeared unto many" (xxvii., 51—53). By this it would seem that the sleeping saints "arose" in their graves, and remained therein from Friday afternoon until Sunday morning. The words are clear. The graves were opened and the saints arose at 3 p.m. on Friday, but they only came out of the graves "after his resurrection". Any persons visiting the cemeteries in the neighborhood of Jerusalem on Saturday would have seen a remarkable sight, and might have held unique and most interesting conversations with these awaked and arisen but yet undesepulchred saints. One cannot help wondering what was the ultimate fate of these perturbed spirits—or were they bodies without spirits? Did they go back to their graves? did they go to sleep again? did they have to die a second time before they were fit for burial? No information is vouchsafed to us on all these grave questions.

Mark, Luke, and John have no knowledge of these "extravagant and erring spirits".

We are bound under peril of our eternal salvation to

believe that Jesus was for "three days and three nights in the heart of the earth" (Matt. xii. 40). Also must we believe, lest we should perish everlastingly, that Jesus was buried on Friday afternoon and left the grave early on Sunday morning, thus remaining in the tomb for two nights and a day, with fragments of two other days. It is hard to believe at one and the same time that he was in the grave for three nights but only remained in it for two, yet the feat must be accomplished, for "he that believeth not shall be damned".

The difficulties attending the actual stories of the resurrection are worse than any others we have found in the gospels, and I cannot put these more pointedly than I have done in my lecture on the "Myth of the Resurrection", which forms No. 9 of the Atheistic Platform Series. I therefore quote the following from that publication:—

"The writer of the first of the six stories bears the name of Matthew in the authorised version of the Bible. He gives the following account of the resurrection:—

"As the dawn was breaking of the first day of the week, two women, Mary Magdalene and 'the other Mary', went to the sepulchre in which Jesus had been buried. On their arrival, an angel came down and rolled away the stone from the mouth of the tomb, and sat thereon, and speaking to the women, he told them that Jesus was risen, invited them to 'see the place where the Lord lay', and bade them go to the disciples quickly, and tell them that they should see their risen Lord in Galilee. As they ran to carry their message Jesus met them, and they held him by the feet and worshipped him. Jesus repeated the command that the disciples should go to Galilee, promising that they should see him there. 'Then the eleven disciples went away into Galilee, into a mountain where Jesus had appointed them. And when they saw him they worshipped him: but some doubted.'

"Comparing this with the account given in Mark, we find one woman added to the company, by name Salome. The three, instead of the two, reach the sepulchre, and instead of seeing an angel descending and rolling away the stone, they find the stone already rolled away. As no angel is there to invite them to enter, they go into the sepulchre without an invitation, and they find inside a young man, sitting on the right side. He speaks to them in almost the same words as did the angel who rolled away the stone, according to Matthew, but the women, instead of running to bring the disciples word, fly trembling from the sepulchre, 'neither said they anything to any man, for they were afraid'. They do not meet Jesus, nor is anything more recorded as far as Mary and Salome are concerned. At this point a new account seems to commence in Mark, for it begins again by saying: 'Now when Jesus was risen early, the first day of the week, he appeared first to Mary Magdalene'. According to Matthew, Mary Magdalene and 'the other Mary' were together, and they both met Jesus, and worshipped him. Mary Magdalene tells the apostles that she has seen him, although two verses before she said nothing to any man. Then Jesus, instead of going into Galilee to meet his apostles, as related in Matthew, meets two of them in the country, and appears to the eleven as they are at meat. . . .

"We turn to Luke:—

"The number of women has increased again: we have now Mary Magdalene, Mary the mother of James, and Joanna—of whom we have not heard before—and 'other women that were with them'. They do not see the rolling away of the stone, nor the angel of Matthew, nor do they find sitting inside the sepulchre the young man of Mark. But as they are puzzling themselves about the empty state of the sepulchre, two men stand by them, and make remarks very similar to those of Matthew's angel and of Mark's solitary young man. They leave the sepulchre, and tell 'all these things to the eleven'. Peter then visits the sepulchre, and departs wondering. On 'that same day' Jesus appears to 'two of them', and these return to the eleven with the story, and while they are speaking Jesus appears. . . .

"We now turn to John:—

"In this account Mary Magdalene goes by herself, 'early, when it was yet dark'. She is alone, and her visit is not, like that in Mark, made with the others 'at the rising of the sun'. The stone has been rolled away before she reaches the sepulchre. She runs straight off to Peter and John, having seen no angel, no young man, no two men; and Peter and John run off at once to the sepulchre. They both go in, but see only the linen clothes in which the dead body had been wrapped. (I have often wondered what clothes Jesus wore after the resurrection, for his own clothes were taken by the soldiers, his body was wound in linen, and this he left in the sepulchre.) Peter and John believe, although we are distinctly told that the account of the resurrection seemed 'as idle tales' to the apostles (Luke), among whom were Peter and John, and that Jesus upbraided the eleven (Mark), of whom Peter and John were two, for their unbelief, 'because they believed not them which had seen him after he was risen'. In John no woman except Mary Magdalene goes near the sepulchre at all, but she remains there, and sees first two angels sitting inside—who speak to her—and then Jesus himself. At first she does not recognise him, but supposing him to be the gardener, she asks if he has taken Jesus away. The information given by the angel, or man, or men, to herself and the other women—according to Matthew, Mark, and Luke—is here omitted, and she knows nothing about the resurrection. Jesus says, 'Mary', and she recognises him, and is not allowed to touch him, although in Matthew she holds his feet. She then goes and tells the disciples that she has seen Jesus. On the same evening Jesus appears to the disciples, and instead of upbraiding them with their unbelief he greets them with 'Peace be unto you'. Eight days later he appears again, still in Jerusalem; afterwards he meets them casually at the sea of Tiberias, and works a miracle. . . .

"In 1 Cor. xv. we hear nothing of the women, but are told that he was seen of Cephas (Peter)—an interview not elsewhere recorded—'then of the twelve'; 'the twelve' included Judas, and except in Corinthians we never hear that the betrayer remained in the company of his former comrades; on the contrary, we read in one account (Matthew) that 'he cast down the pieces of silver in the temple, and departed, and went and hanged himself', while in a second (Acts) he uses the money to purchase a field, and falls headlong in it and bursts. Whichever of these contradictory accounts may be true, neither is compatible with his forming one of 'the twelve' and seeing Jesus. 'After that he was seen of above five hundred brethren at once'; this is quite new, and is a little puzzling, for we are told that after the ascension (Acts) the number of the disciples was 'about an hundred and twenty'. 'After that he was seen of James, then of all the apostles'. James was one of 'the twelve', and the apostles are identical with 'the twelve'. On the whole, the account in Corinthians is rather mixed, and in no single respect agrees with that of the gospels; we are told emphatically by John that the meeting by the sea of Tiberias was 'the third time that Jesus showed himself to his disciples, after that he was risen from the dead'. But this coincides with none of the meetings recorded in Corinthians, and must be at least the sixth meeting if Corinthians is right.

"To sum up the contradictions, leaving Corinthians on the one side, as hopelessly erratic:—

"While it is yet dark, though the sun is rising, Mary Magdalene alone; Mary Magdalene and the other Mary; Mary Magdalene, Mary and Salome; Mary Magdalene, Mary, Joanna, and some 'other women'; goes, or go, to the sepulchre. They find the stone closing the tomb; but an angel comes down, rolls it away, sits on it, and talks to them. They also find the stone not closing the tomb, but rolled away, and see no angel sitting on it, but only a young man sitting inside. They see no angel, no young man sitting, but two men suddenly appear standing by them. They see no angel, no young man sitting, no two men standing, but two angels sitting. After this, they run away, and tell the disciples; but, at the same time, they say nothing unto any man. The apostles do not believe, but two of them do believe. The women meet Jesus, and do not meet him. Mary Magdalene holds him by the feet, but is not allowed to touch him. He meets his disciples for the first time in Galilee, in a mountain, but has seen them twice previously in Jerusalem, and a third time by the sea of Tiberias."

The same hopeless incoherency vitiates the records of the ascension. Matthew records no ascension at all. Mark states that "after the Lord had spoken unto them", apparently on the day of the resurrection, "he was received up into heaven" (xvi., 19). Luke seems to have no break between the morning of the resurrection and the leading of the apostles "out as far as to Bethany", where "he was parted from them and carried up into heaven" (xxiv., 50—51). But according to Mark the apostles went "forth and preached everywhere" after the resurrection (xvi., 20), while according to Luke they returned to Jerusalem and were "continually in the temple" (xxiv., 52, 53).

John, like Matthew, knows nothing of any ascension, but Acts tells us that Jesus remained on earth for forty days, thus agreeing with no other account (i., 3).

We learn from Acts i., 17, 18, that Judas bought a field with the thirty pieces of silver earned by his betrayal of Christ, and that he fell headlong thereon and "burst asunder in the midst". It is blasphemy to deny this buying of the field and the subsequent explosion, but it is equally blasphemy to deny that Judas threw down the thirty pieces of silver in the temple, that the chief priests picked them up and bought with them a "field to bury strangers in", that Judas promptly hanged himself, buying no field and suffering no disruption (Matt. xxvii., 5, 6, 7). It is said in Acts that "all the dwellers at Jerusalem" were acquainted with the fate of Judas, and named the scene of his death Aceldama, the field of blood (i., 19). In Matthew the same name is given for a different reason to the strangers' cemetery bought by the priests (xxvii., 8). The explanation of the discrepancy appears to be that the authors of Acts and of Matthew desired to illustrate different prophecies, and were therefore compelled to make up different stories. In Acts Judas died on his own property because it was written "in the book of Psalms, Let his habitation be desolate" (i., 20). In Matthew the priests buy the field that it may be fulfilled "which was spoken by Jeremy the prophet, saying, And they took the thirty pieces of silver, the price of him that was valued, whom they of the children of Israel did value: and gave them for the potter's field, as the Lord appointed me" (xxvii., 9, 10).

It is difficult to read without a smile verses 23—26 of Acts i. Matthias and Barnabas stand for the vacant apostleship and "the lot fell upon Matthias". One wonders how this queer game of chance, with an apostleship for the pool, was played. Did they deal round cards with the mystic formula, the "first knave has it"? Did Peter hold straws for Matthias and Barnabas to draw, and was Barnabas "surnamed Justus" because he played fair and lost the game?

Of all the queer things characterising the period between A.D. 30 and A.D. 60, the queerest is the serene placidity with which are accepted the most striking and the most wonderful miracles. The cloven tongues only suggested the incoherence of drunkenness (Acts ii., 13); Peter and John healed a cripple, "lame from his mother's womb" (iii., 2), and for reward were imprisoned (iv., 3) and threatened (verse 21); the council absolutely declared "that indeed a notable miracle hath been done by them" (verse 16), and then promptly forbade them to speak in the very name in which the miracle had been worked (verse 18); the apostles wrought "many signs and wonders" (v., 12), the sick were carried into the streets so that the shadow of Peter might fall on them (verse 15), "every one" brought was healed (verse 16), and in consequence the rulers of the people were "filled with indignation" and put the healers in "the common prison" (verses 17, 18); an angel came and opened the prison doors and sent the prisoners to the temple to preach, whereupon the priests again arrested them, beat them, and commanded them not to "speak in the name of Jesus" (verses 19, 20, 26, 40). Yet we blaspheme if we challenge the possibility of the truth of this record. But whether the question be blasphemous or not, I ask: Is it credible that men endowed with the priceless power of healing the sick, men whose word or shadow brought health to the diseased, vigor to the cripple, should have been treated as criminals rather than as benefactors? What nation would be mad enough to permit its rulers to imprison, to beat, to stop the work of those in whose hands lay the power of turning all mourning into joy? These fairy-tales of miracles are stamped as false by the very history that records them. Colonel Ingersoll has well said that if ever the King of Death should stand on our earth, "every knee would touch the ground".

It would be waste of time to analyse further the uninterest-
us long. It is, however, worth while to notice the extreme
ing "Acts of the Apostles", and the Epistles need not delay
brutishness of the view of women taken by the Apostle Paul. His reason for marriage (1 Cor. vii., 9) is worthy in its delicacy to stand beside the exhortation of the Marriage Service of the Church of England; equally high-minded is his declaration that when "the younger widows . . . . have begun to wax wanton against Christ, they will marry" (1 Tim. v., 11). Like his master Christ he disapproves of marriage, except as a preventive of general looseness of living, and says "to the unmarried and widows, it is good for them if they remain even as I . . . .

He that is unmarried careth for the things that belong to the Lord, how he may please the Lord; but he that is married careth for the things that are of the world, how he may please his wife. There is difference also between a wife and a virgin. The unmarried woman careth for the things of the Lord that she may be holy both in body and in spirit; but she that is married careth for the things of the world, how she may please her husband" (1 Cor. vii., 8, 32-34). Those who marry "shall have trouble in the flesh" (verse 28). So again in Hebrews it is urged: "Let marriage be honorable in all" (xiii., 4) as though there were anything dishonorable in the mating of man and woman. [It may be noted that the Reformers, in their eagerness to improve on the Holy Ghost, translated this verse into the much more sensible statement: "Marriage is honorable in all".] In a similar spirit Paul bids women "if they will learn anything" (!) "ask their husbands at home" (1 Cor. xiv, 35). No provision is made for women who have no husbands, or for those whose husbands are ignorant. The woman is to be subject to her husband "in everything", "as the church is subject to Christ" (Eph. v., 24). She is to "learn in silence with all subjection" because "Adam was first formed, then Eve" (1 Tim. ii., 11, 13). If this argument be valid, man should be subjected to the fishes, birds, and lower animals, which were "first formed" (Gen. i., 20, 21, 24, 26, 27). Judging by the analogy of the succession related in Genesis, the woman should be the highest of all created things, since she was the last made. Adam was an intermediate creature, between the lower animals and the woman; by no possible twisting, at whichever end you begin, can the middle be made the highest point.

Many have been the controversies in the Christian Church respecting the relative values of faith and of works as a means of salvation. The immoral doctrine that a man may be saved by faith only finds its support in the writings of the Apostle Paul, while those who declare that good works are necessary to salvation rely upon the Apostle James. When apostles fall out who shall arbitrate between them? It is blasphemy to assert that works avail to save: "We conclude that a man is justified by faith without the deeds of the law" (Romans iii., 28); it is blasphemy to deny that works avail to save:

"Ye see then how that by works a man is justified, and not by faith only" (James ii., 24). The Prayer Book of the Church of England agrees with Paul in this controversy, and in the 11th Article declares: "We are accounted righteous before God only for the merit of our Lord and Saviour Jesus Christ by faith, and not for our own works or deservings. Wherefore, that we are justified by faith only is a most wholesome doctrine and very full of comfort." Wholesome! very full of comfort it may be to evil livers, but wholesome most certainly it is not. Such a doctrine naturally and inevitably tends to immorality, for it relieves people of all trouble about right living, covering them with a garb of imputed righteousness instead of with one of individual well-doing. Paul's teaching has always been popular among loose livers, and we naturally find it vehemently upheld by Luther, who stigmatised the epistle of James as an "epistle of straw". Without entering into the well-worn controversy, we can clearly say that it is necessary for eternal salvation that we should believe both the Pauline and Jamian statements, however contradictory they may be, for they both form part of that infallible Word of God which we are bound to believe, on peril of hell, for "if any man shall take away from the words of the book of this prophecy, God shall take away his part out of the book of life, and out of the holy city" (Rev. xxii., 19). Believe these contradictories, therefore, or——

The old hateful doctrines of the right of men to own men, and of the duty of persecution, are endorsed by the New Testament as well as by the Old. Paul over and over again exhorts slaves to be submissive to their masters—our translation gives "servants" for "slaves", so as to avoid shocking modern civilisation with the sight of an apostle indifferent to the crime of slavery—and he never speaks one indignant word of protest against the wrong, nor makes one claim for human liberty. John commands "the elect lady" to refuse to receive into her house any one who does not hold the "doctrine of Christ" (2 John, 10), thus sanctioning the use of social ostracism as a weapon against those who do not believe incredible dogmas. It may be blasphemy, punishable by law, to declare that slavery and persecution are evil things, that they are brutal, degrading and anti-social. But it would be blasphemy punishable by remorse to accept these vile doctrines and so prove traitor to human liberty and human love.

"The Revelation of St. John the Divine" is a unique production, and it is blasphemy to explain its curious statements by pointing out that it is an astrological document; yet the repetition of sacred numbers and of their multiples and sub-multiples, the seven-headed beasts, the lamb in the midst of the throne, the "Son of Man" with hair "like wool", the four eye-filled beasts, all these mark the character of the book unmistakably to everyone who knows anything of the ancient solar faith.

If it be not a solar symbol, what is the "lamb as it had been slain, having seven horns and seven eyes" (v., 6)? What is the significance of the "woman clothed with the sun, and the moon under her feet, and upon her head a crown of twelve stars" (xii, 1)? Are we to take these things as real existences, and believe that all the queer beasts with superfluous heads, horns, and eyes were really seen by "St. John the Divine"? Are we to believe in the "great red dragon" whose "tail drew the third part of the stars of heaven and did cast them to the earth" (xii., 3, 4)? in the locusts with men's faces, women's hair, lions' teeth, and scorpions' tails (ix., 7—10)? in the great star that fell from heaven "burning as a lamp, and it fell upon the third part of the rivers and upon the fountains of waters", turning them bitter (viii., 10, 11)? in the white, red, black, and pale horses (vi., 2—8)? in the "word of God" sitting on a white horse, wearing "many crowns", and with a "sharp sword" going out of his mouth (xix., 11—15)? It is an insult to our intelligence to present these absurdities for our credence, and to our courage to threaten us with hell if we refuse to believe them. Distinctly and clearly I do refuse to believe any of them, and I prefer being a blasphemer to being a hypocrite. I do not say "to being a believer", because belief in the incredible is impossible for a sane mind. The threat and the enforcement of legal and social penalties against unbelief can never compel belief. Belief must be gained by demonstration; it can never be forced by punishment. Persecution makes the stronger among us bitter; the weaker among us hypocrites; it never has made and never can make an honest convert.

A WORLD WITHOUT GOD.

A REPLY TO MISS FRANCES POWER COBBE

BY

ANNIE BESANT.

LONDON:
FREETHOUGHT PUBLISHING COMPANY,
63, FLEET STREET, E.C.
1885.

PRICE THREEPENCE.

LONDON:
PRINTED BY ANNIE BESANT AND CHARLES BRADLAUGH,
63, FLEET STREET, E.C.

A WORLD WITHOUT GOD.

The Roman Catholic conception of a world over which God is supreme and which is ruled under him by his Church, all authority flowing from that one fount, all duty owing to that one superior, is a logical and a consistent one; the Atheistic conception of a world of which man is the highest product and over which he rules, knowing no superior, and acknowledging no limit to his own rights save the collateral rights of those who share the planet with him, is a logical and a consistent one. On many points of duty the obligation imposed by authority and that deduced from experience will coincide, but the bases of the two schools remain entirely distinct. Between these reasoned and opposing systems float and drift many semi-rational and more or less inconsequent schools—Protestants orthodox and unorthodox, Episcopalian, Presbyterian, Congregational, Unitarian, Theistic, &c., &c.—each of which has partially thrown off authority, here of Rome, there of Canterbury, here of a Kirk, there of a Book, but each of which claims authority for its own remnant of belief; each affirms the right of private judgment over all it rejects, but denies it for all it receives: and often the denial is the more bitter and the more unsparing as the assertion has been wide and sweeping.

Miss Frances Power Cobbe in an article in the *Contemporary Review* on "A Faithless World", and her critics in various religious journals, offer instructive examples of these varying semi-rational schools; herself a Theist and erstwhile at least an opponent of Christianity, she declares that the effects of Atheism in the future cannot be judged by the conduct of Atheists now, because Atheists are surrounded by Christians. "The same holds true", remarks the *Church Times*, "of her own form of Theism, should orthodox Christianity disappear in its favor". Each creed thinks itself necessary to morality and despises all which are more liberal than itself.

Of all creeds, the purely Theistic is the most inconsequent, depending as it does for its "proofs" on the varying emotions of men. "Intuition", "feeling", these for it are the revealers of the Divine, and denying all special revelation, all Divine Incarnation, it leaves each individual to "feel" God for himself and to receive direct inspiration. This plan is obviously the negation of all argument, of all demonstration; a man's feelings may sway his own judgment; they can never convince the judgment of anyone else.

Miss Cobbe takes for her text some words of Mr. Justice Stephen on religion:

> "We can get on very well without one; for though the view of life which science is opening to us gives us nothing to worship, it gives us an infinite number of things to enjoy. . . . The world seems to me a very good world, if it would only last. Love, friendship, ambition, science, literature, art, politics, commerce, professions, trades, and a thousand other matters, will go equally well, as far as I can see, whether there is or is not a God and a future state."

She proceeds to descant on "the chief consequences which might be anticipated to follow the downfall of such religion as at present prevails in civilised Europe and America", and defines religion as "definite faith in a living and righteous God; and, as a corollary therefrom, in the survival of the human soul after death. In other words, I mean by 'religion' that nucleus of simple Theism which is common to every form of natural religion, of Christianity and Judaism." A good deal of dispute might arise as to the meaning of the word "righteous" in connexion with any God common to natural religion, Christianity, and Judaism. The brutal and blood-thirsty Jahveh of the Hebrews was certainly not righteous, and Miss Cobbe does not believe in the God who walked in the Garden of Eden, ate calf with Abraham, showed his back to Moses, and presided over the slaughters of the Canaanites and the Amalekites. It is not straightforward to pretend that her highly-civilised nineteenth century God is identical with the brutal God of Moses and of Joshua, nor is her one indivisible God the God of the Christians, one part of whom became man and in whom there are three distinct persons. After thus lightly waving aside all differences as to God, Miss Cobbe with equal lightness ignores the vast evils wrought by religions: "I absolve myself from weighing against the advantages of religion the evils which have followed its manifold corruptions"! But how can we balance the results of religion and non-religion if we are to leave out of account all the evils accruing from one? We are now to have, it seems, the "religion of Christ—*i.e.*, the religion Christ practised and lived". But that was Judaism, and there is not the smallest sign that Christendom proposes to revert to Judaism.

Miss Cobbe then proceeds: "I confess, at starting on this enquiry, that the problem 'Is religion of use, or can we do as well without it?' seems to me as grotesque as the old story of the woman who said that we owe vast obligation to the moon, which affords us light on dark nights, whereas we are under no such debt to the sun, who only shines by day, when there is always light". If this be a true exposition of the state of Miss Cobbe's mind on the great subject with which she deals, she stands self-condemned as incompetent. No one can argue who is incapable of appreciating the opponent's position, and Miss Cobbe cannot appreciate the Atheistic position if she thinks it comparable to that of her ignorant old woman. I pass the intolerable impertinence of her assumption that her opponents are ignorant fools, as much below herself in knowledge and intelligence as the woman referred to was below the average man and woman; it is one of the results of religion, this intense and arrogant self-conceit. But even Miss Cobbe might deign to consider that it was scarcely worth while to waste fifteen pages of the *Contemporary Review* in solving a grotesque problem, and that the pains she takes to frighten people from Atheism prove that to her it is far more likely that intellectual people will accept it than her insolent parable would imply.

Religion, it seems, is the sun: friendship, science, art, commerce, and politics, are only "moonlike things". "It is the special and unique character of religion to deal with the whole of human nature, *all* our pleasures and pains and duties and affections and hopes and fears, here and hereafter. It offers to the intellect an explanation of the universe (true or false we need not now consider); and pointing to heaven, it responds to the most eager of its questions. It offers to the conscience a law claiming to regulate every act and every word. And it offers to the heart an absolutely love-worthy being as the object of its adoration. Whether these immense offers of religion are all genuine, or all accepted by us individually, they are quite unmatched by anything which science, or art, or politics, or commerce, or even friendship, has to bestow."

Let us consider this most curious paragraph. Religion offers to the intellect an explanation of the universe, "true or false we need not now consider". Pardon me, that is exactly what the intellect must consider, for a false explanation is worthless, and may be mischievous—as when it is accepted as true and prevents further investigation. One religion tells us that God made man out of dust and woman out of a rib; another relates that the earth was populated by Deucalion and Pyrrha throwing stones behind them, Deucalion's stones turning into men, and Pyrrha's into women; a third explains the sexes by saying that Brahma made a figure male and female, and then slit it in half; all these are "explanations". "Take them all", Miss Cobbe says amiably: "never mind whether they are true or false". Yet the value of an explanation depends entirely on the amount of truth it contains. It is idle for Miss Cobbe to answer that the explanation offered by "religion" is not that of any special religion, Jewish or Pagan; belief in God and in immortality offers *per se* no explanation of the universe, and each special religion dogmatises but does not explain. Yet these fables are "quite unmatched by anything which science . . . . has to bestow"! The discoveries of Copernicus and Galileo, of Newton and Laplace, of Lamarck and Darwin, are all thrown into the shade as explanations when compared with these grotesque fancies of religion. I prefer the science.

"Pointing to heaven it responds to the most eager of its questions." And the response, I suppose, may be "true or false" as it happens. Happy hunting-grounds or Elysian fields, the Eastern magnificence of John or the sensual houri-filled paradise of Mahomet, it is all one to Miss Cobbe. Religion says "something" of a life after death. And to her impatient, unbalanced, helter-skelter mind, the crudest and most absurd answers are better than the patient sober silence of Science where knowledge fails.

"It offers to the conscience a law claiming authority to

regulate every act and every word." Where? In the Jewish Scriptures, commanding slavery and persecution? In the Christian Scriptures, commanding non-resistance of evil and celibacy wherever possible? If not in these, where is this law to be found? By intuition? The intuition of the Thug? of the Dyak? of the Fijian? of the Inquisitor? of the Covenanter? of the Sceptic? Or is the moral law evolved by Miss Frances Power Cobbe out of her own inner consciousness to be the law for all humanity?

"It offers to the heart an absolutely love-worthy being as the object of its adoration." Which being? I have never yet met a love-worthy God. The Jahveh of the Jews is detestable. The "Father" of the Christians burns the majority of his children for ever. The God of the Theist has invented the struggle for existence, and looks on unmoved at the immense misery of the world when he might by a word turn all its mourning into joy. Hateful and enemies of man are they, all these innumerable Gods. Love-worthy! it is blasphemy against Love to soil it by joining it to their names. "Whether these immense offers of religion are all genuine", is apparently a matter of small moment from Miss Cobbe's point of view. Yet on their genuineness must depend all their value. If they are not genuine, then the smallest gift of science, art, politics, commerce, or friendship, is more precious than the huge frauds of religion. The man who gives me a pound enriches me more than the man who promises me a million and gives me naught. To promise me the moon would be an "immense offer"; but I should prefer the gift of an acre in Arran.

I have spoken of a few of the gifts of science; what shall I say of those of art, of politics, of commerce, of friendship, the other "moonlike things" so contemptuously regarded by Miss Cobbe? Better the symphonies of Beethoven, the paintings of Turner and of Long, than the jangling of angels' harps and the pearl-gemmed gates of the New Jerusalem. Better the efforts to raise the poor and to bind in brotherhood the nations, than the dull contentment with misery preached by the believers in God. Better the commerce which unites than the religion which divides the nations. And better, a thousandfold better, the sweet trust of human friendship, the priceless wealth of human sympathy, the tenderness, the peace, the perfect joy of human love, than any dream of some non-human, supernatural, unsympathetic Supreme Being, unsympathetic because sympathy implies fellow-feeling and equality, and these can never be between Man and God.

After this introductory statement, Miss Cobbe proceeds to deal with the subject-matter of her enquiry, the changes which may be expected to result from the "downfall of religion in Europe and America". The mere commonplace scientific student would be content to study facts and to deduce conclusions from them; but Miss Cobbe is an Intuitionist, and has methods far less laborious, if more expeditious. She alleges that "after noting the orderly and estimable conduct of many of them [undevout people], the observer might *per contra*, not unfairly surmise that they would continue to act just as they do at present were religion universally exploded. But ere such a conclusion could be legitimately drawn from the meritorious lives of non-religious men in the present order of society, we should be allowed (it is a familiar remark) to see the behavior of a whole nation of Atheists. Our contemporaries are no more fair samples of the outcome of Atheism than a little party of English youths who had lived for a few years in Central Africa would be samples of Negroes. It would take several thousand years to make a full-blooded Atheist out of the scion of forty generations of Christians." This is a fair sample of the argumentative style of Miss Cobbe. She admits that many Atheists—her "undevout" persons—are "orderly and estimable"; now a very large number of "devout" persons are neither orderly nor estimable. Some persons who do not believe in God nor in immortality are moral, some who believe in both are also moral, while many who believe in both are utterly immoral. Such are the facts. The obvious conclusion—by the logical "method of difference"—is that the two thing, belief and conduct, are not causally related. But logic is not Miss Cobbe's *forte*, and she refers the moral conduct of Atheists to "forty [why forty?] generations of Christians". A Pagan of the type of Socrates or of Plato might remark that "it would take several thousand years to make a full-blooded Christian out of the scion of forty generations of Pagans", and as "several thousand years" have not elapsed since the birth of Christ, he might, arguing on Miss Cobbe's model, allege that the Christians of to-day had not yet worked out the degrading results of their creed. Still more forcibly does the *tu quoque* style of argument apply to Miss Cobbe's Theism. Who can plumb the depths of immorality which will be reached by adherents of "mere Theism", when the constraining influence of Christianity has disappeared? All their present parade of virtue is worthless; "full-blooded Theism" is as far off as "full-blooded Atheism". Theists are virtuous members of society, not because they love virtue, but because they are forced into outward decency by their ancestral "forty generations of Christians", and the pressure of Christianity around them. Miss Cobbe's Theism and my Atheism are both products of modern thought. Her arguments against the morality of the one tell with fatal force against the morality of the other. Let Miss Cobbe go back to submissive Christianity, or let her be honest enough to recognise that in seeking a higher truth both she and I have broken with the past, and that while we both owe much to our forerunners, our morality is based on something more reliable than tradition or present pressure.

"As it is, then, impossible", Miss Cobbe goes on, "to forecast what would be the consequences of universal Atheism hereafter by observing the conduct of individual Atheists to-day, all that can be done is to study bit by bit the changes which must take place should this planet ever become, as is threatened, a *Faithless World*". Surely the word "study" is here written in error? To "guess at", to "fancy", to "manufacture", would represent the process, but to study, no! Anyone who desired to write carefully would at least have endeavored in forecasting changes to be guided by some analogy with observed facts, but Miss Cobbe deliberately ignores all the admitted facts, and starts off along a road of pure guess.

Miss Cobbe's bitter contempt for the philosophy she is engaged in caricaturing, and her habit of begging every point in dispute, break out in her next sentences. "Atheists have been hitherto like children playing at the mouth of a cavern of unknown depth. They have run in and out, and explored it a little way, but always within sight of the daylight outside, where have stood their parents and friends calling on them to return. Not till the way back to the sunshine has been lost will the darkness of that cave be fully revealed." I pass the "children playing". In serious controversy such phrases are out of place. But it is well to note the cool assumption that Atheism is "darkness". Whether it be darkness or not is the question at issue; to the Atheist the world is "dark with Gods", and as these awful shadows pass, the sunshine of hope and of love illumines the saddened earth. Nothing is proved by Miss Cobbe's assumption that Atheism is darkness, nor by mine that Atheism is light. Sober investigation, not metaphor, is the only Ariadne's clue through this worse than Cretan labyrinth.

The first of the suggested changes in the "Faithless World" are "the suppression of public and private worship and of teaching; the secularisation or destruction everywhere of cathedrals, churches, and chapels; and the extinction of the clerical profession". And then follows a wail over the "effacement from each landscape of the towers and spires of the churches". "Worship" would certainly vanish under an Atheistic *régime*, but "preaching" not, unless the word "preaching" be confined to dissertations on superstitious dogmas; the teaching of social duties, of civic and personal obligations, will for a long time to come form a necessary part of public education. Why should cathedrals, churches, and chapels be destroyed? Atheism will utilise, not destroy, the beautiful edifices which, once wasted on God, shall hereafter be consecrated for Man. Destroy Westminster Abbey, with its exquisite arches, its glorious tones of soft, rich color, its stonework light as if of cloud, its dreamy subdued twilight soothing as "the shadow of a great rock in a weary land"? Nay, but reconsecrate it to humanity. The fat cherubs who tumble over guns and banners on soldiers' graves will fitly be removed to some spot where their clumsy forms will no longer mar the upward-springing grace of lines of pillar and of arch, but the glorious building wherein now barbaric psalms are chanted and droning canons preach of Eastern follies, shall hereafter echo the majestic music of Wagner and of Beethoven, and the teachers of the future shall there unveil to thronging multitudes the beauties and the wonders of the world. The "towers and spires" will not be effaced, but they will no longer be the symbols of a religion which sacrifices earth to heaven and Man to God.

"The extinction of the clerical profession" would certainly take place in a "Faithless World". Those "barriers to thought" would happily have disappeared. Miss Cobbe thinks that this extinction would "reduce by many perceptible degrees the moral level", and that the "severity of the strictures always passed on the faults of clergymen testifies to the general expectation, not wholly disappointed, that they should exhibit a loftier standard of life than other men". The severity is not so much due to the general expectation of nobler living from them as to the hatred that honest people feel for hypocrisy joined to pretensions of superiority; Pecksniff is detestable not only for the unfathomed depths of his meanness, but for the claim to sanctity above his fellows which is associated with his moral worthlessness.

The "Seventh Day of Rest" will, Miss Cobbe thinks, "survive every other religious institution"; it is, it seems, "so marvellously adapted to our mental and physical constitution". Adapted by whom? Unless Miss Cobbe has turned traitor to her former teaching, she cannot regard the seventh day as God-appointed. The nation is to "enjoy the somewhat doubtful privilege of keeping fifty-six Bank Holidays, instead of four, in the year". Doubtful privilege! Surely a "seventh day rest" will be more recreative to the worker when he may visit picture-gallery, museum, concert-hall, theatre, library, instead of lounging in a gin-palace or at a street-corner, or tramping through the dreary streets.

"Judicial and official oaths of all sorts, and marriage and burial rites, would, of course, be entirely abolished." For the oaths, granted. But why should marriage and burial rites be abolished? People will be married, I hope, and buried, I fear, in a "Faithless World" as in a religious one. The indecent Church marriage service will vanish, to the great gain of refinement and modesty, and the open and notorious evil-liver will no longer be buried in sure and certain hope of a blessed resurrection, but man and woman will still join loyal hands in union unblessed by priest, and the last tender farewell will be given to the dead by lips that speak for love and not for fee.

Next will come "the reduction of the Bible to the rank of an (*sic*) historical and literary curiosity. Nothing (as we all recognise) but the supreme religious importance attached to the Hebrew Scriptures could have forced any book into the unique position which the Bible has now held for three centuries in English and Scottish education. . . . All the golden fruit which the English intellect has borne from Shakspere downwards may be said to have grown on this priceless Semitic graft upon the Aryan stem."

And this from Miss Cobbe's pen! This to be written by a woman who has done so much to degrade the Bible from this unique position by the whole tone and drift of her writings! The position held by the Bible in England has been one of the main obstacles to England's progress. It has been used since Shakspere's time to prop the despotism of the Stuarts, to rivet the manacles on the slave, to delay the enfranchisement of men, to maintain a tyrannical Establishment, to resist the emancipation of Jews and of Dissenters, to justify the imprisonment of civil and religious reformers, to perpetuate the subjugation of women. To the charge of what other book can be laid the crimes against liberty which may be justly laid against the Bible? And this because of its "religious importance". As a book, it has much that is interesting and curious in it. As a religious code it has been a curse to the human race.

The changes dealt with in the preceding paragraphs are those which are regarded by Miss Cobbe as the most obvious; she next considers "those less obvious consequences of the downfall of religion which would take place silently".

"The first of these would be the *belittling* of life .... Only when they disappear will men perceive how the two thoughts—of this world as *God's world* and of ourselves as Immortal beings—have, between them, lighted up in rainbow hues the dull plains of earth. When they fade away, all things, Nature, Art, Duty, Love, and Death, will seem to grow grey and cold. Everything which casts a glamor over life will be gone." I meet this argument by denying the truth of Miss Cobbe's view of earth as well as by objecting to "glamor". The plains of earth are *not* dull; they are musical with birds, green with trees, gemmed with blossoms, sparkling with the silver threads of winding streams; they "Bask in purple, glow in green, exult in gold". "Rainbow hues" would not add to their glory. Wild rose and clematis, mayflower and harebell, wood-sorrel and violet, have hues as lovely and more lasting than those of the rainbow, while earth's garlands fling on the breezes a fragrance that the colored mist of heaven cannot rival. I accept Miss Cobbe's imagery; better the flowers of earth than the unsubstantial rainbows of the sky.

This, of course, is not argument; it is only phrase-making. But the suggestion underlying Miss Cobbe's image is as false as the image is ill-chosen. Art, Duty, Love, are no more "grey and cold" than the literal plains of earth. Art was turned away from its true function when it painted ugly hermits and shrivelled nuns instead of types of human beauty. Sculpture and painting have often given to the world human figures of ideal beauty, and in deference to the superstition of their day have named these Apollo or Aphrodite, Sebastian or Mary, but it has been the human element, not the religious, which has been of value; the ugly Madonnas are as valuable from the religious point of view as are the beautiful ones; indeed, the most sacred of all, the black virgin and child, served for Isis and Horus before worshipped as Mary and Christ. Miss Cobbe admits that "in the purer modern types of religion . . . . we should expect painting and sculpture to be less immediately concerned with it than in old days, because unable to touch such purely spiritual ideas. But", she goes on, "the elevation, aspiration, and reverence which have their root in religion must continue to inspire those arts likewise, or they will fall into triviality on one side (as there seems danger in England), or into obscene materialism on the other, as is already annually exemplified on the walls of the Paris *Salon*". The last phrase is well-chosen to terrify the British Philistine, but is very absurd. I doubt if Miss Cobbe has visited the Paris *Salon* annually, or has even taken the trouble to look over the *Paris Salon* issued by Louis Enault each year. What does she mean by "obscene materialism"? Studies of the nude? To many people the human body as "made by God" is obscene; to make God's work decent the co-operation of Redfern or of Wörth is necessary. But if the nude is indecent, all great sculpture of the human body stands condemned. The statutes of Apollo and of Aphrodite were not, as a rule, dressed; it has been left for the religious feeling of the Vatican to put tin cylinders over the majestic and exquisite nude figures of Pagan Greece. Further, some of the religious statues were really indecent, and the "obscene materialism" of the Paris *Salon* is modesty itself beside the "obscene religionism" of Egypt and of Southern Italy. In painting similar facts might be alleged; *e.g.*, the exquisite Magdalen of Corregio is as voluptuously seductive as any non-religious female figure ever limned by Parisian artist. But the main point is not that of decency and indecency. It is of the true source of inspiration for sculpture and painting. I allege that nature is the only source of inspiration for the graphic arts. Human, brute, vegetable, mineral, forms of beauty —on these alone can the sculptor and the painter draw. The existence of God, the immortality of the human soul, cannot affect the artist's materials. These exist, whether or not there be a God; an invisible, incorporeal being is not well adapted to serve as model for sculptor or painter; souls may wield the chisel and the brush beyond the grave, but it is the human brain and the human hand that guide them here.

Nor do poetry, music, and architecture, need religion for their inspiration now, any more than they have needed it in the past. Belief in God is no more necessary to great poetry than is belief in fairies or in magic, although poets have long used Gods, fairies, and witchcraft as part of their machinery, and will probably continue to do so for many a day to come. They are fancies, not realities, yet fancies often find beautiful poetic setting. Ariel and Caliban need not exist in order that Shakspere may introduce them into a play, and if any of the Gods be coveted by a poet among his *dramatis personæ* their real existence is not necessary for their utilisation. Lucretius among ancients, Shelley and Swinburne among moderns, tell us that poetry is possible without God. It is often alleged that all the grandest music is sacred, but this is prejudice, not fact. No mass or oratorio ever written rivals the sonatas, symphonies, and concerted chamber music of Beethoven; the secular music of Mozart is grander than his masses; the works of Schubert, Bach, Brahms, all bear the same testimony; Berlioz was not the least of the musicians of his day. The masses and oratorios are at present more popular, partly because they are better known, partly because, being inferior, they are better understood by the majority, and chiefly because the religious words "cast a glamor over" the music, and make people fancy that they are performing a work of piety while listening to them. Amusement flavored with religion has a special charm for persons superficially religious and inwardly world-loving. But architecture, at least, it is urged, owes its greatness to religion. Yet the Forum, the Coliseum, can surely hold their own against any cathedral in the world.

Though, however, it may be worth while to find out how unsubstantial is the claim made on the arts by religion, the real answer to that claim is one not of detail, but of principle. Even had man always given his best to his

Gods, yet the gift was of man, not of God. On what ground, then, should it be supposed that while the giver remains the same, the gift should be lessened in value because the recipient is altered?

But, leaving art, what shall we say to Miss Cobbe's allegation that duty will "grow grey and cold" without God and immortality? Yes, for those with whom duty is a matter of selfish calculation, and who are virtuous only because they look for a "golden crown" in payment on the other side the grave. Those of us who find joy in right-doing, who work because work is useful to our fellows, who live well because in such living we pay our contribution to the world's wealth, leaving earth richer than we found it—we need no paltry payment after death for our life's labor, for in that labor is its own "exceeding great reward".

And love "grey and cold" when God has disappeared! None but the unloving can echo Miss Cobbe's words. Love of friend for friend, of parent for child, of man for woman, how should such loves fade because a supernatural love has vanished? Man lives, though Gods die. Those who have been so unfortunate as never to have felt strong human love may fancy that their thin ghost of love for the unseen is the highest emotion that man can feel. But those who know what love is smile at, though they also pitifully sigh over, the twilight life which takes the moonlight of divine for the sunlight of human love.

But what of death? Miss Cobbe may ask. Death in old age, when life is fully lived, should lose much of the sadness it wears when it cuts short the thread of happy days. And annihilation is surely better than the life in torture which religions have offered to the world. Better the death of the beloved than the thought of agony after death. I am aware that Miss Cobbe believes in immortality but not in hell; that she regards all as "doomed to be saved". We are not all dowered with Miss Cobbe's facility for believing in pleasant things because we desire them. For many of us evidence must precede belief. I would gladly believe in a happy immortality for all, as I would gladly believe that all misery and crime and poverty will disappear in 1885—*if I could*. But I am unable to believe an improbable proposition unless convincing evidence is brought in support of it. Immortality is most improbable; no evidence is brought forward in its favor. I cannot believe only because I wish.

Miss Cobbe would keep belief in the unprovable on the ground that it "casts a glamor over life". I desire to see life as it is. If we would judge a landscape rightly we must not look at it through colored glasses. Unhappily, few people really love Truth; they prefer illusions, if the illusions are pleasanter than the truths, and become very angry with those who point out that illusions are not realities, and who are not afraid to recognise painful and disheartening truths. What should we think of a farmer who left undrained a fever-breeding swamp on the ground that the marsh-fires were "so pretty"? Yet there are people who would preserve the swamps of superstition because their dancing flames "cast a glamor over life".

"Again, it will not merely belittle life, it will *carnalise* it to take Religion out of it. . . . . It needs no argument to prove that, as the bestial tendencies in us have scarcely been kept down while we believed ourselves to be immortal souls, they will have it still more their own way when we feel assured we are only mortal bodies." This sentence would be easier to deal with if Miss Cobbe had vouchsafed to tell us which tendencies in man she regards as "bestial". I should have regarded war as one of the strongest examples of a bestial tendency, but judging from her next paragraph Miss Cobbe does not regard war with the detestation felt for it by Atheists. Excuses for the brutality of war, however, may be looked for from anyone who admires the Bible.

It may be frankly acknowledged, however, that man inherits from his brute progenitors various bestial tendencies which are in course of elimination. The wild beast desire to fight is one of these, and this has been encouraged, not checked, by religion. National rivalries have often grown out of the rivalries of national Gods. "I the Lord thy God am a jealous God", quoth Jahveh of the Hebrews, and the bloodiest wars waged by the human race have been the wars waged in the name of God. The "Holy War" has ever been a war of extermination, whether undertaken by the Moabites for Chemosh, by the Hebrews for Jahveh, by the Christians for Christ. Another bestial tendency is the lust of the male for the female apart from love, duty, and loyalty; this again has been encouraged by religion, as witness the polygamy and concubinage of the Hebrews—as in Abraham, David, and Solomon, not to mention the precepts of the Mosaic laws—the bands of male and female prostitutes in connexion with Pagan temples, and the curious outbursts of sexual passion in connexion with religious revivals and missions. Another bestial tendency is greed, the strongest grabbing all he can and trampling down the weaker in the mad struggle for wealth: how and when has religion modified this tendency, sanctified as it is in our present civilisation?

All these bestial tendencies will be eradicated only by the recognition of human duty, of the social bond. Religion has not eradicated them, but Science by tracing them to their source in our brute ancestry has explained them and has shown them in their true light. As each recognises that the anti-social tendencies are the bestial tendences in man, and that man in evolving further must evolve out of these, each also feels it part of his personal duty to curb these in himself and so to rise further from the brute. This rational "co-operation with Nature" distinguishes the scientific from the religious person, and this constraining sense of obligation is becoming stronger and stronger in all those who in losing faith in God have gained hope for Man.

"From the general results on the community, I now pass to consider those on the life of the individual which may be expected to follow the collapse of religion". First of these Miss Cobbe puts the loss of "aspiration, the sacred passion, the *ambition sainte* to become perfect and holy". Needless to say that Miss Cobbe does not explain why the longing after human perfection should disappear with faith in God. To the Atheist it seems that the knowledge that the perfecting of the race is only possible by the improvement of the individual, supplies the most constraining motive which can be imagined for efforts after personal perfection. The Theist may desire personal perfection, but his desire is self-centred; each righteous individual is righteous, as it were, alone, and his righteousness does not benefit his fellows save as it may make him helpful and loving in his dealings with them. The Atheist desires personal perfection not only for his joy in it as beautiful in itself, but because science has taught him the unity of the race, and he knows that each fresh conquest of his over the baser parts of his nature and each strengthening of the higher is a gain for all, and not for himself alone. If, however, by "aspiration" Miss Cobbe only means mere futile longing after good apart from effort to realise it, that will certainly disappear with the invertebrate folk who feel it, as the race grows stronger and more rational.

"Again, repentance as well as aspiration will disappear under the snows of Atheism". Repentance, it is explained, is not the "sense of dissatisfaction" with oneself after having yielded to the lower appetites and passions, as defined by Darwin, but is an "awful convulsion of the soul", an "ordeal", the "vivid experiences of penitence and restoration". Awful convulsions may be seen at any revival meeting, where sinners writhe on the floor, proclaiming their own vileness and crouching and cringing for forgiveness before "an offended God". Such degrading exhibitions will, indeed, have ceased in "a faithless world". To awful convulsions will have succeeded sober and dignified regret for wrong-doing, coupled with a manful resolution to repair as far as is possible any injury inflicted on others, whether of actual aggression or of evil example. It is hardly an argument which will recommend Theism to the rational that losing Theism we shall lose spiritual hysterics.

Private prayer will be given up, of course, when belief in God has vanished, and "with aspiration, repentance, and prayer renounced and forgotten", Miss Cobbe considers that the "inner life" will be made "easy". My blinded eyes fail to see why a man's life should become ignobly easy because he is forced to be self-reliant instead of being dependent on God. A child's legs do not grow strong if he is allowed to walk with the support of leading-strings or of a "go-cart". They grow strong when he is left to trust to them only for support. The easy fashion of leaning on the divine "go-cart" has rendered flabby the muscles of Humanity; they will grow hard and elastic only when men learn to walk alone.

"Christian charity" will vanish in "a faithless world", and this because "the charity of Science is not merely *different* from the charity of religion; it is an *opposite* thing altogether. Its softest word is *Væ Victis!* . . . . Science says, 'The supreme law of nature is the survival of the fittest; and that law, applied to human morals, means the remorseless crushing down of the unfit'." Miss Cobbe's blind and ignorant hatred of Science comes out strongly in this passage; the "survival of the fittest" in the struggle for existence is a *fact* which has underlain past progress; the weak sentimentalist may shriek over the truth, but the thoughtful prefer to recognise a fact as a fact. Miss Cobbe should at least remember, as a Theist, that her God is responsible for the sad truth, and that he deliberately chose that progress should only be possible through struggle and death. But Science does *not* say that this struggle need continue; on the contrary it teaches how man's reason may checkmate the malice of Miss Cobbe's God, and may substitute co-operation for competition, fraternal aid for fratricidal strife. Even if Miss Cobbe points to her *bête noire*, vivisection, as an instance of scientific cruelty, she should remember that if her God had not devised frightful diseases for the torture of men and of brutes, scientists would not need to inflict passing pain to win permanent cure for pain; and that the human vivisector at his very worst limps far far behind the divine vivisector, who daily strews his mangled mutilated victims over the torture-trough of earth, till every forest is stained with blood and every sea and river is sobbing with incalculable pain.

So far from Science teaching us to remorselessly crush down the unfit, Science teaches us not only how to render the unfit more fit to-day, but by laying bare the causes of unfitness she teaches us how to prevent unfitness to-morrow. Those that can be cured, she cures; the incurable, she nurses and relieves; at the same time, she strives to remove the causes of disease, so that a healthier generation may need less of her curative skill. Christian charity! we know its work. It gives a hundredweight of coal and five pounds of beef once a year to a family whose head could earn a hundred such doles if Christian justice allowed him fair wage for the work he performs. It plunders the workers of the wealth they make, and then flings back at them a thousandth part of their own product as "charity". It builds hospitals for the poor whom it has poisoned in filthy courts and alleys, and workhouses for the worn-out creatures from whom it has wrung every energy, every hope, every joy. Miss Cobbe summons us to admire Christian civilisation, and we see idlers flaunting in the robes woven by the toilers, a glittering tinselled superstructure founded on the tears, the strugglings, the grey hopeless misery of the poor.

Miss Cobbe, however, is by no means blind to the suffering which is present in the world, and it is indeed on the existence of suffering here that she partly bases her belief in a future wherein all shall be well with all. By Mr. Justice Stephen's optimistic cynicism she is not unnaturally irritated; he remarked that "a man who cannot occupy every waking moment of a long life with some one or other of these things [friendship, politics, commerce, literature, science, and art] must be either very unfortunate in regard to his health, or else must be a poor creature". In answer to this she writes: "It is not necessary to be either unfortunate oneself or a very 'poor creature' to feel that the wrongs and agonies of this world of pain are absolutely intolerable unless we can be assured that they will be righted hereafter; that 'there is a God who judgeth the earth', and that all the oppressed and miserable of our race, aye, and even the tortured brutes, are beheld by him. . . . . Not that which is 'poorest' in us, but that which is richest and noblest, refuses to 'occupy every moment of a long life' with our own ambitions and amusements, or to shut out deliberately from our minds the 'riddle of the painful earth'." To us there is but small comfort in Miss Cobbe's assurance that earth's "wrongs and agonies" "will be righted hereafter". Granting for a moment that man survives death, what certainty have we that "the next world" will be any improvement on this? Miss Cobbe assures us that this is "God's world"; whose world will the next be, if not also his? Will he be stronger there or better, that he should set right in that world the wrongs he has permitted here? Will he have changed his mind, or have become weary of the contemplation of suffering? To me the thought that the world was in the hands of a God who permitted all the present wrongs and pains to exist would be intolerable, maddening in its hopelessness. There is every hope of righting earth's wrongs and of curing earth's pains if the reason and skill of man which have already done so much are free to do the rest; but if they are to strive against omnipotence, hopeless indeed is the future of the world. It is in this sense that the Atheist looks on good as "the final goal of ill", and believing that that goal will be reached the sooner the more strenuous the efforts of each individual, he works in the glad certainty that he is aiding the world's progress thitherward. Not dreaming of a personal reward hereafter, not craving a personal payment from a heavenly treasury, he works and loves, content that he is building a future fairer than his present, joyous that he is creating a new earth for a happier race.

THE

JESUS OF THE GOSPELS

AND THE

INFLUENCE OF CHRISTIANITY.

VERBATIM REPORT OF THE

TWO NIGHTS' DEBATE

BETWEEN THE

REV. A. HATCHARD & ANNIE BESANT,

At the Hall of Science, 142, Old Street, on Wednesdays, November 25th and December 1st, 1880.

LONDON:
FREETHOUGHT PUBLISHING COMPANY,
28, STONECUTTER STREET, E.C.

PRICE ONE SHILLING

LONDON:
PRINTED BY ANNIE BESANT AND CHARLES BRADLAUGH,
28, STONECUTTER STREET, E.C.

FIRST NIGHT.

SUBJECT:—

"That the Jesus of the Gospels is a Historical Character."

MR. TURPIN IN THE CHAIR.

THE CHAIRMAN in opening the proceedings stated that he had expected his friend, Mr. Cowper, would have taken the chair that evening, and that Mr. Cowper not being able to be present another gentleman had been named; but he also was unable to preside, so that the lot had fallen upon him. It was, however, not the first time he had taken the chair in the Hall of Science, but he was pleased to see that since he last occupied that post there, a change had taken place in the *materialism* of the hall, and he hoped that in course of time a change might also be effected in the *spiritualism* of the hall likewise. He hoped that they would allow him to sit still, by listening quietly and without interruption to both the speakers in the ensuing debate. The Rev. A. Hatchard was to contend that the Jesus of the Gospels was a historical character, and Mrs. Besant would contend that he could not occupy that position. The order of the debate would be as follows:—The Rev. A. Hatchard would open in the affirmative, occupying half an hour; Mrs. Besant would then follow in the negative, occupying another half hour. There would then be four speeches of a quarter of an hour each, two from each speaker; and then Mr. Hatchard would close the debate with another speech of a quarter of an hour's duration. He concluded by asking for a fair hearing for both sides of the argument, which, he said, was better for the subject, better for the debaters, and better for the audience; and he trusted that the dignity and character of the disputants and of the audience would be such that that debate might be looked back upon in the future as a model debate. He then called upon the Rev. A. Hatchard to open in the affirmative.

B 2

The Rev. A. HATCHARD, who was greeted with applause, then rose and said:—Mr. Chairman, Mr. Bradlaugh, Ladies, and Gentlemen: I stand before you here this evening to prove that the Jesus of the Gospels is a historical character. Now I can well understand that some persons may think that a superfluous task in the present day, but as there are those on the present platform who question it it may be necessary for me to go through some of the evidence by which we prove this matter. But as it is utterly impossible to make a jump in the mind from now to more than 1800 years ago, so to speak, I do not intend to ask you to make what I call a "jump" from now to the time when Christ was born. I intend to take you back by what is called the bridge of history—the bridge of history over the gulf of time. Now here is an ordinary English copy of the Scriptures. I put that in the hands of a man, and he looks at it and examines it. After this examination he says: "I see here an account of an extraordinary character, but how do I know that this is a true account; and how do I know that these books really come down from the time you say they come down from?" Now you know very well what the authorised English Bible is, and you find that the same Bibles are in the hands of Christian sects all over the world, for between the Roman Catholic Bible and the English Protestant Bible there is really no difference. Here we have the Church of England and the Roman Catholic Church, and a large number of bodies of Dissenters—of Independents, Baptists, Wesleyans, and many other sects or parties who all accept the same book. Well, now you see that this is the fact that the Christian world receives that book to-day We may make a jump right back from now certainly to the time of Mahomet, who believed in the historical existence of Jesus, and we may make another jump backward to the fourth century. Now you may ask me how do I prove that the Bible was not altered during those centuries, and my answer is that the Bible we have is the same as the book was at the invention of printing, as you may see by the Bibles which are now in the British Museum. Now you are well aware that it is something like 400 or 450 years since printing first came into use, and we may jump back over that period without any difficulty. Now, during the age of manuscripts, we can go back without any difficulty at all to the year 325, where you see the council of Nice. Through that period, the age of manuscripts, what guarantee had we that these manuscripts were not altered? Simply this. These manuscripts, in various languages, were scattered about all over Europe, over a good part of Asia, over the North of Africa; they were in the hands of conflicting sects and parties, so that no one could alter them in the slightest degree. It would be impossible to interpolate the story of Jesus of Nazareth without its being discovered. Now, you see from these diagrams that I have taken you back to this period here (pointing to the diagram fixed on the platform). I have taken you over the easiest period. We now come to the time of Constantine, who was the first Roman Emperor who proclaimed himself a Christian. (Laughter.) I am not going to discuss the character of Constantine. I daresay those of you who have paid any attention to this matter know that in the time of Constantine there was a great dispute between the Arians and the orthodox party, and I suppose you are well aware that Athanasius was the person who maintained orthodox, and that Arius was a man who maintained unorthodox Christianity. Now, Eusebius really is the man who is said to have presented to the Council of Nice the Nicene Creed, and, although some of you are Freethinkers, you have been in the Church of England, and I venture to say that a large number of you have been baptised in the Church of England. Consequently, you know the creed of the Church of England which I refer to when I speak of the Nicene Creed. The Nicene Creed is said to have been presented to the Council of Nice by Eusebius. I stand here to tell you that from the work of Eusebius we receive a very important part of the evidence respecting the Christian Church, that is, as regards its early history. It has been disputed by thinkers whether Eusebius is a truthful historian; but I put him before you to-night as a truthful historian. I stand here boldly to put Eusebius before you as substantially a truthful historian. As to what is said in Taylor's "Diegesis" and other similar works, I do not trouble myself to answer them, for I maintain that the "Diegesis" is an utterly unreliable book, and that its quotations are inaccurate. I could give you plenty of instances to show that Taylor is quite unreliable; and I make nothing at all of the remarks of such writers as Taylor. We have the Christian faith promulgated and pronounced in that Nicene Creed that we read every Sunday in the Communion Service of the Church of England. I have got back now to the time of Athanasius, Arius, Eusebius, and of Constantine, when Christianity was proclaimed as the religion of the Roman Empire, and when, as you know well, it became allied with the State. In this fourth century I find the same Christian Creed maintained by those writers whose names I have placed here (pointing to the diagrams), viz., Augustine, Jerome, Chrysostom, and Basil. Here, then, are these writers belonging to the fourth century, by whom the Christian faith is promulgated and taught as it is put forward in the Four Gospels and in the writings of St. Paul: we find it substantially and practically the same as in those writers whom I have mentioned to you as belonging to the fourth century. I now go back into the third century. I have here the name of Tertullian, who, as you are well aware, was one of the greatest writers of the Christian Church and Cyprian, Minucius Felix, who was a Latin writer, and who wrote what would now be called an "Apology for Christianity." I next come to Origen, who was one of the greatest writers of the Church, against whose name you will see I have placed the dates 184 to 253. Now this Origen was in many respects one of the most eminent writers the Church has produced, according to my own opinion respecting him and his teachings: but he teaches clearly the same Christian faith as we have. We now come to Clement of Alexandria, who was a predecessor of Origen, and we get to Pantænus. It would take me too long to enter into the details, but it is perfectly clear that Pantænus was a Christian teacher. We have only some fragments of his writings preserved to us. He is said to have been a great traveller into the East, and discoverer of a MS. containing an account of the gospel. He is one who is put forward by the Christian thinkers as a link in the chain of historical evidence. I now come to what are called the so-called Apostolic Constitutions. I do not put them before you as the work of the Apostles, but they have come down to us by that name. Mrs. Besant will lose her time in attacking me upon these—(laughter)—don't laugh until you have heard what I have to say. I put them before you as occurring in the third century, simply as a record of Church practices and customs that were popular in the third century. Coming now to the second century, we find an eminent man named Polycarp first mentioned. He, also, was a professor of the Christian faith, and is said to have suffered martyrdom. Tertullian, you will observe, is mentioned in the second century as well as the third century, because he reaches over a part of both of them. I have next the name of Iræneus, who was an eminent Christian of the second century—Iræneus, who also was an eminent believer of the Christian faith. We now come to the *crux* of the whole thing. When we get here, then begins what freethinkers call *the* difficulty. I present to you Justin Martyr. Justin Martyr is really a most important man in the history of the Christian Church, and also in the record of the history of the Christian faith. He was a very popular Christian in his day, and he presented one Apology (so called) for the Christian faith to the Roman Emperor. Of course there are two Apologies, which are known to the world under his name. I stand here to maintain one. I could maintain the two. I maintain the first one. What does he tell us with respect to the Christian faith? He tells us the same thing as we have in the Four Gospels in the present day. I will give you one or two of Justin's quotations. It has been arranged that the quotations shall be printed from the books, so that there will be no mistake whatever about what is read. I give you a quotation from his first Apology, which runs thus: "At the same time an angel was sent to the same virgin, saying, 'Behold, thou shalt conceive in thy womb by the Holy Ghost, and thou shalt bring forth a son, and He shall be called the Son of the Highest, and thou shalt call His name Jesus; for He shall save His people from their sins;' *as they have taught* who have written the history of all things concerning our Savior, Jesus Christ." Another quotation from the same: "For the apostles in those memorials which are written by them, *which are called Gospels*, thus delivered it, 'that Jesus taking bread, blessing it, commanded them to say, Do this in remembrance of me; this is my body; and taking the cup in like manner and giving thanks, to say, This is my blood'"—I need not tell you that that refers to what is called the institution of the Lord's Supper; "For *in the Memoirs* which I say were composed by the apostles, and those who became their followers, it is written, that 'His sweat fell like drops of blood, while he prayed and said, If it be possible, let this cup pass from me.' In giving up the ghost on the cross, He said, 'Father, into Thy hands I commit my spirit,' as *also I learned from the Memoirs*" ["Exeter Hall Lectures," pp. 140, 141]. I have given you now one, two, three quotations from Justin Martyr's Apology. I stand here to tell you most distinctly that the Christian faith, as taught by Justin Martyr in his first Apology, is practically and really the same as what we have in the Four Gospels which exist at the present time. Now, I know that some person may say that it is not quite the exact words, the same as we have them to-day; but I say, What of that? I present you with a short notice from a well-known book, which I got with considerable difficulty. It is an old copy; it is called "Introductory Lectures to the Study of the Books of the New Testament," by John David Michaelis, published by Tonson, in the Strand, 1761. The reason I quote from this is simply this. I could have brought you a number of the modern writers in Germany, but free-thinkers are very fond of quoting from this book—so I was told. I believe it to be a substantially good account of the Gospels. These accounts, "like other ancient writers, they quote merely from memory, and therefore inaccurately." You know that was not an age of printing, but was an age when they had only MS. rolls on which the Scriptures were written; and it was a custom to quote from memory, and, therefore, not so verbally as we should do in the present day with the carefully printed book lying before us. I say that the Four Gospels, as we have them to-day, is substantially what Justin Martyr teaches us here in the second century. Two other confirmatory evidences. All of you present, I suppose, have read what is called the letter of Pliny Junior, or Secundus, to the Emperor Trajan with respect to the treatment of the Christians. If you want outside testimony to the testimony of the Christian sects or societies, and if you want a record as to their practices you have the reference most clearly and unmistakably in the letter of Pliny. He records in the public letter to Trajan, which, of course, was well-known at the time—the existence of this people, who hold substantially the same Christian belief which we hold to-day. I get back now to another heathen writer, Suetonius, who certainly does make distinct allusion to the Christians. He makes an allusion to the Christians, but then again we have here the testimony of Ignatius. This Ignatius is a great name in the early Church. I put Ignatius before you as really one of the Christian writers who bore witness in his day and generation for the Christian faith. Clement, of Rome, comes next, I place him before you to-night boldly—boldly I place him before you as a Christian writer who is well-known, and who bore testimony in the first century to the same facts as we have in the present day. Next to Clement comes Hermas, who wrote what we call "The Shepherd." Under the head Apostolic writers, or writers in their days, we get first of all St. John, who lived according to the Christian Church until the end of the first century. I place before you the testimony of Tacitus, recorded by the sceptical historian, Gibbon—I place before you Tacitus as a witness to the truth substantially of the Christian faith. I also place before you the testimony of Josephus. (Oh!) I know all that Freethinkers say with respect to Josephus, and I may be told that he was a Jew, that he would never have written the passage which, I dare say, you all know, but I say that Josephus seems to be something of the Freethinker himself, and I place him before you as one who just mentioned and alluded to the fact of the Christian Church or sect. I next pass to St. Peter and St. Paul, and I defy all the Freethinkers in Europe to break down the testimony of the Apostle Paul contained in these four epistles—the Epistle to the Romans, the two to the Corinthians, and the Epistle to the Galatians. Even the Freethinkers of Germany have allowed that these are the works of the Apostle Paul. If I understand rightly, Mrs. Besant does not believe in a great first cause and moral ruler of this world. I do. I am not ashamed to say it. To me a universe that has always been, human beings whose life is simply confined to this world and who have no souls are simply ridiculous and monstrous. (Laughter and Applause.) I stand here before the Freethinkers in England, and I am not ashamed to stand upon this platform and say that I believe in a great first cause, a great moral ruler of the universe, whom I believe exercises a superintending providence over all things. (Applause.) The testimony of St.

Paul proves indisputably that Jesus of Nazareth was a historical character, an extraordinary character, and I say a divine character or person. Let me remind you that there can be no dispute that St. Paul was present at Rome in the time of Nero. I find in the time of St. Paul, or about that time, Claudius Cæsar ordered the Jews out of Rome, on account of a disturbance—

The CHAIRMAN: Time.

Mr. Hatchard sat down amid loud applause.

Mrs. BESANT then rose, and when the loud and continued applause with which she was welcomed had subsided, said: Mr. Chairman, Mr. Hatchard, and friends, I am glad that in dealing with a question so important as the present I have the pleasure of meeting one who deals fairly and honestly with the subject; so that if in this debate no satisfactory result comes to the audience it at least will not be the fault of the Christian disputant who opposes me. A very large part of Mr. Hatchard's speech I shall not touch because I do not think that I need in any fashion deal with it. I allude to what he has told you with respect to the fourth century and the time after it. The difficulty of Mr. Hatchard is not to prove that Christ was believed to be a historical personage after the fourth century, but to bridge over the years between A.D. 1 and A.D. 300. I conceive that if he can bridge over that, then my position would be a difficult one to maintain. I admit that from the time of the Council of Nice the Christian Churches were strong and spreading, and that *after* that period Christ was recognised through a large part of the civilised world. But you cannot carry the history of Christ and the history of the Gospels over that terrible chasm of three centuries after the birth of Christ. If even you can get so far as A.D. 200 you have practically knocked away the supports on which the Freethought platform stands. I quite agree that we are not here to discuss the character of the Emperor Constantine, nor even of the Fathers. We have to deal with the reliability of the views of the Christian Fathers: we have nothing in the world to say to their character. They may have been very good, as very bad: we deal with them as witnesses of the truth or falsity of the particular Christian teaching with which we are concerned. The subject for debate is "That the Jesus of the Gospels is a historical person," and clearly the character of Constantine cannot make the historical character of Jesus either more clear or less accurate than my opponent can show it to be. I am obliged to dissent from the view to which my opponent has given utterance, viz., that exactly the same Bible is in the hands of both Protestant and Catholic. The Douay Bible differs in many respects from the Bible received in Protestant Churches; and nothing is more common than for a Roman Catholic to warn his hearers on the peril of their souls not to read the Protestant Bible, while on the other hand the Protestant cautions his followers that the Douay version of the Scriptures is misleading and therefore not to be received. Carrying back the same Bible through the era of printing to the era of MSS., and going back as far as we can, we find that no one pretends that there are any MSS. in existence earlier than those of the fourth century, so that we cannot trace back our MSS. over that critical period of which I spoke. But taking the MSS. which are in existence and comparing them together we find that they are not all alike, and the more we compare one with another the more discrepancies do we find. We have it on the authority of Dr. Angus that there are no less than 100,000 different readings in these MSS. If there were but one set of MSS., so to speak, there surely would be no need for the years that the translators have been spending on their labor of revising the New Testament. If there is one received set of MSS. there would be no difficulty at all. Then again I come to the Arians and the Catholics; but I do not think I need dwell on them, because the Arians admitted the historical character of the Jesus of the Gospels as much as the Catholics. It has been urged by my opponent that the creed known as the Nicene Creed, which was adopted by the Council of Nice in the year 325, and which we are told substantially embodies the Christian teaching of that period, as well as of the present day, is the same creed as the one we now call by that name; but I would remind Mr. Hatchard that the last part of that creed was not adopted at Nicœa, nor presented by Eusebius, but that it was added at the Council of Constantinople, and was not consequently in use until many years after the time at which he alleges the creed was adopted and used as a whole. I now come to Eusebius; and you will observe that I am taking these points which have been raised by my opponent, one by one, before I grapple with the real difficulty. The work of Eusebius is put forward as thoroughly reliable. I would remind my opponent that Eusebius himself says that he chose the materials for his history for edification rather than for accuracy, and that is not a promising beginning for a historian, as you will all allow. But if Eusebius is to be relied on, the letter of Jesus to Agbarus is thoroughly authentic, for that is given with a particularity far greater than is his general wont. We have now come to Justin and the earlier Fathers; and here, with your permission, instead of following step by step the line which my opponent has taken, I will begin at the other end, and work up to these Apostolic Fathers on whom my opponent seems so much to rely. I shall serve the cause, I believe, of Free-thought better not by simply making isolated objections to the views of Mr. Hatchard, but by showing also the heretical view which we hold. I propose, therefore, to try to place before you my own views as to the Jesus of the Gospels. I shall try to give a coherent account of the heretical view, and I shall urge that it is more in accordance with the facts of history, human experience, scientific thought and common sense to take the heretical view which we take, than to accept the view that the Jesus of the Gospels is a historical character. We are agreed apparently that the Jesus of the Gospels is a supernatural character. His birth of a virgin, the marvels surrounding his infancy, his wonderful baptism, his temptation by the devil, his miracles of healing, of destruction and of self-defence, his foreknowledge of his own death, his transfiguration, the mysterious darkness surrounding his cross, his resurrection from the dead, his ascension into heaven; if you take all these, it is impossible to deny that his life is a supernatural and miraculous one from beginning to end. I do not say that you cannot remove all these miraculous and wonderful surroundings, and still leave, untouched, the simple Jew who went about as a teacher of the people; but if you once remove the miraculous, you then have no longer the Jesus of the Gos pels. Clearly, the supernatural is the appropriate frame-work for the incarnation of Deity; the miraculous is the proper paraphernalia of divine royalty. There may have been a Jesus, then, who led a simple human life; but

I have to deal simply with the Jesus of the Gospels, and I shall endeavor to show how I conceive that various myths floating about became crystallised around the figure of Jesus of Nazareth. I cannot admit the supernatural; I cannot admit the miraculous; and, therefore, the very assertion that the Jesus of the Gospels is a miraculous and supernatural character is a great stumbling block at the outset. There are so many incarnate Gods in human history, and they all present the same birthmarks. They are always born at such a remote period, or at some such out-of-the-way place, that it is practically impossible to subject their claims to any kind of scientific investigation. Their births are always surrounded with prodigies; they always work miracles when they grow up; there is always something mysterious in their deaths; they always ascend triumphant at the last; these are the great outline marks of all the incarnate Deities which our world has known; and I allege that Jesus is one of these mythic characters, that the principal features of his life are possessed by him in common with thousands of rivals, and that he cannot, in any fashion, be distinguished from them. The essence of the spirit in which science meets the record of miracles is the spirit of Hume, that it is much more likely that men should have been deceived than that our whole experience of nature should have been contradicted. "A miracle is a violation of the laws of nature; and as a firm and unalterable experience has established these laws, the proof against a miracle, from the very nature of the fact, is as entire as any argument from experience can possibly be imagined. . . . . There must, therefore, be an uniform experience against every miraculous event, otherwise the event would not merit that appellation. And as an uniform experience amounts to a proof, there is here a direct and full *proof*, from the nature of the fact, against the existence of any miracle; nor can such a proof be destroyed, or the miracle rendered credible, but by an opposite proof, which is superior. . . . . Upon the whole, then, it appears, that no testimony for any kind of miracle has ever amounted to a probability, much less to a proof; and that, even supposing it amounted to a proof, it would be opposed by another proof; derived from the very nature of the fact, which it would endeavor to establish. It is experience only which gives authority to human testimony; and it is the same experience which assures us of the laws of nature. When, therefore, these two kinds of experience are contrary, we have nothing to do but substract the one from the other, and embrace an opinion, either on one side or the other, with that assurance which arises from the remainder. But according to the principle here explained, this substraction, with regard to all popular religions, amounts to an entire annihilation; and therefore we may establish it as a maxim, that no human testimony can have such force as to prove a miracle, and make it a just foundation for any such system of religion" ["Essay on Miracles," ed. 1770, pp. 160, 161, 178]. (Applause.) I may say that I at once accept that position of Hume. You all act upon that belief in your daily life, although you don't all act so in regard to the Gospels. We do not trouble ourselves to investigate modern miracles. Even those who accept and believe in the miracles of the Gospels pooh pooh modern ones, and pass them by with contempt. We have so often in our experience found people to be mistaken. We have so often found that testimony breaks down owing to enthusiasm, love, fear, ignorance, inaccuracy of perception or of memory. But we do not find the same changeability in the course of nature. We have not had experience of constant failures in the relation of natural causes to natural effects; and we reject the miraculous because it is contrary to the facts of the world as we know them. We believe that witnesses, however honest, are more likely to have been deceived than that the order of nature should have been violated. (Applause.) We have to deal clearly with this point. If we are to accept miracles, the evidence must be overwhelming in its strength. But when we turn to examine it we find it is lamentably weak—marvellously meagre. Two principal sources of information present themselves. First, we have what is sometimes curiously denominated profane history, but which I will call secular history; and, secondly, we have sacred history, divine history, and to that I will add the testimony of those fathers of the Church on whom my antagonist so much relies. With regard to the outside history—from Pagan writers—I will not give you my own opinion, but I will give you the opinion of Gibbon, and simply allow you to judge whether the life of Christ as it is recorded in the

Gospels could have taken place with so little notice; and with respect to the passage from Josephus and others which my opponent has quoted to you I allege, and shall prove, that they will not bear the slightest investigation. The evidence of the Christian fathers which has been adduced would not be accepted, I will not say in one of our High Courts of Justice, but even in a County Court. Gibbon asks: "But how shall we excuse the supine inattention of the Pagan and philosophic world, to those evidences which were presented by the hand of Omnipotence, not to their reason, but to their senses? During the age of Christ, of his apostles, and of their first disciples, the doctrine which they preached was confirmed by innumerable prodigies. The lame walked, the blind saw, the sick were healed, the dead were raised, dæmons were expelled, and the laws of Nature were frequently suspended for the benefit of the Church. But the sages of Greece and Rome turned aside from the awful spectacle, and pursuing the ordinary occupations of life and study, appeared unconscious of any alterations in the moral or physical government of the world. Under the reign of Tiberius, the whole earth, or at least a celebrated province of the Roman empire, was involved in a præternatural darkness for three hours. Even this miraculous event, which ought to have excited the wonder, the curiosity, and the devotion of mankind, passed without notice in an age of science and history. It happened during the lifetime of Seneca and the elder Pliny, who must have experienced the immediate effects, or received the earliest intelligence of the prodigy. Each of these philosophers, in a laborious work, has recorded all the great phenomena of Nature, earthquakes, meteors, comets, and eclipses, which his indefatigable curiosity could collect. Both the one and the other have omitted to mention the greatest phenomenon to which the mortal eye has been witness since the creation of the globe" [" Decline and Fall," Ed. 1808, pp. 178, 179]. (Applause.) Tacitus is a Pagan writer relied upon by my opponent. Tacitus tells us nothing of the miracles. He tells us only that Christ was put to death as a criminal under Pontius Pilate, but the fact that he was so put to death does not prove the miracles. Allow that this phrase of Tacitus is authentic—even then the passage is worthless from the point of view of my opponent. It simply proves that one Christ was put to death in Judea: it proves nothing as to the supernatural and miraculous Jesus of the Gospels. But I may at once say to you that so far from this testimony of Tacitus being unchallenged, it is very seriously challenged. All the MSS. we possess come down from one copy which belonged to Johannes de Spire in A.D. 1468, and taking the view that this passage may have been inserted, as it is evident that it easily could have been, we find as a strong confirmatory fact that Eusebius is the first to quote it; none of the earlier Fathers quoted it at all, so that you cannot find a trace of it before the fourth century.* We now come to Suetonius. What was it that Suetonius said? He tells us that forty years after Christ's death—no, about A.D. 40—the Jews rioted in Rome and one Chrestus was their leader. If, therefore, this passage from Suetonius be applied to the Christ of the Gospels, then, some years after he had been put to death in Judea, had risen from the dead and ascended into heaven, he is found leading the Jews to insurrection in Rome, and this does not appear to me to be any sort of evidence for his life in Judea. (Applause and laughter.) But there is a very curious remark of the Emperor Adrian which is not generally quoted by Christian writers, so I will give it now: the Emperor wrote from Egypt that the "worshippers of Serapis are Christians, and those are consecrated to the God Serapis who, I find, call themselves the bishops of Christ." This interesting fact is not dwelt upon by Christian apologists. But the silence of Pagan writers is well summed up for me by a Christian writer. The Rev. Dr. Giles, beneficed clergyman of the Church of England, gives us, in this work ["Christian Records"], exactly the points which I have been putting before you. He says: "Though the remains of Grecian and Latin profane literature which belong to the first and second centuries of our era are enough to form a library of themselves, they contain no allusion to the New Testament. . . . . The Latin writers, who lived between the time of Christ's crucifixion and the year A.D. 200, are Seneca, Lucan, Suetonius, Tacitus, Persius, Juvenal, Martial, Pliny the Elder, Silius Italicus, Statius,

* Eusebius does not mention Tacitus, and the statement is a slip, occurring in the rapidity of debate. [A. B.]

Quintilian, and Pliny the Younger, besides numerous others of inferior note. The greater number of these make mention of the Jews, but not of the Christians. In fact, Suetonius, Tacitus, and the younger Pliny, are the only Roman writers who mention the Christian religion or its founder ('Christian Records,' by Rev. Dr. Giles, p. 36)." So much for the arguments regarding Christ which are found in Pagan and Roman writers. I shall have to deal now with the others. Let me say at once that I do not challenge the existence of persons called Christians; on the contrary, I admit that they existed—a long time before Christ was born. (Laughter.) I think they existed long before the birth of Christ into the world, and I may here again remark that no argument brought forward to prove the existence of Christians can have the slightest weight in deciding the question at issue. The point between us is not the existence of Christians, but the historical character of the Jesus of the New Testament. I now come to the passage in Josephus. Mr. Hatchard says that he alleges that this passage was really written by the person whose name it bears; I answer that it is impossible to bring forward the name of one man of note of the present day who accepts it as genuine. It is now almost universally given up, and the evidence of its interpolation is very clear. Take the passage: "Now, there was about this time Jesus, a wise man, if it be lawful to call him a man, for he was a doer of wonderful works—a teacher of such men as receive the truth with pleasure. He drew over to him both many of the Jews, and many of the Gentiles. He was [the] Christ; and when Pilate, at the suggestion of the principal men amongst us, had condemned him to the cross, those that loved him at the first did not forsake him, for he appeared to them alive again the third day, as the divine prophets had foretold these and ten thousand other wonderful things concerning him; and the tribe of Christians, so named from him, are not extinct at this day" [" Antiquities of the Jews," book xviii., ch. iii., sect. 3]. I will now tell you why I do not believe the passage to be true. The Jesus of the Gospels in the first place did not draw many of the Jews unto him; on the contrary, he drew extremely few, and was remarkably unsuccessful as a teacher. Then he did not draw many of the Gentiles; on the con-

c

trary, he alleged, according to the Gospels, that he was not sent save to the lost sheep of the house of Israel; so that you find Josephus distinctly in contradiction with the book he is called to prove. Then, again, it is stated he was the Christ, but how was it possible for Josephus here, a Jew, in his own book to affirm that which his own opinion and religion taught him most strongly to deny? For a man who was not a Christian, but a Jew—who did not accept Jesus as the Messiah, to make this statement in his own book, was practically to call himself "hypocrite," and to stand before the world a self-convicted hypocrite out of his own mouth.

Mrs. Besant's time having expired she sat down amid great applause.

MR. HATCHARD: Mr. Chairman, Ladies and Gentlemen, Mrs. Besant, in her opening remarks, referred to Dr. Angus, and to the fact that he was one of the present company of revisers of the New Testament, and also to the fact that there are a large number of various readings of the New Testament in existence. I am pleased beyond measure, because I lived with Dr. Angus for four years. I know him well, and I know him for a thoroughly trustworthy scholar. Now, Dr. Angus has repeated over and over again in public that all these various readings, in what are called the MSS. of the New Testament, do not alter a single doctrine of Christianity, and do not alter a single important fact in the history of Jesus of Nazareth. I have here Dr. Angus's "Bible Handbook," and if Mrs. Besant has not got this book, I will present her with a copy at the end of this debate. (Laughter.) Here is the book, and Dr. Angus goes very elaborately into the question of those various MSS., and these various readings. Now, Mrs. Besant told you that we had no MSS. in existence older than the fourth century. I suppose that is the fact. But then I say this: Will Mrs. Besant produce to me the original MS. or MSS. of anything—say of any classical work? No! There is no such thing in the world, and it is perfectly well known that there is not a single case where we possess the original MS. or MSS. of any work of antiquity. We have only a few MSS.—certainly three—which are said to be the oldest MSS. of the New Testament in existence. These old MSS. which we have tell us precisely and substantially the same story, and the same tale of Jesus of Nazareth. Reference has been made to the difference which exists between the Douay Bible of the Roman Catholics and the authorised version of the Protestant, but I fail to discover any new or any different facts related in the Douay Bible which do not also find their place in the Bible which the Protestant uses. Why, at one time I acted as a military chaplain, and I have by me now a small Testament which was published by authority, and bearing the imprimatur of the late Cardinal of Westminster (not the present one); and in that book I read the very same facts as I read in the Protestant Bible. The Romish Church published this Testament by authority, and they were not simply content with putting at the top of each Gospel the name of the author which appears at its head in the Protestant Bible, but also the date and circumstances under which it was supposed to be written. We have, therefore, as I have already stated, only a few old MSS., but we have a vast number of a later date. A word about the different readings, and the supposed difference which they make. I hold in my hand what I consider an important little book. It is the New Testament of Tauchnitz, of Germany. If you want to know about what the various readings are, and if you cannot read the Greek Testament, this book (published by the firm of Baron Tauchnitz) will give you the various readings at the bottom of each page in English. I suppose you know that these books in Germany are published by a firm which has gained a good amount of celebrity, whose name I have mentioned. This is the thousandth volume. They thought they would publish the New Testament, and actually here, in this little book, they publish the New Testament, the authorised version, with all the various readings here in English underneath. Was the firm of Tauchnitz, or was Tischendorf himself, afraid to let the public know about these various readings? Certainly not. As you have heard, there is a body of revisers who are sitting at Westminster. They are engaged in revising the Bible, but I challenge Mrs. Besant to prove that they will alter it in any important particular or any Christian doctrine. Here is Scrivener's Greek Testament, in which are condensed all the various readings which are known. This book is one which is considered a very good authority, and it is one which theological

c 2

students are made to read. Here, then, is Scrivener's Greek Testament; here is Tischendorf's English edition of it; prove to me, from these books, that there is any difference between this and the ordinary authorised version. Mrs. Besant has spoken to you at some length upon the subject of miracles, and alleges the impossibility of a single miracle ever having taken place. Now, I beg of all of you here to-night, if you have never read the volume of Bampton Lectures, by Dr. Mozley ["Lectures on Miracles"], to do so at once. This volume I was *ordered* to read by the Bishop of Manchester, and I thank his Lordship for having ordered me to read it. I will tell you why. I am not ignorant of Christian science. I will meet any Freethinker on this platform on philosophy or science if he dares to come. (Laughter, and a voice, "Modesty.") I say, I learn from the examples of Freethinkers, whom I have yet to learn are very modest themselves. You cannot charge me with knowing nothing about physical science. I say that science has no contradictions whatever of the miracles which are recorded in the New Testament. (Laughter.) I tell you that if you like to take the pains, which I do not believe you Freethinkers will do. . . . . ("Question.") If you interrupt me I sit down that minute. (Applause.) I am no paid lecturer of the Christian Evidence Society; I come here entirely upon an independent basis. (Applause.) I tell you that this volume of Bampton Lectures goes elaborately into the question about law. I cannot, in my limited time here to-night, read a passage from this book. I bring it under your notice; but I will read a passage from John Stuart Mill. I suppose all of you know something about him. Now, in his book on "Logic," which I take it that you all know, second volume, and 159th page he says—"But in order that any alleged fact should be contradictory to a law of causation, the allegation must be, not simply that the cause existed without being followed by the effect, for that would be no uncommon occurrence; but that this happened in the absence of any adequate counteracting cause. Now in the case of an alleged miracle, the assertion is the exact opposite of this. It is, that the effect was defeated, not in the absence, but in consequence of a counteracting cause, namely, a direct interposition of an act of the will of some Being, who has power over nature; and in particular of a

Being, whose will being assumed to have endowed all the causes with the powers by which they produce their effects, may well be supposed able to counteract them. A miracle (as was justly remarked by Brown) is no contradiction to the law of cause and effect; it is a new effect, supposed to be produced by the introduction of a new cause. Of the adequacy of that cause, if present, there can be no doubt; and the only antecedent improbability which can be ascribed to the miracle, is the improbability that any such cause existed" ("Exeter Hall Lectures"). (Applause.) Don't cheer too soon. The thing simply means this, that you must deny the existence of a God to deny logically the possibility of a miracle. If I am not mistaken, Paley says the same words; and I think that Mill must have seen it in Paley. I give you John Stuart Mill, not that John Stuart Mill is any great prophet with me, although I have a certain admiration for the man. (Applause.)

Mrs. Besant: There are one or two points which have been alluded to by my opponent in reply to my previous speech, which I will deal with before resuming my criticism on Josephus. The first of these is that of the 100,000 readings which I mentioned—the existence of which is not even challenged—none of them affect any important doctrine in the Bible. I will leave you to judge of the accuracy of that, after I have adduced one or two facts. In the First Epistle of John, chap. v., verse 7, we read: "For there are three that bear record in heaven, the Father, the Word, and the Holy Ghost: and these three are one." Now, that is one of the passages which you do not find in the older MSS.: it is the solitary assertion of the Trinity to be found in the Bible. Surely the Trinity is important. Take next the doctrine of Eternal Punishment. That is a doctrine about which the new reading of the Bible will probably give us very different views to those now held. Some of you may have read a pitiful letter, which appeared in the *Athenæum* a short time back, in which the writer asked whether the rumor which had reached him was true, viz., that the Revisors of the New Testament were going to translate a well-known passage in the Lord's Prayer no longer "Deliver us from evil," but "Deliver us from the evil one." (Laughter.) It is admitted that there are no MSS. which can be traced back beyond the beginning of the fourth century, but Mr.

Hatchard says I may say the same about any classical work. Not one of the originals of the Greek or Latin works which have come down to us is now extant, and it is urged by my opponent that I ought to treat them in the same fashion as I have treated the Bible. My reply to that is that it is precisely because I do treat the Bible in the same way as any other ancient book, that I require some proof as to the authorship and authenticity of what is therein contained. If I find a classical work in which are related a number of miraculous events, I do not believe them as matters of fact or of history any more than I believe in the miraculous events which the Bible narrates. We now come to what has been said about Dr. Tischendorf, and I may tell you that I do not lay much stress upon Tischendorf's authority, and I will tell you why. According to his own confession, he discovered one of these MSS. of which you have heard in a monastery on Mount Sinai, and while believing that he was in possession of the most priceless of treasures, the most ancient copy of the word of God in existence, he kept it to himself for fifteen years before he announced his unparalleled discovery to the world. The man who would thus keep for fifteen years the most valuable of the MSS. in the world is not a man, I say, who ought to be thoroughly relied on. I will now take up Josephus where I laid him down. I will give you the last point, and that is that the second and fourth sections run straight on, while the third section, which consists of this passage which is said to be a forgery, is not connected in sense with those two sections I have mentioned. The end of the second section reads thus: "Since the people were unarmed, and were caught by men prepared for what they were about, there were a great number of them slain by this means, and others of them ran away wounded; and thus an end was put to this sedition. . . . . About the same time also another sad calamity put the Jews into disorder." I allege to you that these two paragraphs which I have read ought to be read consecutively without the intervention of the other paragraph, and that they make sense so read, while the first words of the fourth section have no meaning after the third. I have now disposed of the Latin writers. I have disposed of Josephus. I have said the best I can say briefly about them, and I shall best consult the time and the work before me if, instead of going over any ground twice,

I leave you to judge yourselves between myself and my opponent. I have now got four witnesses absolutely uncorroborated—four witnesses for whom we must try to find some sort of evidence, and I must remind you that we want overwhelming evidence, for no less a question than the supernatural character of Jesus is now at stake. I must say I regret that Jesus only came into the world to a very ignorant and barbarous nation, in an obscure corner, and in such a way that it was quite impossible for any large number of people to become aware of his existence in their midst. We have at least a right to expect that when four of his immediate followers, and witnesses of his alleged miracles sit down to give us an account of what they had seen, the veracity of our witnesses shall be unimpeached, that they shall give us a coherent account of their hero's life. I will take the point as to their competent knowledge first. You do not find it stated in the Gospels who the writers are, and, therefore, it is very difficult to judge of their competency as historians. Further, there is no lack of records in the early Church claiming to be, equally with the Four Gospels now under consideration, authentic narratives of the events which we have here recorded. We have, in fact, no less than thirty-four different Gospels in addition to the four which are now received, and seven of these at least have come down to us at the present day. We only know the others by extracts. Then, in Luke, I find that the author of Luke does not pretend that his Gospel stands by itself. Luke distinctly tells us: "Forasmuch as many have taken in hand to set forth in order a declaration of those things which are most surely believed among us, even as they delivered them unto us, which from the beginning were eye-witnesses and ministers of the word; it seemed good to me also" (Luke i., 1—3). He does not even pretend that he is himself an eye-witness, and I say to my opponent that there is no proof of his accuracy or of the truth of his story. We have no less than ninety-eight other writings, which are said to be written by Peter, James, Matthias, Andrew, and others, fifty-six of which are still extant; so it is not only Matthew and John, among the apostles, who are singled out for the honor of writing Christ's story; the difficulty is to tell which are genuine and which spurious, for according to

Mosheim, it was a habit of the early Christians to take great names in order to cover the want of merit or truth in their compositions. He says: "For, not long after Christ's ascension into heaven, several histories of his life and doctrines, full of pious frauds and fabulous wonders, were composed by persons whose intentions, perhaps, were not bad, but whose writings discovered the greatest superstition and ignorance. Nor was this all: productions appeared which were imposed upon the world by fraudulent men, as the writings of the holy apostles" ("Ecclesiastical History," ed. 1847, p. 31). I quite agree with that view of Mosheim, and I leave it to you as a view of a Christian historian. I am told by my opponent that, passing for a moment the Four Gospels themselves, I shall find them proved by the Fathers of the Christian Church, and I am referred to Polycarp as one of the Christian Fathers on whom my opponent relies. I find my opponent says that he relies upon him, but I am bound to inform you that hardly any quotations can be got from Polycarp which are continuous with texts of the Gospels. My contention with regard to the Gospels is that of Dean Alford.. There were a large number of early traditions floating about from mouth to mouth, which, after thus floating about, and being added to and changed in the course of many years, at last became crystallised in the form in which they are known to us. For instance, Polycarp says: "Beseeching the all-seeing God not to lead us into temptation, as the Lord hath said, the spirit indeed is willing but the flesh is weak;" but such a conjunction of words is nowhere found in our Gospels. Coming now to Irenæus. Irenæus is a man for whom I have always had a considerable amount of sympathy, because he is the first man who really puts forward the idea of *Four* Gospels at all; but I must allow that my faith in him is shaken when I find him giving this as a quotation from John: "John related the words of the Lord concerning the times of the kingdom of God: the days would come when vines would grow, each with 10,000 shoots, and to each shoot 10,000 branches, and to each branch 10,000 twigs, and to each twig 10,000 clusters, and to each cluster 10,000 grapes, and each grape which is crushed will yield twenty-five measures of wine. And when one of the saints will reach after one of these clusters, another will cry: 'I am a better cluster than it;

take me, and praise the Lord because of me'" ("Iren. Hær.," v., 33). I cannot find that in the Gospel of John as we have it to-day. (Applause.) Then, when I find that the reasons which are given by this same Irenæus for accepting the Four Gospels are that there are four corners to the earth, and four spirits, and that Christ sits in the midst of four-faced Cherubims, I begin to be still more doubtful about him. (Laughter.) I allege, then, that I cannot accept such evidence as this, evidence which is absolutely unsatisfactory, and which we can only regard as the nonsensical ravings of a religious enthusiast. (Loud applause.)

The Rev. A. HATCHARD: As our time is precious, I proceed at once to business. If I remember rightly, Mrs. Besant challenged my reference to Suetonius. Mrs. Besant quoted from the Rev. Dr. Giles, from his book on the "Christian Records." I hold in my hand another book, which I shall be happy to give her if she has not got it. (Laughter.) It is called Dr. Giles's "Heathen Records." I quote from this, and there can be no double dealing in the matter, as Dr. Giles gives in the one page the Latin and the other the English. This is what Suetonius says with regard to "*Claudius*—He expelled from Rome the Jews who were continually making disturbances having Chrestus for their instigator." My version of it is this, and you Freethinkers of London may laugh at it if you like: just about that particular time when Claudius Cæsar lived, there was a discussion and a dispute amongst the Jews in Rome about Jesus as to whether he was the Messiah; and Claudius Cæsar says to the Jews, "Depart! Go!" There, you have my version of it. Laugh at it if you like! (Much laughter.) "*Nero*—The Christians, a race of men of a new and baneful superstition, were punished." Now, *here* is the passage, I don't care what you make of it. Well now, I am not going to be led away by any red herring drawn across the trail. (A voice, "Argument!") I am arguing! I have told you that I believe in the miraculous element. Laugh if you like. (Laughter.) Now then, listen again, if you please. Mrs. Besant says that she does not think much of Irenæus, whose name you have mentioned here (pointing to diagram). I simply, and I say as briefly as I can, proceed with my argument. What Mrs. Besant says about Tacitus I will not say a word to you on. I have not the slightest doubt that you will go away and say, "What an ignorant, benighted man"—("Question, question")—at least that is the way I believe you talk about clergymen. (Cries of "Question," and interruption.)

The CHAIRMAN: I think it will be better to go on with the argument, and not indulge in personalities. (Loud applause.)

MR. HATCHARD: Ladies and gentlemen, there is no animosity in my mind. I speak to you fearlessly and frankly. I stand here without fear or favor. If I understand Mrs. Besant's "Freethinkers' Text Book" rightly, she does admit here substantially in this book the accuracy of the passage in Tacitus. I may have misunderstood her. Very good; then I say I put the passage of Tacitus before you, and let me say all the Freethinkers in Europe—or any body of Freethinkers—cannot break it down. I have consulted with men older than myself. I have a knowledge of the Secularist party, not of to-day, but of twenty years or more. (Murmuring, and a voice, "Proceed to business.") I say now Mrs. Besant has told you that the Christians were known, as I understand her to say, before the time of Christ. Freethinkers of London, I stand here to say that there is not an atom of proof of that. I have read that little book ["Chrestos"] which is advertised in the *National Reformer*, and published by Williams and Norgate. I have read that, and I simply say I was rather amused in reading it. I simply pass it by. There is not an atom of proof. There were the sects of what are called the Pharisees, Sadducees, and Essenes. I challenge the proof, and know it can't be brought that Jesus of Nazareth belonged to the sect of the Essenes. Bring to me the proof that Jesus of Nazareth and John the Baptist belonged to the sect of the Essenes. Here let me give you this, and I am glad that Mrs. Besant has let herself into my hands. (Much laughter. and some applause.) I have a great respect for Mrs. Besant. (Applause.) I hope to see Mrs. Besant return to the Church of England. (Renewed laughter.) I hope to know that Mrs. Besant is from this platform preaching the Gospel of Jesus of Nazareth. (Cries of "Question.") Mrs. Besant has challenged the testimony of Josephus to Jesus of Nazareth; but will she challenge it with regard to John the Baptist? Josephus gives you an account. I say that

Josephus substantially confirms the Gospel history when he gives you an account of John the Baptist, which nobody ventures to challenge, as far as I know; and grant me John the Baptist, and I will prove Jesus of Nazareth by collateral evidence. I don't care a straw about that passage about 10,000 this and 10,000 the other: it amounts to nothing. Now, before I sit down I want to drive home to you the testimony of St. Paul the Apostle. You can't tell me that Paul the Apostle never lived, for, if you do, I will overwhelm you with Jewish testimony. (Laughter.) Oh! I know all about this matter. Many of my friends are Jews, and I tell you Jews have armed me for this conflict. (Laughter.) If you want something to read I will make you a present of this (holding up a book); I believe you've got a library here. What do I find in Paul the Apostle's writings? He substantially corroborates the Gospel narrative, and he supplies several instances which the Gospels do not record. Now, then, I shall be told that Paul was deceived! that Paul was an enthusiast! that Paul was a demagogue! that he invented these things! that he was a dishonest man! Great heavens! I open the Epistle of the Romans and I read one of the most logical, convincing, and satisfactory works with regard to Christianity that could be penned. Read them! Are they the words of a dreamer? Are they the words of an enthusiast? Never! Why, ladies and gentlemen—members of Parliament, or who you please—(laughter)—they are the words of a sober, honest, cautious, logical thinker, a man brought up at the feet of the greatest of Jewish Rabbis—Gamaliel. (Slight applause.)

Mrs. Besant, who then rose to make her concluding speech, and was received with hearty applause, said: I will first as briefly as possible finish the argument upon which I entered, showing the weakness of the evidence within the first century on which my opponent relies. The dispute which is supposed to be mentioned in Suetonius has nothing to do with this debate. If the persons there mentioned were Christians, if Suetonius did mention them, it goes for nothing in this argument; I admit the existence of the Christians, and I make this admission in order to show you that I don't trouble to stop and challenge that which might refer to Christians, but which does not refer to Christ. I neither deny, nor challenge, nor accept the reference to John the Baptist in Josephus. It does not come within the limits of this discussion, which has reference only to the question of the existence of the historical Jesus depicted in the Gospels. Paul may have been a very wise man or a very foolish man. It does not touch the subject with which we have to deal to-night. I am still dealing with the first speech of my opponent, the one which contains all his real arguments. Speaking of Ignatius, whose name is put forward by Mr. Hatchard, I may say that I do not accept Ignatius as reliable. He tells us, indeed, that the star appeared to the magi, and further that "all the rest of the stars, with the sun and moon, formed a chorus to this star" (Ep. to the Ephesians, chap. xix.). Why rely on his story of the star and reject his story of the chorus? It is alleged with respect to Justin Martyr that the "Memoirs" of which he speaks are the same as the Gospels; but it is admitted by my opponent that many of the texts are not the same. Printing not being invented, we are told that the MSS. of these works were costly, and not attainable by the people, and that it is very likely in quoting from memory that these slight inaccuracies should occur. But I urge that the only reason for quoting these authorities at all is to show that their Gospels and yours are one and the same, and if you admit that the quotations are inaccurate what becomes of your proof? You have yet to prove that Justin Martyr had access to the same Gospels that we have to-day, and we must also remember that Justin Martyr quotes the Acts of Pilate as authoritative, just as he does the Memoirs. In quoting the text as to the sweat falling down as "drops of blood," I think that my opponent ought to have told you that the words "of blood" do not appear in Justin, and destroy his argument: Justin was trying to prove that the prophesy "My bones are poured out *like water*" was fulfilled in Christ, when "his sweat fell down like drops while he was praying" ("Dial." chap. ciii.). It is hardly fair to insert "of blood" in order to make a resemblance where there is none. Then again, if you take the story of Justin you will find it very different from the story of the Gospels. For instance, that Christ was born in a cave and not in a stable, and so on, with a mass of small discrepancies. You might fairly say: How do you explain the general likeness which you find in the four Gospels? I believe that various

Churches had various oral versions of the life of Christ, and that as the years went on they grew vaguer and vaguer, and it was thought wise to write them down. This is the view taken by Dean Alford, and it is the one which I am inclined to adopt, in common with many others. This is the view which is taken by the Rev. Mr. Sanday, and which is to a great extent held by Canon Westcott. I allege—and I am quoting from Canon Westcott's work on the Canon, where he sums up the value of the evidence from the Apostolic Fathers:—"1. No Evangelic reference in the Apostolic Fathers can be referred certainly to a written record. 2. It appears most probable from the form of the quotations that they were derived from oral tradition. 3. No quotation contains any element which is not substantially preserved in our Gospels. 4. When the text given differs from the text of our Gospels, it represents a later form of Evangelic tradition. 5. The text of St. Matthew corresponds more nearly than the other synoptic texts with the quotations and references as a whole" ("Canon of the New Test.," ed. 1875, p. 62). That is the conclusion come to by Canon Westcott. That is, I should say, substantially accurate, save that I should of course, somewhat demur to his third statement. I turn then from this evidence which is no evidence at all, and I will only say further that if you want to break down the whole of the argument as to the existence of these written Gospels in the first century, turn to that remarkable work called "Supernatural Religion"—there you will find the Apostolic Fathers dealt with one by one with an exactness and detail which I cannot here pretend to use. I have, then, failed to find corroborative evidence outside; I have failed to find in the writings of the Fathers the enormous weight of evidence which I require. Remember, I want evidence of the miraculous. I have now to deal with four uncorroborated witnesses. Do I find that my four witnesses agree with one another? Do I find that their testimony is one? That the voice is one although it comes from four mouths? Remember the story of the birth of Jesus. Reconcile the story in Matthew with the story in Luke. Find how in one Gospel we are dealing with people who come from Nazareth. Read the other where you hear nothing at all of Nazareth in the first place, and when reference is made to it later, it is made in a way that clearly indicates that it was not their own home, but a new place to them—"a city called Nazareth." Take the story of Herod, and I must say that it is strange that Josephus, who has told you the story of Herod with great fulness of detail, has not one word of this remarkable and monstrous crime. Pass around the story of the birth and take it bit by bit. See how Herod, instead of troubling himself about the wise men and their star, might have gone to the Temple, in Jerusalem his own capital, and there have seized the young child; remember how, according to Luke, Jesus was carried to the Temple, had sacrifice offered for him, was greeted by Simon, and rejoiced over by Anna. Take the difficulty that according to one account the young child and his mother fled down to Egypt to escape from Herod, and only returned after Herod's death, while according to the other they went up to Jerusalem, and after quietly performing all the duties imposed by the law, returned peacefully to "their own city, Nazareth." It must, indeed, be a miraculous child who managed to be at Nazareth and in Egypt at one and the same time. Pass to the story of the temptation. Do you believe that that is matter of history and not a myth? Do you believe that there was a wonderfully high mountain, so high and so curiously placed that from it you could see all round a sphere? and that Jesus and the devil went flying through the air to it, and then flew off to Jerusalem and perched on a pinnacle of the Temple, surely to the amazement of the people in the streets? Pass to the comparison of John and the three Synoptics. You will find they bear no likeness: that they are different in incidents, different in place, different in character. Pass to the story of the crucifixion, and learn how Christ was crucified at the third hour, although he was exposed by Pilate at the sixth, and how he was standing in full view of the people at the same hour that he was hanging on the cross, enveloped in miraculous darkness. I am dealing now with the historians themselves, having failed to get any satisfactory evidence outside the records for which we require proof. Pass to the story of the resurrection, the very centre of the Christian creed, and learn how one woman went according to one Gospel, and two, and "two and others," according to the rest; how they went while "it was yet dark," although the sun was rising; how they wondered when they found that the stone was rolled away, although the stone was still there unrolled away, and they saw an angel come down and roll it away and sit on it. Learn how one angel, or two, or a young man, gave them a message to go to the disciples. Learn how Christ overtook them and gave them exactly the same message over again. Learn how the women were so frightened that they said nothing to any man, although they ran and told the disciples all that they had seen. Learn how the disciples went to Galilee although they remained in Jerusalem: how they saw Christ twice at least in Jerusalem, although they did not see him until they got to Galilee: learn how in Galilee some "doubted" his resurrection, although they had him before their eyes. Learn how Christ ascended up into heaven on the day of his resurrection, and then learn how he remained on earth forty days explaining the things concerning the kingdom of God. Don't take the contradictions on my word; but take the four Gospels, make if you can anything which will seem like a reconciliation of one to the other, and give a coherent life of Christ—that was my first step towards heresy. But if you ask me whence does the story come, I reply it is the story of the Sun-god spread through the whole of eastern lands—of the child born in mid-winter, in the sign of the Virgin, surrounded by winter's dangers, passing on through the signs of the Zodiac, struggling with darkness in the critical time of spring, rising at Easter, triumphing over his enemies, rising into mid-heaven, sitting on the right hand of God the Father, sending down his beams to make the bread and the wine, symbols of his very body and blood. Whence does Christ come? He comes not only from the Sun-god, but from Chrishna, the incarnate Indian deity, Chrishna, born of Devaki, hymned by Devas, flying from the wrath of Kansa. Chrishna, who had the children slain around him while he escaped; Chrishna, healing the sick, causing the lame to walk, opening the eyes of the blind, raising the dead, crucified, risen, ascended. You will find him with the sacred stigmata on his hands and feet, carven in the ancient Indian temples which remain to-day. Where does Christ come from? He comes from every place where superstition has been stronger than science. He comes from every land where people have for ages marvelled at the mysteries around them which they could not understand; where they made their theories first and found their facts afterwards. I urge to you that my opponent has failed. The Fathers have lamentably broken down in their evidence. No Pagan writer gives us any fact which can buttress the Christ of the Gospels; and when you come to your four witnesses you cannot for one moment trust them—you cannot for one moment believe them, when they tell you the story of your Christ. I say of him in the words of the Roman poet: "All these figments of crack-brained opiniatry and silly solaces played off in the sweetness of song by deceitful poets, by you, too credulous creatures, have been shamefully reformed and made over to your god." (Loud and continued applause, and cries of "Bravo!")

MR. HATCHARD: I shall not for one moment contend with Mrs. Besant in her eloquence, for to-night I stand here to bear witness for the truth, and on this platform of all places in London. I stand here to vindicate the indisputable, historical, and most important facts that the world knows of. I simply tell you that, beside the Heathen testimony, which I have only briefly alluded to to-night, there is a great deal of Jewish testimony which I have not time to go into. Mrs. Besant has referred to the book entitled "Supernatural Religion." Here it is; and I tell you that that book has been dissected like an anatomist would dissect a body. Get Westcott on the "Canon of the New Testament" 4th edition, and read his Preface, and see what he says. I ask, is not the author of "Supernatural Religion" shown to be untrustworthy? Mr. Cowper told me to be sure and mention here to-night that Mr. Nicholson, of the London Institution, had examined his quotations and found them to be inaccurate. We have heard a good deal from Mrs. Besant in her last speech about Chrishna and such like, but she has made her remarks to the wrong opponent. I spent years in investigating the Indian religion, and next week I will endeavor to go at length into what Christianity has done in India, and I will introduce to your notice Chrishna—that is Vishnu. Why, there is no dispute whatever. (Cries of "Order," and "Question.") I say that the whole story that Mrs. Besant has brought before you is not worth a single mention. I say distinctly about it, that you can't prove that the story of Chrishna was in existence in India at an early period. It was probably known about the sixth century. You shall hear something about Vishnu next week. You shall see him. Chrishna is identified with Vishnu, and if I were not in a public hall I would tell you some nice tales about Chrishna. In the old Jewish traditions there are so many facts of the Gospels corroborated, and there is one fact which is related in the Talmud, which I will mention to you. It is there stated that about forty years before the destruction of Jerusalem the power of life and death was taken away from the Jews, and so it happened that Pilate was the person who had to put Jesus of Nazareth to death. I know all about the Cross in Heathen countries. I know it all. Produce me—you can't produce me—the crucified Saviors besides Jesus of Nazareth. If I had followed the bent of my own inclination I should have brought with me and quoted a whole host of German authorities, but when I went to Stonecutter Street the other day, and there saw Mr. Ramsey, I found that Mr. Ramsey didn't seem to think much of German authorities.* He turned up his nose at them. (Laughter.) Well, I thought, you are a fair specimen of the men I shall have to meet, and I won't quote them. I could have quoted you from a large number of German authorities, for they have been my prophets for many years past. But I bring before you a book, by Grotius, on the "Truth of Christian Religion." I have never seen the book answered. "*Sect. II. The proof that there was such a person as Jesus.*—That Jesus of Nazareth formerly lived in Judea, in the reign of Tiberius the Roman emperor, is constantly acknowledged, not only by Christians dispersed all over the world, but also by all the Jews which now are, or have ever wrote since that time: the same is also testified by heathens, that is, such as did not write either of the Jewish or of the Christian religion, Suetonius, Tacitus, Pliny the younger, and many after these. *That he died an ignominious death.*—That the same Jesus was crucified by Pontius Pilate, the president of Judea, is acknowledged by all the same Christians, notwithstanding it might seem dishonorable to them who worship such a Lord. It is also acknowledged by the Jews, though they are not ignorant how much they lie under the displeasure of the Christians, under whose government they

* It is due to Mr. Ramsey to say that he entirely denies this assertion of Mr. Hatchard.

D

everywhere live, upon this account, because their ancestors were the cause of Pilate's doing it. Likewise, the heathen writers we mentioned have recorded the same to posterity; and, a long time after, the acts of Pilate were extant, to which the Christians sometimes appealed. Neither did *Julian*, or other opposers of Christianity, ever call it in question. So that no history can be imagined more certain than this; which is confirmed by the testimonies, I don't say, of so many men, but of so many people, which differed from each other. Notwithstanding which, we find him worshipped as Lord throughout the most distant countries of the world. *Sect. III. And yet, after his death, was worshipped by wise men.*—And that not only in our age, or those immediately foregoing, but also even in the first, the age next to that in which it was done, in the reign of the emperor Nero; at which time the fore-mentioned Tacitus and others attest, that very many were punished because they professed the worship of Christ." I say, I put this problem to Mrs. Besant, and I should like her to write some articles upon it, which I promise to read. If Jesus of Nazareth never rose from the dead, how comes the belief, not only of the Apostle Paul, but of the early Christians, that such was the fact? You come down, I say, upon the fact, or believed fact, that it was Jesus and the Resurrection that these early preachers of the Gospels believed in, that it was believed that it was decided by abundant witnesses. How came the extraordinary change in the Apostle Peter if the Resurrection never took place? Peter before and Peter after the Resurrection are as opposite as light and darkness. The trembling coward who forsook his master and denied him, the man who afterwards wept bitterly, was the man who stood boldly before the Jewish Sanhedrim, who told them the bitter truth right home as I have told you here to-night; told them that it was this very Jesus who had been raised from the dead. Peter went forth into the world a bold, brave, man to do his duty. Then there was St. John and Paul; but Paul was deceived, you will say. How came it that all the early disciples of Jesus Christ were deceived? How came this doctrine preached in Jerusalem immediately after the Crucifixion if it was myth and fable? I simply tell Mrs. Besant that I know as much about the Sun-god as she can tell me; I simply stop here to say whatever truth there may be in these myths and fables of the Sun-god that immediately after the Crucifixion of Jesus of Nazareth, the story of his Resurrection was proclaimed in Jerusalem. (Cries of "Proof.") Yes, amongst Freethinkers and Sceptics. There is an abundant amount of testimony of every imaginary kind that it was Jesus and the Resurrection which was the belief of the early Christians. All through the Acts of the Apostles, all through the Epistles of St. Paul, all through the early Christian writers in the early centuries, it was the belief in this. It was preached at the city and at the time, by the men, in the place; and I take it such men as St. Paul, Peter, James, John, and others, were far better judges than we are here to-night whether the Resurrection of Jesus of Nazareth, in whom I firmly believe, took place or not. (Applause.)

A vote of thanks to the Chairman, proposed by Mrs. Besant, and seconded by the Rev. A. Hatchard, was then carried unanimously, and the proceedings terminated.

D 2

SECOND NIGHT.

Subject:—

"That the Influence of Christianity upon the world has been Injurious."

Mr. BRADLAUGH in the Chair.

The Chairman in opening the proceedings said: My duty as Chairman is not likely to involve any sort of need for any work on my part provided you of the audience understand two things. First, that you have no right during the time either of the disputants is speaking to challenge any remark that either of them may make. Any cry of "Question"—any cry of disapprobation—is entirely out of place. Those of you who are in favor of either of the speakers may applaud if you please; but you must remember even then that sometimes you waste their time in doing that. To call "Question," or to make any other remark, is entirely out of place, and only does an injury to the debate. I do not know that I need trouble you with anything else except to mention that the rule of the debate is that the opener shall have 30 minutes; Mr. Hatchard 30 minutes in reply; and then five speeches of 15 minutes alternately, the opener concluding as on the last occasion. The subject for debate for this evening is the proposition to be affirmed by Mrs. Besant—"That the influence of Christianity on the world has been injurious." I now call upon Mrs. Besant to open the debate. (Applause.)

Mrs. Besant, who was warmly greeted, said: Mr. Chairman, Mr. Hatchard and Friends: The affirmation that I make to-night is "That the influence of Christianity upon the world has been injurious." I propose, in my first speeches, to give you a mass of facts on which I rely for proof of this affirmation, and, even at the risk of wearying you, to give you a condensed statement of historical occurrences which serve as foundation for the position I take to-night. In my last speech I will sum these up, but in the earlier ones, I shall merely pile up my facts which you can verify for yourselves. In order to lend clearness and vigor to the affirmation, and to render it, if false, more easy to refute, I propose not to make a general and discursive attack, but to endeavor to prove five special propositions. I allege of Christianity: 1. That it has discouraged learning. 2. That it has supported tyranny, and has been the enemy of liberty. 3. That it has used persecution more largely than any other creed. 4. That it has upheld and aggravated slavery. 5. That it has not ensured purity of morals. If I can prove these propositions, it will be fair for me to say "that the influence of Christianity on the world has been injurious." I allege, further, that the whole of this mischief has its root in the Christian theory, and that each of the faults alleged in the propositions may be defended by Holy Writ. That, therefore, these faults are not excresences on Christianity, due to the wickedness of man, but are portions of the creed itself, and that modern Christianity in partly escaping from them has become less Christian while becoming more civilised. I propose to show the root of each of these faults in Christian theory, and then to demonstrate its development in Christian practice. (Applause.) 1. *That Christianity has discouraged learning.* Throughout the Bible knowledge is an accursed thing. For eating of the tree of knowledge man was expelled from Paradise; Solomon, said to be the wisest of men, gives his judgment as follows: "Lo, I am come to great estate, and have gotten more wisdom than all they that were before me in Jerusalem; yea, my heart had great experience of wisdom and knowledge. And I gave my heart to know wisdom, and to know madness and folly: I perceived that this also is vexation of spirit. For in much wisdom is much grief; and he that increaseth knowledge increaseth sorrow" (Eccles. i., 16—18). Isaiah prophesied against Babylon: "Thy wisdom and thy knowledge it hath perverted thee" (Isa. xlvii., 10). Jesus proclaimed: "I thank thee, O Father, Lord of heaven and earth, because thou hast hid these things from the wise and prudent and hast revealed them unto babes" (Matt. xi., 25). Paul wrote: "For ye see your calling, brethren, how that not many wise men after the flesh, not many mighty, not many noble are called: but God hath chosen the foolish things of the world to confound the wise" (1 Cor. i., 26-27). Again: "Let no man deceive himself. If any man among you seemeth to be wise in this world, let him become a fool that he may be wise" (Ibid ii., 18). Again: "Knowledge puffeth up, but charity edifieth" (Ibid viii., 1). There are many more of the same type which time forbids me to quote. This beatitude of nescience was very acceptable to the classes among which Christianity first spread, and the natural result of canonising ignorance and anathematising knowledge was very soon seen. Mosheim tells us of even the great lights of the second century, that "they are worthy of little admiration on account of the accuracy or depth of their reasonings. The most of them appear to have been destitute of penetration, learning, order, application and force" ("Ecclesiastical History," ed. 1847, p. 53). As the centuries went on the darkness grew deeper and deeper; Hallam tells us that schools were "confined to cathedrals and monasteries" and were "exclusively designed for the purposes of religion": that Charlemagne and Alfred were the greatest scholars of their time, but that Charlemagne could not read, and Alfred had but an imperfect knowledge of Latin: of the "prevailing ignorance," he says, "it is easy to produce abundant testimony. Contracts were made verbally, for want of notaries capable of drawing up charters; and these, when written, were frequently barbarous and ungrammatical to an incredible degree. For some considerable intervals, scarcely any monument of literature has been preserved, except a few jejune chronicles, the vilest legends of saints, or verses equally destitute of spirit and metre. In almost every council, the ignorance of the clergy forms a subject for reproach. It is asserted by one held in 992, that scarcely a single person was to be found in Rome itself who knew the first element of letters. Not one priest of a thousand in Spain, about the age of Charlemagne, could address a common letter of salutation to another. In England, Alfred declares that he could not recollect a single priest south of the Thames (the most civilised part of England), at the time of his accession, who understood the ordinary prayers, or could translate Latin into his mother-tongue. Nor was this better in the time of Dunstan, when it is said, none of the clergy knew how to write or translate a Latin letter. The homilies which they preached were compiled for their use by some bishops, from former works of the same kind, or the writings of the Christian fathers" ("Europe during the Middle Ages," ed. 1869, pp. 595-596). In the tenth century a little light struggled to penetrate from Moorish Spain into Christendom, but for a long time with small success, for wherever a mind struggled to think, Christianity promptly shut it up; in Spain itself 119 men were imprisoned by the Inquisition, not for heresy, but for science; Roger Bacon, a monk of the thirteenth century, bears witness to the prevailing ignorance: "Without mathematical instruments no science can be mastered," he complains sadly, "and these instruments are not to be found among the Latins, and could not be made for two or three hundred pounds. . . . . The admirable books of Cicero de Republicâ are not to be found anywhere, so far as I can hear, though I have made anxious inquiry for them in different parts of the world, and by various messengers. I could never find the works of Seneca, though I made diligent search for them during twenty years and more. And so it is with many more most useful books connected with the science of morals" (Green's "Short History of the English People," ed. 1878, pp. 133-134). His own studies were rewarded with bread and water and a dungeon, and pen and paper were taken from him; he died in the prison of his monastery. In the same spirit Torquemada burned 6,000 priceless oriental books. Not a single great discovery lightens Christendom from the time whereat Christianity destroyed Pagan science until the stir of mental life brought about by heresy. Calvin, among Reformers, hated knowledge as Torquemada among Romanists; Calvinists hunted Bruno from Geneva if Catholics burned him at Rome. Later, Buckle gives a long list of learned men imprisoned merely for their science. (See "History of Civilisation," vol. ii., pp. 230—242, ed. 1869.) To-day, all the chief leaders of thought are outside the pale of the churches. Mill, Darwin, Spencer, Bain, Huxley, Tyndall, Clifford—these, the moulders of this century's thought, are alien to the Christian creed, and hated by the Christian Churches. I affirm, therefore, that "Christianity has discouraged learning." (Applause.) 2. *That Christianity has supported tyranny, and has been the enemy of liberty.* Passive submission has ever been the political doctrine of the

Church. Paul commanded: "Let every soul be subject to the higher powers. For there is no power but of God: the powers that be are ordained of God. Whosoever, therefore, resisteth the power resisteth the ordinance of God, and they that resist shall receive to themselves damnation" (Romans xii., 1-2). Peter, in the same spirit, taught: "Submit yourselves to every ordinance of man for the Lord's sake; whether it be to the king as supreme; or unto governors. . . . . . Honor the king" (1 Peter ii., 13, 14, 17). Kings have granted huge wealth to priests, and priests, in return, have taught absolute submission to kings. Mosheim thinks that Constantine turned Christian because he saw "the admirable tendency of the Christian doctrine and precepts to promote the stability of government, by preserving the citizens in their obedience to the reigning powers" (Ibid, p. 87). According to the same historian, Charlemagne converted the Saxons to Christianity for the same reason, hoping that the Gospel would "induce them to submit more tamely to the Government of the Franks" (Ibid, p. 170). It is noticeable that dissent, which is always a step towards Freethought, is, in civil struggles, on the side of freedom, while the orthodox creed is always on the side of passive obedience. Thus Cromwell the Independent, Milton the Socinian, and Martin the Atheist, fought side by side for liberty against Charles and his bishops. In the same spirit, during the struggle under James II., the Church taught the duty of passive obedience, and preached that resistance to the king was a sin against God. I affirm, therefore, "that Christianity has supported tyranny." (Applause.) (3) *That it has used persecution more largely than any other creed.* The duty of persecution is taught both in the Old and New Testaments. The passages in Deuteronomy are well known: it is commanded touching the heretic: "Thou shalt not consent unto him, nor hearken unto him; neither shall thine eye pity him, neither shalt thou spare, neither shalt thou conceal him: But thou shalt surely kill him; thine hand shall be first upon him to put him to death, and afterwards the hand of all the people" (Deut. xiii., 8, 9); touching a city of heretics: "Thou shalt surely smite the inhabitants of that city with the edge of the sword, destroying it utterly, and all that is therein, and the cattle thereof, with the edge of the sword" (Ibid 15): this we are assured "is right in the eyes of the Lord thy God" (Ibid 18). Many other passages of like spirit are familiar to you. In the New Testament the Christians are weak, and the vengeance against heretics is partly delayed till the next world. In fact, as they could not burn in this world, they were comforted with the hope that their enemies should burn on the other side of the grave. (Laughter and applause.) Jesus promised: "Whosoever shall not receive you, nor hear your words, when ye depart out of that house or city, shake off the dust of your feet. Verily I say unto you, It shall be more tolerable for the land of Sodom and Gomorrha in the day of judgment, than for that city" (Matthew x., 14, 15). The same spirit is shown in Luke xix., 27: "But those mine enemies, which would not that I should reign over them, bring hither, and slay them before me." Nay, persecution was to enter into social life: John writes to the "elect lady:" "If there come any unto you, and bring not this doctrine, receive him not into your house" (2nd John, 10). The power of the sword passed into the hands of Christianity when Constantine ascended the throne A.D. 324. In 380–394 fifteen statutes were passed, by which Pagans and heretics were forbidden to meet, were made incapable of making wills or of receiving legacies and so on. In fact, you have some of the same wicked enactments that still disgrace your English Statute Book in the nineteenth century. At this same date the first heretic was burned in Spain; in 1784 in the same country the last human sacrifice by fire was offered up to Christ. Between these two stakes who can measure the misery wrought by Christian hands? I give you a few instances; you can fill in more from your own reading. The Empress Theodora in Armenia, in the ninth century, put 100,000 Paulician heretics to death; in the twelfth 60,000 Albigenses were massacred in one town alone; in the fifteenth 3,000 persons were burned alive, and 17,000 fined or imprisoned for life in Andalusia during one year; during another 950 persons were burned alive in the town of Ville Reale; in another the Jews were expelled and died by thousands, while in 1502 the number of the expelled was raised to three millions, the Moors being driven out, and a vast number perished on the way. Torquemada has the following record: "Burnt at the stake alive, 10,220; burnt in effigy, the persons having died in prison or fled the country, 6,860; punished with infamy, confiscation, perpetual imprisonment, or loss of civil rights, 97,321: total, 114,401" ("Freethinker's Text-Book," Part II., p. 472). Cardinal Ximenes has 52,855 victims. In Spain alone 31,912 persons were burned alive, and 291,450 more perished for heresy; in the Netherlands Alva put 18,000 heretics to death, by his own confession, and 50,000 were put to death in the year 1566 only; in 1572, 14,000 Huguenots were slain in Paris, and tens of thousands more throughout France; Henry VIII. of England slew 500 heretics who rejected his "Six Articles;" Mary killed 277 Protestants, Elizabeth a large number of Roman Catholics; in Ireland Roman Catholics were under the most cruel laws; the misery there to-day is largely due to Christianity, Orange fanaticism and Popish bigotry being equally bloodthirsty, and Ireland will never be at peace until heresy has cured the brutality generated by Christianity; in Scotland Dissenters were killed and tortured. Christian leaders proclaimed the duty of persecution: "In Germany, Luther cried, 'Why, if men hang the thief upon the gallows, or if they put the rogue to death, why should not we with all our strength, attack these popes and cardinals, these dregs of the Roman Sodom? Why not wash our hands in their blood?' Sandys, Bishop of London, wrote in defence of persecution. Archbishop Usher, in an address signed by eleven other bishops, said, 'Any toleration to the papists is a grievous sin.' Knox said, 'The people are bound in conscience to put to death the queen, along with all her priests.' The English Parliament said, 'Persecution was necessary to advance the glory of God.' The Scotch Parliament decreed death against Catholics as idolators, saying 'it was a religious obligation to execute them'" ("Freethinker's Text-Book," Part II., p. 474). I admit that most religions persecute more or less, but let my opponent, if he can, produce the record of any superstition drenched in blood as is this Christianity; until such a record is produced I affirm "*that Christianity has used persecution more largely than any other creed.*" (4) *That it has upheld and aggravated slavery.* Slavery is admittedly taught in the Old Testament (Lev. xxv., 44); it is nowhere denounced in the New. On the contrary, slaves, euphemistically translated servants in our Bible, are exhorted to be obedient and submissive, and Paul sent back to his master a fugitive slave, recognising his rights of property. Let me say at once that slavery was universal in the Old World. But it was surely the duty of Christianity to strive against this universal curse. Instead of so doing it was silent respecting the wrong, and even aggravated the bad condition of the slave. A very remarkable testimony is given in a most unexpected quarter to the supreme vileness of Christian slavery. Charles Dickens was admittedly a Christian, yet here in his own journal, we have the following: "Indeed, one of the most horrible features in this most horrible traffic is the fact that fathers sell their children, and brothers their brothers, without thought or care; that fathers and brothers do worse than sell to another master their daughters and sisters; that all natural duties are violated, and all natural boundaries overpassed. In no other country, and under no other condition of slavery, have such things been done before. In Mohammedan slavery, natural ties are respected as sacredly as the most perfectly legal ties, and the moralities of society are regarded and enforced from bond as well as from free. . . . . Slave-owners would as soon think of preserving conjugal fidelity among their sheep and horses as among their slaves. The farmer who sells his calf, and the planter who sells the suckling from the mother's breast, act with exactly the same feeling, and from the same motive. . . . . This has never been in any age of the world's history before. Judaism, the Greek and Roman times, Mohammedanism, all recognised the rights of nature in their slaves. Christianity is the only faith whose professors have violated and destroyed these rights" (*Household Words*, Vol. XIV., p. 137). (Loud applause.)

Mr. HATCHARD, who was greeted with applause, then rose to reply. He said: Mr. Chairman, Ladies and Gentlemen, before I enter to-night upon what I have really to say I want to say one word, and that is this, I am exceedingly obliged to all those friends who have written me a lot of letters regarding this debate, telling me what I was to say and what I was not to say. But I can only use my own brains and not other people's, and if I don't follow the course that some persons present say that I ought to take, it is because I think I am doing the right thing in what I am about to do. I may say at once that I don't intend to follow Mrs. Besant over all the ground she has gone upon, but to tell you another story. I fully expected that she would follow the course which she has to-night, because she has printed these opinions. I will give you another picture, which is a contrast to the picture which she has presented to you. It has been said by some persons that Christianity did not introduce many new intellectual truths to the world. That is directly the fact, but my contention is that, in short, both the revolution and the revelation of Christianity—that the change effected by Christianity—was a moral one and not an intellectual one. I say that Christianity has nothing at all that is not in harmony with the highest philosophy and the highest science, and I am prepared to prove that; but I do say most distinctly that Christianity was intended to be a moral revelation to the world, and I stand here to challenge the world to-night to contradict that which I am about to set before you. I suppose there is no person present who has not read at some time or other the first chapter of St. Paul's Epistle to the Romans. If you have not read that I do most earnestly request you to do so when you get home, and to ponder it and think most carefully over it. I may be told at once that it is only St. Paul who speaks this, and, in short, that he is not worth attention. Let me tell you that St. Paul simply gives the words of many of the writers of antiquity—he exactly gives us a picture of the heathen vices of his time, which, Ladies and Gentlemen, are so truly abominable and defiling that before an audience in which there are a great many ladies I would rather not read the verses. If there were only Mr. Bradlaugh and a few gentlemen here, and the doors were locked, I would not mind going into these subjects. (Much laughter.) I have told you that that was the state of the heathen world, and that it was a true and faithful picture of what the heathen world was at the time of St. Paul. Now, mind you, St. Paul is corroborated by a mass of testimony, and by a number of evidences which are literally overwhelming. You may ask me what were some of the prominent vices which were practised at the time of St. Paul. Slavery was one, and slavery was universal. I may be a most ignorant person, but I say that Jesus Christ had love to man; I see that St. Paul had this: I see in the principle of Christian brotherhood that there was laid the great principle which opposed slavery in the ancient Roman world; and, with all due deference to our Chairman, I say that it was Christian principle and Christian feeling which opposed slavery in the Southern States of America. ("Oh!") You may think I am a very ignorant man in saying this, but I say it was Christian feeling in the Roman Empire, too, that was the cause of slavery being gradually given up. From different councils and different ancient authors we see that it was the Church of which you have heard so much to-night that stood between the slaves and their masters—that extended the power of her protecting hand or arm on their behalf. A Roman Catholic friend of mine—a Roman Catholic mark you!—has taken the trouble to collect in the British Museum for me a whole mass of authorities upon this question, and I tell you that they are so voluminous that they have astonished me. I will give Mrs. Besant my notes if they are of any use to her. (Laughter and cries of "Oh!") I speak respectfully. Just for a moment or two let me refer you to Juvenal. Juvenal is truly what is called a satirist. Juvenal, mind you, was not a burlesque writer. Now let me tell you that Juvenal is one of the greatest names in Roman literature; and any of you who cannot read the Latin may buy a translation for about a shilling. Now I say distinctly that what is taught here is exactly the truth. This is Dryden's translation. I wish there were no ladies here. (Laughter.) The sixth satire is so bad that I cannot read it before this audience. I say the picture of vice, and immorality, and profligacy here is something which is simply alarming. Now our Chairman knows the Luxembourg, in Paris. They have a collection of beautiful pictures there, and amongst them there is a splendid painting of "The Romans of the decadence," and of the profligacy depicted by Juvenal and St. Paul. There is shown what Juvenal says and what St. Paul says. I hold in my hand "Horace." Listen just to this. This is a quotation which I looked out this afternoon. It occurs in the first book of his Satires and in the third Satire. He is speaking about the punishment of the slaves and he goes on in this way: "Lastly, since the vice of ire, likewise other vices adhering to fools, cannot be cut off entirely; why does not reason use her own weights and measures, and, as each thing is, so coerce offences by punishment? If anyone should fix that slave on a cross, who having been ordered to take away a dish shall have licked the half-eaten fishes and warm sauce; among sane persons he would be called more insane than Labeo." [" The Classical Student's Translation of Horace," ed. 1844, pp. 160, 161]. Do you understand what this means? (No!) It means this, that a man—mind you, this Horace was a heathen!—a slave who simply partakes of a piece of any delicacy—say a fish, is punished, his master having supreme power over him, by ordering him away to be crucified on that account, and that is the custom or practice which Horace alludes to. The cruelty, the vice, and the immorality of the Roman Empire is something that you can hardly credit. There are no common books which give a good account of this, simply because the majority of authors do not like to defile their pages with the immorality and licentiousness that abounds in these classics, but here is one which does. This is a well-known book which was published some hundred years ago. It is called "The Advantage and Necessity of the Christian Revelation shown from the state of Religion in the Ancient Heathen World." It is by John Leland, Doctor of Divinity, who Mr. Bradlaugh well knows is the author of a book against the Deists. I say that that book is a black, appalling, fearful picture of what the state of the heathen world was morally. I say nothing about Jerusalem when Jesus of Nazareth came into the world. Don't take my word for it, but listen attentively to what I say, and I stand here against all the Freethinkers of England; I stand here before all the world to bring evidence of what I have said of the awful and appalling vices in Rome and the neighboring nations at the time when Jesus came into the world. It was because Christ came with the pure Gospel, because it reproved and denounced the follies of the time; because it taught purity of morals and uprightness of life that a large number of the heathens were so opposed to it and Him. Why, if you will only get these two small volumes you will see for yourselves. These two books are "The Early Empire" and the "Age of the Antonines," by Mr. Capes, the Reader of Ancient History in the University of Oxford. Now the truth is this, these two books give the same kind of account, but not so extended as I have told you with regard to Leland. I am going on at great length showing you the state of the heathen world because I think it is very important that you should know what the world was like at that time, and what Christianity has done to make it better. If you will only look carefully over the pages of another author, Mosheim, you can see most clearly what were some of the vices, and how Christianity operated in correcting these follies, in teaching these people higher and nobler views of life. I say the influence of these truths was such that at the time they were preached they purified the people. Within the first few years their effects were not so apparent, but as time rolled on—between the time of Paul and the time of Constantine—the rapid advance in teaching men nobler and higher ways of life was apparent in that age, and is apparent on the page of history. Why, Ladies and Gentlemen, I should hardly dare to tell you what so great a man as Plato taught! What did Plato teach? Did Plato allow fornication? Did Plato appoint a community of women in his Republic? That is men were to have wives in common. Read Plato's "Republic"! You see how these vices were the great curse of the Heathen world. They were really a large part of the means of the decline of the Roman Empire. If I do nothing else to-night than leave this upon your minds let me tell you again that the change wrought by Christianity was a moral change. I did not hear the book mentioned by Mrs. Besant, but the view placed before you by Mrs. Besant was much the same as is presented in Draper's "Conflict between Science and Religion." In that book you get a one-sided view, and I tell you that there might be a very different picture painted by another hand. Christianity was not so much intended to be an intellectual change as a moral change, and I stand here to-night to tell you that that moral change was effected in the Roman Empire by Christianity to a very great extent. I believe I may say entirely so. You will say it may be true, but Christianity is now worn out, and people do not believe in it, in short that it is dead. I stand here to-night to bring before you facts as to what Christianity effected in the Roman Empire in the first three centuries, between the time of Jesus of Nazareth and the time of Constantine, and also facts as to the great change which has been effected in India during the last eighty years. I stand before you to-night to defend Christianity from this charge of being dead. I can defend it, and have done so through a large part of England and Ireland before to-night. Mrs. Besant told you last week in very eloquent words about Chrishna. There is not an atom, not a tittle of proof that the story of Chrishna existed before the time of Jesus of Nazareth. I hold in my hand a book that is somewhat well-known. It is this; "Christ and other Masters: an Historical Enquiry," by Archdeacon Hardwick. This book is published by Macmillan. His object is to draw a picture of the various religions of the ancient world, and he goes very elaborately into the question of the religions in India. I stand here before you to-night to tell you that there is not a tittle of proof to show that the story of Chrishna, as we know it in the Indian books of to-day, existed before the time of Jesus of Nazareth; but there is a very great amount of evidence to show that the story of Chrishna became popular in India, about the sixth century, in the form in which we know it now, and you would be astonished to see the evidence which Archdeacon Hardwick gives in this book. His notion appears to be that the original story about Chrishna got mixed up with the story of our Gospels, when they found their way into India. (A laugh.) Let me tell the gentleman who laughs that I can prove it to be the truth, and I tell the gentleman who laughs that I have made it my business to understand these things. I cannot finish my subject to-night. Sometime in January or February I hope to come here and lecture on these subjects. (Applause.) I can lecture for an hour, and I shall be happy to meet Mrs. Besant in the same way as we meet now if she likes. In India they chiefly worship three gods—Brahma, Vishnu, and Siva. Now, I only, to-night, have to do with Vishnu. Vishnu is the second person of the Hindu Triad or Trinity. Don't confound this with our doctrine of the Trinity. Only ignorant persons do so! (Laughter.) There is no similarity or resemblance, and no one who knows anything of the subject would confound them. This person, Vishnu, whose name means to enter or pervade, the Hindus believe has had nine incarnations in the past, and one incarnation in the time which is to come. I say this Vishnu is supposed to have been nine times incarnate, and he has one to come in the future. In one of these incarnations he is called Chrishna, and he is

E

one of the most popular gods in India in some parts. Ladies and gentlemen, I wish to be a free man! I don't challenge persecution or prosecution, and, therefore, I am not going to tell you about Chrishna to-night; but I have books on this platform that if the Chairman likes to read to you I will see that he is sent to prison for doing it. (Laughter.) I hold in my hands Ward's "History, Literature, and Religion of the Hindus." What is Ward's evidence? These books are the original, and they were printed in India. What does Ward, who stands unchallenged before the world, say? He gives a picture of degradation, of fearful immorality, in India, which he dare not print in English. I could tell you a tale, but I won't. (Laughter, applause and hisses.) Ladies and gentlemen, you know I have been brought on to the Freethinkers' platform, and I must do my duty; and the heads of the Church in London, who know well I am here and what I am doing, and who have sanctioned my coming, will hold me responsible if I don't do my duty. (Applause, mingled with laughter.) Now, then, besides the evidence which is supplied by Ward, I hold in my hand the memoirs read before the Anthropological Society of London, volume ii., page 264. Dr. James Hunt, an intimate friend and acquaintance of mine, was the President. It is headed "Some Remarks on Indian Gnosticism or Sacti Puja, the worship of the Female Powers," by Edward Sellon, Esq. I don't wish to get sent to prison, and I don't wish to read it to you. The worst of this is in Latin, and it shows distinctly the same kind of black picture of degradation, of vice, of immorality that existed in the Roman Empire at the time when Juvenal wrote his satires, and when Horace wrote his satires which I have referred to. What about Christianity? I stand here to-night fearlessly before all the Freethinkers of this country, and I say, Christianity has so altered the whole tone of Indian society during the last eighty years—has so completely and thoroughly altered the moral tone that now there is a totally opposite state of things to what there was eighty years ago. I came here armed for the fray, I told you last week. I have brought with me testimonies to the results of Christian Missions which I trust that our Chairman and Mrs. Besant will look at—at least I earnestly pray that they will.

(Laughter and applause). There are testimonies from the late Lord Lawrence, Lord Northbrook, Lord Napier, Sir Bartle Frere—(Oh! oh! laughter and hisses)—Sir Donald Macleod, late Lieutenant-Governor of the Punjaub, and Sir Richard Temple; there are so many that I won't go over more of them, except Professor Monier Williams. Let me tell you, Freethinkers, that these testimonies no one can shake down, that there is a mass of evidence to show what Christianity has done in India—(interruption)—of what Christianity has done in India. Keep quiet. That they are simply overwhelming, and before I have done with you this night I will show it you, and more still. It will be said that Christianity is dead. Gracious! how ignorant you must be!

Mr. Hatchard's time here expired, and he sat down amid slight applause.

The CHAIRMAN: In calling upon Mrs. Besant now to address you, I must request both disputants to address themselves to the question, and not to personal remarks. (Applause.)

Mrs. BESANT: Let me say at once that in dealing with my opponent's speech I shall not take up to-night the question of the likeness between Chrishna and Christ. Our subject for debate to-night is not "The historical character of the Jesus of the Gospels," but "That the influence of Christianity upon the world has been injurious." The proper place to have dealt with Chrishna, about whom my rev. opponent has told you so much to-night, was in last week's debate. It is out of place to do so in the present debate, and I trust he will not think me wanting in courtesy if I entirely leave the question of Chrishna in presenting to you my view of the subject at issue. There are various points, however, which distinctly challenge my position. We are told about the moral change that Christianity has wrought in the world. You may remember that my fifth proposition was that Christianity has not purified public morals. Therefore, I have come prepared to deal with that part of the subject. I will first take the allusions to slavery which we have heard, because I have not quite finished what I was about to say on that subject. Mr. Hatchard has urged that it was the custom, dealing with a remark of Horace's, to crucify slaves in Rome for very slight faults. I do not think it is fair to say, that because a Roman poet says that a master would be mad to crucify his slave for a small fault, therefore crucifixion of slaves for small faults was general. Allow, as I do allow, that wherever you get slavery you get the brutalisation of the masters as well as of the slaves, yet I will ask you to contrast the words of the Roman poet, stamping cruelty as madness, with the words of Jehovah, the God of the Jews: "If a man smite his servant, or his maid, with a rod, and he die under his hand; he shall be surely punished. Notwithstanding, if he continue a day or two, he shall not be punished: for he is his money" (Exodus xxi., 20-21). I think Horace was a better moralist than Jehovah. But I am told that Christian feeling opposed slavery in the Southern States of America. I shall have to deal with that in a moment, but I will now take up the question of slavery where I laid it down. So far from Christianity discouraging slavery, if you turn to Hallam's history you will find the following. I quote Hallam because he is often called the judicious Hallam, and it throws a halo of respectability over my arguments. "It is an humiliating proof of the degradation of Christendom, that the Venetians were reduced to purchase the luxuries of Asia by supplying the slave-market of the Saracens. . . . . This trade was not peculiar to Venice. In England, it was very common, even after the Conquest, to export slaves to Ireland; till, in the reign of Henry II., the Irish came to a non-importation agreement which put a stop to the practice" ["Europe during the Middle Ages," pp. 613-614]. And in a note he adds: "William of Malmsbury accuses the Anglo-Saxon nobility of selling their female servants, even when pregnant by them, as slaves to foreigners. I hope there were not many of these Yaricoes; and should not perhaps have given credit to an historian rather prejudiced against the English, if I had not found too much authority for the general practice." That is the testimony of Hallam that Christians were wont to sell slaves, and female slaves, not only to their fellow-Christians, but even to the Mahommedans, the Saracens, and sold them in a condition which at least should have aroused a feeling of humanity. I pass from the testimony of Hallam, and I draw your attention to the very different way in which the Mahommedans, who were not Christians, were taught to treat their slaves.

Everyone who knows the history of slavery in America knows how the female slaves had their children born to their masters torn from them, and how you absolutely thus found the father selling his own daughter, and the brother selling his own sister. If you turn to the false prophet, Mahomet, you find him saying: "Whoso among you hath not means sufficient that he may marry free women who are believers, let him marry with such of your maidservants whom your right hands possess, as are true believers. . . . Ye are the one from the other; therefore marry them with the consent of their masters, and give them their dower according to justice" (Koran, chap. iv.). And again: "And unto such of your slaves as desire a written instrument allowing them to redeem themselves on paying a certain sum, write one if ye know good in them; and give them of the riches of God, which he hath given you. And compel not your maidservants to prostitute themselves, if they be willing to live chastely" (Ibid, chap. xxiv.). This is not Christian teaching, but it is the teaching of the heretic; but I will ask you to contrast that with the teaching you will find in the Book of Exodus. You will find there that a man may sell his own daughter, and that having taken a wife from those who may have been taken captive, he may, if it suits him, send her away if he does not care for her any longer. And then you find Moses saying that the slave is the owner's "money." There is a striking resemblance between the teaching of Moses and the practice in Christian lands; but it is alleged by Mr. Hatchard that it was Christian feeling and Christian teaching which opposed slavery in the Southern States of America. That is rather a rash statement to make in a hall which is filled with those who know that Christians were opponents of the abolition of slavery, and are acquainted with the general testimony which comes to us from all directions. I take a quotation from an admirable article lately written for the *N. R.* by one of our vice-presidents, Mr. Symes: "The Charleston Union Presbytery, 7th April, 1836, 'Resolved, that in the opinion of this Presbytery, the holding of slaves, so far from being a sin in the sight of God, is nowhere condemned in his holy word: that it is in accordance with the example and consistent with the precepts of patriarchs, apostles and prophets,' etc. The Missionary Society of the South Carolina Conference of the Methodist Episcopal Church, by their board of managers, said: 'We denounce the principles and practice of the abolitionists *in toto*. . . . . We believe that the holy scriptures, so far from giving any countenance to this delusion, do, unequivocally, authorise the relation of master and slave.' The Hopewell Presbytery, South Carolina, said: 'Slavery has always existed in the Church of God, from the time of Abraham to this day.'" This I admit to be true. "The Presbyterian Synod of Virginia 'Resolved, unanimously, that we consider the dogma, that slavery as it exists in the slave-holding States is necessarily sinful, and ought to be immediately abolished, and the conclusions which naturally follow from that dogma, as directly and palpably contrary to the plainest principles of common sense and common humanity, and the clearest authority of the word of God.'" That was the view, not of individuals, but of the Churches in America, when the slavery question was in agitation; and I will ask you to remember one terrible proof of the Christian opposition to all those who argued for slave abolition. The name of William Lloyd Garrison is identified with the struggle against slavery. Remember how he went to Boston and found that every church there closed its doors against him, how he could find no place to speak in, until the pulpit of Theodore Parker was opened to him, Theodore Parker who had been expelled even from the Unitarian body for the rank heresy which he thought it his duty to preach. (Applause.) I urge Mr. Hatchard to be good enough to give us some proofs of the statements he has made, to point out to us the resolutions of one church or of one sect tending to show us that the Christians were foremost in the trial to get abolition, to show that they preached abolition from their pulpits, when to preach it involved danger of life. I know that they joined in afterwards, when the battle was over and won. (Applause and laughter.) I will ask you to remember that the opposition to Clarkson's Bill came chiefly from the Christians in the House of Commons and the House of Lords, and that Lord Chancellor Thurlow, speaking from the woolsack, stigmatised it as a "miserable and contemptible Bill," and as utterly "contrary to the word of God." These are quotations which can easily be verified, and I will ask my opponent, when he next rises, to explain how, with this evidence before him, he can say that Christians were in favor of the abolition of the slave trade. I submit to him that this is absolutely unsupported by any kind of evidence, and is directly negatived by what I have laid before him. Remembering the general mildness of Greek and Roman slavery, remembering how slaves were the teachers of the young, and how freedmen often rose to places of honor and of dignity, I allege "*That Christianity has upheld and aggravated slavery.*" (Loud applause.) We now come to the curious statement which my opponent makes to us that Christianity is consonant with science; and I propose here to put the argument in the hands of a very capable writer, one of whose works I will bring before you. I notice that my opponent the other night, in his last speech to which I had no right of reply, laid very great stress upon German authority; but that, in pity for our ignorance, he refrained from quoting a single German writer to us. I will ask your patience for a moment, because I think it as well to meet the challenge. I will read a passage of Strauss, so that we may see whether he, a representative German Freethinker, shares Mr. Hatchard's opinion with respect to Christianity and science being in harmony with each other. I have here a German edition of a work by Strauss, and I propose to read the extract in German, asking your pardon for doing so. Strauss deals with Christianity and science in a very interesting way, and it is an extract from him by which I will answer this part of my opponent's speech. The title of the book from which the quotation is given is "Der alte und der neue Glaube." "Den Hauptwiderspruch mußte die Stellung erregen, die sie der Erschaffung der Himmelskörper gab. Diese kommen bei ihr in jedem Betrachte zu spät. Die Sonne wird erst am vierten Tage geschaffen, nachdem bereits drei Tage lang der Wechsel von Tag und Nacht, der ohne die Sonne nicht denkbar ist, stattgefunden haben soll. Ferner wird die Erde mehrere Tage vor der Sonne geschaffen, und dieser wie dem Monde nur eine dienende Beziehung zur Erde gegeben, der Sterne aber nur ganz nebenher gedacht. Eine Verkehrung der wahren Rangverhältnisse unter den Weltkörpern, die einem geoffenbarten Berichte schlecht anstand." (Laughter and applause.) I have a word to say about one part of my opponent's speech which was most startling. He told us that, in the first chapter of the Epistle to the Romans, the language was so bad that he would not defile your ears by reading it to you. I would ask Mr.

Hatchard to remember that these words are read in the churches when the first chapter of Romans happens to be the lesson for the day, unless, indeed, the clergyman be better than his creed, and feels that he ought not to read it before decent men and women. Does not my opponent know that there are passages in the Bible infinitely worse than this chapter which he refuses to read before you on account of its language? Does he not put this Bible into the hands of little children, though he will not read it before grown men and people to whom the world has taught the knowledge of evil? Not read the New Testament aloud before women because of its foulness! But oh Sir (turning to Mr. Hatchard), that I would not defile my little daughter's ears with this foulness was one of the charges against me when your creed took away from me my child. (Loud and continued applause, mingled with cries of "bravo," during which Mrs. Besant resumed her seat.)

Mr. HATCHARD: Mr. Chairman, Ladies, and Gentlemen, before I go on with some of the remarks which Mrs. Besant has made, I wish to say distinctly that we both came to discuss the influence of Christianity, and as far as I am concerned I have distinctly kept to the subject. ("Oh, oh," and laughter.) I say that I have not wasted a word from the subject, nor wandered a word, because I know this subject moderately well. I did not come here to discuss the Old Testament—I came here to discuss Jesus Christ, and his teaching and his influence on the world. I know perfectly well that it is a very cheap argument, indeed, about what is related in the books of Moses about slavery; but I want to see the same thing in the New Testament. I find nothing in the teaching of the New Testament about this treatment of these slaves, about the women and such-like. I have cut off that part of the argument——(laughter and interruption.)

The CHAIRMAN: I shall be obliged if our friends will remain perfectly quiet, except so far as they may applaud during Mr. Hatchard's speech.

Mr. HATCHARD: I did not come here to discuss slavery, and I allege most distinctly that it has nothing to do with the subject of the influence of Christianity upon the world. It would take me too long to give you the evidence—chapter and verse—how Christianity did ameliorate the world. But down to the time of Constantine—roughly 300 years—it was Christian sentiment and Christian teaching that taught the doctrine of Christian brotherhood, that put down the slavery that existed in the ancient world. With regard to what Mrs. Besant has told you about persecution, the unfortunate thing is that I agree with every word she says; and if I had to come out on this platform to lecture on what has been called Christianity in the world, I should say the same thing as Mrs. Besant. I say when, not only the Romish Church, but the Protestant Church likewise, persecuted and burnt people at the stake, or did all the other awful things which we read about in history, that they were not acting upon Christian principles in any sense whatever. They were acting in the same intolerant way that an ancient heathen nation acted when they compelled Socrates, as you have so often heard, to put himself to death. I find that all sects and parties have in their turn persecuted those that opposed them. I find a most extraordinary history of persecution with regard to Protestantism. I find that Elizabeth burnt a large number of Catholics, and I find that Mary persecuted a large number of Protestants. When I go to India I find a similar display of intolerance. Why did not the Brahmins let the followers of Buddha alone in India? How comes it that they persecuted each other? Why, ladies and gentlemen, the story ought to be well known to you. It was because of the persecuting spirit of the Brahmins who could not tolerate the free spirit of the Buddhists, because the Buddhists opposed the followers of Brahma the Buddhists were driven out and persecuted most fearfully. I say most distinctly—and let this be my answer in full, whether you think it is a good answer or not—when the Christian Church was guilty of persecuting various persons and burnt them at the stake, that it was not acting upon Christian principles—it was not acting upon the principles of the New Testament. Lest you should go away from here to-night without hearing the truth let me hasten on. I told you that I had here in my hands these testimonies by various great Indian authorities. These men are witnesses—witnesses to the truth. I know Sir Bartle Frere does not meet the approbation of some people; but I tell you most distinctly that as an officer of the Government he is a competent witness to what has been done——(interruption).

The CHAIRMAN: If any interruption is offered I shall allow Mr. Hatchard time for it.

Mr. HATCHARD (resuming): Thank you! Mr. Bradlaugh is certainly one of the fairest chairmen I ever met. These men are competent witnesses of what takes place under their own cognisance and their own observation. But you will say "after all, these testimonies are only the testimonies of single men;" but, ladies and gentlemen (holding up a Blue Book), I have brought you a document which nobody can challenge. Our chairman knows what that is. (Much laughter and some applause.) These—I have two of them here. (Renewed laughter). I wish to read this with all the earnestness that my strength will allow me. This one was broken like this for a printer—but, friends, I hold here a Blue Book. The covers are gone. It is called, "Statement respecting the Moral and Material Progress of India during the year 1871-2." I have here the next volume, I believe, showing the progress of India morally and materially during 1873. These are, of course, official books, and I take the trouble to get these in order that I may show that my statements can be supported by indisputable evidence. I find here one, two, three, four, five pages with respect to the progress of Missions—Christian Missions in India, and what they have done; and I may tell you that the Church Missionary Society had these reprinted to take about the country to read to the people. I only have time to read briefly, so to speak, an extract, the last extract. It is called "General Influence of Missionary Teaching." This is not the word of a missionary deputation; it is not the word of a single official governor; it is the word of the Official Report in the Blue Book, and it says this. Ladies and gentlemen, I ask you to remember these words: "But the Missionaries in India hold the opinion that the winning of these converts, whether in the cities or in the open country, is but a small portion of the beneficial results which have sprung from their labors. No statistics can give a fair view of all that they have done. They consider that their distinctive teaching, now applied to the country for many years, has powerfully affected the entire population. The moral tone of their preaching is recognised and highly approved by multitudes who do not follow them as converts. The various lessons which they inculcate have given to the people at large new ideas, not only on purely religious questions, but on the nature of evil, the obligations of law, and the motives by which human conduct should be regulated. Insensibly a higher standard of moral conduct is becoming familiar to the people, especially to the young, which has been set before them not merely by public teaching, but by the millions of printed books and tracts which are scattered widely through the country." Christianity they tell us is opposed to education and knowledge! "On this account they express no wonder that the ancient systems are no longer defended as they once were; many doubts are felt about the rules of caste; the great festivals are not attended by the vast crowds of former years; and several Theistic schools have been growing up among the more educated classes, especially in the Presidency cities, who profess to have no faith in the idol-gods of their fathers." Now, there is much more that I might have read, and if I might be allowed to publish it in the *National Reformer*, I should like to do so. Now, perhaps you would like to see what things were in India before the introduction of Christianity. I think I have about three minutes left, and I will show you some pictures I have brought with me of the gods they used to worship in India. That (showing the first of a series of large colored diagrams fixed at the back of the platform)—that is one of the idols—that is Siva.

A VOICE: Will you bring them to the front, if you please?

The CHAIRMAN: Please don't interrupt. You can see well enough.

Mr. HATCHARD: That represents Kali or Durga. She has a thousand names, and it used to be that human sacrifices were constantly offered to her. It would take me a full night to tell you of the horrors of the worship of that most horrible and disgusting goddess. That is one of the old things which has been put down. There you have what is called the Swing Festival, and I tell you here to-night that the Swing Festival—one of the most horrible things—has almost entirely died out because of what Christianity has taught. Here is another thing, the Exposing of Infants by the banks of the Ganges. That is dying out. Here you have the Festival of Juggernaut, and I stand here to-night to tell you that this festival, which used to be attended by say 250,000 Hindus, has now only about 10,000. I cannot tell you all that Christianity has done in India during the last eighty years. Is it dead? Here is another picture. Here you have the burning of the Indian widow. Was it not Christianity and Christian sentiment which put that down? and you know how deeply rooted it was in the Indian mind. The testimony with regard to what Christianity has done in India in effecting a moral change, a moral alteration, a moral revolution, is something alarming. I have testimonies in this book ("Indian Missionary Manual," 1870, John Murdoch,) which are enough to convince anybody. I say distinctly, what I have told you about the moral progress in India, the alteration in the public mind, has been brought about by Christian teaching and Christian preaching in the land. The late Miss Mary Carpenter was a friend of mine, and she, and I, and Sir Mutu Coomaru Swarmy with some other friends, established a "National Indian Association" in Manchester some years ago, to make known in this country what was being done in India. You say, perhaps, that you don't take my word for it; but I can bring forward chapter and verse to prove all that I have told you. Well, then, you have seen what I have tried to do to-night. I have tried to show a parallel between these two things: What Christianity effected morally in the Roman Empire during the first 300 years down to the time of Constantine, and What Christianity has effected in India in the last seventy or eighty years. (Applause.)

Mrs. Besant: I understand that Mr. Hatchard is not prepared to defend the Old Testament. Of that I am glad, although it is strange that a Christian clergyman should say so, for I find in the New Testament that Christ laid it down that anyone who should break the least of these commandments of Moses, he shall be called the least in the Kingdom of Heaven; and while I find Christ altering some of them, and saying that it was said "by them of old time" do so and so, "but I say unto you," do something else, yet he never said: "It was said by them of old time, you may flay your slaves nearly to death, but I say unto you, set them free." If slavery in the old world was as abominable as Mr. Hatchard has said, that makes the conduct of the Apostle Paul in sending back the fugitive slave to his master worse than I have pictured it, where slaves were constantly the instructors of the young, and where freed slaves rose to the highest positions in the polity of the Roman Empire. Mr. Hatchard says that India is totally different now from what it was when we took it. I am sorry to say that I admit that contention, although I do not think it will help his argument very much. I may say in explanation of the groans with which the name of Sir Bartle Frere was greeted that he is regarded here as a man who has done more harm and shed more blood than any living man. And when I am told of the few lives rescued from the car of Juggernaut I wonder how many thousand people have been offered up as sacrifices to the War-God to please Sir Bartle Frere. The change is indeed alarming since Christianity first made its way into India. Before then the natives "had reared cities larger and fairer than Saragossa or Toledo, and buildings more beautiful and costly than the Cathedral of Seville. They could show bankers richer than the richest firms of Barcelona or Cadiz; viceroys whose splendor far surpassed that of Ferdinand the Catholic; myriads of cavalry and long trains of artillery which would have astonished the Great Captain" (Macaulay's Essays p. 502). Instead of persecution, as put by Mr. Hatchard, Mr. Torrens draws the following picture: "Neither Moslem nor Hindu was incapacitated for public employment on account of the belief in which he had been brought up. Mahommedan princes gladly confided to learned and astute Brahmins civil trusts of importance; and many a Mussulman rose to honor and won fortune in a Maharajah's camp. . . The governments of Southern Asia, when we began to meddle in their affairs, were strangers to the system of penal laws, which were then among the cherished institutions of our own and nearly every other European State. While no Catholic in Ireland could inherit freehold, command a regiment, or sit on the judicial bench; while in France the Huguenot weaver was driven into exile beyond the sea; and while in Sweden none but Lutherans could sit as jurors, and in Spain no heretic was permitted Christian burial—Sunis and Sheahs, Mahrattas and Sikhs, competed freely for distinction and profit in almost every city and camp of Hindustan" (Torrens' "Empire in Asia"). In order to strengthen that, I read again in the *Quarterly Review*—

"Philip IV. and our own Elizabeth were the contemporaries of Akber; and while Europe was convulsed and desolated with the wars which arose out of the Reformation, India reposed in unexampled prosperity under the tolerant sway of her Mussulman autocrat. While Philip was extinguishing the last embers of industry and commerce in Spain, by the unremitting persecution of Morisco, Jew and heretic, and waging the most sanguinary warfare against the civil and religious liberties of the Low Countries, Akber was endeavoring to blend, under one peaceful and equitable government, the discordant elements of the vast Indian population" (Vol. lxviii.). We have not only introduced Christianity, but we have driven the people to a misery that they never knew in the old days. Hear the words of Mr. Phillimore: "There is no spot of the earth where all that is necessary for the support of its inhabitants is raised with more facility. . . . Spices, grain, indigo, sandal-wood, opium, pepper, vegetables and fruit are equally abundant. Sugar, though it requires more labor, can be raised with the same success. The cattle, though small and yielding little milk, more than compensate by their numbers for their want of strength. Fish swarm in the rivers, the woods are full of game. . . When we seized upon this land, the overflowing of its soil fed distant regions" ("History of England during the Reign of George III., vol. i.). [The quotations were read from "England, India and Afghanistan."] Now these people die of starvation by hundreds and by thousands. Christianity has indeed progressed to a remarkable and alarming extent. But I am told that the persecutions I allege are the effect of *what is called* Christianity, and not of *true* Christianity. I can only judge the tree by its fruits. I only know that every Christian Church did persecute; there was nothing to choose between one and another; and I say that wherever you get religion there you get persecution; wherever you get religion sincere, there you will have persecution. Persecution is less to-day, because Freethought is so widely spread that even Christians themselves are not sure of the eternal damnation of the heretic, and they do not like to burn him. But the suttee is abolished we are told. The suttee has been very much exaggerated; Abbè Dubois has told us that out of a population of thirty millions only about thirty widows a-year committed suicide in that way. But I ask are there not in every Christian country more suicides in one single month than you find in a year by this Indian suttee? I put one other point. Mr. Hatchard admits that other religions have gone wrong, and I agree with him. Christianity, however, claims to be what no other religion is, the revelation of an almighty god, and I urge that it is no excuse for its errors to say that it has done no worse than the other religions of the world have done. It will be my duty in my last speech to sum up the various points which my opponent has not dealt with, but I should like him to deal with that remarkable argument from Strauss which I read to him. My 5th allegation is *that Christianity has not succeeded in purifying morals*, that it has not insured their purity. I am glad however to be able to say that the Christian scriptures are not, on the whole, as bad as Christian practice; the New Testament, at least, does not teach gross vice, although very faulty morality, but the influence of Christianity has not insured purification of morals. I know that it is urged that although Greece and Rome were great intellectually, they were very bad morally; could not exactly the same be said of Paris and London to-day? It is not enough to say that they were bad, unless you can prove that you have made things better. Christianity has utterly failed to improve upon the morality of Paganism on most points, and while it sinks far below it in intellect it does not rise above it in morals. I admit that in Plato's Republic there is a community of women, a thing of which I utterly disapprove. But I might very fairly urge that there is plenty of authority in the Bible for the foulest polygamy. Let us see the condition of society after 400 years of Christianity. Salvian, a Christian minister, writes: "Who is there who is not rolling in the mire of fornication? And what more? What I am about to state is grave and mournful. The very Church of God, which ought in all things to please God, what does it but provoke Him to anger? With the exception of a *very few*, who fly from vice, what is almost every Christian congregation, but a sink of vices? For you will find in the church scarcely one who is not either a drunkard, or a glutton, or an adulterer, or a fornicator, or a ravisher, or a robber, or a manslayer, and, what is worse than all, almost all these without limit.

I put it now to the conscience of all Christian people, whether it be not so that you will barely find one who is not addicted to some of the vices and crimes I have mentioned; or rather, who is it that is not guilty of all? Truly you will more easily find the man who is guilty of all than one who is guilty of none" (Miall's "Memorials of early Christianity," pp. 366-367). That is the purity of morals which was insured by Christianity after four centuries of work. It is extremely useful to us that Christians have quarrelled as much as they have, for it is from the mouth of a Christian who wants to do away with Episcopacy and to prove that the early Church was not perfect that I am able to bring you this very valuable testimony on my side of the argument. Again, let us see what Mosheim says of the third century: "Many were sunk in luxury and voluptuousness, puffed up with vanity, arrogance, and ambition, possessed with a spirit of contention and discord, and addicted to many other vices" [p. 73]. That is the Christian historian on the Church even in the third century. And shall I not find in the Middle Ages that vice was literally everywhere? Shall I not find, if I want to discover the very worst characters, I must go to the centre of the Christian Church, to Rome under the rule of the Popes? Shall I not find that the priests encourage the people to commit crime by the sale of indulgences, by virtue of which they could do whatever their passions led them to do with impunity? Shall I not find that the first movement towards a purer morality came from those very heretics whom they put to death? There was no difficulty in the way of the sin, because there was no difficulty in the way of the forgiveness; and the Christian doctrine of the New Testament has entirely destroyed the chance of stopping sin. By the gifts of the sinners the Church grew wealthy. Every day brought riches to them. You find that the riches of the Church are made up by the riches which came from the death-bed when men tried to buy their way to heaven. The Roman Catholic opened heaven's gate with a golden key; later, the Protestant used the key of the blood of Christ, to be had for the asking; and so you find that Christianity did not insure purity of morals, because it did not teach that crime was unpardonable, because it taught that however wrongly you acted you might easily escape punishment from God by giving something to his priests before your last hour came. (Applause.)

MR. HATCHARD: Mr. Chairman, ladies and gentlemen, Mrs. Besant has thrown out some very bold challenges. I proceed as briefly as I can to answer one or two of them. She has drawn you a very black picture, indeed, of what the Church was in what I call the middle ages. But the unfortunate thing is that I perfectly agree with her, because I was taught the same thing in a Theological College. Let me ask you another question. During the dark ages, as they are called, when the people were many of them very profligate, and I regret to say that many of the clergy were not much better—(laughter)—I say, where were the scriptures, and where was the New Testament? I do ask you most distinctly to carefully read over some good ecclesiastical history. There are a great many small histories which you can easily buy, if you do not care to read the large work of Mosheim, as Mrs. Besant has done. You will find this unless I am greatly mistaken. As the ages rolled on from the time of Christ, say to that of Constantine—take the year 325, the Council of Nice—gradually it appears to me that the Bible was laid aside, the people were very little acquainted with it, and we, to-day, cannot understand the ignorance of the clergy of the twelfth and thirteenth centuries. The truth is, that when Martin Luther found the Bible, and read it, it was like a revelation to him. The New Testament, as far as the intelligence of the people was concerned, was non-existent. Now, therefore, it appears to me that true religion—such as read in the New Teatament—that true religion gradually declined during the fourth, fifth, sixth, and seventh centuries, and so on, over a large part of Europe. Curiously enough, learning died out in Europe in the same way. With the rise of Christianity in the earliest times there was a new school of Greek learning; but, as the ages rolled on, curiously enough true religion died out: I freely admit it; and gradually it seems that learning died out as well; and curiously enough again at the Reformation they came back at the same time; at least, that is my version of it. I have here "The Life of Leo X." I learn here that learning and true religion—that is New Testament religion—came in together. I am surprised that Mrs. Besant brought in the Epistle of Paul to Philemon. What do I

F

find here? I read in the sixteenth verse, with regard to sending this slave or servant back again I read these words: "Receive him not now as a servant, but above a servant, a brother beloved, specially to me, but how much more unto thee." This man, the poor, broken-down slave, who fled to the Apostle Paul for refuge, was sent back to his master, not simply as a slave to be crushed and beaten and trodden down, but as a beloved brother to be treated well, honestly, and kindly. (Applause). I hold in my hands a book which I dare say Mrs. Besant knows well, "The Education of the Human Race," by Lessing. Of course I don't put Lessing forward as orthodox by any means whatever. Lessing has been discussing the education of the world and the various systems of the world. I hold myself that the human race has been educated—educated in the same way as you educate a child, and Lessing here says: "A better Instructor must come and tear the exhausted Primer from the child's hands. Christ came! That portion of the human race which God had willed to comprehend in one Educational plan, was ripe for the second step of Education. He had, however, only willed to comprehend on such a plan, one which by language, mode of action, government, and other natural and political relationships, was already united in itself." ("Education of the Human Race," pp. 46—47, ed. 1858). And then he goes on to discuss Christianity. My version of it is this, that the world in various ways, by modes of government, by systems of philosophy or science so-called, educated itself up to a certain point. Christ came into the world, and when he came he made a moral change, or rather, the beginning of a change; because Christianity has not effected a violent revolution in the world and a violent change. I am not afraid of any comparison between Jesus of Nazareth and Buddha. It is only those who don't know about Jesus and about Budda who are afraid. I will come here some night and show you the difference and the relation. (Laughter.) Jesus of Nazareth left his words upon the world in the minds of his disciples to produce fruit. In the early ages they did produce this fruit. Then, unfortunately for the world, the world disregarded them, till by-and-bye, at the time of the Reformation, Martin Luther arose. There was John Wicliff, Jerome of Prague, and others, who helped the Reformation forward; and by-and-bye there comes Martin Luther, and he was followed by a great number, as you well know, throughout Germany and throughout Europe. Perhaps, with the exception of Russia, you had this New Testament—the words of Jesus of Nazareth—again brought to the front, which our friend Strauss, in his "Life of Jesus" (of which I make Mrs. Besant a present), tried curiously enough to upset, but failed. Strauss was driven away completely out of the field by Neander and such-like writers. There is hardly a single thing which Strauss has put forward that even the very Freethinkers of to-day have not given up. I say that Strauss as a power has died out. I made it my business to inquire from one of the best German houses, a publishing firm, as to what was the influence of Strauss in Germany now. They told me that Strauss was practically dead, that only those who put forward Strauss-and-water—*ie.*, Strauss disguised, had any influence with the public. I proved to you beyond dispute and against the cavil of all the Freethinkers in Europe, Strauss included, that Jesus of Nazareth, the Jesus of the Gospels, actually lived as a historical character; that the Gospels and Epistles are substantially a true account of what he said and did; and in consequence of the teaching of the early Christian teachers, that Christian churches were established in the East certainly and in a large part of the Roman Empire. By the teaching of these disciples and Christian teachers a great moral change was effected. Now then, I say most distinctly, and I wish you not to go away from this place and forget it, that I don't stand here to-night to defend persecution. I also say distinctly I know some little of what such men as Professors Huxley and Tyndall put before the public, and I have yet to learn that there is any real contradictions between the highest science as taught by these men and Christianity as taught in the New Testament. (A voice, "Keep to the point.") I am to the point, Sir; much too near to the point to suit you. Mrs. Besant is, I have no doubt, sincere in the view she has taken of Christianity, and which she has published to the world in her book and various writings. But I say she has drawn you one picture to night—the picture which you Freethinkers most like to hear; but I stand here to paint the other picture—that there is no real contradiction between the highest science as taught in the present day and true religion as taught in the New Testament. I deny emphatically that the highest intellects are against religion. I ask who is Professor Owen? Who is Dr. Carpenter of the London University? Dr. Carpenter believes as much as I believe in the historical existence of Jesus of Nazareth, and also that Jesus of Nazareth was the teacher which I put before you last week. Ladies and Gentlemen, answer me this if you can. You Freethinkers ("Oh, oh!" laughter and groans,) are indebted to Christian scholars for the very knowledge that you have of the Bible, and of its past history in Europe during the last eighteen centuries; and it is out of the armory of Christianity that you have got the weapons that you have turned against me. (Applause.)

Mrs. BESANT: It is my duty to sum up the results of this debate so far as they appear to touch the question, to point out the arguments which my opponent has omitted to notice, and, lastly, to put before you a brief sketch of what the world was before Christianity, what the world became under Christianity, and what the world is to-day. I must first remark that my challenge touching Strauss has remained entirely unanswered. Not only has my opponent failed to answer the argument drawn from Strauss, but he has even mistaken the very book used. He has jumped to the conclusion that I was using Strauss's best known work, the "Leben Jesu," although I twice gave the title of the book really used. In the quotation read, Strauss points out the utter disagreement between the Mosaic account of the creation and the facts known to science. But my opponent says that Strauss is not now read in Germany; well, the book is in its sixth edition, and that is pretty good for an unread man. My reason for using Strauss will have been very obvious to you. My opponent, in a way which was scarcely courteous either to the audience or to myself, sneered at us as ignorant of German, and said that he could have overpowered us with German authorities, but did not, as we should know nothing about them. So I thought I would test his own knowledge of German, and I am inclined to think that the result is hardly satisfactory. (Loud laughter and cheers.) Now for the missionaries and their work. Major-General Stuart, in a book I have here, implores the Government to stop them, on the ground that they are undermining our rule in India and are rendering revolt probable. As to their moral influence, listen to the words put into the mouth of a Hindu by Abbé Dubois: "You speak of morality, and of purity of manners, and you boast of a great superiority over me in these respects. But pray, how comes it that from the very accounts you are not ashamed to publish even in this my supposed thoroughly corrupted country, it appears that in each of your respective metropolises, London and Paris, you reckon no less than forty thousand prostitutes? . . . You speak in high terms of your civilisation, of your refined education and manners, bu how comes it that amidst the advantages you claim over me in these respects, crimes and vices of every kind are more prevalent in your countries than in mine. From whence comes it that, with the superior education and civilisation you boast of, your cities and towns are filled with thieves, sharpers, pickpockets, swindlers, gamblers, forgers, false coiners, and other knaves of every description, most of them happily unknown in my supposed thoroughly corrupted country?" But we are told, Dr. Owen and Dr. Carpenter are Christians. I do not know if Dr. Owen be a Christian; if so, it may explain his taking the wrong side on Evolution. But Dr. Carpenter no more believes in the Deity of Christ than I do; he is a Unitarian, and it is not fair to bring forward in defence of orthodoxy a man who is three-parts a heretic. Mr. Hatchard admits that Christianity brought forward no new intellectual truths, and he has not denied —indeed, he could not—the ignorance which reigned while Christianity was supreme, so my first proposition stands. Christianity took hundreds of years before it tried to abolish slavery. Mr. Hatchard asserted that it abolished it in the Southern States of America. I gave three important authorities in contradiction, and though Mr. Hatchard has spoken twice since he has not given one authority in support of his statement, so that, as regards slavery, you have Mr. Hatchard's bare assertion on one side and all the facts on the other. (Applause.) The persecution on the part of the churches is admitted; in the face of history it could not be denied. Has not the influence of Christianity on the world tended to horrible persecution? But we are told that Christianity was practically dead during the Middle Ages, and revived at the Reformation, when Christianity and learning came back together. But if so Christianity died when it was wanted and came back when it was superfluous. But, says Mr. Hatchard, the human race was educated like a child. Is that so? are the laws of Moses fit for a child to follow, or even to read? Are these cruel, persecuting, bloodthirsty laws the laws by which god educated his creature man? Why, the worst father or mother among you would not train their children as god is said to have trained his. Friends, I urge to you that Mr. Hatchard has utterly failed to prove his own position and that he has left my points absolutely unshaken. (Applause.) The only place wherein he even tried to show that Christianity had been useful was in India, and here he did not touch the terrible evidence I gave you on the other side. So much for the debate. Now for a general review of the influence of Christianity on the world. Carry back your minds to the old days, long, long before the birth of Christ. Come with me to India, and see the wise men studying astronomy, mapping the heavens, recording the motions of the stars. Come to Egypt, and see the learned there gazing at the starry worlds around them, climbing to a knowledge which Christendom afterwards destroyed. Come from the East. come from India and from Egypt into Europe, and stay awhile in Greece. Remember Greece in the days of the paganism, in the days of her glory. Vicious? aye, but Christendom had the vices, but where had it the magnificent intellect which Greece and Rome gave to the world? (Applause.) I would ask you now, friends, not to cheer me, for I have much to say and brief time for speech. Wait in Greece and look around you. See the canvas glow under the pencil of Apelles. See the marble grow to life under the chisel of Phidias. Art was beautiful, and lent her grace to life, and hand in hand with Art went Science, her sister. Philosophy rose in the writings of Democritus and Epicurus. The golden groves of Athens were musical with the voice of Socrates, with the teachings of Plato; mathematics found such mastery in Euclid that you send your children to school to-day at the feet of the old Pagan. Greece gave birth to the drama. Tragedy rose to her most majestic expression, comedy found the mirthfullest utterance, for art was there as many sided as nature. And the sterner sciences had too their place; physical science was cultivated, nature was questioned, natural philosophy was built up. And all this without Christianity. Science grew, and life was beautiful. The very idolatry had its beauty, for it worshipped the natural. But Christianity was born, and instead of the glow and the glory of paganism, the "world grew grey at the breath" of the Galilean. Pass from Greece to Rome. Cicero is to-day the model of the purest eloquence. Statesmen go to school to these old teachers, who were Pagan and not Christian in their thought, and learn from them the stately eloquence which they use to sway the nations. Such were the might, the glory, and the beauty of Pagan Greece and Rome. And now Christianity is born—born in Judæa among an ignorant and a barbarous people. Christ comes with words of love on his lips and a destroying sword in his hand. See the cross is in the hand of his servant the Church, and she goes among the poor, and her influence spreads until she climbs the throne of the Cæsars. And now she bears the crucifix in one hand and the sword in the other, and she reigns from the imperial throne. The crucifix is her symbol, and look at it well. A dead man hangs on the cross, turning men's thoughts to death instead of to life. See from his riven side flow water and blood, water for the tears that shall be shed for his sake, blood for the lives that shall be spilled in his name. See how she walks over Europe, the cross in her hand. The land is as the garden of Eden before her, but behind her a desolate wilderness. The arts decay; the schools disappear; all knowledge is withered at the breath of the Church. Intellectual death everywhere meets our eyes. Gloom and darkness envelope Christendom, darkness only lightened up by the lurid flames from the stake where the heretic is burning, and yet more lurid flame of the hell beyond the grave. But see, there is a gleam of light breaking through the blackness of the sky. It comes from Spain, where the followers of the false prophet are. Science is born, new born to bless the earth. But round the cradle of the infant Hercules gather the serpents of the Church, they hiss, and bite, and struggle; their fangs are the dungeon and the stake, and the child is in sore peril of life, but he fights and catches the hydra necks and strangles them, and the serpents no longer can bite. Yet the struggle is not over; it continues even till to-day. The crucifix is stricken to the earth, the sword is broken and dashed from the hands of the Church. It can no longer touch the body, it can only cramp the soul. But we will free the souls of men as we have freed their bodies. Instead of religion we will give them science. Instead of heaven we will give them earth. Instead of credulity we will give them knowledge. Instead of fear we will give them love. Love on the earth which Christianity has darkened instead of fear of the hell which the churches have dreamed. We raise a nobler temple and we bring a grander creed. Our morality is based on experience not on revelation, on man's needs not on god's command. Thus at length shall the world regain its old beauty, and it shall be beautiful because it shall be consecrated to man, and shall no longer be darkened because it belongs to god.

Mrs. Besant resumed her seat amid tremendous applause, accompanied by the waving of hats and handkerchiefs and shouts of "Bravo!" which continued for some minutes.

When silence was at length restored the Rev. A. Hatchard rose and said:—I trust you will have the courtesy of Englishmen on my motion to accord to Mr. Bradlaugh a hearty vote of thanks for his taking the chair here to-night. It is the first time I have been present on this platform before you, but I trust it will not be the last. I sincerely hope that Mrs. Besant and myself will meet again under similar circumstances in the early part of the coming year. There are one or two points to which I should like to refer——

The CHAIRMAN here rose and intimated that this could not be allowed.

Mr. HATCHARD (to the Chairman): May I just say one word respecting Strauss?

The CHAIRMAN: I say that I must stop anything but the mere motion.

Mr. HATCHARD then moved a vote of thanks to the Chairman which was seconded and put by Mrs. Besant, and carried unanimously with loud applause.

The CHAIRMAN briefly responded, thanking the audience for the attention paid on both nights, and declared the meeting closed.

THE

WORLD AND ITS GODS.

BY

ANNIE BESANT.

LONDON:

FREETHOUGHT PUBLISHING COMPANY,

63, FLEET STREET, E.C.

1886.

PRICE THREEPENCE.

LONDON:
PRINTED BY ANNIE BESANT AND CHARLES BRADLAUGH,
63, FLEET STREET, E.C.

THE WORLD AND ITS GODS.

There are many who acknowledge that Christianity has made for the retardation of scientific thought, the hindering of human progress. By thousands of educated men and women, the question I lately asked, "Is Christianity a success?" has been answered in the negative. Face to face with the evidence borne by history, honesty forces from them this one answer. They read of the countless frauds out of which struggled its "historical" books; of its success among the most ignorant and superstitious of an uninstructed populace; of the horrible crimes of its first imperial supporter; of the violence, treachery, and bribery by which it won its way through Europe; of its shocking barbarities towards heretics and unbelievers; of its crusades and its Inquisition; of its ferocious struggles against each new truth, and its fawning supple acceptance of each when it had won its way by agony and martyrdom. Glancing over Europe, they see that to-day the most backward and the most ignorant countries are those over which Christianity still rules unchallenged, while those which are in the van of civilisation are penetrated through and through with all the forms of scepticism, from moderate doubt of Biblical inspiration up to the most pronounced and aggressive Atheism. As the result of all this cumulative evidence, they pronounce Christianity to be a failure. But very many of them still cling to a belief in "God", whether as a "personal Deity", a "great First Cause", a "pervading Power" that "makes for righteousness", and is the Creator, Upholder, Father of all. They think that the world would be hopeless were it not for God, and that humanity walks the more strongly for leaning on a divine crutch. I propose to traverse this contention and to show, by surveying the Gods of the world, that they have been its hindrances rather than its helpers.

For what is God? He is the black cloud of the Unknown. Vast, stretching in every direction, brooding over existence from horizon to horizon, such was God in the childhood of the race. He was huge as its ignorance, omnipresent as its wonder and its fear. As man has grown in knowledge, God has diminished in extent. Each acquisition of new truth has lessened the domain of uncertainty over which he spreads. The telescope has chased him from his throne beyond the stars; navigation has left him no "heaven above" towards which prayer can be directed; the understood forces of nature render him unnecessary; "there is no" longer "need for such a hypothesis".

That man's belief in God was natural, and indeed inevitable, every student must admit. Theism is a stage through which the race must pass in its intellectual evolution. The supernatural, being the unknown portion of the natural, must needs play a large part in the thoughts of the race as it begins to study and to question. The Gods believed in will vary as their creators vary, some cruel, some brutal, some lustful, some noble, some beautiful, some stately. Men who desire to use God for personal gain will proclaim cruel Gods who need to be propitiated by sacrifice and gift; on the other hand, the most poetic and most advanced minds of a semi-civilised community will body out their best thoughts into God, will picture him as the realisation of their loftiest ideal, will claim his authority for their most beneficent legislation.

But while belief in God was inevitable, human progress has consisted in growing out of it. The advanced thought of each generation, the thought which moulded the intellect of the succeeding one, has ever been branded as Atheistic. For every popular God is the fossil of a dead thought, while the fresh living thought bodies itself into a new form, a higher God. So was Socrates Atheist in the eyes of the populace, though he had not reached what would be called Atheism to-day. In truth he was a Theist of type higher than his fellows, but being without *their* God he was to them without God.

In this survey of the world and its Gods we may class

them for convenience of presentation into: I. The world with Jewish Gods; II. The world with Pagan Gods; III. The world with Christian Gods; IV. The world with a Mahommedan God. Under the word Pagan I include all Gods that are not Jewish, Christian, or Mahommedan; but it is hardly necessary to say anything of the Gods of absolutely savage nations, such as Mumbo-Jumbo and his congeners; no European will probably be found to contend that belief in such as these is elevating.

I. The world with Jewish Gods.

"Gods," not "God", I have written advisedly, for the God of the earlier Hebrew mythology is a deity of lower type than the one of the later books. Were the Gods of the Jews a helping or a hindering force in the national development?

And first, be it noted, all religious wars were directly due to the national belief in Jahveh. They were waged wholly in his name and for his glory, and the terrible bloodshed attendant on them was essentially an offering to God. The Cherem, or sacred war, was a custom prevalent among all the tribes to which the Hebrew nation belonged. Moab carried out wars dedicated to Kemosh just as the Hebrews carried out wars dedicated to Jahveh. The characteristic of the war was the same in all cases—the total destruction of the people against whom it was waged, and of the whole of their property, animate and inanimate. Two instances of such wars will suffice.

The city of Jericho was declared "accursed [rather, as given in the margin, "devoted," with reference to Lev., xxvii., 28], even it, and all that are therein, to the Lord" (Joshua vi., 17); "And they utterly destroyed all that was in the city, both man and woman, young and old, and ox and sheep, and ass, with the edge of the sword. . . . And they burnt the city with fire, and all that was therein, only the silver, and the gold, and the vessels of brass and of iron, they put into the treasury of the house of the Lord" (verses 21 and 24). One of the Hebrews, however, stole some of the spoil devoted to Jahveh, and the offended deity would not again give victory to his people until he was appeased by the return of the spoil and the slaughter of his enemy and his family: "Joshua sent messengers, and they ran unto the tent; and behold, it was hid in his tent and the silver under it. And they took them out of the midst of the tent, and brought them unto Joshua, and unto all the children of Israel, and laid them out before the Lord. And Joshua, and all Israel with him, took Achan the son of Zerah, and the silver and the garment, and the wedge of gold, and his sons and daughters, and his oxen and his asses, and his sheep, and his tent, and all that he had; and they brought them unto the valley of Achor. And Joshua said, Why hast thou troubled us? The Lord shall trouble thee this day. And all Israel stoned him with stones and burned them with fire, after they had stoned them with stones" (vii., 22—25). The scene of horror can be imagined; the groaning men, the shrieking women, falling under showers of stones hurled at them by a mob drunk with religious fury; the unhappy brutes, rushing hither and thither, bewildered by the stony hail, trampling on each other and on their owners in their terror; at last nothing but a bruised, quivering mass of men, women, and brutes, moaning their lives out in torture; and Jahveh gloating over the scene of agony, propitiated by the awful sacrifice; "so the Lord turned from the fierceness of his anger" (verse 26).

The second instance, also selected as typical of many, is the sacred war against Amalek, recorded in 1 Sam. xv. The command from Jahveh ran: "Go and smite Amalek, and utterly destroy all that they have, and spare them not; but slay both man and woman, infant and suckling, ox and sheep, camel and ass" (verse 3). Saul, the king of Israel, did not carry out the divine command, but saved Agag, the king of the "devoted" nation, and some of the cattle. Samuel, the prophet of Jahveh, hereupon wrathfully reproved Saul for not obeying "the voice of the Lord", and declared, "thou hast rejected the word of the Lord, and the Lord hath rejected thee from being king over Israel" (verses 19 and 26). Moreover the brutal and pious Samuel actually "hewed Agag in pieces before the Lord in Gilgal" (verse 33), the sacred place where was one of Jahveh's altars.

The instances are, as above said, typical, not exceptional. The general command authorising the Cherem within Israel may be read in Deut. xiii., 12—18: "If thou shalt hear say in one of thy cities, which the Lord thy God hath given thee to dwell there, saying, Certain men, the children of Belial, are gone out from among you, and have withdrawn the inhabitants of their city, saying, Let us go and serve other Gods, which ye have not known; then shalt thou inquire, and make search, and ask diligently; and, behold, if it be truth, and the thing certain, that such abomination is wrought among you; thou shalt surely smite the inhabitants of that city with the edge of the sword, destroying it utterly, and all that is therein, and the cattle thereof, with the edge of the sword. And thou shalt gather all the spoil of it into the midst of the street thereof, and shalt burn with fire the city, and all the spoil thereof every whit, for the Lord thy God: and it shall be an heap for ever; it shall not be built again. And there shall cleave nought of the cursed [margin, devoted] thing to thine hand: that the Lord may turn from the fierceness of his anger, and show thee mercy, and have compassion upon thee, and multiply thee, as he hath sworn unto thy fathers; when thou shalt hearken to the voice of the Lord thy God, to keep all his commandments which I command thee this day, to do that which is right in the eyes of the Lord thy God."

Can it be said that the God who demanded such bloody service, was a God who promoted the civilisation of the Hebrew race?

The religious wars were by no means the only bloodshed directly due to Jahveh among the Jews. Whole classes of persons were condemned to death for offences which would have had no existence save for the belief in this ferocious deity.

I. *Unbelievers in him were all to be slain:* "He that sacrificeth unto any God, save unto the Lord only, he shall be utterly destroyed" (Ex. xxii., 20); "If thy brother, the son of thy mother, or thy son, or thy daughter, or the wife of thy bosom, or thy friend, which is as thine own soul, entice thee secretly, saying, Let us go and serve other Gods, which thou hast not known, thou nor thy fathers; namely, of the Gods of the people which are round about you, nigh unto thee, or far off from thee, from the one end of the earth, even unto the other end of the earth; thou shalt not consent unto him, nor hearken unto him; neither shall thine eye pity him, neither shalt thou spare, neither shalt thou conceal him; but thou shalt surely kill him;

thine hand shall be first upon him to put him to death, and afterwards the hand of all the people. And thou shalt stone him with stones, that he die; because he hath sought to thrust thee away from the Lord thy God, which brought thee out of the land of Egypt, from the house of bondage. And all Israel shall hear, and fear, and shall do no more any such wickedness as this is among you" (Deut. xiii., 6—11).

II. *All witches were to be slain.* "Thou shalt not suffer a witch to live" (Ex. xxii., 18). "A man also, or woman, that hath a familiar spirit, or that is a wizard, shall surely be put to death; they shall stone them with stones" (Lev. xx., 27).

III. *All Sabbath-breakers, who did work on Jahveh's day, were to be slain.* "Six days shall work be done, but on the seventh day there shall be to you an holy day, a Sabbath of rest to the Lord: whosoever doeth work therein shall be put to death (Ex. xxxv., 2, and see xxxi., 13—15). "And while the children of Israel were in the wilderness, they found a man that gathered sticks upon the Sabbath day. And they that found him gathering sticks brought him unto Moses and Aaron, and unto all the congregation: and they put him in ward, because it was not declared what should be done to him. And the Lord said unto Moses, the man shall be surely put to death: all the congregation shall stone him with stones without the camp. And all the congregation brought him without the camp, and stoned him with stones, and he died; as the Lord commanded Moses" (Numb. xv., 32—36).

IV. *All blasphemers were to be slain.* "The Israelitish woman's son blasphemed the name of the Lord and cursed. And they brought him to Moses; . . . . and they put him in ward, that the mind of the Lord might be showed them. And the Lord spake unto Moses, saying, Bring forth him that hath cursed without the camp; and let all that heard him lay their hands upon his head, and let all the congregation stone him. And thou shalt speak unto the children of Israel, saying, Whosoever curseth his God shall bear his sin. And he that blasphemeth the name of the Lord, he shall surely be put to death, and all the congregation shall certainly stone him: as well the stranger, as he that is born in the land, when he blasphemeth the name of the Lord, shall be put to death" (Lev. xxiv., 11—16).

V. *All who intruded into the priestly office, not being of Aaron's family, were to be slain.* "Thou shalt appoint Aaron and his sons, and they shall wait on their priest's office: and the stranger that cometh nigh shall be put to death" (Numb. iii., 10).

VI. *All who approached Jahveh's tabernacle, not being Levites, were to be slain.* "When the tabernacle setteth forward, the Levites shall take it down: and when the tabernacle is to be pitched, the Levites shall set it up: and the stranger that cometh nigh shall be put to death" (Numb. i., 51). Little wonder was it that the Israelites impatiently exclaimed to Moses: "Behold, we die, we perish, we all perish. Whosoever cometh any thing near unto the tabernacle of the Lord shall die: shall we be consumed with dying?" (Numb. xvii., 12, 13).

VII. *All who imitated the holy oil of Jahveh, or his incense, were to be slain.* "Whosoever compoundeth any like it [the oil], or whosoever putteth any of it upon a stranger, shall even be cut off from his people. . . . Whosoever shall make like unto that to smell thereto [the incense], shall even be cut off from his people (Ex. xxx., 33 and 38).

In all the cases named above there were absolute laws inflicting the death penalty. In addition to these, the readiness with which Jahveh slew his people when they were discontented was something marvellous. 14,700 were slain by plague for murmuring at the cruel slaughter of Korah and his company and of 250 men who offered incense (Numb. xvi., 49). 3,000 were slain by the sword for worshipping the golden calf, the Levites being commanded, "Consecrate yourselves to-day to the Lord, even every man upon his son and upon his brother; that he may bestow upon you a blessing this day" (Ex. xxxii., 28, 29). It is useless to accumulate the cases.

We must not omit from this sketch of the bloodshed due solely to belief in Jahveh, the terrible custom of direct human sacrifice. Abraham, the reverenced ancestor of the Jewish race, was blessed for his willingness to offer up his only son (Gen. xxii., 16—18), and this readiness was carried out to complete sacrifice among his descendants. Jephthah, having promised to offer "up for a burnt offering" whatsoever came out to meet him on his return home, and being met by his daughter, declared: "I have opened my mouth unto the Lord, and I cannot go back," and took her and "did with her according to his vow" (Judges xi., 31, 34, 35, 39). When the Lord sent a famine on Israel, and declared it was in punishment of Saul's crime, he was appeased when seven of Saul's family were "hanged in the hill before the Lord", and "after that, God was entreated for the land" (2 Sam. xxi., 1, 9, 14). The command to sacrifice human beings is found in Lev. xxvii., 28, 29: "No devoted thing that a man shall devote unto the Lord of all that he hath, both of man and beast, and of the field of his possession, shall be sold or redeemed: every devoted thing is most holy unto the Lord. None devoted, which shall be devoted of men shall be redeemed; but shall surely be put to death." Dr. Kalisch has written on this subject a learned and interesting essay, and speaking of the sacrifice of Jephthah's daughter he remarks that "the fact stands indisputable that human sacrifices offered to Jehovah were possible among the Hebrews long after the time of Moses" (Commentary, Leviticus, Part I., p. 391). After dwelling on the sacrifice of the sons of Saul, he alludes to that offered by Mesha, king of Moab, when hard pressed by the Jews, and points out that the withdrawal of the Jewish armies shows "the consternation into which the sacrifice, designedly performed in public, threw the troubled Hebrews," and says that "it remains an undeniable fact that the Israelites were terrified by the power, supposed to be irresistible, of the human sacrifice to such a degree, that they abandoned the certain prospects of victory" (Ibid, p. 394). He concludes that "it is, therefore, undoubted that human sacrifices were offered by the Hebrews from the earliest time up to the Babylonian period, both in honor of Jehovah and of heathen duties, not only by depraved idolators but sometimes even by pious servants of God; they probably ceased to be presented to Jehovah not much before they ceased to be presented at all; for being prized as deeds of singular piety, they were efficiently opposed and ultimately abolished only when the notions of piety itself were purified and refined" (Ibid, p. 396).

The penal code of the Jews, apart from offences against Jahveh, was bloody in the extreme, but that was due to their own savagery, not to their belief in God. They suffered, however, under the disadvantage that all their code was supposed to be given by him, and the sanction of religion perpetuated the barbarities which otherwise they might have more rapidly outgrown. Judging of their condition by their penal code, the Hebrews certainly did not need to be taught to add the death penalty for religious offences to the numerous death penalties adjudged for immoral acts; they were brutal enough without the added brutality of Jahveh. Of course Jahveh was but the reflexion of their own savagery, and my object in quoting their religious laws is merely to show how much added bloodshed was due to their belief in God.

The original God of the Jews was of a peculiarly brutal and ferocious type, brought as he was out of the desert and the hardships of a nomadic life. When we see him cursing man and his whole posterity for eating forbidden fruit; slaying all his creatures in a flood, save a few he selected to survive; ravaging Egypt with his plagues, and hardening the heart of its king so that he might have an ostensible reason for working them; sending sword and fire over Canaan, and strewing with the corpses of its inhabitants the fair land which "flowed with milk and honey"; we shrink back appalled at the monstrous shape, and marvel how man could worship one so revolting in his cruelty. When we come to glance at the facts of the neighboring and allied tribes we shall see how closely alike were the Gods of the Israelites, the Moabites, and the Canaanites.

As the more settled life of the Hebrews in Palestine gave opportunities of civilisation, and the Hebraic type became less barbarous and more human, Jahveh lost his most revolting features and became a comparatively civilised deity. The Gods share in the evolution of Man, and while religion has a retarding influence, it can never absolutely stop Man's upward growth.

II. The World with Pagan Gods.

Turning now to the study of the Gods worshipped by the tribes allied to the Hebrews we shall find them to resemble closely the terrible Jahveh of the latter people. In fact the highest deity of all these tribes bore the general name of El, recognisable equally in the Bethel of the Hebrews and the Bel of the Babylonians. But each had its special deity, its tribal God. Thus Israel had Jahveh, Moab had Kemosh, Ammon had Moloch, and all these tribal Gods were ferocious and bloodthirsty, Gods of the desert, of fire and of storm.

We have seen that human sacrifices were offered to Jahveh (p. 199); similar offerings were presented to Moloch and to Chemosh; as Jahveh claimed the firstborn, so were children "passed through the fire to Moloch". Just as the priests of Jahveh were "to cause the lamp to burn always" (Ex. xxvii., 20) before him, so was a fire kept ever burning on the altars of Moloch at Gades and at Tyre. Says Jules Soury in his essay on "The Religion of Israel", pp. 44, 45: "The worship and the rites of the religion of Jahveh are naturally those of Kemosh, Baal, Moloch, and Milcom, in short of the deities of all the other Terahite tribes, belonging to the same race and of the same psychological constitution as the Hebrews. How should the worship rendered by Israel to his national God differ from that rendered by Moab to his, when the race, the language, and the civilisation of these two Semitic families had arrived at almost the same stage of development? Among all these nations the idea of God was associated with that of fear; their Gods were the Gods of blood and of fire, of insatiable furnaces. The *Cherem*, which devoted to extermination the towns of infidels in revolt against Jahveh, and destroyed by fire everything, down to plants and animals, in order that the sacrifice might be worthy of deities so terrible, reveals the sinister and ferocious nature of the national God of Israel. Here again we may ask: How did the Cherem of the people of Jahveh (a part of the Mosaic institutions) differ from the Cherem of the people of Kemosh, which is known to us by the tablet of Mescha, the king of Moab? In both peoples we find the same religious frenzy of massacre and destruction. It was the will of the God. It was the holy war of Kemosh or of Jahveh."

Baal, again, was a God closely allied to Jahveh, Kemosh, and Moloch. Despite the professional jealousy of the priests and prophets of Jahveh, the Hebrews constantly offered sacrifices and incense to Baal, and the altars of Baal at Bethel drew worshippers from those of Jahveh at Jerusalem. Often both were worshipped together, much to the wrath of the more zealous Jahveists. The Phœnicians also worshipped Baal under the form of a metal bull, into whose brazen body were thrust the sacrificial victims, and therein they were roasted to death by a fire kindled round the symbol of the deity. In truth these various Gods are scarcely distinguishable from each other; each added to the world's sorrows by the bloodshed attendant on his worship, and the wars supposed to be commanded by him. Men slew each other in the names of their rival Gods, and race hatreds were embittered and prolonged by the celestial jealousies, which seemed to turn earthly quarrels into acts of piety towards the Gods.

But not only among the Hebrews and their congeners were human sacrifices offered to the Gods. The Greeks had their Iphigenia, as the Hebrews had their Jephthah's daughter; if the Phœnicians had their brazen bull, the Druids had their wickerwork figure in which they burned their offerings to their God. And there is one crime wrought for the sake of the Gods which cannot be omitted in the most cursory survey of the effects of religion on the world—the murder of Socrates. That noble and unique figure is swept off the world's stage enwrapt in a cloud from the Gods. As Atheist the hemlock-cup was pressed on him, and Greek religion robbed Greece of the teacher of Plato and of Xenophon.

Even on the other side of the world, the Gods were served in similar fashion. When Cortes invaded Mexico, he found human sacrifices common there. We read in Prescott's "Conquest of Mexico" of the sacrifices to Tezcatlepoca, in which the victim was stretched on his back on a block of jasper, with upper surface convex, and the high-priest opened his breast with a sharp razor and tore out his heart, throwing it at the feet of an image of the deity. The skulls of the victims were preserved as memorials of the sacrifices, and "the companions of Cortes counted one hundred and thirty-six thousand in one of these edifices". Go where we will, the footsteps of a God are stained with blood.

III. The World with Christian Gods.

Turning to the world with Christian Gods, we shall find reproduced the horrors of Jahveistic worship, the Cherem and the burnt-sacrifice.

First, it must not be forgotten that Christianity, the child of the Semitic races, is founded on a human sacrifice. The torture of Christ upon the cross and his death in agony was an expiatory sacrifice to an angry God. A fresh horror is added to the picture in that the sacrifice is that of a son to his own father; there is an exquisite refinement of cruelty in the notion of pleasure being taken by the parent in contemplating the anguish of his own child. The bloodthirsty nature of the Christian God is marked out with terrible distinctness in the epistle to the Hebrews: "By his own blood he entered in once into the holy place, having obtained eternal redemption for us . . . . without shedding of blood is no remission . . . . once in the end of the world hath he appeared to put away sin by the sacrifice of himself" (Heb. ix., 12, 22, 26). What more could be demanded by Moloch or by Kemosh, than the torture of the victim in the Prætorium and the cruel and prolonged death-agony on Calvary?

The Church founded on a human sacrifice, has demanded thousands of such sacrifices during its bloodstained existence. What were the burnings of heretics save burnt offerings to the Christian God, "acts of faith", as they were termed by the pious Spaniards.

Of all the Gods of the world, the Christian Gods have, perhaps, wrought the most harm, and this both because of their genealogy and of the doctrines of the religion which belongs to them. They descend from the Semitic deities, whose bloodthirsty and cruel characters have already been dealt with, and they inherit the qualities of their ancestors. And these qualities appear in the doctrines of the Christian religion. Christians worship the Hebrew Jahveh, with all his hideous cruelties: they believe that this God made a world and peopled it with sentient beings who prey upon each other; that he created a man and woman who he foreknew would become the parents of a fallen race; that he placed them in an environment which would mould them into "sinful" beings; that he gave an arbitrary command, the breach of which was to ruin them, but the wrongness of breaking which they were not to know until they had broken it; that when they had broken it, he cursed them for the act he foreknew and fore-ordained; that, not content with cursing them, he entailed his curse on their helpless innocent posterity; that the curse for the trifling act of eating some fruit by two people included heavy toil, pain, disease, death in this world, and unending torture in another, for countless millions unborn when their doom was pronounced; that, having brought about a detestable state of things in his own world, he drowned it in a fury, slaying all living beings, save a few whom he kept alive in order that the entail of the curse should not be broken; that the posterity of these selected ones turned out as badly as their fore-runners; that he threatened to burn the world up instead of drowning it again; that he sent his son to become a man, and then, as man, to suffer, to die in agony, that by his pain a few elected from the cursed race might escape the doom of the majority; that these "few chosen" shall be eternally happy, while the myriads of the lost shall suffer the inherited curse. This is the teaching of the Christian religion; these Gods, the Avenger and the Redeemer, are the Gods that the Christians worship. They have also a third, God the Holy Ghost, much overlooked and under-worshipped; and some of them, the great majority, believe in a fourth, a curious composite of incompatible attributes, a virgin and a mother, the creature of God yet his mother. The puzzle becomes yet more complex when we are taught that the son is "begotten of the father before all worlds", but is as old as his begettor; that the son is "conceived by the Holy Ghost", who is therefore presumably his father also; so that in the Trinity we have two fathers of different dates, one "before all worlds", and the other nine months B.C., of the same son, the first father being identical with the son ("I and my father are one"), and the second father being identical with the first father and the common son ("they are not three Gods, but one God")—the family arrangements being so complex that plain men can only gape at them, yet of such vital importance that "he therefore which will be saved must thus think of the Trinity". Think! Belief in the Trinity is the negation of thought.

Out of this chaos has been evolved the superstition and the ignorance of the Christian world. Those who cannot pretend to believe are accursed.

The whole biblical scheme of creation and divine providence is as revolting to morality as is its salvation to intelligence. The late Winwood Reade, in the "Outcast", has made on this a bitterly sarcastic and effective attack. A dreamer enters the kingdom of the Demigods, who amuse themselves by creating worlds much as earthly authors write plays. These works are submitted to a Demigod audience, and one of them is seen by the dreamer; of this a review appears in a Demigod periodical, and after describing the drama—which is the story of our own earth—a severe criticism is passed on the way in which progress has been produced in the animal world. "We are almost ashamed to explain a law which, in its recklessness of life and prodigality of pain, almost amounts to a crime. In cold forethought, the Creator so disposed the forces of nature that more animated beings were born than could possibly obtain subsistence on the earth. This caused a struggle for existence, a desperate and universal war; the best and improved animals were alone able to survive, and so in time Evolution was produced. We shall not deny that there is a kind of perverted ingenuity in the composition of this law; but the waste of life is not less clumsy than it is cruel. . . . Evil unhappily exists, and we do not condemn its employment in art. We are not in favor of those impossible dramas in which only the virtues are displayed. But we do condemn this confusion of evil and good, and maintain that nothing can be more immoral than to make crime the assistant of progress, and vice the seed of which virtue is the fruit. Again, Death is a useful and perhaps indispensable appliance in works of this kind, but so potent a means of exciting sympathy should be employed with moderation. Now what do we find here? The law of evolution is the law of death. Massacre is incessant; flowers, animals, and men die at every moment; the earth is a vast slaughter-house, and the ocean reddened with blood. Nor, incredible as it may seem, is that the worst. With a talent for torture which rouses our wonder only next to our disgust, the Creator has smitten the animated world, even to the insects, with numerous painful and lingering diseases, while the intellect is also afflicted with maladies peculiar to itself. The affections which at first would appear to afford some meagre consolation in the martyrdom of man are themselves too often the cause of mental pain and incurable despair. What can be said for such a world? What kind of defence or excuse can there be for its Creator? . . . Who could view that melancholy Earth, and those writhing masses of humanity; who could hear those agonising cries without a shudder of pain and a glow of honest indignation against the author of such woes and wrongs? Many of the audience withdrew, while others hooted the Creator, and at one time we thought his planet would be damned. . . . We do not wish to be too hard upon a young beginner whose talents cannot be disputed, and we trust that this critique, which is not unkindly meant, in spite of its severity, will induce him to reform. When next he produces a world let it be one which we can take our wives and daughters to see." Who can wonder that Christians should be cruel when they worship such a God as the Creator of the world!

Out of this cruelty of nature, and out of the belief in hell, have grown the horrible persecutions which have distinguished Christianity beyond every other creed. What other God can reckon among his victims so many of human kind as can the Christian? To him Spain offered up by fire her noblest sons from the fourth century to the eighteenth; her Inquisition offered to him 31,912 burnt sacrifices, each of a living human being; Germany, France, England, the Netherlands, all brought their burnt offerings, and for fourteen centuries Jahveh smelled a sweet savor of roasting human flesh. Torquemada and Ximenes were the very high priests of the Christian God; Torquemada's victims were 114,401, and of these 10,220 were burned alive: Ximenes offered his God 52,855. Spain's full total of sufferers came to 323,362 human beings. In addition to these, three millions of Jews and Moors were expelled from her soil, and many thousands of these died of privation. In the ninth century the Empress Theodora put to death 100,000 heretics. In the Netherlands Alva slew 18,000 heretics; in one year, Buckle tells us, 8,000 were executed or burned; and altogether more than 50,000 were offered to God. 14,000 Huguenots at least were slain in the massacre of St. Bartholomew in 1572. The hosts of slain heretics are practically innumerable. The command of Jahveh, "Thou shalt not suffer a witch to live," met with full obedience, and thousands of foolish human beings were burned and drowned and tortured to death for their supposed commerce with the evil one.

If from these judicial murders we turn to religious wars, to the *Cherem* of the Christian Gods, we shall find them as bloody as any of those of the more ancient deities. In the crusades alone the slaughter was horrible; Hallam puts that of the first as, "at the least computation," exceeding half a million on the Christian side, and says: "We should be warranted by contemporary authorities in stating the loss of the Christians alone during this period at nearly a million". We have no data for the loss among the invaded peoples, but we know that at the the taking of Jerusalem the Christians slaughtered men, women, and children, till none remained alive. When Bézières, a city of the Albigenses, was taken by the Catholics, 60,000 persons were slain. "Kill them all," quoth the leader, emulating Joshua; "God will know his own." Not a God of antiquity can hope to rival the Christian God in the huge roll of his victims.

Nor is bloodshed the only evil which must be ascribed to this terrible deity. The dense darkness of ignorance that shrouded Europe like a pall for centuries; the cruelty with which each effort to gain knowledge was crushed out; the poisoning of education with superstition after some slight education had at length been won; the diseases which scourged Christendom for its filth and its poverty, and were met with prayer instead of with knowledge; the poverty which was blessed by the priests and unshared by the Church; these horrors lie at the feet of the Christian Gods, in awful amount, piled up as offering.

Is it needful here to recount how Greek learning was crushed out by the Church as it grew strong? Justinian absolutely forbade the teaching of philosophy, and the famous Athenian schools were closed. Schools were only to be found, after a few conturies of Christianity, in connexion with cathedrals and monasteries, and these, according to Hallam, were "exclusively designed for the purposes of religion". According to the same authority, in a Council of the Church held A.D. 992, it was asserted "that scarcely a single person was to be found in Rome itself who knew the first element of letters. Not one priest of a thousand in Spain, about the age of Charlemagne, could address a common letter of salutation to another. In England Alfred declares that he could not recollect a single priest south of the Thames (the most civilised part of England) at the time of his accession who understood the ordinary prayers, or could translate Latin into his mother-tongue. Nor was this better in the time of Dunstan, when it is said none of the clergy knew how to write or translate a Latin letter" ("Europe during the Middle Ages," p. 596). Roger Bacon, in the 13th century, complains that mathematical instruments were not to be found among the Latins; that "the admirable books of Cicero De Republicâ are not to be found anywhere so far as I can hear, though I have made anxious enquiry for them in different parts of the world, and by various messengers. I could never find the works of Seneca, though I made diligent search for them during twenty years and more. And so it is with many more most useful books connected with the science of morals." But why accumulate facts so well known? What can be more eloquent than the one fact that for the twelve centuries of the domination of Christianity not one great scientific discovery was made in Christendom?

Even now their influence causes misery; broken hearts, marred lives, ruined homes, liberty outraged, honesty punished, slander virulent, hypocrisy wellnigh general, all these still bear witness to the maleficent power of the Christian Gods.

IV. The World with a Mahommedan God.

Of all the Gods of the world the Mahommedan God is the one who has done least mischief and most good. In his revelation, the Koran, there is brutality, but there is also much of generous feeling, of love of justice, of insistence on virtue. It is on the whole far superior in moral teaching to the Hebrew and Christian Scriptures, and the average Mahommedan trained in the Koran is a more upright, veracious, honest, and temperate man than the average Christian trained in the Bible. The contrast between the highminded generous Saracen and the treacherous bloodthirsty Christian during the crusades is known to every reader of history. It is probable that this superiority is largely due to the fact that in Mahommedanism there is little dogma and much attention to conduct. The unity of God and the apostleship of Mahomet are the only dogmas of the faith: "There is one God, and Mahomet is his prophet"; such is the simple and all-sufficient formula of the Mahommedan religion.

None the less does the Koran contain much which is wholly barbarous. Thus we find in it the same teaching as to hell that is prominent in the New Testament: "Verily, those who disbelieve our signs, we will surely cast to be broiled in hell fire; so often as their skins shall be well burned, we will give them other skins in exchange, that they may taste the sharper torment; for God is mighty and wise" (chap, iv.). "The companions of the left hand (how miserable shall the companions of the left hand be!) shall dwell amidst burning winds, and scalding fire, under shade of a black smoke, neither cool nor agreeable" (chap. lvi.). All Gods have these horrors for those who do not believe in them. It is needless to insist on the degradation which must follow belief in such doctrines.

Again, the Koran is disfigured by commands to war against infidels and to destroy them, although it does not go to the lengths of the Hebrew Scriptures, commanding the absolute destruction of all living things; on the contrary, those who yield are to be saved, and none are to be attacked without provocation having been given. "Fight for the religion of God against those who fight against you, but transgress not by attacking them first, for God loveth not the transgressors. And kill them wherever ye find them, and turn them out of that whereof they have dispossessed you; for temptation to idolatry is more grievous than slaughter: yet fight not against them in the holy temple, until they attack you therein; but if they attack you, slay them there. This shall be the reward of the infidels. But if they desist, God is gracious and merciful. Fight therefore against them, until there be no temptation to idolatry and the religion be God's: but if they desist, then let there be no hostility, except against the ungodly" (chap. ii.). "Think not that the unbelievers have escaped God's vengeance, for they shall not weaken the power of God. Therefore prepare against them what force ye are able, and troops of horse, whereby ye may strike a terror into the enemy of God, and your enemy, and into other infidels besides them, whom ye know not, but God knoweth them. And whatsoever ye shall expend in the defence of the religion of God, it shall be repaid unto you, and ye shall not be treated unjustly. And if they incline unto peace, do thou also incline thereto; and put thy confidence in God, for it is he who heareth and knoweth. . . . O prophet, stir up the faithful to war: if twenty of you persevere with constancy, they shall overcome two hundred, and if there be one hundred of you, they shall overcome a thousand of those who believe not; because they are a people which do not understand. . . . It hath not been granted unto any prophet, that he should possess captives, until he had made a great slaughter of the infidels in the earth" (chap. viii.). It is clear that these restrictions on warring against the unbelievers were not observed by the Mahommedans as their numbers grew, and that they spread their religion by the sword as did the Christians; but taking their history as a whole the Mahommedan nations have proved singularly unaggressive, though stubborn and heroic in self-defence. On this point Gibbon writes: "The military laws of the Hebrews are still more rigid than those of the Arabian legislator. The Lord of hosts marched in person before the Jews: if a city resisted their summons, the males, without distinction, were put to the sword: the seven nations of Canaan were devoted to destruction; and neither repentance nor conversion could shield them from the inevitable doom, that no creature within their precincts should be left alive. The fair option of friendship, or submission, or battle, was proposed to the enemies of Mahomet. If they professed the creed of Islam, they were admitted to all the temporal and spiritual benefits of his primitive disciples, and marched under the same banner to extend the religion which they had embraced" ("Decline and Fall of the Roman Empire," vol. vii., pp. 128, 129; Ed. 1809). While various trivial but humiliating restraints have been imposed on unbelievers in Mahommedan countries, yet the Christians have been left free to hold their own religion; and, while Christians persecuted and burned heretics, unbelievers of every sort, Christians included, lived peacefully under the milder rule of the followers of Mahomet.

Mahommedanism in the Koran shows the same anti-social spirit as does Christianity. "O true believers, take not the Jews or Christians for your friends; they are friends the one to the other; but whoso among you taketh them for his friends, he is surely one of them" (Chap. v.)

From time to time, but rarely, massacres, bloody as those wrought by Jews and Christians, disgraced the later religion. Mahomet, God's own prophet, forced 700 Jews into a huge grave prepared for them, and had them slaughtered under his own eyes—an exceptionally cruel act for the usually generous-tempered Arabian. When Damascus was taken by the Arabs, Caled charged down the streets of the city; "No quarter!" was his cry, "no quarter to the enemies of the Lord!" Happily his superior, Abu Obeidah, was of gentler mood, and swiftly stayed the slaughter. The instructions of Abukeker, the successor of Mahomet, to the chiefs of the Syrian army of invasion, are worthy of note: "Remember that you are always in the presence of God, on the verge of death, in the assurance of judgment, and the hope of paradise. Avoid injustice and oppression; consult with your brethren, and study to preserve the love and confidence of your troops. When you fight the battles of the Lord, acquit yourselves like men, without turning your backs; but let not your victory be stained with the blood of women or children. [Contrast the instructions of Moses to his captains, Numb. xvi.] Destroy no palm-trees, nor burn any fields of corn. Cut down no fruit-trees, nor do any mischief to cattle, only such as you kill to eat. When you make any covenant or article, stand to it, and be as good as your words. As you go on, you will find some religious persons who live retired in monasteries, and propose to themselves to serve God that way: let them alone, and neither kill them nor destroy their monasteries. And you will find another sort of people that belong to the synagogue of Satan who have shaven crowns [Christian priests]; be sure you cleave their skulls, and give them no quarter till they either turn Mahommedans or pay tribute" (Gibbon, vol. vii., pp. 188, 189).

The wonderful Moorish empire, and the scientific culture of the Arabs and Spanish Moors, have thrown a glory over the Mahommedan religion which does not altogether belong to it. The most earnestly pious Mahommedans were not favorable to learning, and the science of the Arabs and Moors was disapproved by the more zealous religionists. The story of the Khalif Omar's answer when Amrou sent to him to ask whether John Philoponus might be given the poor remnant of the once great Alexandrian library, is typical of the hatred ever shown to knowledge by religion. "If the books agree with the Koran, the

Word of God, they are useless, and need not be preserved; if they disagree with it, they are pernicious. Let them be destroyed." The story of the library of Alexandria after half of it had been destroyed in Cæsar's war, is, in truth, an impeachment of religion. "The Patriarchs of Alexandria had not only permitted but superintended the dispersion of almost all the rest. Orosius expressly states that he saw the empty cases or shelves of the library twenty years after Theophilus, the uncle of St. Cyril, had procured from the emperor Theodosius a rescript for its destruction. . . . . There can, then, be no more doubt that Omar did order the destruction of this library, under an impression of its uselessness or its irreligious tendency, than that the Crusaders burnt the library of Tripoli, fancifully said to have consisted of three million volumes. . . . Bigotry, however, has often distinguished itself by such exploits. The Spaniards burnt in Mexico vast piles of American picture-writings, an irretrievable loss; and Cardinal Ximenes delivered to the flames, in the squares of Granada, eighty thousand Arabic manuscripts, many of them translations of classical authors" (Draper's "Conflict of Religion and Science," 103, 104). Than this destruction of the literature of the past there is no worse crime against humanity. The books of the dead enshrine past phases of human history which are lost for ever in the destruction of the books. No human genius, no human skill, can ever fill up the gap in the history of the human race which has been made by the barbaric act of the Spaniards in Mexico. They murdered the past; and for that crime no atonement can ever be made. For all the centuries to come humanity is the poorer for their sin. Listen to the words of Milton: "Books are not absolutely dead things, but doe contain a potencie of Life in them to be as active as that Soule was whose progeny they are; nay, they doe preserve as in a violl the purest efficacie and extraction of that living intellect that bred them. I know they are as lively, and as vigorously productive, as those fabulous Dragons teeth; and being sown up and down, may chance to spring up armed men. And yet on the other hand unlesse warinesse be us'd, as good almost kill a Man as a good Booke; who kills a Man kills a reasonable creature, God's Image; but hee who destroyes a good Booke, kills Reason it selfe, kills the Image of

God, as it were, in the eye. Many a Man lives a burden to the Earth; but a good Booke is the pretious life-blood of a master spirit, imbalm'd and treasur'd up on purpose to a Life beyond Life. 'Tis true, no age can restore a Life, whereof perhaps there is no great losse; and revolutions of ages doe not oft recover the losse of a rejected Truth, for the want of which whole Nations fare the worse. We should be wary therefore what persecution we raise against the living labours of publick men, how we spill that season'd Life of Man preserv'd and stor'd up in Books; since we see a kinde of homicide may be thus committed, sometimes a martyrdome; and if it extend to the whole impression, a kinde of massacre, whereof the execution ends not in the slaying of an elementall Life, but strikes at that ethereall and fift [fifth] essence, the breath of the Reason itselfe, slaies an Immortality rather than a Life" ("Areopagitica," pp. 17, 18; Ed. 1819).

The Khalifs soon showed themselves lovers of education; thus, Haroun-al-Raschid, A.D. 786, ordered that every mosque should have a school in connexion with it. Al-Mamun, A.D. 813, collected books, and made the learned his companions: but when he ordered "his mathematicians and astronomers to measure a degree of a great circle upon it [the earth], Takyuddin, one of the most celebrated doctors of divinity of that time, denounced the wicked Khalif, declaring that God would assuredly punish him for presumptuously interrupting the devotions of the faithful by encouraging and diffusing a false and atheistical philosophy among them" (*Ibid*, p. 109). So true is it that religion is ever the foe of science. None the less may we say for Mahommedanism that it has done less harm than any other of the world's Theistic creeds.

Thus has the world fared at the hands of its Gods: useless bloodshed, needless discord, religious hatreds, delayed progress, all these come from the Gods. All that is hopeful with promise for the future comes from man's unaided efforts, man's strenuous labor. The day is coming, already its dawn is on the mountains of knowledge, when man shall live free in a

WORLD WITHOUT GOD.

LIFE, DEATH, AND IMMORTALITY.

BY

ANNIE BESANT.

LONDON:
FREETHOUGHT PUBLISHING COMPANY,
63, FLEET STREET, E.C.
1886.

PRICE TWOPENCE.

LONDON:
PRINTED BY ANNIE BESANT AND CHARLES BRADLAUGH,
63, FLEET STREET, E.C.

LIFE, DEATH, AND IMMORTALITY.

Of all the questions which, throughout the centuries, have escaped from the lips of man, there is none which has been asked with such persistence, none which has possessed interest more perennial, than "Whence do I come? Whither shall I go?" Man's origin, man's hereafter, have ever been of intensest interest to man. When Paulinus stood before Eadwine of Northumbria and preached the faith of Christ, it is said that an aged ealderman of Eadwine's court cried out: "As a swallow's flight across a lighted hall, so seems the life of man. The swallow flieth in at one door, tarrieth awhile in the light, and thereafter flieth out again into the darkness. So for a moment is the life of man in our sight, but of what it was before and what it shall be after we know nought. If the message of the stranger tell of this, let us hear it." As the flight of the swallow, from darkness to darkness, man's life has been in the past. Out of the darkness of the womb, into the darkness of the grave, man passes across his narrow strip of life. Two vast eternities stretch ocean-like on either side of the island of individual existence, and through the darkness that enshrouds them no human eye, it has been thought, could ever pierce. On this mystery religions have claimed to cast light, but the darkness has only been as a screen, on which the magic-lantern of faith has thrown strange figures, fanciful resemblances of human life on earth. In later time the true light of science has rippled over the space where darkness had reigned, and human life is seen to be no isolated phænomenon, but a part of one great cycle, wherein that which we call death is as natural as that which we call life.

The answers of the various religions of the world are all of the nature of guesses, and are unsupported by proven fact. Hinduism says that all life is an emanation from the divine existence; the creative power is ever emitting, ever reabsorbing, individual lives; it alone IS; all else is *maya*, illusion. Hence the reverence shown to all living things by the Brahmin; he will not slay the lowest creature, since it shares with him the divine essence, and all the forms with which the deity clothes itself are to him sacred.

Buddhism sees life as a state of unrest, each individual life passing through a circle of changes so long as it continues imperfect; the life rises through stage after stage, or if unworthy in one stage it is degraded to a lower for its next probation; at length, becoming perfect, it passes into Nirvana, is absorbed into the All. To escape from life's unrest, from the circle of existence, is the aim of the Buddhist philosopher; the unruffled serenity of unconsciousness is his goal; the loss of the One in the All is the hope on which his world-weary eyes are fixed.

These mystic Oriental religions are profoundly Pantheistic; one life pulsing through all living things; one existence bodying itself forth in all individual existences; such is the common ground of those mighty religions which number among their adherents the vast majority of human kind. And in this magnificent conception they are in accord with modern science; the philosopher and the poet, with the far-reaching glance of genius, caught sight of that unity of all things, "the One in the Many" of Plato, a belief which it is the glory of modern science to have placed upon the sure foundation of ascertained fact.

Hebraism, a growth so curiously crude when regarded in the light of the elaborated creeds of the surrounding cults, had no idea of this grandiose view of human life. To it the value of life lay in life's pleasures. The joy of a man in a woman, not in *the* woman but in the sex alone; the delight in wine and flesh, in overbrimming treasure-bin, in "basket and store"; the pride of laden orchard and golden heads of corn; the gladness in the autumn ripening, and in the gathering for the winepress, and in the foaming torrent of the trodden fruit; all these—glad and beautiful truly as they are, but not the greatest gladness or the fairest beauty of human life—were to the Hebrew the one thing needful, the sign of the favor of the Most

High. And it was not the sheer beauty of them all, not the radiance of the glad exuberance of Nature; but rather the physical comfort and the luxurious enjoyment which they promised; the rich flavor of the purple scented draught, rather than the gracious beauty of the vine-tendrils, and the exquisite contrast of color in the deep ruby of the grape-juice and the brown and creamy ancles around which it bubbled under the rays of the setting sun.

In horrible contrast with the scenes in which he delighted stood to the Hebrew—the grave. His sensuous, or rather his sensual, delight in life gave a vivid horror to his shrinking from death, from the worm and the corruption, the silence and the gloom. Therefore Hezekiah turned his face to the wall, weeping, when he was like to die, and on his recovery he cried: "The grave cannot praise thee; death cannot celebrate thee: they that go down into the pit cannot hope for thy truth. The living, the living, he shall praise thee, as I do this day" (Is. xxxviii., 18, 19).

The Hebrew, ere he came into contact with the more cultured Babylonians, had no idea of immortality. To him death was the end of the individual life. The blessings and the curses of his God applied only to human life. Nothing can be plainer than the declarations of Solomon, "the wisest of men", regarding the end of personal consciousness. "The living know that they shall die: but the dead know not anything, neither have they any more a reward, for the memory of them is forgotten. Also their love, and their hatred, and their envy, is now perished: neither have they any more a portion for ever in anything that is done under the sun. . . . . Whatsoever thy hand findeth to do, do it with thy might; for there is no work, nor device, nor knowledge, nor wisdom, in the grave, whither thou goest" (Eccles. ix., 5, 6, 10). "That which befalleth the sons of men befalleth beasts; even one thing befalleth them; as the one dieth, so dieth the other; yea, they have all one breath; so that a man hath no pre-eminence above a beast: for all is vanity. All go unto one place: all are of the dust, and all turn to dust again. Who knoweth the spirit of man that goeth upward, and the spirit of the beast that goeth downward to the earth? Wherefore I perceive that there is nothing better, than that a man should rejoice in his own works; for that is his portion: for who shall bring him to see what shall be after him?" (Ibid, iii., 19—22). It would be impossible to put into words a more complete negation of immortality.

After the Babylonian captivity, the books of the Hebrews change their tone, and a life after death becomes a definite object of belief. "The souls of the righteous are in the hand of God, and there shall no torment touch them. In the sight of the unwise they seemed to die; and their departure is taken for misery, and their going from us to be utter destruction: but they are in peace. For though they be punished in the sight of men, yet is their hope full of immortality. And having been a little chastised, they shall be greatly rewarded: for God proved them, and found them worthy for himself" (Wisdom iii., 1—5).

Christianity inherited this idea of personal immortality, and adding thereto the asceticism of the Essenes, it described this world as a state of probation and death as a release, as the gate of everlasting joy. "Having a desire to depart and to be with Christ; which is far better" (Phil. i., 23). "Looking for and hasting unto the coming of the day of God" (2 Peter iii., 12). To the true Christian life is only valuable as a preparation for death, and before the vast range of eternity human life shrivels to a span.

From these manifold religions, with their unproven assertions, their dogmatic spurious revelations, let us turn to Science, in whose "light we shall see light".

Scientifically regarded, life is not an entity, but a property; it is not a mode of existence, but a characteristic of certain modes. Life is the result of an arrangement of matter, and when re-arrangement occurs the former result can no longer be present; we call the result of the changed arrangement death. Life and death are two convenient words for expressing the general outcome of two arrangements of matter, one of which is always found to succeed the other.

The difficulty found in defining life is due to this fact; properties are far harder to define than things; thus it is harder to define color than to define rose. And the difficulty is increased when the property varies much in different cases, and all the varieties are called by the same name: the activities of the oyster and the man, of the elephant and of the rotifer, differ considerably, yet we call the totality of these activities in each case "life". On this Dr. Maudsley well says: "It is desirable to examine into that which is generally deemed to constitute the specialty of life. Now it is certain, when we consider the vast range of vitality, from the simple life of a molecule or cell to the complex life of man, that valid objections may be made to any definition of life. If it be wide enough to comprise all forms, it will be too vague to have any value; if narrow enough to be exact, it will exclude the most lowly forms. The problem is, to investigate the conditions of the manifestation of life. A great fault in many attempted definitions has been the description of life as a resistance or complete contrast to the rest of nature, which was supposed to be continually striving to destroy it. But the elements of organic matter are not different from those of the inorganic, whence they are derived and to which they return; and the chemical and mechanical forces of these elements cannot be suspended or removed within the organism. What is special is the manner of composition of the elements; there is a concurrence of manifold substances, and they are combined or grouped together in a very complex way. Such union or grouping is, however, only a further advance upon, and by no means a contrast to, the kind of combination which is met with in inorganic bodies. Life is not a contrast to non-living nature, but a further development of it. The more knowledge advances the more plainly is it shown that there are physical and chemical processes upon which life depends. Heat is produced by combustion in the organism, as it is in the fire; starch is converted into sugar there, as it is in the chemical laboratory; urea, which is so constant a product of the body's chemistry, can be formed artificially by the chemist; and the process of excitation in a nerve, on the closure of a constant stream, appears to be analogous to the process o electrolysis, in which hydrogen is given off at the negative pole. The peculiarity of life is the complexity of combination in so small a space, the intimate operation of many simultaneously acting forces in the microcosm of the organic cell." ("Body and Mind", p. 162.)

It is perhaps a little difficult for the non-chemical reader to appreciate the extreme difference of results that may flow from mere re-arrangement of the atoms forming a substance. Even in the case of a single element, we may have very different bodies consisting of it alone, different because of some differences of combination of its atoms; thus a lump of the element carbon may be lampblack, or graphite, or diamond, according to whether it is amorphous (without form, *i.e.* non-crystalline), or is a rhombohedral or an octohedral crystal. Yet a non-chemist would scarcely identify the carbon which sparkles on his finger in a diamond, with that in the pencil with which he writes, or that which floats down on his paper from a smoky chimney. It has been found, also, that the mere action of heat will suffice to turn into a product characteristic of animal bodies, urea, a body that can be built up from its elements. If ammonium cyanate, thus obtained, be heated, a change of arrangement of its atoms takes place, and urea is formed.

$$\left.\begin{matrix} H_4N \\ CN \end{matrix}\right\} O \text{ heated} = CO \left\{\begin{matrix} H_2N \\ H_2N \end{matrix}\right.$$

Ammonium cyanate. Urea.

The reactions given by these bodies are quite different, yet each is composed of four atoms of hydrogen (H), one of carbon (C), one of oxygen (O), two of nitrogen (N). It is the *grouping* which causes the difference of the results. Such bodies as these are called isomerides (or sometimes metameres), and these isomerides become more numerous as the compounds forming them become more complex. Now organic compounds are, as a rule, far more complex than inorganic, and this complexity has probably, as Maudsley suggests, much to do with life. The more complex a compound is the more unstable it is, the readier to break up and recombine into new forms; in a living body this disassociation and re-association are ceaselessly going on; these rapid constant chemical changes are one of the conditions of life.

We may borrow an illustration from another science to show how result depends upon arrangement of matter. Everyone knows the exquisite irridescence of mother-of-pearl, the tender delicate hues which melt into each other, glowing with soft radiance. How different is the dull dead surface of a piece of wax. Yet take that dull black wax and mould it so closely to the surface of the mother-of-pearl that it shall take every delicate marking of the shell, and when you raise it the seven-hued glory shall smile at you from the erstwhile colorless surface. For though it be to the naked eye imperceptible, all the surface of the mother-of-pearl is in delicate ridges and furrows, like the surface of a newly ploughed field; and when the waves of light come dashing up against the ridged surface they are broken like the waves on a shingly shore, and are flung backwards, so that they cross each other and the oncoming waves; and as every ray of white light is made up of waves of seven colors, and these waves differ in length each from the others, the fairy ridges fling them backward separately and each ray reaches the eye by itself; so that the color of the mother-of-pearl is really the spray of the lightwaves, and comes from arrangement of matter once again. Give the dull black wax the same ridges and furrows, and its glory shall differ in nothing from that of the beautiful shell.

To apply our illustration: as the color belongs to one arrangement of matter and the dead surface to another, so life belongs to some arrangements of matter, and is their resultant, while the resultant of other arrangements is death.

Once grasp this view of life, and the question "Where does the life go to at death?" becomes meaningless. A result "goes" nowhere when its cause is no longer present; it simply ceases. Raise a gas to incandescence, and the result is light; shut the gas off, and the light goes out; it does not go somewhere else, and continue as light in some other sphere; you have removed the cause, and the effect ceases. When the combinations and disassociations of compounds in the body cease to go on within certain limits, life ceases, and other phænomena set in which we class together as death.

Further, the degree of life varies with the complexity of the combination and the co-ordination of many diverse organs. The life of the vegetable differs in much from the life of the animal, when we compare together the complex organisms of the vegetable and animal kingdoms. The simple organisms of each are almost indistinguishable, and the simplest organisms which exist form the common stem of the two diverging branches of living things. The life of the single cell consists in very limited activities; how far it is "conscious" who shall say? the organism moves, feeds, and reproduces itself; it has no senses, no nerves, no muscles, no digestive or respiratory or circulatory system;

yet it lives. Stage by stage the simple is succeeded by the complex; cells unite to form tissues, first of similar cells; then differences arise in the cells from differences of external conditions; pressure, contact, action of heat and light, all help to modify the various cells, and differentiated tissues are gradually formed. These differentiated tissues perform different works, and the activities of the body increase—the life increases. Yet another complexity arises; these differentiating tissues become co-ordinated in their growth; integration proceeds step by step with differentiation; until, in the most highly evolved organism, we have the greatest complex of activities working in perfect harmony, and the totality of these forms the life of the human being. He shares "life" with the Amœba, but what definition can adequately include the twain?

If life be thus analysed, what is to be said of death? Death is re-arrangement; it is the disassociation of the compounds whose resultant was life; the breaking up of the complex organic products, and their gradual resolution into the simpler inorganic forms; until the living body, with its compounds of wonderful variety and intricacy, is resolved through stage after stage of ever-increasing simplicity into those ultimate fates of all living things, carbon dioxide, water, and ammonia; and then these recommence the upward building once more.

Nor are the changes we call death simultaneous over the whole body; the body does not die at once; it dies gradually, tissue after tissue. The muscles die when their semi-fluid substance begins to coagulate, and the *rigor mortis* sets in; the glandular tissues die later, and they work (and are therefore living), as every nurse knows, for some little time after "death"; hair and nails grow in similar fashion; the brain is sometimes dead ere the body is regarded as a corpse. It is the death of the heart and lungs only that is recognised as "death"; when the pulse ceases, and when the mirror held to the lips is not dulled by a breath, then the bystanders say: "He is gone". And in this there is some truth, since with the ceasing of the circulation and with the non-supply of oxygen to the tissues chemical changes must set in in them all, which tend to disintegration. And though some few tissues may for a brief while continue to live, yet their life must needs be very limited; the nervous system cannot work without the gaseous and solid materials brought to it by the blood, and when the nervous stimulus is withdrawn life must cease, even in the lowest tissues. But it is interesting to note that the tissues in which life persists the longest are those whose cells most resemble the lower cellular forms of living things. Retaining more independence, they do not at once die with the death of the higher tissues.

It is obvious that if the reasoning applied to life and death in the preceding pages be accepted, the word "immortality" is not predicable of any of the material arrangements there spoken of. Nor, indeed, do the believers in immortality now claim it for what they call the "perishable body". It is true that in the Apostles' Creed, accepted by the whole Catholic Church, Christians constantly repeat their belief in "the resurrection of the body", as well as in "the life everlasting". It is true that in the Visitation of the Sick, in the authorised Book of Common Prayer, the priest is directed to examine the sick person as to his belief, and to ask: "Dost thou believe in . . . . the resurrection of the flesh; and everlasting life after death?". And to this the sick person answers: "All this I stedfastly believe". But it is very generally understood that these words must be taken in a non-natural sense, and that while they may have, and indeed did, represent the belief of the very ignorant primitive Christians, they are absolutely meaningless at the present day. Knowing, as we now do, what becomes of "the body", "the flesh"; knowing that it passes through various stages of "decay", that is, of disassociation and recombination into simpler and simpler forms, until water, ammonia, and carbon dioxide are all that remains; knowing that many of the intermediate products have been taken up by the roots of plants, and have been broken up and recombined in the wonderful chemical laboratory of the vegetable cells, and that these ultimate products will have the same fate; knowing that many of the vegetables thus built up have supplied food to animals —is not the churchyard a favorite pasture-ground for sheep in many country districts?—and that these animals have in their turn formed food for man, and have thus built the materials of past generations into the living tissues of the present: knowing all this, how can the Christian say with full faith: "I believe in the resurrection of the flesh"?

That some curious heredity of faith does act on the nineteenth century Christian mind—at least when that mind is episcopal—may be surmised from the ground set forth by Dr. Wordsworth, late Bishop of Lincoln, as that on which he founded his antagonism to the wholesome and decent disposal of the bodies of the dead by cremation. The Bishop alleged that the destruction of the body by fire would tend to produce doubt in the minds of the faithful touching the resurrection of the flesh; and he certainly thereby showed some obscure idea that the very body placed in the grave had some future resurrection in store for it. Yet he must most surely have known that the work wrought swiftly by the flames in the crematorium is slowly, but no less completely, wrought on the buried corpse beneath the ground; and that while the one is more manifest to the eye than is the other, the ultimate result differs not.

The later Jews and the Egyptians—from both of which nations Christianity took much of its creed—were firm believers in the absolute resurrection of the body. The curious vision of the valley of dry bones, narrated in Ezekiel xxxvii., may be taken as a partial rehearsal of the expected resurrection drama. And the Jews held the curious fancy that one very hard bone in the human skeleton—named from this belief the *os sacrum*, or holy bone—never suffered decay, but remained as a nucleus for the resurrection body; which would be formed therefrom, I presume, as Eve was formed from out a rib. The Egyptians did not trust to a single bone; they preferred to ensure the continuance of the whole body. Hence their custom of embalming the dead, so that the spirit on the resurrection morning might not fail of lodgment in its own dwelling-place. And I cannot help thinking that if there is really to be a resurrection of the flesh, the Egyptians were far more rational than modern-day Christians. For under the present plan, we use up our ancestors' bodies for the building of our own frames, as countrymen use the stones from ruined castles to make walls for their fields; and it will be no more possible for everyone to reclaim the materials which erstwhile formed his body, than it would be to build up both castle and walls at the same moment out of the same stones.

Apart, however, from any of these fables of the resurrection of the flesh, there exists a widespread belief in the prolongation of the individual consciousness after death. Man is regarded as consisting of two things, a body and a spirit; the body is considered to be dead *per se*, and the spirit is the living agent which animates the body, inhabiting it and using it as an instrument, as a man goes into an animal in a pantomime, and gives to the inanimate piece of mechanism the gestures of the living creature. It is this spirit for which immortality is now alone claimed by the educated; it is this which "leaves the body" at death, and which, "freed from the burden of the flesh", continues to exist while its former body decays, and will, it is alleged, continue to exist for ever.

Now to this claim it might be sufficient to say, "Not proven"; for the duty of proving an allegation lies on the person who makes it, not on the one who declines to accept it without some demonstration being brought forward in its support. On this, again, Dr. Maudsley speaks with admirable sense and clearness: "The burden of proving that the *Deus ex machinâ* of a spiritual entity intervenes somewhere, and where it intervenes, clearly lies upon those who make the assertion, or who need the hypothesis. They are not justified in arbitrarily fabricating an hypothesis entirely inconsistent with experience of the orderly development of nature, which even postulates a domain of nature that human senses cannot take any cognisance of, and in then calling upon those who reject their assumption to disprove it" (Body and Mind, p. 162).

Let us see how far mental activity, which is the supposed domain of the "spirit", is dependent on the bodily organisation. When the babe is born, it shows no sign of mind. For a brief space hunger and repletion, cold and warmth, are its only sensations. Slowly the specialised senses begin to function; still more slowly muscular movements, at first aimless and reflex, become co-ordinated and consciously directed. There is no sign here of an intelligent spirit controlling a mechanism; there is every sign of a learning and developing intelligence, developing *pari passu* with the organism of which it is a function. As the body grows the mind grows with it, and the childish mind of the child develops into the hasty, quickly-judging, half-informed, unbalanced youthful mind of the youth; with maturity of years comes maturity of mind, and body and mind are vigorous and in their prime; as old age comes on, and the bodily functions decay, the mind decays also, until age passes into senility, and body and mind sink into second childhood. Has the immortal spirit decayed with the organisation, or is it dwelling in sorrow bound in its "house of clay"? If this be so, the spirit must be unconscious, or else separate from the very individual whose essence it is supposed to be; for the old man does not suffer when his mind is senile, but is contented as a little child. And not only is this constant simultaneous growth and decay of body and mind to be observed, but we know that mental functions are disordered and suspended by various physical conditions. Alcohol, many drugs, fever, disorder the mind; a blow on the cranium suspends its functions, and the "spirit" returns with the surgeon's trepanning. Does the "spirit" take part in dreams? Is it absent from the idiot, from the lunatic? Is it guilty of manslaughter when the madman murders, or does it helplessly watch its own instrument performing actions at which it shudders? If it can only work here through an organism, is its nature changed in its independent life, severed from all with which it was identified? Can it, in its "disembodied state", have anything in common with its past?

Professor Clifford, in his essay on the "Unseen Universe" criticises the notion of a supposed ether which prepares for the life immortal. "Far greater, indeed, is the work which the second ether has to perform: nothing less than the fashioning of a 'spiritual body'. While our consciousness proceeds *pari passu* with molecular disturbance in our brains, this molecular disturbance agitates the first ether, which transfers a part of its energy to the second. Thus is gradually elaborated an organism in that second or unseen universe, with whose motions our consciousness is as much connected as it is with our material bodies. When the marvellous structure of the brain decays, and it can no more receive or send messages, then the spiritual body is replete with energy, and starts off through the unseen, taking consciousness with it, but leaving its molecules behind. Having grown with the growth of our mortal frame, and preserving in its structure a record of all that has befallen us, it becomes an organ of memory, linking the future with the past, and securing a personal immortality. Can another body, then, avail to stay the hand of death, and shall man by a second nervous system escape scot free from the ruin of the first? We think not. The laws connecting consciousness with changes in the brain are very definite and precise, and their necessary consequences are not to be evaded by any such means. Consciousness is a complex thing made up of elements, a stream of feelings. The action of the brain is also a complex thing made up of elements, a stream of nerve-messages. For every feeling in consciousness there is at the same time a nerve-message in the brain. This correspondence of feeling to nerve-message does not depend on the feeling being part of a consciousness, and the nerve-message part of the action of a brain. How do we know this? Because the nervous system of animals grows more and more simple as we go down the scale, and yet there is no break that we can point to and say, 'above this there is consciousness or something like it; below there is nothing like it'. Even to those nerve-messages which do not form part of the continuous action of our brains, there must be simultaneous feelings which do not form part of our consciousness. Here, then, is a law which is true throughout the animal kingdom; nerve-message exists at the same time with feeling. Consciousness is not a simple thing, but a complex; it is the combination of feelings into a stream. It exists at the same time with the combination of nerve-messages into a stream. If individual feeling always goes with stream of nerve-messages, does it not follow that when the stream of nerve-messages is broken up, the stream of feelings will be broken up also, will no longer form a consciousness? does it not follow that when the messages themselves are broken up, the individual feelings will be resolved into still simpler elements? The force of this evidence is not to be weakened by any number of spiritual bodies. Inexorable facts connect our consciousness with this body that we know; and that not merely as a whole, but the parts of it are connected severally with parts of our brain-action. If there is any similar connexion with a spiritual body, it only follows that the spiritual body must die at the same time with the natural one. Consider a mountain rill. It runs down in the sunshine, and its water evaporates; yet it is fed by thousands of tiny tributaries, and the stream flows on. The water may be changed again and again, yet still there is the same stream. It widens over plains, or is prisoned and fouled by towns; always the same stream; but at last

'even the weariest river
Winds somewhere safe to sea!'

When that happens, no drop of the water is lost, but the stream is dead."

BIBLICAL BIOLOGY.

A CONTRIBUTION TO RELIGIOUS NON-SCIENCE.

By ANNIE BESANT.

"Avoiding profane and vain babblings, and oppositions of science, falsely so-called."—1 Tim. vi., 20.

In these later days, when science is carrying devastation into the land of faith, and godless education is everywhere offering the fruit of the tree of knowledge to the children of men, it behoves those who still cling to the faith once delivered to the saints to offer such small aid as they may in defending the citadel of Christianity, the Holy Bible, against its foes. And above all things is it necessary to know thoroughly what is in the Bible, so that those who "turn the Bread of Life into stones to cast against their enemies" may not suddenly shoot one out of an unsuspected catapult. Let us search the Scriptures, as did the noble Bereans, and we shall be rewarded by discovering therein biological facts that we shall never find if we confine ourselves to works written by mere uninspired scientific men.

And, first, let us reject with indignation the idea that the Bible is not written to teach us science. All that is in the Bible is written "for our learning" (Rom. xv., 4), and if scientific statements are made therein they must be made for our instruction. It is not conceivable that when "holy men of God spake as they were moved by the Holy Ghost" (2 Peter i., 21) they spake wrong. The very thought is blasphemy, and must be at once rejected by every reverent mind. How should we be able to trust the Bible in its revelations about heaven if we refuse to credit its revelations about earth? If it is worthy our faith in celestial matters, surely we may believe it in matters terrestrial. If it is to be our guide to eternal, much more must it be our guide to temporal, truths. Surely no one will be foolish enough to accept a light to his feet and a lamp to his paths (see Ps. cxix., 105) if that light is delusive on the road along which he walks, and only throws a glare on the far-off mountains beyond the river of death?

No! Against all such "oppositions of science falsely so-called" let us set our faces as flint (see Isa. l., 7). Give up one of these precious words, and we give up all. If God has not "at sundry times and in divers manners" spoken "in times past unto the fathers by the prophets" how can we be sure that he "hath in these last days spoken unto us by his Son" (Heb. i., 1, 2)? Rather let us "receive with meekness the engrafted word which is able to save" our "souls" (James i., 21), and thank God, who has hidden these things from the wise and prudent Darwins and Huxleys, and has revealed them unto babes (see Matt. xi., 25).

Gen. i. contains some biological facts of great interest and novelty. Herein we learn that trees brought forth fruit, and herbs yielded seed, and the earth brought forth grass, before the sun existed to "divide the day from the night" (verses 11—14). These were the first living things that existed on the earth. At that time there was no animal life in existence; no sound of life broke the silence of those vast woods; for two days the vegetable world triumphed in security; no snail smeared the delicate fronds of the fern; no caterpillar ate the dainty new-born leaves; no sparrow pecked the cherry; no blackbird feasted on the strawberry. Dogmatic science asserts that these grasses and herbs and fruit-trees could not have brought forth their seeds and fruits without the sunrays, but Genesis knows better. Foolhardy science produces miserable pieces of rock, containing fossil animals older than any plants, and sets them against our glorious revelation. But are men moles or rabbits, that they should burrow in the earth and bring out these deceiving pebbles which God mercifully hid out of sight, clearly showing that he intended them to be out of mind? Far better leave the earth as God made it, and live on the surface, where God placed us. The fossils cannot injure the moles, whereas it is plain that they are a serious danger to a child-like faith. Are we not told that except we "become as little children" we "shall not enter into the kingdom of heaven" (Matt. xviii., 3), and I ask you, as sensible persons, "I speak as to wise men, judge ye what I say" (1 Cor. x., 15), would any child you ever heard of trouble its little head about Terebratula biplicata, Thecodontosaurus, Pterodactylus crassirostris, Noeggerathia cuneifolia, Homalonotus Delphinocephalas, Gorgonia infundibuliformis? Would not the mere names be enough to bring on croup? And if we are to become as little children, is it not clear that creatures possessing names of this description are, by the merciful dispensation of Providence, stamped as utterly inappropriate to our present state?

There is one beautiful suggestion, it would be going too far to call it thought, of a man of God, which the truly pious may well ponder over. It is this. Perhaps God created the earth, just as it is, full of fossils, placing these apparent records of the past out of the sight of simple people, but ready to entrap the carnal geologist, as it is written: "He taketh the wise in their own craftiness" (1 Cor. iii., 19). Who can say that fossils are not among the means prophesied of by Paul when he says that "God shall send them strong delusion, that they should believe a lie: that they all might be damned" (2 Thess. ii., 11)? At any rate, no one ever alleges that people will be damned for refusing to believe in fossils, while if Christianity be true, people may be damned for believing them, and it is surely wiser to be on the safe side. Fossils would be no consolation in hell, especially as they would probably all become metamorphic rocks.

It is most interesting and comforting to know that God gave man and woman "dominion over the fish of the sea, and over the fowl of the air, and over every living thing that moveth upon the earth" (Gen. i., 23). It is a little difficult, perhaps, for a man to exercise this dominion when his leg is seized by a shark, or his body is carried off by a tiger; but doubtless if he reminded the animals of Gen. i., 28, they would at once mend their ways, and restore his property.

Gen. ii., 21, 22, are verses that have been the source of wide-spread error—I mean of divine correction of so-called science. Adam clearly went through life short of one rib, and it has been generally supposed that his sons have inherited this peculiarity, and that man has normally an uneven number of ribs, twelve on one side and eleven on the other, thus affording a beautiful hereditary proof of ancestral generosity. This pious faith has been rudely shaken by the study of anatomy, and by the unpleasant discovery that the number of male ribs is not odd; it now exists only, I fear, in country villages where science classes under South Kensington have not yet exerted their sceptic-making influence, and where people do not enquire too curiously into their internal arrangements.

Gen. iii. presents us with a pleasant picture of intercourse with the lower animals before the fall of our first parents brought sin into the world. What does scientific zoology know of a talking serpent? Can any scientist of to-day pretend that he has ever met with a specimen able to talk? Yet this remarkable snake talked with great effect, and we owe to his well-directed eloquence the inestimable blessing by which, as God said, "the man is become as one of us, to know good and evil" (v. 22). The serpent in question was remarkable in ways other than his gift of speech. After God had cursed him, he went about as snakes do now, but before that he progressed on his back, or his head, or his tail, in a manner since become as old-fashioned as the minuet.

The tree of knowledge of good and evil, and the tree of life, are plants quite beyond the reach of modern botany. It would have been a priceless blessing for mankind if Adam and Eve had smuggled some cuttings of these out of the garden, for knowledge now has to be painfully acquired, while life closes when experience has brought its highest utility. It is, perhaps, comforting to know that in the middle of the street of the throne of God and of the Lamb, and on either side of the river, there is a tree of life (Rev. xxii., 1, 2), which bears a different sort of fruit every month—proving incidentally how very much horticulture has advanced in that neighborhood—but the thought intrudes, despite all effort, that we could dispense with the tree of life after we have risen to immortality, while it would be invaluable to us as mortals here. It requires great faith to feel that God is good in withholding the tree of life while it would be useful, and in giving it to us when it will be superfluous.

Gen. xxx., 37—42, gives some suggestions which breeders of cattle will find useful. Peeled rods of green poplar, hazel, and chesnut will influence the color of the young of sheep and cattle. There is no reason why they should, and the whole idea is absurd, but we are assured that by this means Jacob cheated his uncle Laban in the most scandalous manner.

The bush which burned with fire and was not consumed (Ex. iii., 2.) and the rod which became a serpent and then retransformed into a rod (*Ibid* iv., 2—4), offer much subject for study to the pious mind, while the kinds of dust that became lice (*Ibid* viii, 16, 17), and of ashes that became boils (*Ibid* ix., 8, 10), are fortunately confined to Egypt. The cattle that were all killed of murrain (*Ibid* ix., 6) and subsequently plagued with boils (*Ibid* 9), and later smitten with hail, so that they died again (*Ibid* 18—25), and of which some died a third time (*Ibid* xii., 29), smitten by the Lord, and others a third time drowned in the sea (*Ibid* xiv., 28) are also confined to that same curious land; in other countries animals only die once.

Lev. xi. gives some interesting facts of animal life. Now-a-days the camel's leg does end in two toes, although not very obvious ones, but in Moses' time it was not so (v. 4). The hare that chews the cud (v. 6) has become extinct, though all hares have a deceptive habit of munching, and the bat is not now classified as "a fowl" (compare verses 13 and 19). Probably at that time the bat was not a mammal, and it has only become one since with the object of damning the scientific biologist. The "fowls that creep, going upon all four" (v. 20) have also become extinct, and have left no fossils behind them to perpetuate their memory; four-legged fowls given to creeping are wholly unknown. So again with the "flying creeping things which have four feet," and go "upon all four" (verses 23, 21), such as locusts, beetles, etc. These have six legs now-a-days, having acquired two more since the days of Moses, and I desire to point out to scoffing sceptics that were it not for this blessed book these remarkable quadrupedal birds and insects would have remained unknown. Who after this can dare to say that the Bible makes no contributions to science?

I say nothing of the pregnant suggestion contained in the reference to the flying, creeping things that "have *legs above their feet*" (v. 21). To me this verse contains a hint that at that time there existed some four-legged birds with feet above their legs, a peculiarity that would necessitate a unique anatomical re-arrangement of the appendages, and, to our purblind eyes, seems to present certain difficulties in locomotion. This speculation is full of interest, but perhaps it is dangerous to press too far inferences from the sacred text. We must ever remember that he who adds to the words of this holy book is cursed with him who takes away from them (Rev. xxii., 19), but perchance we avoid this danger by not regarding the existence of these supracrural-footed, flying, creeping things as a matter of faith, like that of the four-legged fowls, but only as a pious opinion.

The Israelites must have had serious difficulties during the period of transition between the queer beasts and their modern namesakes. Thus a four-legged beetle was "clean" (Lev. xi., 22), but "whatsoever hath more feet [than four] among all creeping things" was "unclean" (*Ibid.* 42), as, for instance, everything now known as a beetle. Perhaps beetles had four legs until the Jewish ceremonial law was supplanted by Christianity, and thereupon they suddenly changed into the modern six-legged kind. This change may have taken place even in the time of Moses, for it is remarkable that in Deut. xiv., 19 "every creeping thing that flieth" has become unclean and may not be eaten, and it would reconcile this apparent contradiction if we suppose that all the insects had suddenly developed an extra pair of legs, and so had come under the head of flying creeping things with more legs than four. Thus beautifully does science throw light on the dark places in scripture, and cause apparently discordant texts to harmonise.

In Numbers xvii. we read of a remarkable rod which in the space of a single night "budded and brought forth buds, and bloomed blossoms and yielded almonds." So greatly can God expedite natural processes when he wills. Indian jugglers can now perform these marvels, but no one would dream of being so blasphemous as to suggest that Moses, who was "learned in all the wisdom of the Egyptians" (Acts vii., 22), played a conjuring trick in order to substantiate his brother's claim to the priesthood.

The unicorn is another animal of which we should know nothing were it not for the Bible. We find it mentioned in Deut. xxxiii., 17, in Job xxxix., 9—12, and in Ps. xcii., 10. There must therefore have been such an animal, as the Holy Ghost would not talk about a non-existent creature, and yet there is not a trace of its existence outside this book of God.

Ezekiel is a book of priceless value from our present point of view. Who can read without his heart thrilling of the living creatures that "had the likeness of man," and such a man—a man with four faces, with four wings, with a calf's feet, and a man's hands, sparkling like burnished brass, looking like burning coals of fire and like the appearance of lamps (Ezek. i., 5—13). The likeness is clearly not to any man of the past, so it must be to a man of the future, and under these circumstances well might John the Apostle say that "it doth not yet appear what we shall be" (1 John iii., 2). In the tenth chapter of Ezekiel the same creatures appear again and are named cherubims, and we learn the additional fact that "their whole body, and their backs, and their hands, and their wings, and the wheels were full of eyes round about" verse 12), a superfluity of visual organs that must have been almost confusing to the possessors. First cousins to these extraordinary creatures must be the four beasts of Revelation, who are "full of eyes within" (Rev. iv., 8), an arrangement admirable for introspection, but otherwise slightly unsatisfactory. I am almost inclined to think that these four beasts are made out of one of Ezekiel's, for a careful comparison shows that, barring the multiplication of wings, one beast is exactly a quarter of a cherub.

Jonah's experiences are full of valuable biological information. The whale (compare Matt. xii., 40), which was a "great fish" (Jonah i., 17) living in the Mediterranean Sea, and the internal arrangements of which were suitable for swallowing a prophet and affording him lodging for three days; the gourd which grew up in a night, and the worm which "smote" the gourd (*Ibid* iv., 6, 7)—are not these known to and admired by every student of holy writ?

Space fails to draw attention to all the biological revelations made in this blessed book, but I cannot pass over the withered fig-tree without a word. As against the story so beautifully told (Matt. xxi., 18, 19; Mark xi., 12—14, 20, 21) of this unhappy tree, on which Jesus "found nothing but leaves, for the time of figs was not yet," it is alleged by infidel critics that if the season for figs had not arrived it was absurd for Jesus to expect to find any, and they scoff at the explanation given by the true believer that fig-trees at that time in Judæa (although at no other time and in no other place) bore figs before they bore leaves, and that this fig-tree was therefore guilty of false pretences, whereby it deceived its Creator. It is perfectly true that now the fig-tree is covered with leaves long before its remarkable inflorescence has ripened into fruit, but it is clear that this particular fig-tree began at the other end and worked backward, otherwise we should be obliged to come to the horrible and blasphemous conclusion that Jesus was both silly and ill-tempered, and that he behaved like a petulant child, howling because it cannot obtain impossibilities.

The Revelation of St. John the Divine offers a rich feast of creatures unknown to science; I have already mentioned the quarter-cherubs, and we have in addition a seven-horned seven-eyed lamb (v. 6); locusts shaped like horses, with men's faces, women's hair, lions' teeth, scorpions' tails, wearing crowns and breast-plates (ix., 7—10); a red dragon, with seven heads, ten horns, and a wonderful tail, who casts a flood of water out of his mouth (xii. 3, 4, 15): a beast like a leopard, with seven heads and ten horns, with a bear's feet and a lion's mouth, and another with two horns, who "spake as a dragon" (xiii., 1, 2, 11), however that may be; yet another, scarlet in color, "full of names of blasphemy," as others were full of eyes, and with seven heads and ten horns (xvii., 3); never was there such a menagerie full of most curiously composite animals as that seen by the beloved Apostle from "the isle that is called Patmos" (Rev. i., 9).

My task is ended; I have shown something of the treasures of biological knowledge laid up for us in this most precious book, and I commend my humble effort to all true believers, beseeching them to aid it by their prayers.

London: Printed by Annie Besant and Charles Bradlaugh, 63, Fleet Street, E.C.—1884.

THE SINS OF THE CHURCH.

VII.

A BURDEN ON LABOR.

By ANNIE BESANT.

The cry, "Disendow the Church!" is that which lends most vigor to the attack on the Establishment, and the fear of disendowment is that which causes the chief bitterness of the defence. Argument for disendowment is regarded as an "attack on property", and is resisted with all the anger which is apt to be shown when property is touched. An added cause of wrath is that the property is supposed to have some special kind of sacredness, and the proposal to disendow the Church is not only a proposal of robbery but one of "sacrilege." With this idea I am not concerned; it is natural that an ecclesiastical body should try to fence about its wealth with special protections, but these ecclesiastical pretences cannot be taken into account in serious discussion. My contention will be that the State has set aside certain revenues, raised by taxation, to pay certain officials for the purpose of performing certain duties; and that if the State chooses to suppress its ecclesiastical department, and assign the portion of its revenues hitherto expended in it to other uses, it is acting within its admitted rights. And this contention I propose to establish by indubitable historical facts.

Before adducing these, however, it will be well to consider the peculiar nature of the "property" claimed as belonging to the Church. First and foremost there is no corporation capable of holding property known in law as "the Church of England". The Church is made up of a large number of corporations, each of which is distinct in law as a holder of property. No bequest can be made to, no endowment conferred on, the "Church of England". A benefice may be endowed, or a church or a cathedral, but the endowment goes to the special distinct "corporation", and not to "the Church" as a whole. Thus every bishop, or parochial clergyman, is a "corporation sole", and is distinct from every other; no collection of these have power over "Church" property, but each man has power over the property attached to his office, and over none other. "The Church" cannot interfere with these independent corporations with regard to their disposal of their property; "the Church" does not own, nor does it control the disposition of, one single penny piece. It is not therefore possible to rob "the Church"; it has no property. If a new parish or a new see is to be created, the Church has nothing to do with arranging its revenue; this is done by the State, and by the State alone, which disposes of its ecclesiastical revenues as it pleases. Individual Church people may, if they please, give money to the new parish, or the new see; but it can only be given to the parish or see, the new separate corporations created by the State, and not to "the Church" in general. As Mr. Effingham Wilson well says: "There is no community between the property of one parish and the property of another. Every parish, in respect to its common property, is as distinct and separate from any other parish as the Corporation of London is from the Corporation of Bristol; there is a community of faith and discipline, but no community of temporal goods in the Church of England" ("The Church, Church Property and Church Rates," quoted in Mr. Miall's "Title Deeds of the Church of England", p. 82, ed. 1885).

A very important practical result flows from this absence of any single corporate body capable of holding property as "the Church of England". The holding of property has been attached to certain offices by the State, not to a collection of individuals. If the State chooses to abolish those offices, no one has right of complaint; all that any individual can claim is, possibly, some compensation for his personal loss by the abolition of the office he has held.

Further, the property of the holder of any such office in the emoluments attached to it is of a very limited character. The cleric has merely a life-interest in his benefice; he cannot alienate it, sell it, bequeath it, or charge it after his death for any purpose. When the holder of a benefice dies, no other person can claim the benefice as of right: its bestowal depends on a purely arbitrary choice, generally exerted by a layman, who is unable to hold it himself: if the State assumed the disposal of it, no cleric would be robbed; the only individual injured would be the lay owner of the living, who would be deprived of the market price of the advowson.

Hallam, who holds very Conservative principles on the rights of private property, draws a very clear line of division between Church and other property. He says: "I cannot, until some broad principle is made more obvious than it ever has been to me, do such violence to all common notions on the subject, as to attach an equal inviolability to private and corporate property. The law of hereditary succession, as ancient and universal as that of property itself, the law of testamentary disposition, the complement of the former, so long established in most countries as to seem a natural right, have invested the individual possessor of the soil with such a fictitious immortality, such anticipated enjoyment, as it were, of futurity, that his perpetual ownership could not be limited to the term of his own existence, without what he would justly feel as a real deprivation of property. . . . But in estates held, as we call it, in mortmain, there is no intercommunity, no natural privity of interest, between the present possessor and those who may succeed him; and as the former cannot have any pretext for complaint, if, his own rights being preserved, the legislature should alter the course of transmission after his decease, so neither is any hardship sustained by others, unless their succession has been already designated or rendered probable. Corporate property, therefore, appears to stand on a very different footing from that of private individuals, and while all infringements of the established privileges of the latter are to be sedulously avoided, and held justifiable only by the strongest motives of public expediency, I cannot but admit the full right of the legislature to new mould and regulate the former in all that does not involve existing interests upon far slighter reasons of convenience" ("Constitutional History," pp. 66, 67).

Nor is even the clergyman's life-tenure of his benefice absolute; it is dependent on his good behavior, and on his regular discharge of the duties laid upon him by Act of Parliament. If he is drunken or profligate, he can be "deprived"; but no one under such circumstances would say that the "rights of property" were interfered with, so limited are these rights in the case of a clergyman and his benefice. A rector might have an income of £500 a year from his parish and of £500 a year from private property. If he were deprived for drunkenness, his £500 a year from the parish would be taken away from him, but his own £500 a year would remain untouched. So different is the clerical property in a benefice from ordinary private property. Above all his holding of his office depends on his discharge of the duties *laid on him by Act of Parliament*—by the State, be it noted, not by the Church. A clergyman would forfeit his living if he obeyed the command of the Church issued by Convocation in opposition to the law of the land. Parliament can at any time vary the duties attached to the offices held in the Establishment: and, as a matter of fact, has done so over and over again. In the reigns of Henry VIII., Edward VI., Mary, Elizabeth, James I., Charles I., Charles II., William and Mary, and during the Commonwealth, thousands of clergymen were ejected from their benefices because they would not accept the new conditions successively attached to them by the State. There has been talk of "persecution" by their friends, but never of their being robbed of property. In truth, if Parliament determined to attach the revenues now held by clerics to the office of village schoolmaster, the cleric would have either to discharge those duties or give up his office. Property would not be touched; only the duties of a certain office would be changed, as they have been so often changed before.

We come to the crucial point in dispute. The Church says that the property claimed by it was given by pious persons for the support of religion; we say by far the greater part of the property now used in support of the Establishment was given by the State for certain public purposes, and was raised by taxation levied by State authority, and that the State has changed and can change the purposes for which the money is assigned.

The greater part of the revenues of the Church is derived from tithes, and it is beyond dispute among instructed persons that the origin of compulsory tithes is purely civil. Priests claimed tithes as a religious duty long before tithe became a legal tax, enforceable by process of law. Its origin in England dates from the reign of Offa, King of Mercia, who in A.D. 794 summoned his nobles into Council and decreed that all should pay tithe.

In A.D. 855, Ethelwolf being king, a Parliament sitting at Winchester decreed that a tenth part of the kingdom should belong to God, the Virgin and the Saints, and should be applied "to the service of God". This law of Offa, says Burn, "enabled the clergy to gather and recover them [tithes] as their legal due, by the coercion of the civil power. Yet this establishment of Offa reached no further than to the kingdom of Mercia, over which Offa reigned; until Ethelwulph, about sixty years after, enlarged it for the whole realm of England" ("Ecclesiastical Law," vol. iii., p. 680). Alfred followed in his father's steps, and ordained fines against any who should "withhold his tithes"; his successors enacted similar laws, and in A.D. 697 a law of King Edgar runs: "If any one shall refuse to pay his tithes in such manner as we have prescribed, then let the king's sheriff, and the bishop of the diocese, and the minister of the parish come together, and let them by force cause the tenth part to be paid to the church to which it was due, leaving only the ninth part to the owner. And for the other eight parts, the lord of the manor shall have one four parts, and the bishop of the diocese the other four" ("Title Deeds," p. 23). "A curious illustration this", caustically remarks Mr. Miall, "of spontaneous and private liberality in endowing the church with parochial tithes!". The pious founder theory, in truth, somewhat breaks down under the weight of historical facts; and we find that tithe is merely a tax, levied by the State like any other tax, and that the clergy who receive tithes are as much maintained out of the taxes, as much State-paid, as are our soldiers and sailors.

Other laws of the same description were enacted in the reigns of succeeding monarchs, but we may pass to the reign of William I., who in reissuing various laws of Edward the Confessor included the following among them: "Of all corn the tenth sheaf is due to God, and therefore is to be paid unto him. If any shall have a herd of mares, let him pay the tenth colt, but if he have only one or two mares, let him pay a penny for every colt which he shall have of them. In like manner, if he shall have many cows, he shall pay the tenth calf; if he shall have but one or two cows, then he shall pay a halfpenny for every calf. And he who shall make cheese must give unto God the tenth cheese; but he that shall make none must give the milk of every tenth day. And so likewise must be paid the tenth lamb, the tenth fleece, the tenth part of the butter, and the tenth pig. And so, in like manner, of the bees, the tenth part of the profit. And so likewise of woods, of meadows, of waters and mills, of parks, of ponds, of fisheries, of copse, of orchards and gardens, and of trade, and of all things which the Lord shall give, the tenth part is to be rendered to him who giveth unto us the other nine parts with that tenth. Whosoever shall withhold this tenth part shall, by the justice of the bishop and of the king, be forced to the payment of it, if need be" ("Title Deeds", p. 25).

What here becomes of the pious founder? Is a payment enforced by law to be paraded among the ignorant as due to the voluntary gifts of religious persons for the support of a religion they venerated? The constant reference to the enforcement of the payment proves that tithe was on a level with other legal taxes, and that it is no more sacred than the excise, or the income-tax. But suppose that the tithes which support the parochial system had been voluntary gifts of pious Papists to their Church, is it to be pretended that we are to be bound to pay tithe of all our possessions because Papists did so a thousand years ago? Are Kentish farmers to pay tithe of their hops, because some Mercian semi-barbarian paid tithe of his agricultural produce ten centuries since? Or is it to be pretended that because the said Mercian paid tithe, therefore all succeeding people, living on the district of English soil once inhabited by him, are to tithe their multifarious products, the majority of which were wholly unknown to his pious savage-ship? Equally preposterous is the pretence that the tithe laws of Ethelwolf, Alfred, or William, should be regarded as binding upon us. All laws ordaining taxes are wholly within the power of Parliament to confirm, to alter, to repeal. This tax upon industry levied first for the support of the Roman Catholic Church, and later for that of the Protestant Establishment, can either be wholly abolished, or its results can be appropriated to some useful national purpose, without even touching the "sacred rights of property".

The claim of reverence for the supposed intentions of these constrainedly pious donors sits rather oddly on the Established Church of England. The tithes were clearly enforced on behalf of the Roman Catholic Church; they were given to the Virgin and the Saints as well as to God. But the Establishment which cries out "sacrilege!" if the State now proposes to alienate tithes from its clergy, actually justifies the action of the State in alienating them from the Romish priests to whom by law they were payable; and it can only defend the receipt of them by its clergy, by claiming for the State in the sixteenth century a power which it denies to it in the nineteenth.

Further, tithe was not originally appropriated merely for the support of the clergy. The unmarried priesthood of Rome did not need for its support the large incomes necessary for the many-childed Protestant pastor. According to Blackstone, "at the first establishment of the parochial clergy, the tithes of the parish were distributed in a fourfold division; one for the use of the bishop, one for maintaining the fabric of the church, a third for the poor, and a fourth to provide for the incumbent" (Commentaries, bk. i., chap. xi., sec. v). The rapacity of the Protestant clergy has appropriated the whole; the repair of the church was thrown by them on the ratepayers, and the portion of the poor was dispensed in accordance with the maxim that "charity begins at home". But it is noteworthy that in many parishes, in which the "great tithes" have passed into lay hands, the cost of repairing the chancel of the parish church still falls on the lay rector, thus recalling the ancient division of tithes.

There is, however, one place in which the pious founder does come in, namely in the endowment of monasteries. But the amusing thing is that the pious founders endowed monasteries by alienating for the benefit of the monastery the parochial tithes paid by the people on their lands! So that their piety consisted in making presents out of other people's goods. Sometimes, on their deathbeds, if they had been particularly disreputable, they endowed monasteries and chantries out of the property they could no longer enjoy, charging their gift with the obligation of saying masses for their sinful souls. Mr. Miall gives the following specimen of such an unjust alienation of tithe from the parish by which it was paid: "I, Robert Waste, have granted to God, and to Holy Mary of Beck and St. Neots the Confessor, and to his Church of Ernelesbury, and to the monks who serve therein, two parts of my tithe over all my estate in Wereslay, of corn and animal on which tithes should be paid. And this is done especially for the soul of Sœnus of Essessa, and for the salvation of my Lord Robert, son of the aforesaid Sœnus, who gave me this land, and for the salvation of Gonnor his wife, and for my own salvation and that of my wife, and of William, son of Gereus, her father, and for the soul of my father, and my mother, and my brother, and all my friends, and all my ancestors, etc." When the property held by monasteries was seized by Henry VIII. all these "gifts of pious founders" were confiscated, and disposed of according to the good pleasure of the prince. Burn gives a list of 194 monasteries of the value of £200 a year and upwards, dissolved by a single statute (31 Hen. VIII., c. 13); those suppressed by the 27 Hen. VIII., c. 28 were under £200 a year in value, and numbered no less than 3,760. The property thus appropriated amounted to about one-third of the whole property assigned to ecclesiastical purposes in the kingdom, and included all the gifts of "pious founders"; this was distributed among laymen, and several of the great houses of the aristocracy owe their wealth to this confiscation. The Establishment, by abolishing purgatory, rid itself of the charges for dead people's souls; and pocketed any money left for masses for the dead, which was not appropriated by the State, on the ground that purgatory was a fond conceit.

Returning to the parochial tithes which were not meddled with at the Reformation, save in so far as the duties attached to them were completely changed—a very important and significant fact as proving the full control over their disposition exercised by the State—we turn to Burn to note exactly in what they consisted: "Tithes, with regard to the several kinds or natures, are divided into prædial, mixt, and personal. Prædial tithes are such as arise merely and immediately from the ground; as grain of all sorts, hay, wood, fruits, herbs . . . . Mixt tithes are those which arise not immediately from the ground, but from things immediately nourished by the ground, as by means of goods depastured thereupon, or otherwise nourished with the fruits thereof; as colts, calves, lambs, chickens, milk, cheese, eggs. Personal tithes are such profits as do arise by the honest labor and industry of man, employing himself in some personal work, artifice, or negociation;

being the tenth part of the clear gain, after charges deducted. Tithes, with regard to value, are divided into great and small. Great tithes: as corn, hay, and wood. Small tithes: as the prædial tithes of other kinds, together with those which are called mixt, and personal" (vol. iii., p. 680). Originally, all these tithes went to the parochial clergy, the bishop, the parochial poor, and the maintenance of the parochial church. By deed of gift, as we have seen, some were alienated, and it was the great tithes that were usually dealt with in this way. The receiver of the great tithes was the "rector" of the parish, while the "vicar" received the small. Hence the large number of lay rectors now existing, and it is significant of the parochial origin of tithes that these rectors are all rectors of given parishes, and take tithe of them. Wherever a clergyman is a vicar, the great tithe of the parish has passed into lay hands.

Tithe is not now paid in kind. The constant friction between parishioners and parson on the subject gave rise to so much ill-feeling that it was thought expedient to get rid of it, and to conceal tithe under a yearly rent-charge, which coming as "rent" should not be recognised as a tax for the benefit of the Establishment. Accordingly in 1836, 1837, 1838, and 1839, were passed Tithe Commutation Acts, which substituted "a corn-rent, payable in money and permanent in quantity, though fluctuating in value, for all tithes" (Burn, vol. iii., p. 698). In some cases land has been given to the incumbent in lieu of this rent-charge. Extraordinary tithe, about which there is now so much commotion, is the tithe of hop grounds, orchards, or gardens, newly cultivated since the passing of the Commutation Acts. The idle clergy claim a tenth part of the results of industrious men's labor, in virtue of the preposterous laws of old Offa and Ethelwolf and the rest, which form part of "the common law" of England. So if anyone plants an orchard or a market garden he must pay a tenth part of his produce to the Establishment, whether he belongs to it or not. And the clergy pretend that it will be "robbing God" if the State puts an end to their robbery of the cultivators. And be it noted that this extraordinary tithe is not even an old tax continued; it is a claim of the Establishment to plunder everyone who shall, at any time, commence a special industry at a new spot.

A crushing argument brought by Mr. Miall against the pretence that tithe owes its origin to voluntary lay liberality, is the fact that one-third of the cultivated land now paying tithe has only been brought under cultivation during the last century; another five-twelfths has been brought under cultivation since the time of Edward VI., leaving only one-fourth as originating before this time. But the arbitrary appropriation of tithes ceased from the reign of King John, and at that time only some 2,500,000 acres of land were cultivated (see pp. 53—60). So that the theory of the Establishment involves the assumption not only that the then landlords might determine for ever to whom should be paid tithe on the lands they owned, but that they might also direct the taxing of all land that in after ages should be brought under cultivation, for the benefit of the Church!

Not only may the parochial endowments which support the Establishment be historically proved to originate in the State, and to be of the nature of a State-levied tax; but the State has always treated these endowments as wholly subject to its own control. It has, as we have already noted, changed over and over again the conditions on which were held the offices to which tithes were attached. In the tremendous convulsion of the Reformation, the tithes were transferred from the clergy who served the churches in obedience to Rome to those who accepted the new lay head of the State Establishment. They were attached to the public reading of the Roman Breviary under Henry VII.; to the reading of the changed service under Henry VIII.; to the reading of two successive Books of Common Prayer under Edward VI.; back to the reading of the Roman breviary under Mary; once more to the Book of Common Prayer under Elizabeth; to the reading of the Directory during the last few years of Charles I.; to the reading of the Book of Common Prayer under Charles II. and his successors. Other conditions were attached to the holding of tithes, *e.g.*, the taking of the oaths of supremacy and allegiance to whomsoever might chance to be on the throne; or, during the Commonwealth, the abstinence from loyalty to the Crown. To illustrate this phase of tithe-receiving, it is sufficient to remind the reader of two remarkable historical cases thereof; the ejection of 2,000 Puritan clergy under Charles II., and of 400

Jacobite clergy, an Archbishop, and eight Bishops, under William and Mary. Acceptance of whatever ceremony may be laid down by Parliament is another condition of receiving tithes; as witness the deprivation of several High Church clergy in our own time. Under the Commonwealth tithes were treated wholly as State property. We read in Whitelock, under date September 9th, 1652: "That the tithes were all employed to the uses directed by the Act of Parliament. (1) To maintain Godly ministers. (2) Schoolmasters. (3) The fifth part to the wives and children of the ejected clergy. (4) To pay taxes. (5) To pay the officers." There are also very many references to the sale of Church Lands. A somewhat ludicrous instance of the complete subordination of the Church to the State occurred during the last two months with the Bishop of Ely. He had been duly consecrated, and all the Church could do to make him into a Bishop had been done. But he could not touch one penny of episcopal revenue, nor exercise a single episcopal function, until he had done homage to the Queen and acknowledged that he held all his temporalties from her. As some royal whim delayed the receipt of this homage, the Bishop, who had received the Holy Ghost for the work of a Bishop in the Church of God, had to wait patiently for five weeks before he could begin that work! In truth, the clergy are just State officials, paid by the State, and holding office under conditions laid down by the State, and changeable at its pleasure; the very rites that make them capable of receiving tithes are part of an Act of Parliament, and their capacity does not even give them a right to receive tithes, but only makes them eligible to do so, if arbitrary whim should bestow on them a benefice.

The amount raised by the tithe-tax yearly is nowhere stated with exactitude, and Parliament would do well to appoint a Royal Commission to ascertain exactly the revenues raised for its ecclesiastical service. The tax is variously estimated as producing from £4,054,000 to £5,000,000 per annum. In addition to this, a large amount of land has been given in lieu of tithes in various parts of the country, but here no exact figures are ascertainable.

Bishops, to whom originally went, as we have seen, one-fourth of the tithe, have for many centuries been maintained otherwise than by this tax. Most bishoprics were of royal foundation, and the 31 Hen. VIII., c. 9, authorised the king to create as many new bishoprics as he pleased, endowing them at his pleasure; and he accordingly created several, bestowing on them some of the confiscated property of the monasteries. The exact value of the episcopal and capitular estates is doubtful. In the "Case for Disestablishment", published by the Liberation Society in 1884, it is stated, on the authority of Parliamentary returns, "that the [capitalised] value of the estates is £39,457,613" (p. 60).

Another curious sort of "Church Property" is that connected with the fund known as "Queen Anne's Bounty." Up to the time of Henry VIII. certain monetary dues were regularly paid to the Pope as Primate of Christendom, the chief Bishop of the Church. Burn says: "Annates, primitiæ, or first fruits, was the value of every spiritual living by the year, which the pope, claiming the disposition of all ecclesiastical livings within Christendom, reserved out of every living. What pope first imposed first fruits historians do not agree" ("Ecclesiastical Law," vol. ii., pp. 273 n., 274). Which pope made the levy is not, to us, a matter of the smallest importance; that the levy originated with the pope is of interest, since Protestants base claims on it to-day. *Tenths* are the tenth part of the yearly income of a benefice, and are paid on a valuation made in the time of Henry VIII.! By this admirable arrangement the living of Halsall—to take a single instance—which has a value according to Crockford of £3,500, pays first fruits and tenths calculated on its value of £25 in the Liber Regis of Henry VIII., so that it contributes £2 10s. a year instead of £350 a year as tenths, and £25 instead of £3,500 as first fruits. In calculating the payment of tithes the clergy are not willing to have them reckoned on the prices current in the reign of Henry VIII. By the 26th Henry VIII., c. 3, these dues, hitherto paid to the Pope, were made payable to the Crown, and so came ultimately under the control of Parliament. They were, in fact, a special tax levied on the clergy, for the benefit of their head, whether that head were ecclesiastical, as the Pope, or lay, as the King. The monarchs of England—with the exception of Mary I.—regularly received these payments from Henry VIII. down to Queen Anne, as part of the revenues attached to the Crown, out of which was discharged the whole cost of civil government. Queen Anne, generous to the Church with national funds, surrendered them into the hands of a corporation created for that purpose in the year 1703, in order that they might be applied to the improvement of poor livings. This fund, known by the name of Queen Anne's Bounty, is really public property, for the nation has had to take into account this diminution of the revenues appointed for the Crown, and to make it up in fixing the Civil List. The royal successors of Queen Anne are not a penny the poorer for her "bounty", for the money given out of one royal pocket for the support of the poorer clergy has to be put back into the other royal pocket by the nation. The nation is, in every case, the milch cow. From time to time Parliament has largely added to the Bounty, and between 1809 and 1829 grants were made to it out of the taxes to the amount of £1,100,000. It can hardly be pretended that this fund is not under the complete control of the State, and ought not to be disposed of at its pleasure. It might be enormously increased if the duties were levied on the real value of Church benefices, and not on their nominal worth as given in the Liber Regis; and it is clearly monstrous that the clergy should be allowed to appropriate amounts which have increased as the people have labored, without paying back dues which were laid upon them by law as one of the conditions of their holdings. The curious adhesiveness shown by the clergy to all money in any way connected with the Establishment has so worked that actually, in the popular mind formed by them, it has changed these moneys—which were originally taxes levied on the clergy, first for the benefit of a foreign prelate, and later for the benefit of a State official—into a fund which is supposed to be "Church Property".

The question has probably been complicated in the minds of many by the fact that considerable sums of money have been paid into the Fund from time to time by private persons who desired to help the poorer clergy. Part of the Fund would therefore come under the head of recent private endowments, if distinctions are to be drawn between private and public gifts when the details of disendowment come to be considered. The Fund is now a very important one. In 1884 it had a revenue of £166,304, and possessed £4,398,159 in trust, invested, in addition to £1,088,836 lent on mortgage.

Glebe land is land attached to a parochial church, and in old times no church could be consecrated until house and land had been assigned to it (see Burn, vol. ii., p. 296). Mr. Arthur Arnold in the *Nineteenth Century* for April, 1878, calculated the value of glebe houses at £750,000 a year, or at a capitalised value of £15,000,000 sterling, and of glebe lands at £400,000, or at a capitalised value of £10,000,000.

The "Ecclesiastical Commissioners for England" are a corporation established by 6 and 7 Will. IV., cap. 77, 3 and 4 Vict., cap. 113, and 4 and 5 Vict., cap. 39 (see Burn, vol. ii., p. 237 *et seq*). The gross scandals of the disposal of ecclesiastical funds, of sinecures, etc., led to the establishment of this commission, in which were vested a large number of endowments to be disposed of and controlled by them. Here again is a body appointed wholly by the State, made capable of receiving and managing the so-called property of the Church, and it is slightly absurd to admit that such a body can be appointed by one Parliament, and that another might not be appointed by a second Parliament to again change the disposal of the ecclesiastical funds. This commission at the present time disposes of some £700,000 a year.

Mr. Arnold, in the before-mentioned article in the *Nineteenth Century* for April, 1878, gives the following list of funds now used in support of the Establishment (I omit his capitalised values as unimportant):

Bishops' estates	£40,854
,, palaces	12,400
Deans and Chapters' estates	136,488
,, ,, residences, etc.	50,000
Tithes	5,000,000
Glebe houses	750,000
Glebe lands	400,000
Churchwardens', etc., lands	21,000
Queen Anne's Bounty	30,000
Ecclesiastical Commissioners	700,000
Property omitted from the New Domesday Books	361,860
	£7,502,602

The absurd pretence that the clergy are not State paid may be exposed yet further. Unhappily, we have no complete return of Parliamentary grants to the Establishment for various purposes; but it is easy to take a few instances as examples. Thus in Queen Anne's reign we find a grant of £370,000 towards building fifty new churches; a tax on coals brought into the port of London was levied from 1710 until 1728 for building these churches and for forming a fund for the endowment of the clergy belonging to them; for some time a yearly grant of £100,000 was made; in 1812 there was a grant of £400,000, and a relinquishment of £200,000 of land tax; in 1818, a grant of £1,000,000; in 1824, of £500,000, and another of £89,406. Between 1817 and 1845 duty remitted on materials used for building churches amounted to the respectable sum of £336,340 13s. 8d. Until compulsory Church rates were abolished, half a million a year was raised by them, and many thousands are still extracted annually under this head under local "rights", reserved when churchrates in general were abolished. How much money has been taken from the public for building churches it is impossible to discover. For instance, Oldham parish church was rebuilt in 1828, at a cost to the rates of £30,000, levied *pro rata* on the four parishes of Oldham, Crompton, Royton, and Chadderton. It is tolerably obvious that under these circumstances Oldham parish church is as much the property of the ratepayers as is Oldham Town Hall; yet most people regard it as "Church property", and would consider it scandalous if it were turned to some useful public purpose. It would be interesting to know how many parish churches have been built thus out of the money of ratepayers.

There is one ancient source of wealth that I have not referred to, which comes nearer to the pious founder fiction than any other—the gifts to the Roman Church of frightened scoundrels lying on their deathbeds, whereby they hoped to win pardon for their sinful souls. But I leave Hallam to describe this, and other yet more disreputable sources of clerical wealth: "Some gave their wealth to the Church before entering on military expeditions; gifts were made by some to take effect after their lives, and bequests by many in the terrors of dissolution. Even those legacies to charitable purposes, which the clergy could with more decency and speciousness recommend, and of which the administration was generally confined to them, were frequently applied to their own benefit. They failed not, above all, to inculcate upon the wealthy sinner, that no atonement could be so acceptable to heaven, as liberal presents to its earthly delegates. To die without allotting a portion of worldly wealth to pious uses was accounted almost like suicide, or a refusal of the last sacraments. . . . . The canonical penances imposed upon repentant offenders, extravagantly severe in themselves, were commuted for money or for immovable possessions: a fertile though scandalous source of monastic wealth, which the popes afterwards diverted into their own coffers, by the usage of dispensations and indulgences. The church lands enjoyed an immunity from taxes, though not in general from military service, when of a feudal tenure. But their tenure was frequently in what was called frankalmoign, without any obligation of service. Hence it became a customary fraud of lay proprietors to grant estates to the church, which they received again by way of fief or lease, exempted from public burdens. And as if all these means of accumulating what they could not legitimately enjoy were insufficient, the monks prostituted their knowledge of writing to the purpose of forging charters in their own favor, which might easily impose upon an ignorant age, since it has required a peculiar science to detect them in modern times" ("Europe during the Middle Ages," pp. 333, 334, ed. 1869). It is to wealth acquired in these nefarious ways by the Church of Rome in England that the Establishment lays claim today, oblivious of the fact that if any rights of property over this wealth exist in any ecclesiastical body, save by act of the State, they must exist in the Romish Church alone. To that Church the wealth was given, or by it it was stolen; and such part of it as has remained in ecclesiastical hands is vested in the officials of the present Establishment wholly by the action of the State.

Printed by ANNIE BESANT and CHARLES BRADLAUGH, 63, Fleet St., E.C.—1886.

VIII.

A CREATURE OF CROWN AND PARLIAMENT.

By ANNIE BESANT.

Before dealing with the practical side of disendowment, it is well to substantiate the position that the Church is the mere creature of Crown and Parliament, an ordinary department of the State which may be either modified in any convenient fashion, or entirely abolished. And to this end it is important to define clearly the difference between a free and a State Church. Of a free Church, the great Church of Rome serves best as model; it has its supreme head, the Pope, who has no ecclesiastical superior and to whom all its members owe implicit obedience; it has its own discipline, its rites and ceremonies, its doctrines, and over these no civil power has any control; it appoints its own officials; it enters into arrangements with various civil governments, negotiating with them, and entering into treaties with them, as an independent power. If a new doctrine is to be incorporated in the faith of the Church, its bishops are summoned into council from every land; they meet together, discuss and decide; their decision is binding on the conscience of every member of the Church; no Parliamentary authority is asked for in any land; no crowned head is consulted; the decree of the General Council goes forth into every land; from every high altar it is read out by the ecclesiastical official; and the new doctrine becomes "of faith". Thus in our own times have been added to the dogmas of Rome those of the immaculate conception and of papal infallibility. Such is the method of a free Church. Contrast with this the condition of an Establishment like our own; its highest clerical official, the Archbishop of Canterbury, has for ecclesiastical head a layman or laywoman; Queen Victoria is now the supreme head of the Church of England; its discipline, rites, ceremonies, and doctrines are laid down for it by Act of Parliament; its chief officials are appointed over it by the Crown; it can no more enter into treaty with a foreign power than could the Admiralty or the Exchequer. If any addition to, or substraction from, its doctrines is to be made, it can be made only by a Parliament of laymen, in which sit dissenters of every shade of opinion, from orthodox presbyterianism to avowed atheism. This Parliament can alter its creed at will, and the only terms on which the State permits its clergy to hold their benefices is that they shall submissively yield whatever subscription Parliament may ordain. It is this submission to Parliamentary authority, this impuissance of the Church to act as an organised body, this laying down by Parliament of every doctrine that may be taught, and of every ceremony that may be practised in the services of the Church, that we mean when we speak of the Church as "established". It has been reduced from a self-governing organisation to a department of the State.

It is alleged by those who contend for the autonomy of the Church that the Church in England is older than Parliament; and it is perfectly true that there was a Christian Church in England before there was a Parliament. There were some Christian churches in Britain in very early times, before the invasion of the country by the non-Christian Teutons, who swept the Britons and their Christianity into Wales and the south-west. Augustine, landing in A.D. 597, planted among the triumphant Teutons churches which owned the obedience of Rome, and was by Pope Gregory created primate of these English churches, receiving from his hands the archiepiscopal pall. These churches were welded into a firm and centralised organisation by Theodore of Tarsus, sent to England for that work by the Pope in A.D. 668; he built up the scattered churches into a single body, with the Archbishop of Canterbury for its national head, and he holding his office from Rome. It is unnecessary even to sketch the subsequent history of this Church and of its struggles with the State. Throughout all these it acted as the independent body that it was, and constantly as the civil power strove to encroach on its temporal jurisdiction, and endeavored to diminish the independence of the State of its great officers and their dependence on Rome, it never dreamed of meddling in "spiritual" matters, and the Church had its synods and its central Parliament, and in all questions of faith and conscience was supreme; the State, indeed, was merely its tool in some matters, as where it burnt, without any trial on its own part, any offenders handed over to it for that purpose by the ecclesiastical courts. The Church paid tribute to the Pope as its supreme head in the shape of first fruits and tenths (see pp. 108 and 109, Tract VII.), in token that all its officers held from him.

In the reign of Henry VIII. the links between the State and the Church of Rome in England were roughly broken; the vast possessions of the Church were confiscated; some of them were taken by the Crown, some distributed among court favorites, and the remainder—mostly endowments of the parochial churches—were left in connexion with the Roman foundations, these being bestowed on men who were willing to bear office in the new ecclesiastical department of the State. The first distinct step in this change was taken in A.D. 1531, when the convocation of the Church separated itself from Rome by acknowledging King Henry VIII. as the "supreme head of the Church and clergy of England". A clause was inserted, "so far as the law of Christ permits", but this was later withdrawn. In the following year an Act was passed forbidding the payment to Rome of first fruits and tenths. And the bishops and clergy bound themselves to make no new canon or constitution ecclesiastical save by the king's leave. In 1533 a further Act was passed that no excommunication from Rome should have any effect, and all appeals to Rome from English ecclesiastical courts were forbidden. In 1534 the final separation was made; anyone submitting to papal authority was rendered liable to a *præmunire;* the appointment of bishops was vested in the crown; monasteries were made subject to the king only; the Parliament conferred on the king the title already acknowledged by convocation, of "the only supreme head in earth of the Church of England", and declared the refusal of this title to him to be treason. Further, Parliament declared "that our said sovereign lord, his heirs and successors, kings of this realm, shall have full power and authority from time to time, to visit and repress, redress, reform, order, correct, restrain and amend, all such errors, heresies, abuses, offences, contempts and enormities, whatsoever they be, which by any manner of spiritual authority or jurisdiction ought or may lawfully be reformed, repressed, ordered, redressed, corrected, restrained, or amended most to the pleasure of Almighty God, the increase of virtue in Christ's religion, and for the conservation of the peace, unity, and tranquility of this realm". And as a further proof of the reality of this headship it was declared, "that towards the augmentation, maintenance, and defence of the king's royal estate and dignity of supreme head, the first-fruits of all benefices, dignities, offices, etc. spiritual, shall be paid to his highness" (Herbert's Life and Times of King Henry VIII., pp. 530, 531).

After thus abolishing the Pope's authority and establishing that of the Crown, Parliament next concerned itself with the doctrines of the new church. These, as might be expected, varied much from time to time. In 1539 was passed the famous Statute of the Six Articles, the first standard of doctrine of the Parliamentary church. In 1549 the first Act of Uniformity was issued, commanding the use of the new "Book of Common Prayer", and in 1552 this Prayer Book was considerably altered, and was annexed to the Act of Parliament ordering its use. Queen Mary changed the service back to that used in the last year of Henry VIII., and Elizabeth on her accession changed it again to that commanded in 1552; a few months later some slight alterations were made, and imposed by Act of Parliament; in the first year of James I. the Prayer book was again amended to a very considerable extent, having thus been once abolished and four times altered within the brief space of fifty-four years. The Long Parliament swept away the Book of Common Prayer altogether, and issued in its stead a "Directory for Public Worship", which it enforced in lieu of the Prayer Book. Charles II. restored the Prayer Book, altering it for the fifth time, and thus changing for the seventh time, since Henry VIII., the service which the ministers of the Establishment were ordered to read. In the face of all these variations, all made by Act of Parliament, it is a little difficult to see how it can be pretended that the Church is anything more than the mere creature of the State. If it accepts from the dictation of Parliament the actual words in which it shall worship its God, there is surely no depth of submission to which it may not stoop.

The ministerial ranks in the new Church were partially the same as those of the old. Abbots, abbesses, monks, and nuns, disappeared with the Roman Church: archbishops, bishops, priests, and deacons were retained. The Long Parliament for a short time established the presbyterian form of ecclesiastical government, but it did not take root in England, any more than did episcopacy in Scotland, and the traditional form returned with Charles II. The power, however, of the bishops was very much curtailed, in comparison with that they wielded when they were the official chiefs of an independent organisation. In 1547, the whole bench of bishops surrendered their offices into the hands of Edward VI., and in the new commissions granted to them a clause was inserted stating they held their offices during the royal pleasure. The Duke of Somerset, as protector, actually suspended all the bishops, while a general visitation of their dioceses was made by a commission, partly clerical and partly lay. In every way they were made to feel that they were no longer princes of a Church, but merely heads of a department of the State, administering its affairs under complete State control, and clothed only in delegated authority.

Dr. Heylyn, in his "History of the Reformation", dwells on this complete change in the status of the bishops. He says: "But that which made the greatest alteration, and threatened most danger to the state ecclesiastical, was the Act entitled 'An Act for the election of bishops, and what seals and styles shall be used by spiritual persons', etc. In which it was ordained—(for I shall only repeat the sum thereof)—that 'Bishops should be made by the King's letters patent, and not by the election of the deans and chapters: that all their processes and writings should be made in the King's name only, with the Bishop's *teste* added to it; and sealed with no other seal but the King's, or such as should be authorised and appointed by him'. In the compounding of which Act there was more danger than at first appeared. By the last branch thereof it was made plain and evident that the intent of the contrivers was by degrees to weaken the authority of the episcopal order, by forcing them from their stronghold of divine institution, and making them no other than the King's ministers only—his ecclesiastical sheriffs (as a man might say), to execute his will, and disperse his mandates" (vol. i., pp. 104, 105).

The bishops were further weakened by the disuse of excommunication: "The wings of their authority had been so clipped, that it was scarce able to fly abroad; the sentence of excommunication, wherewith they formerly kept in awe both priest and people, not having been in use and practice since the first of this king [Edward VI.]" (Heylyn, vol. i., p. 198).

One small scrap of pretended freedom was left to the State Church; it was still permitted to have its own Parliament—Convocation—although this Church Parliament was reduced to impotence, and could only talk, not legislate. As, however, it happened in the reign of George I. to talk in a manner disapproved of by the Head of the Church and his lay ministers, Convocation was quietly swept away (A.D. 1717), and has only been revived during the present reign.

It is very commonly pleaded on behalf of the present Establishment that the Church was only purified, not changed, at the Reformation. But this plea is utterly inconsistent with historical facts. The Reformation was resisted by the hierarchy, by the clergy, and by the laity of the Church then existing, and was forced on the country by the Tudor monarchs and the supple Parliaments they controlled. These Parliaments also, it must be remembered, were to a considerable extent composed of men who profited by the ecclesiastical change. Henry, advised by his minister Cromwell, had counted on enlisting the cupidity of his courtiers in his service, when he distributed among them the broad lands of the monasteries whose property he confiscated. Even under Mary, the nobles had clung to their Church lands, and under Elizabeth they gladly aided in destroying the Church they had plundered. Zeal for "religion" had very little to do with the Reformation in England. The ambition of the Crown and the cupidity of the nobles were the principal factors in the change. The old hierarchy was swept away, the clergy deprived by hundreds, and thousands of the laity were slain, ere the new Church was firmly established.

How great was the change in the *personnel* of the Church officials is not as a rule recognised by members of the Establishment. Passing over the execution of Cardinal

Fisher and of a large number of clergy and monks under Henry VIII. for denying the royal supremacy, we find that under Edward VI. five bishops were deprived, and three impoverished by the alienation of their lands, for lack of zeal in forwarding Court views of religion (see Heylyn, vol. i., pp. 210–214). When Elizabeth came to the throne no less than nine out of the twenty-seven dioceses of England and Wales lay vacant (including the Archbishopric of Canterbury) in consequence of death; a terrible fever had swept over the land, and most of these bishops had fallen a prey to it. Two more fled the kingdom soon after Elizabeth's accession, leaving only sixteen prelates in the country; of these the Bishop of Sodor and Man does not appear to have taken active part in the struggle between the Crown and the Roman Church, though he also was later deprived. Strype tells us that all the bishops present in Parliament dissented from the Bills which restored the Established Church after Mary's death, and that they strove to prevent the passing of the Act of Uniformity (Annals, vol. i., cap. 2). He gives a long account of the way in which the bishops struggled against Queen and Parliament; how they strove to prevent the alienation of lands given to the Roman Church, and the putting into the Crown's hands of the power of deprivation. They argued and voted against the transference to the Crown of all "abbeys, priories, nunneries, hospitals, and chantries, founded since the reign of Queen Mary". In fact, they made a very gallant fight for the liberty of their Church, and struggled hard to prevent its destruction. But despite all their efforts, as Strype triumphantly relates, by Acts of this first Parliament of Elizabeth was "popery overthrown, true religion founded upon the word of God, brought in again and established. . . . And all this work done within little more than three months; and that even while all the bishops, zealous creatures of Rome, and many other popish lords, sat in the parliament house, and had free votes there" (p. 105). The immediate consequence of the defeat of the bishops was the tendering to them of the oath of supremacy. This was done in July 1559, and the Archbishop of York, and every bishop, save Dr. Kitchin of Llandaff, refused to take it. The only prelate thus left for the new Church was Dr. Kitchin, a man of great flexibility of principles, who—says Dr. Heylyn, a

Protestant—"having formerly submitted to every change, resolved to show himself no changeling in not conforming to the pleasure of the higher powers" (vol. ii., p. 293). The bishops were not only deprived, but they were fined and imprisoned, and four bishops-elect and one suffragan were also rejected. Strype and Heylyn both rejoice over the ravages made in the hierarchy by death and deprivation, as facilitating the great change. The former remarks that "this voidance of so many bishoprics happened well for the furthering of the reformation of religion; that their places being vacant, men of other principles, and such as favored true religion, might succeed therein" (vol. i., p. 106). But it was not enough to get rid of the bishops. Other dignitaries of the Church, the clergy, and the Universities, had to be dealt with. Heylyn says that only "fourteen bishops, six abbots, priors, and governors of religious order, twelve deans, and as many archdeacons, fifteen presidents or masters of colleges, fifty prebendaries of cathedral churches, and about eighty parsons" were deprived; but while this may be true of actual deprivations of dignitaries who refused the oath of supremacy, it is utterly false if it be meant to represent the whole clerical changes in the first two years of Elizabeth's reign. For the great sweeping away of the clergy was not in consequence of the oath of supremacy, but in consequence of the enforcement of the Book of Common Prayer by Act of Parliament. Strype's Annals show us the condition of the country, and the straits to which the Establishment was reduced to find clergy reveal the completeness of the refusal of the educated classes to accept the new Church. We read that one of the earliest acts of Elizabeth was to prohibit all preaching, because the great body of the clergy was Popish. The new prayer book was to be used for the first time in the parish churches on June 24th, 1559. This prescribed reading "the popish priests, that is, the majority of them, utterly refused", on the ground "that this manner of ministering of the sacrament, set forth in the book of Common Prayer, was never allowed nor agreed upon by the universal Church of Christ in a General Council", "that it was only agreed upon by the laity, who had nothing to do in spiritual matters" (vol. i., p. 201). So determined were the majority of the clergy not to submit, that they vacated their cures and "since many churches were left destitute, the ministers that remained, and that were put into the places of the popish priests, especially in London, were fain to serve three or four churches on Sundays and holy days, in reading the prayers, and administering the sacraments to the people. And yet they sufficed not. So that in this year, and some years following, until the year 1564 inclusive, many of the laity, who were competently learned, and of sobriety and good religion, were appointed to read the service in the churches, by letters of toleration from the bishops" (p. 203). But the supply of "laity who were competently learned" proved utterly insufficient. The bishoprics were filled up first, and by May 4th, 1561, the bench was reconstituted; but as Dr. Kitchin was incompetent alone to consecrate a bishop, four of the deprived prelates were forced to assist him in starting the new set. "After the Church was thus furnished with some Protestant bishops, it was necessary to supply it with inferior clergy" (p. 233), and, failing the "competently learned", and "the Church standing in need of sober persons to serve in it, the bishops were fain to take many laymen that had little more learning than ability of reading well" (p. 234). But even "ability of reading well" became too severe a test, and "another inconvenience the want of clergymen now brought was the ordination of illiterate men to be readers: which likewise many were offended at. These readers had been tradesmen, or other honest, well-disposed men; and they were admitted into inferior orders, to serve the Church in the present necessity, by reading the common prayer and the homilies, and orders unto the people" (p. 265). Bitter complaints arose about the incompetent men who were thrust into the parishes from which the priests of Rome had been expelled. It was alleged that "of late tinkers, cobblers, cowherds, fiddlers, broommen, and such like were created divines"; and the accusation was not denied by the new dignitaries of the Establishment. All that the Dean of St. Paul's could urge in defending the action of the bishops was "that indeed the Papists' cruel murdering of so many learned men had forced them of mere necessity to supply some small cures with honest artificers, exercised in the Scriptures" (p. 266). When to all this we add that no fewer than one hundred and twenty clergymen were absolutely executed for celebrating the old worship, we shall be able to estimate the value of the pretence that "the Church of England reformed itself".

The great Universities of Oxford and Cambridge, like the parishes of England, were swept by the ecclesiastical storm. Dodd, in his "Church History", quotes the evidence of several great Protestants as to the desolate condition of the seats of learning. He remarks: "The strength of the party that opposed the reformation, appears still more from the account which the Protestant writers give of the desertion that happened in our Universities, and scarcity of persons sufficiently qualified to instruct the people. 'It must be known (saith Anthony Wood) that in the beginning of the reign of Queen Elizabeth, the University of Oxford was so empty after the Catholics had left it upon the alteration of religion, that there was very seldom a sermon preached in the University church called St. Mary. There was not one then [an. 1564] in that society [of Merton College] that could or would preach any public sermon in the college turn; such was the scarcity of theologists, not only in that house, but generally throughout the University'. The same Oxford historian also gives us several particulars of this grand defection. He names twenty-three persons of note ejected out of New College only; seven out of St. John's College, and great numbers out of the colleges of St. Mary Magdalen, Lincoln and Trinity; so that the University seemed to be entirely destroyed; that the persons left were few, and so illiterate that an order came out for everyone to con over the Bible, and lessons, being unable to read them distinctly otherwise; that a like order came out for liberty to make use of the common prayer in the Latin tongue, there being some danger of losing that language in the University: Thomas Sampson and Dr. Humphrey were the only two that could preach with any reputation, unless we join to them Richard Taverner, the high sheriff, who, though a layman, was sometimes permitted to preach in St. Mary's Church. . . . . This desolate condition of Oxford is in like manner taken notice of by Jewel, Parker, and others. 'Our universities, saith Jewel, are in a most lamentable condition—there are not above two in Oxford of our sentiments.' Archbishop Parker tells the Queen, 'There were not two men able or willing to read the lady Margaret's lecture; and though they had a great many preachers, yet he was afraid several of them were but slenderly furnished for that employment'" (vol. ii., pp. 8, 9).

Nor did the laity, any more than the clergy, receive quietly the overthrow of the old Church and the setting up of the new one. In 1536 the whole north of England was convulsed by risings in defence of the old faith. First in Lincolnshire and then in Yorkshire the people rose, demanding the reinstatement of the monks in their possessions, and the "depressing of heretics". Doncaster, Carlisle, Hull, and other towns were attacked, and the rebellion was ultimately suppressed in 1537 only by martial law. In 1549, the imposition of the Parliamentary Prayer Book was bitterly resisted, and on the very day after its first use in Devonshire the parish priest of Samford Courtney was forced by his parishioners to read mass instead, and the rising in support of the old Church was soon joined by some 10,000 men. They sent to the king a demand for the restitution of the mass "celebrated as it was in times past", and marched with the consecrated host carried under a canopy in front of their army. The rebellion was put down with great slaughter, "most of the rascal rabble executed by martial law; and the Vicar of St. Thomas, one of the principal incendiaries, hanged on the top of his own tower, apparelled in his Popish weeds, with his beads at his girdle" (Heylyn, vol. i., p. 159). A rebellion broke out in Norfolk at the same time, in which more than 20,000 men took part; in their complaint they urged "Secondly, that holy rites, established by antiquity, were abolished, new ones authorised, and a new form of religion obtruded, to the subjecting of their souls to those horrid pains which no death could terminate" (*Ibid*, p. 160). This rising also was put down with terrible severity, as was a third in Yorkshire in the same year. Whereupon says Dr. Heylyn gleefully: "The necessary execution of so many rebels, and this seasonable severity against Bishop Bonner [his deprivation], did much facilitate the King's proceedings in the Reformation" (*Ibid*, p. 163). Dodd also remarks: "Upon the alterations that were made in the discipline of the Church, a general discontent appeared all over the nation. They saw plainly all was going to ruin, and that the system of religion was aimed at, no less than the revenues of the Church" ("Church History", vol. i., p. 352). In truth no pretence can be more opposed to the facts of history than the pretence that the Reformation was the work of the Church of England reforming itself. The abolition of the Church of Rome, and the setting up of a Parliamentary Church with a Royal Head, were due wholly to the imperious will of Henry VIII.; had the Pope granted him a divorce from Catherine, he would never have rejected the Papal supremacy; but he "who never spared man in his anger, or woman in his lust" found the Roman Church standing in his path to Anne Boleyn, and he struck it down and cast it out of his way. One of the earliest acts of the new Church through its archbishop, Cranmer, was to legalise Henry's union with Anne, and it as readily divorced her when Henry was weary of her as it had divorced Catherine. It was born of royal will mated to royal lust, and was forced on a reluctant people by Henry, Edward VI. and Elizabeth with all the dogged determination of the Tudor race. The old Church was stripped of its possessions; its doctrines and ceremonies were proscribed; its hierarchy was destroyed; its faithful laity were kept down, impoverished, murdered; with sword and penal law the State imposed on its members a new Church, dowered it with some of the wealth it had taken from its forerunner, bound its creature strictly in every detail, and from time to time remoulded it at its pleasure. Well may the adherents of the old Church denounce the impudence with which the Parliamentary cuckoo claims to be the original owner of the nest whence it has ousted the true fledglings. The present Roman Catholic Bishop of Nottingham in his "Pastoral Letter for Lent", Part II., 1886, takes the ground that "the Church of England is not the representative of the early English Church, nor the rightful heir to her goods." After quoting the "Profession of Faith unanimously agreed to by the English bishops and the Convocation of the English Clergy, and presented to the House of Lords, with a protest against the Bill of Supremacy, in the first year of Elizabeth", the bishop says: "By this noble act, the last act of the ancient Church of England, the English Bishops and Clergy bore witness not only to their own faith, but to the faith of their predecessors, that it was both Catholic and Roman." The bishop proceeds to show how the country resisted the new Church forced on it, and then continues: "Hallam tells us that 'such a deficiency of Protestant Clergy was experienced at the Queen's accession, that for several years it was a common practice to appoint laymen, usually mechanics, to read the service in vacant churches'. We read also in the life of Parker, that in the diocese of Ely, in the year 1560, only fifty-two out of one hundred and fifty-two benefices were served. In 1560 again Lever wrote Bullinger: 'Many of our parishes have no clergymen, and some dioceses are without a bishop. And out of that very small number who administer the Sacraments throughout this great country, there is hardly one in a hundred who is both able and willing to preach the Word of God'. And in the same year Horne, Dean of Durham, wrote to Cecil: 'In the Diocese of Durham the ministry is destitute of a sufficiency of worthy men, there and in other places'." He further argues that in rejecting the "Papal Supremacy and the Sacrifice of the Mass" "they have ever taught the direct contrary of the teaching of the early English Church", and that the Parliamentary bishops are no true bishops, since they receive their spiritual jurisdiction from one of the laity, instead of from a spiritual authority, appointed by God; and he asks: "Has any Anglican bishop ever ventured to enquire how her Majesty has received from Christ any commission to feed his sheep, or any power whatsoever to give spiritual jurisdiction, or assign limits for its exercise?" He taunts the bishops and clergy with having "to learn their faith and take their worship from a handful of lawyers", quoting the address of the English bishops to their clergy after the passing of the Public Worship Regulation Act, in which they "seriously remind our brethren of the clergy of the solemn obligation which binds us all to be ready to yield a willing obedience to the law of the Church of England, of which we are ordained ministers, and to recognise the necessity of submitting our own interpretations of any points in that law which may be considered doubtful to the judicial decisions of lawfully-constituted courts. We, the Clergy, are bound by every consideration to obey the law when thus clearly interpreted." After quoting a number of the Elizabethan bishops who denounced the older Church and laid stress on their divergence from it, he concludes: "Thus did Elizabeth's so-called bishops blaspheme, outrage, and endeavor to abolish, the Supreme authority in God's Church, and its central act of Divine worship; and thus cruelly did they persecute and hound to death the devoted priests of God, and other adherents to the ancient Faith of England. And yet we sometimes hear the successors of these impious and usurping persecutors of God's Church impudently styling themselves the successors of the Catholic bishops, and claiming for the Anglican Establishment, with an almost incredible audacity, that it is the true successor and representative of that very Church and Faith which it sacrilegiously did its best to root out and utterly abolish from this land."

It is not surprising that the adherents of the older Church should feel indignant at the pretensions of the new. And truly a Church that ruthlessly crushed the men and women whose only offence was that they did *not* change their religion, but remained true to the faith into which they had been baptised, can scarcely rationally claim to be the same Church as that to which the persecuted admittedly belonged.

In considering the Church as the creature of Crown and Parliament, it is impossible to overlook the fashion in which it was completely remodelled by the Long Parliament. When that body met in 1640, a movement commenced that soon resulted in the destruction of Episcopacy and the setting up of Presbyterianism. The Bishop of Ely was impeached for Popish leanings in December, 1640, and the king was requested to depose him. Twelve Bishops, in December, 1641, petitioned the king, alleging that they could not reach Parliament in consequence of mob violence, and that all things done in Parliament during their absence were null and void; they were thereupon impeached for high treason, and imprisoned in the Tower for eighteen weeks; then released on bail (see Howell and Cobbett's State Trials, vol. iv., pp. 63—82). Laud, Archbishop of Canterbury, was also attacked, and after a trial that dragged on from 1640 to 1644 was condemned, nominally for high treason. And truly, if capital punishment be ever justifiable, it was justifiable in the case of the cruel and bloodthirsty Archbishop Laud. In 1642, the Bishops were relieved from their attendance in Parliament, much to the benefit ef Parliament and, let us hope, to the benefit of their ecclesiastical duties. In 1643 the Covenant was taken by the Commons, and in the following year it was imposed as a test for office. Hundreds of clergy left their livings rather than accept the new conditions laid down by the State. The "Directory of Public Worship" took the place of the Book of Common Prayer, and became the service book of the Establishment. The "Confession of Faith" was debated in Parliament over and over again; the "Business of the Church" is one of the frequent items recurring in Whitelock's "Historical Account"; and the disposition of "Bishops' Lands" was often discussed. The revenues accruing to the ecclesiastical department were freely disposed of by Parliament; in October, 1647, it was voted by the Commons "that the Presbyterian Government be established, till the end of the next Session of Parliament. That the Tenths and Maintenance belonging to any Church shall be only to such as can submit to the Presbyterian Government, and none other" (p. 276). We find them also from time to time directing tithes to be used for non-ecclesiastical purposes. In October, 1648, the king "consented to the abolishing of Archbishops, Chancellors, Deans, and Chapters, etc., and the whole Hierarchy, save Bishops"; and he confirmed the Presbyterian Government "for three years; and no other to be used, and the exercise of episcopal government to be wholly suspended, during that time" (p. 339). Thus the Crown and Parliament that had set up Bishops pulled them down, and down they remained until Crown and Parliament set them up again on the accession of Charles II.

My position that the Establishment is the creature of Crown and Parliament is, I contend, historically proved; and Parliament, in once again changing the disposition of the revenues now allocated to the ecclesiastical department of the State, will be acting strictly in accord with precedent, and not entering on a new path.

There remains the question: To what purposes shall this property be put? Two objects, above all others, it seems to me, are the best to which it could be devoted under present conditions—the education of children and the relief of the poor. Let the clergyman be replaced by the schoolmaster in every parish, and let those who want a clergyman hire him and pay him themselves. Let the whole income of each parish be paid into the hands of a diocesan board, or other district authority; let the salaries of the parish schoolmasters be paid by this board; let the school buildings be maintained out of it; and let the remainder of the funds be devoted to the assistance of the sick and the aged who may be in want of such help. Until poverty is done away with by a saner social system than now prevails, the relief of the poor is a duty incumbent on the community; and it might be a good use for the rectories and vicarages to turn them into parochial homes for the aged poor, making the gardens the pleasure resort of the parish. The parish income might be increased by letting the church for lectures, concerts, and religious services, to any who require it, without distinction of sect.

How to make the change is too large a subject for the conclusion of this tract; but I may suggest as a plan that would avoid much friction, that parish clergymen over sixty years of age should be allowed to hold their livings till death, without any change being made in their parishes; that parish clergymen under forty should be offered the duty of teaching secular subjects, under control of the new district board, any who declined vacating their livings without compensation; parish clergymen between forty and sixty should have the same offer made to them, with the alternative of receiving £150 a year till death, no lump sum being paid to them under any circumstances. All advowsons should pass to the district boards on the death of the present proprietors; the patrons now living to be permitted only to present schoolmasters to any benefices that fall vacant, such presentation to be confirmed by the district board.

On these lines the change might be made without an "interference with vested interests" such as would not be sanctioned by public opinion at the present time. If however, the Establishment should last very much longer, and should endure into a period in which public opinion shall have grown more rational, the change will come in far more sweeping fashion, and the only compensation offered to the dispossessed clergy will be openings for useful work.

Printed by Annie Besant and Charles Bradlaugh, 63, Fleet St., E.C.—1886.

WHY I DO NOT BELIEVE IN GOD.

BY

ANNIE BESANT.

LONDON:
FREETHOUGHT PUBLISHING COMPANY,
63, FLEET STREET, E.C.
1887.

PRICE THREEPENCE.

LONDON:
PRINTED BY ANNIE BESANT AND CHARLES BRADLAUGH,
63, FLEET STREET, E.C.

WHY I DO NOT BELIEVE IN GOD.

THERE is no doubt that the majority of people in most parts of the world—save in those in which Buddhism is supreme—believe in the existence of a God. The kind of God may vary indefinitely, but there is generally "some God or other". Now a growing minority in every civilised country finds it intellectually impossible to make the affirmation which is necessary for belief in God, and this growing minority includes many of the most thoughtful and most competent minds. The refusal to believe is unfortunately not always public, so cruel is the vengeance worked by society on those who do not bow down to its fetishes; but as John Stuart Mill said: "The world would be astonished if it knew how great a proportion of its brightest ornaments—of those most distinguished even in popular estimation for wisdom and virtue—are complete sceptics in religion" ("Autobiography," p. 45).

It is sad that all should not recognise that, as the late Professor Clifford put it, Truth is a thing to be shouted from the housetops, not to be whispered over the walnuts and wine after the ladies have left; for only by plain and honest speech on this matter can liberty of thought be won. Each who speaks out makes easier speech for others, and none, however insignificant, has right of silence here. Nor is it unfair, I think, that a minority should be challenged on its dissidency, and should be expected to state clearly and definitely the grounds of its disagreement with the majority.

Ere going into detailed argument it may be well to remind the reader that the burden of affording proof lies on the affirmer of a proposition; the rational attitude of the human mind is not that of a boundless credulity, accepting every statement as true until it has been proved to be false, but is that of a suspension of judgment on every statement which, though not obviously false, is not supported by evidence, and of an absolute rejection of a statement self-contradictory in its terms, or incompatible with truths already demonstrated. To remove this position from the region of prejudice in which theological discussion is carried on, it may be well to take the following illustration: a man asks me, "Do you believe that Jupiter is inhabited by a race of men who have one eye in the middle of their foreheads, and who walk about on three legs, with their heads under their left arms?" I answer: "No, I do not believe it; I have no evidence that such beings exist". If my interlocutor desires to convince me that Jupiter has inhabitants, and that his description of them is accurate, it is for him to bring forward evidence in support of his contention. The burden of proof evidently lies on him; it is not for me to prove that no such beings exist before my non-belief is justified, but for him to prove that they do exist before my belief can be fairly claimed. Similarly, it is for the affirmer of God's existence to bring evidence in support of his affirmation; the burden of proof lies on him.

For be it remembered that the Atheist makes no general denial of the existence of God; he does not say, "There is no God". If he put forward such a proposition, which he can only do intelligently if he understand the term "God", then, truly, he would be bound to bring forth his evidence in support. But the proof of a universal negative requires the possession of perfect knowledge of the universe of discourse, and in this case the universe of discourse is conterminous with the totality of existence. No man can rationally affirm "There is no God", until the word "God" has for him a definite meaning, and until everything that exists is known to him, and known with what Leibnitz calls "perfect knowledge". The Atheist's denial of the Gods begins only when these Gods are defined or described. Never yet has a God been defined in terms which were not palpably self-contradictory and absurd; never yet has a God been described so that a concept of him was made possible to human thought. Again I fall back on an illustration unconnected with theology in order to make clearly apparent the distinction drawn. If I am asked: "Do you believe in the existence of a triangle in space on the other side of Saturn?" I answer, "I neither believe in, nor deny its existence; I know nothing about it". But if I am asked: "Do you believe in the existence there of a boundless triangle, or of a square triangle?" then my answer is: "I deny the possibility of the existence of such triangles". The reason for the different answers to the two questions is that as I have never visited the other side of Saturn I know nothing about the existence or non-existence of triangles there; but I deny the possibility of the existence of a boundless triangle, because the word triangle means a figure enclosed by three limiting lines; and I deny the possibility of the existence of a square triangle, because a triangle has three sides only while a square has four, and all the angles of a triangle taken together are equal to two right angles, while those of a square are equal to four. I allege that anyone who believes in a square triangle can have no clear concept either of a triangle or of a square. And so while I refuse to say "there is no God", lacking the knowledge which would justify the denial, since to me the word God represents no concept, I do say, "there is no infinite personality, there is no infinite creator, there is no being at once almighty and all-good, there is no Trinity in Unity, there is no eternal and infinite existence save that of which each one of us is mode". For be it noted, these denials are justified by our knowledge: an undefined "God" might be a limited being on the far side of Sirius, and I have no knowledge which justifies me in denying such an existence; but an infinite God, *i.e.*, a God who is everywhere, who has no limits, and yet who is not I and who is therefore limited by my personality, is a being who is self-contradictory, both limited and not-limited, and such a being cannot exist. No perfect knowledge is needed here. "God is an infinite being" is disproved by one being who is not God. "God is everywhere" is disproved by the finding of one spot where God is not. The universal affirmative is disproved by a single exception. Nor is anything gained by the assertors of deity when they allege that he is incomprehensible. If "God" exists and is incomprehensible, his incomprehensibility is an admirable reason for being silent about him, but can never justify the affirmation of self-contradictory propositions, and the threatening of people with damnation if they do not accept them.

I turn to examine the evidence which is brought forward

in support of the existence of God, taking "God" to mean some undefined being other than and superior to the various forms of living and non-living things on this earth—or those forming part of the "material universe" in which we exist—and related to these as creator and controller. Now the existence of anything may be sensated or it may be inferred; the astronomer believed in the existence of Saturn because he saw it; but he also believed in the existence of the planet afterwards named Neptune before he saw it, attaining this belief by way of induction from the otherwise inexplicable behavior of Uranus. Can we then by the senses or by the reason find out God?

The most common, and to many the most satisfactory and convincing evidence, is that of the senses. A child born into the world has open to him these sense avenues of knowledge; he learns that something exists which is not he by the impressions made on his senses; he sees, he feels, he hears, he smells, he tastes, and thus he learns to know. As the child's past and present sensations increase in number, as he begins to remember them, to compare, to mark likenesses and unlikenesses, he gathers the materials for further mental elaboration. But this sensational basis of his knowledge is the limit of the area on which his intellectual edifice can be built; he may rear it upward as far as his powers will permit, but he can never widen his foundation, while his senses remain only what they are. All that the mind works on has reached it by these senses; it can dissociate and combine, it can break in pieces and build up, but no sensation no percept, and no percept no concept.

When this fundamental truth is securely grasped it will be seen of what tremendous import is the admitted fact that the senses wholly fail us when we seek for proof of the existence of God. Our belief in the existence of all things outside ourselves rests on the testimony of the senses. The "objective universe" is that which we sensate. When we reason and reflect, when we think of love, and fear, when we speak of truth and honor, we know that all these are not susceptible of being sensated, that is, that they have no objective existence; they belong to the Subject universe. Now if God cannot be sensated he also must belong to the Subject world; that is, he must be a creation of the mind, with no outside corresponding reality. Granted that we can never know "the thing in itself"; granted that all we know is only the effect on the mind produced by something which differs from the effect it produces; yet this fundamental physiological distinction remains between the Object and the Subject worlds, that the Object world announces itself by nervous action which is set up at the periphery, while the Subject world results from the centrally initiated travail of the brain.

It might, indeed, be argued by the Theist that God may exist, but may be incognisable by our senses, we lacking the sense which might sensate deity. Quite so. There may be existences around us but unknown to us, there being no part of our organism differentiated to receive from them impressions. There are rays beyond the solar spectrum which are invisible to us normally, the existence of which was unknown to us some years ago, but some of which apparently serve among light rays for the ant; so there may be all kinds of existences in the universe of which we are unconscious, as unconscious as we were of the existence of the ultra-violet rays until a chemical reagent rendered them visible. But as we cannot sensate them, *for us they do not exist.* This, then, cannot avail the Theist, for an incognisable God, a God who can enter into no kind of relation with us, is to us a non-existent God. We cannot even conceive a sense entirely different from those we possess, let alone argue over what we should find out by means of it if we had it.

It is said that of old time the evidence of the senses for the existence of God was available; the seventy elders "saw the God of Israel"; Moses talked with him "face to face"; Elijah heard his "still small voice". But these experiences are all traditional; we have no evidence at first hand; no witness that we can examine; no facts that we can investigate. There is not even evidence enough to start a respectable ghost story, let alone enough to bear the tremendous weight of the existence of God. Yet, if some finite "God" exist—I say finite, because, as noted above, the co-existence of an infinite God and a finite creature is impossible—how easy for him to prove his existence; if he be too great for our "comprehension", as some Theists argue, he might surely bestow on us a sense which might receive impressions from him, and enable us to reach at least a partial, an imperfect, knowledge of him. But if he exist, he wraps himself in darkness; if he exist, he folds himself in silence. Leaning, as it were, over the edge of being, men strive to pierce the dark abyss of the unknown, above, below; they strain their sight, but they see nothing; they listen, but nothing strikes their ear; weary, dizzy, they stagger backwards, and with the darkness pressing on their eyeballs they murmur "God!".

Failing to discover God by way of the senses, we turn to such evidence for his existence as may be found by way of the reason, in order to determine whether we can establish by inference that which we have failed to establish by direct proof.

As the world is alleged to be the handiwork of God, it is not unreasonable to scrutinise the phænomena of nature, and to seek in them for traces of a ruling intelligence, of a guiding will. But it is impossible even to glance at natural phænomena, much less to study them attentively, without being struck by the enormous waste of energy, the aimless destruction, the utterly unintelligent play of conflicting and jarring forces. For centuries "nature" has been steadily at work growing forests, cutting out channels for rivers, spreading alluvial soil and clothing it with grass and flowers; at last a magnificent landscape is formed, birds and beasts dwell in its woods and on its pastures, men till its fertile fields, and thank the gracious God they worship for the work of his hands; there is a far-off growl which swells as it approaches, a trembling of the solid earth, a crash, an explosion, and then, in a darkness lightened only by the fiery rain of burning lava, all beauty, all fertility, vanish, and the slow results of thousands of years are destroyed in a night of earthquake and volcanic fury. Is it from this wild destruction of slowly obtained utility that we are to infer the existence of a divine intelligence and divine will? If beauty and use were aimed at, why the destruction? If desolation and uselessness, why the millenniums spent in growth?

During the year 1886 many hundreds of people in Greece, in Spain, in America, in Ne v Zealand, were killed or maimed by earthquakes and by cyclones. Many more perished in hurricanes at sea. Many more by explosions in mines and elsewhere. These deaths caused widespread misery, consigned families to hopeless poverty, cut short careers of use and of promise. They were caused by "natural" forces. Is "God" behind nature, and are all these horrors planned, carried out, by his mind and will? John Stuart Mill has put the case clearly and forcibly:

"Next to the greatness of these cosmic forces, the quality which most forcibly strikes everyone who does not avert his eyes from it is their perfect and absolute recklessness. They go straight to their end, without regarding what or whom they crush on the road. Optimists, in their attempts to prove that 'whatever is, is right', are obliged to maintain, not that nature ever turns one step from her path to avoid trampling us into destruction, but that it would be very unreasonable in us to expect that she should. Pope's 'Shall gravitation cease when you go by?' may be a just rebuke to anyone who should be so silly as to expect common human morality from nature. But if the question were between two men, instead of between a man and a natural phænomenon, that triumphant apostrophe would be thought a rare piece of impudence. A man who should persist in hurling stones or firing cannon when another man 'goes by', and having killed him should urge a similar plea in exculpation, would very deservedly be found guilty of murder. In sober truth, nearly all the things which men are hanged or imprisoned for doing to one another, are Nature's everyday performances. Killing, the most criminal act recognised by human laws, Nature does once to every being that lives; and in a large proportion of cases, after protracted tortures such as only the greatest monsters whom we read of ever purposely inflicted on their living fellow creatures. If, by an arbitrary reservation, we refuse to account anything murder but what abridges a certain term supposed to be allotted to human life, nature also does this to all but a small percentage of lives, and does it in all the modes, violent or insidious, in which the worst human beings take the lives of one another. Nature impales men, breaks them as if on the wheel, casts them to be devoured by wild beasts, burns them to death, crushes them with stones like the first Christian martyr, starves them with hunger, freezes them with cold, poisons them by the quick or slow venom of her exhalations, and has hundreds of other hideous deaths in reserve, such as the ingenious cruelty of a Nabis or a Domitian never surpassed. All this, Nature does with the most supercilious disregard both of mercy and of justice, emptying her shafts upon the best and noblest indifferently with the meanest and worst; upon those who are engaged in the highest and worthiest enterprises, and often as the direct consequence of the noblest acts; and it might almost be imagined as a punishment for them. She mows down those on whose existence hangs the wellbeing of a whole people, perhaps the prospects of the human race for generations to come, with as little compunction as those whose death is a relief to themselves, or a blessing to those under their noxious influence" ("Three Essays on Religion," pp. 28, 29, ed. 1874).

It is not only from the suffering caused by the undeviating course of the phænomena which from the invariable sequence of their happening are called "laws of nature" that we infer the absence of any director or controller of these forces. There are many absurdities as well as miseries, caused by the "uniformity of nature". Dr. Büchner tells us of a kid he saw which was born perfect in all parts save that it was headless ("Force and Matter", page 234, ed. 1884). Here, for weeks the kid was a-forming, although life in the outer world was impossible for it. Monstrosities occur in considerable numbers, and each one bears silent witness to the unintelligence of the forces that produced it. Nay, they can be artificially produced, as has been shown by a whole series of experiments, eggs tapped during incubation yielding monstrous chickens. In all these cases we recognise the blind action of unconscious forces bringing about a ridiculous and unforeseen result, if turned slightly out of their normal course. From studying this aspect of nature it is certain that we cannot find God. So far from finding here a God to worship, the whole progress of man depends on his learning to control and regulate these natural forces, so as to prevent them from working mischief and to turn them into channels in which they will work for good.

If from scrutinising the forces of nature we study the history of the evolution of life on our globe, and the physical conditions under which man now exists, it is impossible from these to infer the existence of a benevolent power as the creator of the world. Life is one vast battlefield, in which the victory is always to the strong. More organisms are produced than can grow to maturity; they fight for the limited supply of food, and by means of this struggle the weakest are crushed out and the fittest survive to propagate their race. Each successful organism stands on the corpses of its weaker antagonists, and only by this ceaseless strife and slaying has progress been possible. As the organisms grow more complex and more developed, added difficulties surround their existence; the young of the higher animals are weaker and more defenceless at birth than those of the lower, and the young of man, the highest animal yet evolved, is the most helpless of all, and his hold of life the most precarious during infancy. So clumsy is the "plan of creation" that among the most highly-evolved animals a new life is only possible by peril to life already existing, and the mother must pass through long weeks of physical weariness and hours of acute agony ere she can hold her baby in her arms. All these things are so "natural" to us that we need to think of them, not as necessary, but as deliberately planned by a creative power, ere we can realise the monstrous absurdity of supposing them to be the outcome of "design". Nor must we overlook the sufferings caused by the incomplete adaptation of evolving animals to the conditions among which they are developing. The human race is still suffering from its want of adaptation to the upright position, from its inheritance of a structure from quadrupedal ancestors which was suited to the horizontal position of their trunks, but is unsuited to the vertical position of man. The sufferings caused by child-birth, and by hernia, testify to the incomplete adaptation of the race to the upright condition. To believe that all the slow stages of blood-stained evolution, that the struggle for existence, that the survival of the fittest with its other side, the crushing of the less fit, together with a million subsidiary consequences of the main "plan", to believe that all these were designed, foreseen, deliberately selected as the method of creation, by an almighty power, to believe this is to believe that "God" is the supreme malignity, a creator who voluntarily devises and executes a plan of the most ghastly malice, and who works it out with a cruelty in details which no human pen can adequately describe.

But, again, the condition and the history of the world are not consistent with its being the creation of an almighty and perfect cruelty. While the tragedy of life negates the possibility of an omnipotent goodness as its author, the beauty and happiness of life negate equally the possibility of an almighty fiend as its creator. The delight of bird and beast in the vigor of their eager life; the love-notes of mate to mate, and the brooding ectasy of the mother over her young; the rapture of the song which sets quivering the body of the lark as he soars upwards in the sun-rays; the gambols of the young, with every curve telling of sheer joy in life and movement; the beauty and strength of man and woman; the power of intellect, the glory of genius, the exquisite happiness of sympathy; all these things could not find place in the handiwork of a power delighting in pain. We cannot, then, from the study of life on our globe infer the existence of a God who is wholly good ; the evil disproves him: nor can we infer the existence of a God who is wholly evil; the good disproves him. All that we learn from life-conditions is that if the world has a creator his character must be exceedingly mixed, and must be one to be regarded with extreme suspicion and apprehension. Be it noted, however, that, so far, we have found no reason to infer the existence of any creative intelligence.

Leaving the phænomena of nature exclusive of man, as yielding us no information as to the existence of God, we turn next to human life and human history to seek for traces of the "divine presence". But here again we are met by the same mingling of good and evil, the same waste, the same prodigality, which met us in non-human nature. Instead of the "Providence watching over the affairs of men" in which Theists believe, we note that "there be just men, unto whom it happeneth according to the work of the wicked; again, there be wicked men, to whom it happeneth according to the work of the righteous". A railway accident happens, in which a useful man, the mainstay of a family, is killed, and from which a profligate escapes. An explosion in a mine slays the hardworking breadwinners at their toil, and the drunken idler whose night's debauch has resulted in heavy morning sleep is "providentially" saved as he snores lazily at home in bed. The man whose life is invaluable to a nation perishes in his prime, while the selfish race-haunting aristocrat lives on to a green old age. The honest conscientious trader keeps with difficulty out of the bankruptcy court, and sees his smart, unscrupulous neighbor pile up a fortune by tricks that just escape the meshes of the law. If indeed there be a guiding hand amid the vicissitudes of human life, it must be that of an ironical, mocking cruelty, which plays with men as puppets for the gratification of a sardonic humor. Of course, the real explanation of all these things is that there is no common factor in these moral and physical propositions; the quantities are incommensurable; the virtues or vices of a man are not among the causes which launch, or do not launch, a chimney pot at his head.

Outside these "changes and chances" of human life, the thoughtful mind feels conscious of a profound dissatisfaction with many of the inevitable conditions of human existence: the sensative faculties are at their keenest when the intelligence is not sufficiently developed to utilise them; the perceptive faculties begin to fail as the reflective touch their fullest development; and when experience is ripest, judgment most trained, knowledge most full, old age lays its palsy on the brain, and senility shakes down the edifice just when a life's toil has made it of priceless value. To recognise our limitations, to accept the inevitable, to amend—so far as amendment is possible—both ourselves and our environment, all this forms part of a rational philosophy of life; but what has such self-controlled and keen-eyed sternness of resolve to do with hysterical outcries for help to some power outside nature, which, if it existed as creator, must have modelled our existence at its pleasure, and towards which our attitude could be only one of bitterest, if silent, rebellion? To bow to the inevitable evil, while studying its conditions in order to strive to make it the evitable, is consistent with strong hope which lightens life's darkness; but to yield crushed before evil deliberately and consciously inflicted by an omnipotent intelligence—in such fate lies the agony of madness and despair.

Nor do we find any reliable signs of the presence of a God in glancing over the incidents of human history. We note unjust wars, in which right is crushed by might, in which victory sides with "the strongest battalions", in the issue of which there appears no trace of a "God that judgeth the earth". We meet with cruelties that sicken us inflicted on man by man; butcheries that desolate a city, persecutions that lay waste a province. In every civilised land of to-day we see wealth mocking poverty, and poverty cursing wealth; here, thousands wasted on a harlot, and there children sobbing themselves in hunger to sleep. Our earth rolls wailing yearly round the sun, bearing evidence that it has no creator who loves and guides it, but has only its men, children of its own womb, who by the ceaseless toil of countless generations are hewing out the possibility of a better and gladder world.

Similar testimony is borne by the slow progress of the human race. Truth is always fighting; each new truth undergoes a veritable struggle for existence, and if Hercules is to live to perform his labors he must succeed in strangling the serpents that hiss round his cradle. The new truth must first be held only by one, its discoverer; if he is not crushed at the outset, a few disciples are won; then the little band is persecuted, some are martyred, and, it may be, the movement destroyed. Or, some survive, and gain converts, and so the new truth slowly spreads, winning acceptance at the last. But each new truth must pass through similar ordeal, and hence the slowness of the upward climb of man. Look backwards over the time which has passed since man was emerging from the brute, and then compare those millenniums with the progress that has been made, and the distance which still separates the race from a reasonably happy life for all its members. If a God cannot do better for man than this, man may be well content to trust to his own unaided efforts. We turn from the phænomena of human life, as from those of non-human nature, without finding any evidence which demonstrates, or even renders probable, the existence of a God.

There is another line of reasoning, however, apart from the consideration of phænomena, which must, it is alleged, lead us to believe in the existence of a God. This is the well-used argument from causation. Every effect must have a cause, therefore the universe must have a cause, is a favorite enthymeme, of which the suppressed minor is, the universe is an effect. But this is a mere begging of the question. Every effect must have a cause; granted; for a cause is defined as that which produces an effect, and an effect as that which is produced by a cause; the two words are co-relatives, and the one is meaningless separated from the other. Prove that the universe is an effect, and in so doing you will have proved that it has a cause; but in the proof of that quietly-suppressed minor is the *crux* of the dispute. We see that the forces around us are the causes of various effects, and that they, the causes of events which follow their action, are themselves the effects of causes which preceded such action. From the continued observation of these sequences, ourselves part of this endless chain, the idea of causation is worked into the human mind, and becomes, as it were, part of its very texture, so that we cannot in thought separate phænomena from their causes, and the uncaused becomes to us the inconceivable. But we cannot rationally extend reasoning wholly based on phænomena into the region of the noumenon. That which is true of the phænomenal universe gives us no clue when we try to pass without it, and to penetrate into the mystery of existence *per se*. To call God "the first cause" is to play with words after their meaning has been emptied from them. If the argument from causation is to be applied to the existence of the universe, which is, without any proof, to be accepted as an effect, why may it not with equal force be applied to "God", who, equally without any proof, may be regarded as an effect? and so we may create an illimitable series of Gods, each an assumption unsupported by evidence. If we once begin puffing divine smoke-rings, the only limit to the exercise is our want of occupation and the amount of suitable tobacco our imagination is able to supply. The belief of the Atheist stops where his evidence stops. He believes in the existence of the universe, judging the accessible proof thereof to be adequate, and he finds in this universe sufficient cause for the happening of all phænomena. He finds no intellectual satisfaction in placing a gigantic conundrum behind the universe, which only adds its own unintelligibility to the already sufficiently difficult problem of existence. Our lungs are not fitted to breathe beyond the atmosphere which surrounds our globe, and our faculties cannot breathe outside the atmosphere of the phænomenal. If I went up in a balloon I should check it when I found it carrying me into air too rare for my respiration; and I decline to be carried by a theological balloon into regions wherein thought cannot breathe healthily, but can only fall down gasping, imagining that its gasps are inspiration.

There remain for us to investigate two lines of evidence, either of which suffices, apparently, to carry conviction to a large number of minds; these are, the argument from human experience, and the argument from design.

I have no desire to lessen the weight of an argument drawn from the *sensus communis*, the common sense, of mankind. It is on this that we largely rely in drawing distinctions between the normal and the abnormal; it is this which serves as test between the sane and the insane; no thoughtful student can venture to ignore the tremendous force of the consensus of human experience. But while he will not ignore, he must judge: he must ask, first, is this experience universal and unanimous? Secondly, on what experimental or other evidence is it based? The universal and unanimous verdict of human experience, based on clear verifiable experience, is one which the thinker will challenge with extreme hesitation. Yet cause may arise which justifies such challenge. Perhaps no belief has at once been so general, and so undeniably based on the evidence of the senses, as the belief in the movement of the sun and the immobility of our globe. All but the blind could daily see the rising of the sun in the eastern sky, and its setting in the west; all could feel the firmness of the unshaken earth, the solid unmoving steadfastness of the ground on which we tread. Yet this consensus of human experience, this universality of human testimony, has been rejected as false on evidence which none who can feel the force of reasoning is able to deny. If this belief, in defence of which can be brought the *ne plus ultra* of the verdict of common sense, be not tenable in the light of modern knowledge, how shall a belief on which the *sensus communis* is practically non-existent, on which human testimony is lacking in many cases, contradictory in all others, and which fails to maintain itself on experimental or other evidence, how shall it hold ground from which the other has been driven?

The reply to the question, "Is the evidence universal and unanimous?" must be in the negative. The religion of Buddha, which is embraced by more than a third of the population of the globe, is an Atheistic creed; many Buddhists pay veneration to Buddha, and to the statues of their own deceased ancestors, but none pretend that these objects of reverence are symbols of a divine power. Many of the lower savage tribes have no idea of God. Darwin writes: "There is ample evidence, derived not from hasty travellers, but from men who have long resided with savages, that numerous races have existed, and still exist, who have no idea of one or more Gods, and who have no words in their language to express such an idea" ("Descent of Man," pp. 93, 94, ed. 1875). Büchner ("Force and

Matter," pp. 382—393) has collected a mass of evidence showing that whole races of men have no idea of God at all. Sir John Lubbock has done the same. When savages reach a stage of intelligence at which they begin to seek the causes of phænomena, they invariably postulate many Gods as causes of the many objects around them. A New Zealander who was told of the existence of the one God by a missionary, asked him scoffingly if, among Europeans, one man made things of every sort; and he argued that as there were various trades among men, so there were various Gods, each with his own business, and one made trees, another the sea, another the animals, and so on. Only when intelligence has reached a comparatively high plane, is evolved the idea of one God, the creator and the ruler of the universe. Moreover this idea of "God" is essentially an abstract, not a concrete idea, and the fancy that there is an entity belonging to it is but a survival of Realism, a theory which is discredited in everything save in this one theological remnant.

It has been alleged by some writers that, however degraded may be the savage, he still has some idea of supernatural existences, and that error on this head has arisen from the want of thoroughly understanding the savage's ideas. But even these writers do not allege that the belief of these savages touches on a being who can be called by the most extreme courtesy "God". There may be a vague fear of the unknown, a tendency to crouch before striking and dangerous manifestations of natural forces, an idea of some unseen power residing in a stone or a relic—a fetish; but such things—and of the existence of even these in the lowest savages evidence is lacking—can surely not be described as belief in God.

Not only is the universal evidence a-wanting, but such evidence as there is wholly lacks unanimity. What attribute of the divine character, what property of the divine nature, is attested by the unanimous voice of human experience? What is there in common between the Mumbo-Jumbo of Africa, and the "heavenly Father", of refined nineteenth century European Theism? What tie, save that of a common name, unites the blood-dripping Tezcatlepoca of Mexico with him "whose tender mercy is over all his works"? Even if we confine ourselves to the Gods of the Jews, the Christians, and the Mahommedans, how great is the clash of dissension. The Jew proclaims it blasphemy to speak of a divine Trinity, and shrinks with horror from the thought of an incarnate God. The Christian calls it blasphemy to deny the deity of the man Christ Jesus, and affirms, under anathema, the triune nature of the Godhead. The Mahommedan asserts the unity of God, and stamps as infidel everyone who refuses to see in Mahommed the true revealer of the divinity. Each is equally certain that he is right, and each is equally certain that the others are wrong, and are in peril of eternal damnation for their rejection of the one true faith. If the Christian has his lake of fire and brimstone for those who deny Christ, the Mahommedan has his drinks of boiling water for those who assert him. Among this clash of tongues, to whom shall turn the bewildered enquirer after truth? All his would-be teachers are equally positive, and equally without evidence. All are loud in assertion, but singularly modest in their offers of proof.

Now, it may be taken as an undeniable fact that where there is confusion of belief there is deficiency of evidence. Scientific men quarrel and dispute over some much controverted scientific theory. They dispute because the experimental proofs are lacking that would decide the truth or the error of the suggested hypothesis. While the evidence is unsatisfactory, the controversy continues, but when once decisive proof has been discovered all tongues are still. The endless controversies over the existence of God show that decisive proof has not yet been attained. And while this proof is wanting, I remain Atheist, resolute not to profess belief till my intellect can find some stable ground whereon to rest.

We have reached the last citadel, once the apparently impregnable fortress of Theism, but one whose walls are now crumbling, the argument from design. It was this argument which so impressed John Stuart Mill that he wrote in his Essay on "Theism": "I think it must be allowed that, in the present state of our knowledge, the adaptations in Nature afford a large balance of probability in favor of creation by intelligence. It is equally certain that this is no more than a probability" ("Three Essays on Religion", p. 174). This Essay was, however, written between the years 1868 and 1870, and at that time the tremendous effect of the hypothesis of evolution had not yet made itself felt; Mill speaks (p. 172) of the "recent speculations" on "the principle of the 'survival of the of the fittest'", and recognising that if this principle were sound "there would be a constant though slow general improvement of the type as it branched out into many different varieties, adapting it to different media and modes of existence, until it might possibly, in countless ages, attain to the most advanced examples which now exist" (p. 173), he admits that if this be true "it must be acknowledged that it would greatly attenuate the evidence for" creation. And I am prepared to admit frankly that until the "how" of evolution explained the adaptations in Nature, the weight of the argument from design was very great, and to most minds would have been absolutely decisive. It would not of course prove the existence of an omnipotent and universal creator, but it certainly did powerfully suggest the presence of some contriving intelligence at work on natural phænomena. But now, when we can trace the gradual evolution of a complex and highly developed organ through the various stages which separate its origin from its most complete condition; when we can study the retrogression of organs becoming rudimentary by disuse, and the improvement of organs becoming developed by use; when we notice as imperfections in the higher type things which were essential in the lower: what wonder is it that the instructed can no longer admit the force of the argument from design?

The human eye has often been pointed to as a triumphant proof of design, and it naturally seemed perfect in the past to those who could imagine no higher kind of optical instrument; but now, as Tyndall says, "A long list of indictments might indeed be brought against the eye—its opacity, its want of symmetry, its lack of achromatism, its absolute blindness, in part. All these taken together caused Helmholtz to say that, if any optician sent him an instrument so full of defects, he would be justified in sending it back with the severest censure" ("On Light", p. 8, ed. 1875). It is only since men have made opical instruments without the faults of the eye, that we have become aware how much better we might see than we do. Nor is this all; the imperfections which would show incompetence on the part of a designer become interesting and significant as traces of gradual development, and the eye, which in the complexity of its highest form seemed, notwithstanding its defects, to demand such great intelligence to conceive and fashion it, becomes more intelligible when we can watch it a-building, and, as it were, see it put together bit by bit. I venture to quote here from a pamphlet of my own a very brief statement of the stages through which the eye has passed in its evolution: "The first definite eye-spot that we yet know of is a little colored speck at the base of the tentacles of some of the Hydromedusæ, jelly-fish in common parlance. They are only spots of pigment, and we should not know they were attempts at eyes were it not that some relations, the Discophora, have little refractive bodies in their pigment spots, and these refractive bodies resemble the crystalline cones of animals a little higher in the scale. In the next class (Vermes), including all worms, we find only pigment spots in the lowest; then pigment spots with a nerve-fibre ending in them; pigment spots with rod-shaped cells, with crystalline rods; pigment spots with crystalline cones. Next, the cones begin to be arranged radially; and in the Alciopidæ the eye has become a sphere with a lens and a vitreous body, layer of pigment, layer of rods, and optic nerve. To mark the evolution definitely in another way, we find the more highly developed eye of the adult appearing as a pigment spot in the embryo, so that both the evolution of the race and the evolution of the individual tell the same story. In the Echinoderma (sea-urchins, star-fishes) we find only pigment spots in the lower forms, but in the higher the rod-shaped cells, the transparent cones projecting from pigment cells In the Arthropoda (lobsters, insects, etc.,) the advance continues from the Vermes. The retina is formed more definitely than in the Alciopidæ, and the eye becomes more complex. The compound eye is an attempt at grouping many cones together, and is found in the higher members of this sub-kingdom. In the lowest vertebrate, the Amphioxus, the eye is a mere pigment spot, but in the others the more complex forms are taken up and carried on to the comparative perfection of the mammalian eye" ("Eyes and Ears", pp. 9, 10). And be it noted that in the most complex and highly developed eye there is still the same relation of pigment layer, rod layer, cone layer, seen in its earliest beginnings in the Discophora and the worms.

The line of argument here applied to the eye may be followed in every instance of so-called design. The exquisite mechanism of the ear may be similarly traced, from the mere sac with otoliths of the Medusæ up to the elaborate external, middle, and internal ears of man. Man's ear is a very complex thing. Its three chambers; the curious characteristics of the innermost of these, with its three "semi-circular canals", its coiled extension, like a snail-shell, called the cochlea, its elaborate nervous mechanism; the membrane between the middle and outer chambers, which vibrates with every pulsation of the air; we can trace all these separate parts as they are added one to one to the auditory apparatus of the evolving race. If we examine the edge of the "umbrella" of the free-swimming Medusa, we shall find some little capsules containing one or more tiny crystals, the homologues of the inner ear; the lower forms of Vermes have similar ears, and in some there are delicate hairs within the capsule which quiver constantly; the higher worms have these capsules paired and they lie close to a mass of nervous matter. Lobsters and their relations have similar ears, the capsule being sometimes closed and sometimes open. In many insects a delicate membrane is added to the auditory apparatus, and stretches between the vesicle and the outer air, homologue of our membrane. The lower fishes have added one semicircular canal, the next higher two, and the next higher three: a little expansion is also seen at one part of the vesicle. In the frogs and toads this extension is increased, and in the reptiles and birds it is still larger, and is curled a little at the further end. In the lowest mammals it is still only bent, but in the higher it rolls round on itself and forms the cochlea. The reptiles and birds have the space developed between the vesicle and the membrane, and so acquire a middle ear; the crocodile and the owl show a trace of the external ear, but it is not highly developed till we reach the mammals, and even the lowest mammals, and the aquatic ones, have little of it developed. Thus step by step is the ear built up, until we see it complete as a slow growth, not as an intelligent design.

And if it be asked, how are these changes caused, the answer comes readily: "By variation and by the survival of the fittest". Since organisms and their environments re-act on each other, slight variations are constantly occurring; living organisms are ever in very unstable equilibrium, chemical association and disassociation are continually going on within them. Some of these changes are advantageous to the organism in the struggle for existence; some are indifferent; some are disadvantageous. Those that are advantageous tend to persist, since the organism possessing them is more likely to survive than its less fortunate competitors, and — since variations are transmissible from parents to progeny—to hand on its favorable variation to its young. On the other hand the disadvantageous variations tend to disappear, since the organism which is by them placed at a disadvantage is likely to perish in the fight for food. Here are the mighty forces that cause evolution; here the "not ourselves which makes for righteousness", *i.e.*, for ever-increasing suitability of the organism to its environment.

It is, of course, impossible in so brief a statement as this to do justice to the fulness of the explanation of all cases of apparent design which can be made in this fashion. The thoughtful student must work out the line of argument for himself. Nor must he forget to notice the argument from the *absence* of design, the want of adaptation, the myriad failures, the ineptitudes and incompetences of nature. How, from the point of view of design, can he explain the numerous rudimentary organs in the higher animals? What is the meaning of man's hidden rudimentary tail? of his appendix cœci vermiformis? of the branchial clefts and the lanugo of the human being during periods of ante-natal life? of the erratic course of the recurrent laryngeal? of the communication between the larynx and the alimentary canal? I might extend the list over a page. The fact that uninstructed people do not appreciate these difficulties offers no explanation to the instructed who feel their force; and the abuse so freely lavished on the Atheist does not carry conviction to the intellect.

I do not believe in God. My mind finds no grounds on which to build up a reasonable faith. My heart revolts against the spectre of an Almighty Indifference to the pain of sentient beings. My conscience rebels against the injustice, the cruelty, the inequality, which surround me on every side. But I believe in Man. In man's redeeming power; in man's remoulding energy; in man's approaching triumph, through knowledge, love, and work.

THE

TEACHINGS OF CHRISTIANITY.

A DEBATE BETWEEN

ANNIE BESANT, *Atheist*,

AND THE

REV. G. F. HANDEL ROWE,

Of Halifax, Clergyman of the Church of England.

LONDON:

FREETHOUGHT PUBLISHING COMPANY,

63, FLEET STREET, E.C.

1887.

LONDON:
PRINTED BY ANNIE BESANT AND CHARLES BRADLAUGH,
63, FLEET STREET, E.C.

THE TEACHINGS OF CHRISTIANITY.

Mr. Rowe's First Article.

The subject of the present debate is as follows: "Are the teachings of Christianity calculated to promote adequately the welfare of humanity in this life?" My task is to substantiate an affirmative answer; Mrs. Besant has undertaken to prove the negative. It may be useful to state at once that I regard the whole New Testament as containing the teachings of Christianity, and not the Four Gospels only. Therefore I claim the right of quoting from any portion of the New Testament.

Inasmuch as any and every human being may be viewed from various standpoints, "the welfare of humanity in this life" is capable of manifold aspects. A human being may be surveyed as an individual endowed with bodily powers and mental faculties; secondly, as having family relationships; thirdly, as a member of society; fourthly, as a political citizen. How far, then, can the individual, having this four-fold character, find guidance in this life from "the teachings of Christianity"? My respected opponent will doubtless agree with me that the welfare of humanity is promoted when progress is achieved. So that if I show that Christian teachings aid human progress, and necessarily tend so to do, I shall have maintained my position. The very fact that the avowed purpose of Christianity is to provide means for the redemption of man from vice, and to sustain him in the path of virtue in this life, is a sufficient indication that the fundamental conception of the Christian religion is consonant with human progress. This is so obvious a truism that I need not quote New Testament passages bearing on the point. If required to do so, I will immediately comply.

But what says Christianity to the individual as a being endowed with bodily powers and mental faculties? Progress is won by the exercise of those. Individual happiness is similarly promoted. Accordingly in Matt. xxv., 14–30, and Luke xix., 12–26, we have the parable of the talents setting forth that human faculties are not bestowed with any implied sanction of their neglect; rather is the failure to use them strongly condemned. Again, our Savior declares it to be a part of the first and greatest commandment of all that man is to love God with all his "mind and strength" (Luke x., 27, 28). On the assumption that God has bestowed on the individual both mind and strength, which is the Christian theory, it is superfluous to enter on any labored argument on behalf of the conclusion that God can only be loved with the human mind and strength when both are developed by culture to their utmost capacity. How could an absence of love for the Giver of both be more effectively displayed than by dooming both to disuse?

Nor are the teachings of Christianity less outspoken on family relationships. Parents and children are alike plainly addressed in regard to their family duties in the New Testament. Thus husbands are exhorted to love their wives (Eph. v., 25), and children to obey their parents (Eph. vi., 1). It follows inevitably that a wife-loving husband will provide for her and the family. A wife-loving husband will be no wife-beater, no faithless one, no drunkard, neither gambler nor spendthrift; and what a tremendous advance towards the foremost vanguard of human progress would be realised if husbands only conformed to this Christian teaching. Such a lofty platform of civilisation would then have been reached as would cause the hearts of tens of thousands of wives in our land to leap for joy. Even the representation of God as a Heavenly Father in Christian teachings, providing food and clothing for the fowls of the air and the lilies of the field, His creatures, is of itself sufficient, without a positive precept, to remind human parents how they should act towards those dependent on themselves. What a magnificent portrait of our Heavenly Father in this respect is drawn by Jesus Christ in the last eleven verses of St. Matthew's sixth chapter! Will my Atheistic readers kindly peruse them once more? And lest it should be supposed that the obedience to parents inculcated on children by the New Testament is meant to be a harsh, arbitrary, slavish one, conferring on parents an unlimited and vexatious control, St. Paul, in Ephesians vi., 4, carefully writes: "Ye fathers, provoke not your children to wrath". Moreover, in the same verse, the duty of educating children is enjoined. If it be answered that religious training only is specified, my reply is two-fold. First, even religious training involves and embodies the principle of education, and thus suggests the enquiry in what direction education ought to be extended. Secondly, Christian parents, knowing that their children as well as themselves are desired to love God with their mind and strength, will expand these faculties in their children to the uttermost, aware that the more this is done the better will they be enabled to love God, the original Giver. Hence had parents been faithful to the teaching of Christianity, the inhabitants of the world would have been further ahead in the highway of progress and civilisation than at present, and there would have been no need for Education Acts in the British Statute Book to compel the fulfilment of parental functions.

Probably the social relations of each individual, and the line of conduct which is thereby required, will be deemed not the least important test of the adequacy of Christian teachings for the promotion of human welfare in this life. It is commonly alleged that the whole fabric of society is mischievously inverted to-day, resting on the narrow apex of selfishness instead of the broad basis of allied interests. In so far as this is true, doubtless it is a stumbling-block to human welfare, arresting the march of civilisation and progress. But in so far also as it is true it is equally a departure from Christian teachings. Selfishness in humanity is annihilated by the doctrine of the fatherhood of God. That tenet inevitably points to its correlative, viz., the brotherhood of man. So Jesus Christ taught his disciples —"all ye are brethren" (*vide* Matt. xxiii., 8). St. Paul expressed the same idea in another form (*vide* Acts xvii., 26), when he declared to the Athenians that God "hath made of one blood all nations of men". In another place, viz., Epistle to Philippians, ii., 4, he again plants a safeguard against selfishness by enjoining that no man should look simply on his own things, but every man also on the things of others. In the succeeding verse he adduces the self-sacrificing example of Christ Jesus as a model for imitation. Numerous other instances might be adduced. Were these Christian teachings put into practice society would speedily be re-formed, a new and more kindly spirit would pervade it, the sharpness of commercial competition would be mollified, poverty and distress would disappear before the remedies suggested by brotherly love. Christian Socialism, if carried out in daily life, would bridge over the gulf between the rich and the poor. Linking them together as brethren it would teach the wealthy eagerly to embrace every opportunity for ministering to the necessitous, and thus it would remove out of the hearts of the poor the poison of envy and jealousy cherished towards those in affluent circumstances. How beautifully changed would society become if re-modelled in this fashion! Socialism so-called, with its naked schemes of forceful type. would then have no excuse for its advocacy. Why do not the disciples of Comte, who to-day loudly plead for the conversion of humanity into a brotherhood as a cure for social ills, candidly admit that while they repudiate Christianity, they nevertheless thus borrow from Christian teachings one of their chief fundamental ideas?

Stress is often laid by political economists on the injury wrought by the non-producing members of a community. Christian teachings afford no shelter to idlers, but encourage industry. Thus St. Paul, 1 Epistle to Thessalonians, iv., 11, repeats a command previously given, that all should do their own business, and work with their own hands. Slothfulness in business is likewise rebuked by the same Apostle in Romans xii., 11. Evidently St. Paul believed in and taught commercial diligence and energy, for the condemnation of sloth involves an approbation of the opposite. Our Savior also reminded employers of labor that a fair day's work deserved a fair day's wage, when he affirmed that the laborer was worthy of his hire (*vide* Luke x., 7). Quarrels between capital and labor which so frequently culminate in disastrous strikes, would be avoided if both sides would deal fairly with each other. Workmen complain that masters refuse to them the share of profits due to labor. Christian teaching corrects masters by insisting in Jesus Christ's words that the laborer is worthy of his hire. On the other hand masters avow that their workpeople are at fault in the strife. Christian teaching again admonishes servants that they must not labor grudgingly "with eye-service, as men-pleasers" (*vide* Eph. vi., 6); on the contrary "whatsoever ye would that men should do unto you even so do unto them" (see Matt. vii., 12). "Love worketh no ill to his neighbor" says St. Paul. Can Mrs. Besant deny this, and furnish a better sentiment than that of love to rule the relationships of society? If so, I ask for it. If not, then Christian teaching must promote adequately the welfare of humanity in this life in so far as it is affected by the proper discharge of social duties, for its second great precept is: "Thou shalt love thy neighbor as thyself" (*vide* Matt. xxii., 39).

We now approach the fourth division of human welfare in this life, viz., that connected with the political citizenship of the individual. Christian teaching nowhere inspires a ruler to acts of despotism. Instead, it adopts the hypothesis that government ought to be for the benefit of the people. Thus St. Paul depicts a ruler as "the minister of God *for good*" (*vide* Romans xiii., 4). He expresses the same thought in another form in the prior verse: "Do that which is good and thou shalt have praise of the same (ruler)". Is it possible for a moment even to imagine that any political ruler, guided by such Christian teachings as I have just quoted, would feel himself at liberty to treat his subjects as he pleased? Take another view of the case. The beneficent character of Jesus Christ is universally conceded. Had I available space I would gladly present as one proof the striking eulogy pronounced on the Founder of Christianity by that conspicuous unbeliever in Christianity, the late John Stuart Mill. In a future article I may find room for it. Now Jesus Christ is declared in the New Testament (*vide* Rev. xix., 16) to be "king of kings and lord of lords". Consequently, it behoves earthly sovereigns and rulers so to shape their sway that it shall conform to all the features of conduct found in the life of Christ, their superior. When they do this, instead of being self-assertive, they will minister to the welfare of others; instead of exacting excessive taxation, they will rather be sympathetic and helpful towards the needy; they will try to remove the ills of humanity as Christ did; and so they will win the affections of the masses, as Jesus Christ gained the hearts of the multitudes clustering around him wheresoever he travelled. What numberless wars, and what wasteful expenditure, have been occasioned by the freakish, cruel ambition of some earthly rulers! Civilisation has thereby been seriously retarded. Human progress has well-nigh been forced out of remembrance at the same time. All this would have been avoided had the spirit of Christ dwelt in earthly rulers. Again and again have they wielded the sceptre as though subject citizens had no rights. Jesus Christ emphatically asserted the inherent rights of citizens and subjects by his independent, yet courteous and rational demeanor before the Jewish High Priest, and Pontius Pilate, the Roman procurator. My opponent will hardly venture to dispute that utilitarian government, and a recognition of the rights of subjects, are strongly conducive to human welfare; and as I have demonstrated that Christian teachings foster each of them, it follows that Christian teachings in this way are calculated adequately to promote human welfare.

If professing Christians have not uniformly practised Christian teachings, the latter must not on that account be blamed. Christianity is not responsible where its precepts have been set aside, and when its ideals have been ignored. I invite Mrs. Besant to specify the impediment to human welfare, human progress, and human civilisation, which Christian teachings, honestly and faithfully followed, would not remove. Further, if Christian teachings are not calculated to promote adequately the welfare of humanity in this life, can better teachings be named? If so, let it be done. If not, then at least we shall have the acknowledgment that Christian teachings are superior to all others within the reach of humanity.

Annie Besant's First Article.

At the outset of a debate which turns on the teachings of the Bible, it is necessary to remind the reader that the Bible is a collection of books of unknown authorship, and unknown dates, and that the moral teachings of these books are of the most diversified kind. By a careful process of selection it would be possible to prove that the

Bible teaches a lofty and a base morality, that its precepts are useful and mischievous, that it is the friend and the enemy of progress. The algebraical sum of its teachings is clearly mischievous, but I freely admit that odd texts may be quoted which are on the right side. It will be for me to show that the teachings of Christianity are destructive of human progress, and are therefore in antagonism to human welfare; I shall prove that the spirit and the words of the teachings of Christianity are fatal to the welfare of humanity in this life, and while Mr. Rowe may quote some dislocated texts on the other side, he will fail in maintaining his position unless he can disprove my quotations. Any success he may have in proving that Christian teachings form a chaos of self-contradictions will be of small avail in commending them to the thoughtful mind.

I note that in Mr. Rowe's first paragraph he identifies the New Testament with the teachings of Christianity. I shall be glad to know if, as a priest of the Established Church, he repudiates the divine authority of the Old Testament? He is bound either to explicitly state that he rejects the Old Testament, as forming no part of Christian teachings, or else to prove that the infamous precepts on slavery, sexual relations, etc. of the "Mosaic code" are calculated to promote human progress. Until I know his position on this question, I leave the Old Testament out of our discussion.

Passing to paragraph 2, I deny "that the avowed purpose of Christianity is to provide means for the redemption of man from vice, and to sustain him in the path of virtue in this life". The avowed purpose of Christianity is the saving of man from punishment in another life for acts that may, or may not, be vicious. A man's life is of no importance in comparison with his belief. Thus Paul writes: "A man is justified by faith without the deeds of the law" (Rom. iii., 28). "To him that worketh not, but believeth on him that justifieth the ungodly, his faith is counted for righteousness" (Rom. iv., 5). "Being now justified by his blood, we shall be saved from wrath through him" (Rom. v., 9). "Believe on the Lord Jesus Christ, and thou shalt be saved" (Acts. xvi., 31). "He that believeth, and is baptized, shall be saved: but he that believeth not, shall be damned" (Mark xvi., 16). This importance of orthodoxy of belief over purity of life is further enforced by the promise of paradise by Jesus to the dying thief, and by his declaration that one repentant sinner caused more joy in heaven than ninety and nine just persons. Dozens of other passages might be quoted to prove the same point. Now since those who sincerely believe in life beyond the grave must needs regard that eternal existence as of far more vital importance than anything in this mortal life, and since that eternity is to be spent either in bliss unspeakable or woe immeasurable, their supreme concern here must of necessity be the insuring of that bliss and the avoidance of that woe. Thence follows it that *that* will to them be of uttermost importance which opens to them the gate of heaven. But heaven's gate is opened by the key of faith, not by that of works. Christ's *imputed* righteousness is to be their salvation, and the blessedness is for the man whose "iniquity is *covered*", not for the man of righteous life. "He that believeth not shall be damned", no matter how pure his conduct, how lofty his morality. In strict accordance with this morality-destroying teaching of the New Testament, are the articles of the Established Church. "We are accounted righteous before God, only for the merit of our Lord and Savior Jesus Christ by faith and not for our own works or deservings" (Art. xi.). "Works done before the grace of Christ and the inspiration of his Spirit, are not pleasant to God, forasmuch as they spring not of faith in Jesus Christ, neither do they make men meet to receive grace, or (as the School-authors say) deserve grace of congruity; yea rather, for that they are not done as God hath willed and commanded them to be done, we doubt not but they have the nature of sin" (Art. xiii.). So that justice, and honesty, and purity, and candor, and generosity, are all sins when manifested by an Atheist! Now I readily admit that many of the less virile virtues are held up to Christians as part of their duty after they have secured their salvation by faith; but I contend that putting faith above works, resting salvation on belief instead of on conduct, and making the righteousness of another the justification of the sinner, is to encourage carelessness of life and to sap the springs of morality. The low tone of public morality in every Christian land bears eloquent witness to the small power of Christianity as a moralising agent.

In paragraph 3 the parable of the talents is used to prove that Christianity urges the utilising of human faculties; the parable merely extols successful trading, and blames the "slothful servant" because he had not given his master, on his return, "his own with usury". Why the sordid and grasping character of the "lord" should be glorified into a condemnation of the neglect of human faculties it is hard to see; a smart shopkeeper might enforce the parable on his apprentices, but the less said of its morality the better. If God "can only be loved with the human mind and strength when both are developed by culture to their utmost capacity", the vast majority of Christians cannot obey the precept, and the odd thing is that most of the highly-cultivated minority do not love him at all. Besides, how does Mr. Rowe's doctrine agree with the words of God? "I thank thee, O Father, Lord of heaven and earth, because thou hast hid these things from the wise and prudent, and hast revealed them unto babes" (Matt. xi., 25). "Not many wise men after the flesh . . . . are called; but God hath chosen the foolish things of the world to confound the wise" (1 Cor. i., 26, 27). "The wisdom of this world is foolishness with God" (1 Cor. ii., 19). The apostles of Jesus, chosen by himself as the fittest messengers for his teaching, were "unlearned and ignorant men" (Acts iv., 13).

Paragraph 4, quoting the injunction to husbands to love their wives, omits to notice the degrading position assigned to the wife by Christianity. She is to be subject to her husband "in everything", as the Church to Christ (Eph. v., 24). She is to "learn in silence with all subjection" (1 Tim. ii., 11). She is to take as example Sarah, who "obeyed Abraham, calling him lord" (1 Pet. iii., 6). The "magnificent portrait of our heavenly father . . . . drawn by Jesus Christ in the last eleven verses of St. Matthew's sixth chapter" is not true to nature. The birds starve to death in a hard winter, the heavenly father not feeding them; the squirrels who lay up a store of nuts for themselves instead of trusting to God come off better. The lilies of the field constantly die from want of rain or from too much of it. And the heavenly father lets his human children die of starvation, both rapid and slow. The portrait-painter drew on his imagination for his facts, and the human father who modelled his conduct to his children on that of the heavenly father would be likely to find himself in the police-court for neglect. Bringing children up "in the nurture and admonition of the Lord" is translated by Mr. Rowe into an injunction to educate them. This extraordinary gloss is at least a testimony to the changed views of the clergy on education.

In paragraph 5 the brotherhood of man is extolled, but we are not told how we are to reconcile this brotherhood with the recognition by Paul and Peter of the institution of slavery. "Servants, be obedient to them that are your masters according to the flesh, *with fear and trembling*" (Eph. vi., 5). "Servants, be subject to your masters with all fear . . . . what glory is it, if, when ye be buffeted for your faults, ye shall take it patiently?" (1 Pet. ii., 18, 20). The teaching that is wanted to change society is the destruction of the class distinctions that make brotherhood a farce; not the "ministering to the necessitous" by the rich, but the alteration of the system which leaves the industrious in a necessitous state.

Paragraph 6 touches a sound point in Christian teaching when the injunction to work is quoted. But the allusion to "our Savior's" views inevitably recalls the praise of cheating in the parable of the unjust steward, and the curious views of justice in the parable of the laborers hired at a penny apiece. "Can Mrs. Besant", asks Mr. Rowe, "furnish a better sentiment than that of love to rule the relationships of society?" Yes: justice. It is not possible for everybody to love everybody else, unless the word love is to be emptied of all meaning, but a man can learn to be just alike to friend and foe.

In paragraph 7 Mr. Rowe says that "Christian teaching nowhere inspires a ruler to acts of despotism"; but it makes the committal of acts of despotism certain by teaching craven submission to injustice and tyranny. "I say unto you that ye resist not evil; but whosoever shall smite thee on thy right cheek turn to him the other side also" etc. (Matt. v., 39–41). "Let every soul be subject to the higher powers, for there is no power but of God: the powers that be are ordained of God. Whosoever, therefore, resisteth the power, resisteth the ordinance of God: and they that resist shall receive to themselves damnation" (Rom. xiii., 1, 2). With this declaration Christianity brands as damned every hero who has resisted a tyrant, every martyr in the cause of civil liberty. The passage from J. S. Mill on the character of Jesus is familiar to every Freethinker, if only from its constant quotation by Christian advocates. Personally I do not agree with Mr. Mill's view of Jesus, and his opinion is, of course, not binding on any Freethinker. But it is interesting to note that Mr. Mill, despite his admiration, did not believe in Jesus, and one would therefore like to know whether he regarded him as self-deceived or a deceiver of others. If Jesus were not divine, he must have been either deluder or self-deluded; neither hypothesis is reconcilable with *both* high mental and moral character. Jesus, Mr. Rowe tells us, "gained the hearts of the multitudes"; it may be so; but the multitudes shouted "crucify him", and out of them all only one hundred and twenty are said to have represented the results of his life-work. I do not desire to be uncourteous to Mr. Rowe, but really I do not know how to argue formally against a proposition which seems to me so utterly preposterous as the one that "Jesus Christ emphatically asserted the inherent rights of citizens and subjects by his independent, yet courteous and rational demeanor before the Jewish High Priest and Pontius Pilate". Let us suppose the accounts in the gospels are roughly accurate; what did Jesus do? Before the High Priest he remained silent, refusing to answer, and his demeanor must have appeared to be either sullen or stupid, most certainly not courteous: when at last, in answer to a solemn adjuration, he opened his lips, he gave an answer which, from the Jewish point of view, was a blasphemy (Matt. xxvi., 59–65). Before Pontius Pilate he was equally rude, remaining stolidly silent (Matt. xxvii., 12–14). In the fourth gospel the silence is broken with some futile and enigmatical remarks to Pilate; but in what way he maintained the rights of citizens and subjects I should be glad to learn from Mr. Rowe.

But my reasons for regarding Christianity as the enemy of progress are not based on isolated texts, nor can they be removed by the quotation of isolated texts which contain ethical doctrines on elementary moral duties which are common to every religion. Apart from the distinctly immoral doctrines mentioned above, such as those of the subjection of women and of unresisting submission to evil-doers—doctrines which strike at the welfare of the family and of the State—there are fundamental teachings of Christianity fatal to human progress. There are two chief factors in progress, intellect and character. Christianity strikes at both. Raising faith to the rank of a cardinal virtue, it opens the door to the most irrational superstitions; making it perilous to doubt, it deprives man of his best weapon against traditional error. Unreasoning credulity has ever been the favorite "virtue" of the Church, and the fear of hell has guarded her myths and fables from exposure. The result of her canonisation of faith is seen in her history, in the ignorance that spread over Europe during the ages that were the Dark Ages and also the ages of faith. In my criticism of paragraph 3 I quoted a few of the passages in which ignorance is put as preferable to knowledge.

At character Christianity strikes with its doctrines of substitutionary atonement, vicarious righteousness, salvation by faith not works, easy forgiveness to the sinner. A far sterner doctrine is needed for the improvement of man. That there is no such thing as the washing away of sin; that no forgiveness of a God can undo the harm wrought to man; that character can only be built up by patient effort, long-continued vigilance, stern self-judgment, keen self-analysis; that the grace of God can no more turn a sinner into a saint than it can turn a mongrel cur into a prize-dog; such is the kind of teaching needed for the regeneration of society. The angels of God may rejoice over the blood-washed murderer as he joins them from the gallows, more than over ninety and nine just and righteous men. By all means let the angels have the repentant sinner, but it is the ninety and nine just persons who make for progress.

Mr. Rowe's Second Article.

In answer to the assertion that I am bound to state explicitly whether I reject the Old Testament as forming no part of Christian teachings, I reply that the New Testament is the source of these teachings. Where the New Testament appeals to the corroborative authority of the Old Testament in relation to Christian teachings I am obviously bound by the specific reference, but not further, in regard to the subject matter of this debate. It is open for Mrs. Besant to prove otherwise, if that be possible. I should have thought my respected opponent would have been aware of the description of the Mosaic dispensation in the Epistle to the Hebrews, chap. 10, as "a *shadow* of good things to come, and *not the very image* of the things". Our discussion relates not to "*the shadow* of good things to come", but to the actual good things, or Christian teachings themselves; which, as already affirmed, are to be discerned in the New Testament. Mrs. Besant's prefatory investigation of the character of all the books in the Bible is therefore superfluous; as much so as is her quotation from the Thirty-nine Articles of the Church of England. Were I to cite from the latter any passage as an authoritative declaration of Christian teachings, Mrs. Besant would immediately reply that these Articles belong to a secondary document, and only profess to be interpretative of the primary records of Christian teachings. Henceforth, if similar irrelevant appeals be made, I must pass them over in silence, inasmuch as I cannot allow the discussion to wander out of its proper course. Nevertheless, in her disquisition on the books of the Bible, Mrs. Besant has made some admissions damaging to her cause. It is confessed that the Bible, in which the New Testament is included, teaches a lofty morality, contains useful precepts, and is the friend of progress. So far my case is conceded. Such lofty morality, such useful precepts, and such a friendship for progress, must be "calculated to promote adequately the welfare of humanity in this life", the very position which I have to establish. All these features of the New Testament, therefore, my respected opponent will thus warrant me in placing before Atheists for their guidance. But it has also been alleged by her that the Bible, comprehending I suppose the New Testament, teaches a base morality, embodies mischievous precepts, and is the enemy of progress. Many reflecting minds will not unreasonably enquire whether in view of the pronounced eulogy, this commingling of censure may not be due to a misunderstanding of the things condemned. My earnest contention is that Mrs. Besant has exhibited a strange misunderstanding of the New Testament. Let me now place before the reader the evidence.

It is denied that "the avowed purpose of Christianity is to provide means for the redemption of man from vice, and to sustain him in the path of virtue in this life". Note here that the issue is not whether the machinery of Christianity is efficacious for its purpose, but what is the purpose itself. A few references will suffice, viz., Epistle to Titus ii., 11, 12: "The grace of God that bringeth salvation hath appeared to all men, teaching us that, denying ungodliness and worldly lusts, we should live soberly, righteously, and godly in this present world". Again, in the 14th verse of the same chapter we read that the purpose of the coming and sacrifice of Christ was that "He might redeem us from all iniquity, and purify unto Himself a peculiar people, zealous of good works". Both these passages correspond with Jesus Christ's own words, Luke 19, 10: "The Son of Man is come to seek and to save that which was lost". Could language be plainer? My position as to the purpose of Christianity is thus demonstrated to be correct. Perhaps Mrs. Besant's error in denying the virtuous purpose of Christianity may now be apparent to the reader, if not to herself. Inasmuch, then, as the professed aim of Christianity is to foster virtue, its fundamental conception must be "calculated to promote the welfare of humanity".

Mrs. Besant has argued that the avowed purpose of Christianity is the saving of man from punishment in another life for acts that may, or may not, be vicious. But, first of all, let us be told whether Christianity at least assumes the punishable acts to be positively vicious. I fearlessly invite Mrs. Besant to establish the contrary. It is impossible to cite such proof. Therefore, it again appears that Christianity *professes* anyhow to promote virtue and to lessen vice, whereby we see once more that its fundamental conception tends to promote human welfare in this life. And how does my opponent seek to establish that Christianity threatens punishment in another world for acts which may not be vicious? By representing that in the eye of Christianity a man's life is of no importance in comparison with his belief. Orthodoxy of belief, she alleges, is exalted over purity of life. Five Scriptural texts are arrayed on this behalf, the third of which has not the faintest bearing on the point; and of the remaining four, the two following are typical:—"A man is justified by faith without the deeds of the law" (Romans iii., 28), and "Believe on the Lord Jesus Christ and thou shalt be saved" (Acts xvi., 31). Surely Mrs. Besant is aware that the former passage is a part of St. Paul's argument for convicting every man of vice. How else are we to understand the third chapter of Romans, especially verses 10 to 16? His aim is to show how sinful man, under the stain of guilt, may approach a righteous God, viz., by Jesus Christ who has obeyed God's law on man's behalf. Hence, in God's sight, through forgiving mercy, man is accounted righteous, not with a total disregard of virtue and vice, but because of Christ's perfect obedience on his behalf, an obedience which each repentant man confesses ought to have been rendered by himself; and yet "without the deeds of the law", because each man's very sinfulness establishes that he is unable completely to obey the law. Instead, therefore, of justifying faith setting aside "purity of life", it actually rests upon the perfect compliance with the moral law by Christ, and involves man's shelter in Christ through the proof of his own sinfulness, which will necessarily prompt him the more to strive after perfect purity. And what is meant by the second text "Believe on the Lord Jesus Christ, etc."? Not a mere fruitless sentiment, as Mrs. Besant would suggest. The believer in Christ above all things regards Christ as his example how to live. Thus 1 St. Peter ii., 21, expressly declares that "Christ left us an example that we should follow His steps". In the very nature of the case, Christ being the head of the Church (Ephes. i., 22) there must be some correspondence between His life and the conduct of the Church's members. A disciple will inevitably imitate the actions and bearing of his master. Hence, to believe in Christ is to be like Him in life. Jesus Christ "went about doing good" (Acts x., 38). His truly believing disciples will thus do likewise. When our Savior, after uttering the touching parable of "The Good Samaritan" concludes with the command—"Go and do thou likewise", is it possible that any Christian believer can deem himself at liberty to ignore the injunction? Certainly not; and so it becomes marvellous how Mrs. Besant can possibly assume that believing in Christ is limited to a mere capricious sentiment, and not intended to become the mainspring of changed and virtuous conduct.

If Mrs. Besant will examine the New Testament more carefully she will find that orthodoxy of belief, instead of supplanting purity of life, is pourtrayed as inseparably allied with it, just as the cause is allied with its effect. See Epistle of James, ii. 18: "Show me thy faith without thy works, and I will show thee my faith *by my works*". Again, in verse 22, alluding to Abraham: "by works was faith make perfect". Once more in verse 20: "faith without works is dead". If Mrs. Besant knew of these passages, why was no mention made of them? Of course, if unaware of them it at once follows that her contentions against Christian teachings have simply rested upon an incomplete acquaintance with them, which fact alone is sufficient to decide the issue between us. Nor is it in St. James alone that the necessary and inevitable alliance between faith and works is proclaimed. St. Paul enunciates similar teaching in Galatians v. 6, where he expressly speaks of "faith which *worketh by love*".

Mrs. Besant having appealed to St. Paul as inculcating the sole requirement from a Christian to be sheer faith regardless of "purity of life", one is curious to ascertain how it comes to pass that St. Paul's exaltation of a wonderfully fruitful charity over faith in 1 Corinthians xiii., 13, has been overlooked. What a splendid catalogue of the good works produced by charity which he deems superior to faith, is furnished in that same chapter! It is all ignored by Mrs. Besant as if the chapter were not contained in the New Testament; and in presence of it we are told, on the contrary, that purity of life is altogether supplanted by empty orthodoxy of belief in Christian teachings. My readers will now know differently.

Moreover, respecting the nature of the works which Christianity seeks to suppress, many catalogues are found in the New Testament. Let me adduce one list from Gal. v., 20: "adultery, fornication, uncleanness, lasciviousness, idolatry, witchcraft, hatred, variance, emulations, wrath, strife, seditions, heresies, envyings, murders, drunkenness, revellings, and such like". My task in this debate is to establish that Christian teachings are calculated to promote adequately the welfare of humanity in this life. Would not human welfare be immensely advanced by the extinction of the evil deeds just cited as banned by Christianity? In the first Epistle to Cor., xiii., which has already been mentioned, we have a glimpse of the life which Christian teachings commend. Another may be read in Ephes. iv., 31–32: "Let all bitterness, and wrath, and anger, and clamor, and evil speaking, be put away from you with all malice. And be ye kind one to another, tender-hearted, forgiving one another, even as God for Christ's sake hath forgiven you." Would not human welfare be greatly promoted if this ideal were practised universally? Surely there is abundance of outline of conduct here. Why, then, has Mrs. Besant depicted Christianity as requiring but a barren faith? We have been reminded, but without a shadow of evidence, by my respected opponent, of the low tone of public morality in every Christian land. This is outside the region of our discussion, which is the nature of Christian teachings, and not the manner of life exemplified by professing Christians. Assuming, however, for argument's sake alone, the existence of this low tone of public morality; Mrs. Besant has carefully refrained from indicating that it proceeds from Christian teachings. Until it is proved to be the consequence of Christian teachings, its mention appears to be doubly irrelevant. How is it, moreover, if Atheism be sublimely more moral than Christianity, that it has allowed this low tone of public morality to continue?

The replies furnished to my former illustrations of the manner in which Christian teachings promote human welfare in this life, seem to me somewhat feeble. It cannot be denied that the parable of the talents inculcates the development of human faculties. Mrs. Besant says the parable merely extols successful trading, and blames the slothful servant who failed to return to a lending lord his own with usury. Is not successful trading the mark of exercised faculties? Is not the condemned slothful servant an instance of the opposite? My point, then, is tacitly conceded. To lavish censure on the "lord", as Mrs. Besant does, is not to disprove that the parable favors the exercise of human talents; nor is it any more reasonable than would be a condemnation of any working man who asked for interest when he had lent money to a neighbor. Further, Mrs. Besant is unable to question that the requirement to love God with the mind and strength equally fosters the cultivation of both. Her retort is that most of the highly cultivated minority do not love Him at all. Where is the evidence? Once more it is not forthcoming. There is no basis for the retort, for it cannot be disputed that the vast majority of "the highly cultivated" in the whole world accept Christian teachings for their guidance, and that, too, in proportion to their culture. Mrs. Besant asks me to reconcile my representation that Christian teachings encourage the expansion of human powers, with certain Scriptural passages where worldly wisdom is placed at a discount. My answer is that in some of these passages human pride is depicted as turning worldly wisdom into a lever for resisting Christian teachings, and therefore such use is inevitably condemned. And does not Mrs. Besant see the peculiar fitness of the choice of "unlearned and ignorant men" to be Christ's Apostles? It was an exceptional case. It presented room for the exceptional exercise of miraculous powers by them on behalf of Christianity, so that the evidences for the Christian revelation might be the more convincing. Further, on the one hand, their lack of knowledge was supplied by Divine inspiration, according to promise, whenever required (Matt. xviii., 19); while on the other, the calling of that eloquent, powerful, philosophic reasoner Paul (Acts xxiv., 25) testifies that the highest talents are meant to be employed in the exposition and elucidation of Christian teachings.

In regard to family life, I formerly showed that Christian teachings placed before parents and children with plainness their duties, exhorting husbands to love their wives, fathers to provide for those dependent on them, and children to be obedient. Why has Mrs. Besant dismissed with silence the happy consequences which, as I stated, would follow in this and other lands if men would be wife-loving? Is my respected opponent afraid to admit the accuracy of the delineation, and of the social reformation which Christian teachings would thus effect? Oh, why this silence, when tens of thousands of wives in our population daily dread the echoes of the footsteps of their cruel partners? Instead of admitting my accuracy, Mrs. Besant twists the death of a few birds from starvation into a reproach of the Divine Fatherhood, without specifying the relation of the fact to the whole economy of Nature; and forgetful that, on the assumption of a Heavenly Father's existence, the instinct with which untrained birds build their nests, and the largeness of the varied sustenance which they meet with, evidence that He does feed the birds after all. Mrs. Besant thinks my effort to point out that Christian teachings press for the education of children is a testimony to the changed views of the clergy on the value of education. Here is a fatal mistake. In 1868 Mr. Gladstone confessed at Ormskirk that even the much abused clergy of the Church in Wales were bearing the brunt of the work of educating the people of the Principality. But I am reminded that Christian teachings reduce wives to the "degrading position" of being subject to their husbands. The pattern of the subjection, however, is the Church's subjection to Christ, which harmonises with the Church's love of Christ. Wherein, then, consists the degradation which love leavens?

My portraiture of the brotherhood of humanity contained by the Christian ideal stands in its integrity. Nor is it disputed that the disciples of Comte borrow the ideal without acknowledgment. I am asked to reconcile this Christian brotherhood with the recognition of slavery by St. Paul and St. Peter. Their recognition was mere cognizance of a fact, not approbation of the principle. St. Paul practically condemned slavery by counselling Philemon to receive back the runaway Onesimus as not a slave, but "a brother beloved". Christian brotherhood and love will ring and have rung the death-knell of slavery.

Mrs. Besant impugns the conduct of Jesus Christ before the high priest and Pontius Pilate as not asserting the inherent rights of citizens and subjects. Therefore I appeal to St. John xviii., 19 to 23rd verses, and from the 33rd to the 38th verses of the same chapter. The former shows that he exemplified dignified innocence without being "rude"; the latter acquits him of "remaining stolidly silent".

Mrs. Besant's closing rhetoric against Christianity is unavailing. We rather need fact and argument. Am I to take her as a typical representative of Atheism in clinging to the ninety and nine just persons only, and leaving somewhat scornfully to the angels of Christianity "the repentant sinner"? Let those who yearn for the moral reformation of themselves mark this. Atheism disdains them. Beholding them struggling to snap the fetters of vice, it loftily passes by on the other side. It courts the society of the already virtuous, of the ninety and nine just ones who need no repentance. Methinks Mrs. Besant has thus rightly unveiled Atheism as cold-hearted. How sharp the contrast thus afforded to the ever-flowing sympathy for helpless ones presented by what even Professor Tyndall has pronounced to be "the incomparable life of Christ".

Annie Besant's Second Article.

I note that in his first paragraph Mr. Rowe declines to defend the Old Testament, although it is part of the Canonical Scriptures put forth by his Church as of divine authority. I note also that he waves aside the Thirty-nine Articles, to which he has declared his unfeigned consent and assent, finding that in debate with an unbeliever it is inconvenient to maintain the Christian doctrines which he teaches to his uncritical Christian flock, and his acceptance of which gives him privileged position in the community. I do not complain of the repudiation. I merely note it as a significant admission of the indefensibility on the platform of the doctrines which are safely taught from the law-defended pulpit. It would indeed be difficult to prove that Ex. xxi. 1–11, 20, 21, Deut. xxi. 10–14, were shadows of good things, or anything but the vilest immorality. If I cared to imitate the veiled insolence which is, I presume, the Christian way of dealing with an unbeliever, I might ask Mr. Rowe if he does not know the passage, Matt. v., 17—19, and if he knows it why he does not quote it. It is fatal to his repudiation of the Old Testament. Still more pointedly might I regret his apparent ignorance of the phrase, "algebraical sum". Mr. Rowe's argument on the "admissions" supposed to be damaging to my cause amounts to the following: A and B dispute on the direction in which a body is moving; A says: "It is moving northwards"; B says: "There is a force of 2 lbs. propelling it northwards; there is an opposite force of 50 lbs. propelling it southwards: therefore the body moves southwards with a force proportionate to 48 lbs." "Oh," says A, "you have made an admission damaging to your contention that the body moves southwards; you have admitted the existence of a force of 2 lbs. propelling it northwards; therefore you admit that the body moves northwards." If Mr. Rowe can convince anyone by such a line of argument, he is heartily welcome to his converts. The "reflecting minds" will take the sensible view that where there is some good and much evil eclecticism is useful, and while they will gladly get any good they can out of the Bible, as out of any other book, they will laugh to scorn the pretence that its jumble of contradictory propositions can be a revelation from a Supreme Intelligence. Its effect on human progress they will judge by its total effect, and finding that the good in it is common to Buddhism, Zoroastrianism, Hinduism, Confucianism, Christianity, and Mohammedanism, while its evil is its own and is most shockingly marked in history, they will disentangle from it and cling to the common good which is the outcome of human experience, and cast on to the dust-heap of dead faiths all that is distinctively "Christian".

Paragraphs 2 and 3. In paragraph 2 Mr. Rowe quotes some of the stray texts in which Christianity teaches moral truisms, current in the world before Christianity was dreamed of. The fact that Christianity repeats some of the lessons taught much more effectively by the older religions proves nothing. A species is marked by its differentia, and the differentia of Christianity is mischievous. But in paragraph 3 Mr. Rowe asks to be told "whether Christianity at least assumes the punishable acts to be positively vicious. . . . . Therefore it again appears that Christianity *professes* anyhow to promote virtue", etc. Yes, Christianity does assume that unbelief, which is one of the punishable acts, is positively vicious, and in so assuming it makes itself the enemy of progress. My phrase, "acts that may, or may not, be vicious", was purposely chosen. Christianity damns a man for unbelief (Mark xvi. 16); it classes unbelief with vice: "The fearful and unbelieving, and the abominable, and murderers, and whoremongers, and sorcerers, and idolators, and all liars, shall have their part in the lake which burneth with fire and brimstone" (Rev. xxi. 8). It threatens one fate for the sceptic and the scoundrel, for J. S. Mill and Charles Peace, save that at the foot of the gallows it pardons the scoundrel and bears him heavenward, while it writes on the tombstone of the blameless philosopher, "He that believeth not shall be damned". The angels welcome

Peace, the devils exult over Mill, and I deny that a religion which saves the murderer and damns the philosopher is a force for human progress.

My answer to Mr. Rowe's argument about sinful man approaching a righteous God by Jesus Christ, is that his statement completely confirms the objections I urged. Man is "accounted righteous" though he is sinful, because somebody else "has obeyed God's law". Mr. Rowe appears to be unconscious of the profound immorality of this whole transaction, for he seems to fancy that re-stating my charge is a defence. How is human progress helped by this substitution of a righteous person for a criminal? It is surely man's observance of moral duty, not his escape from deserved punishment, that helps progress. Progress is not helped when I, being a scoundrel, make a compact that God shall make believe that I am a saint because somebody else is one. On the contrary, I, being a scoundrel, am encouraged to remain one, by being told that all will come right if I only believe; and Christian preachers may exhaust themselves in preaching virtue, so long as they point out that virtue is a matter of quite secondary importance, since I can get to Paradise as I am dying by saying, "Lord, remember me". Let me put to Mr. Rowe a parallel case, suggested by a phrase of Mr. Cotter Morison. I am a trainer of horses for the Derby; I pay large sums to get good stock, and have a thoroughbred mare and a three-thousand guinea stallion; I take great care of my colt, feed him and groom him and train him sedulously; my thoughts and my time are devoted to his nurture and education. My neighbor, the day before the Derby, goes to the knacker's yard, buys a screw brought to be killed, for 10s., prays over it, brings it up next day to the starting point, and it runs neck-and-neck with my carefully reared colt. Shall I next year spend my time, and thought, and money, on training my Derby candidate? Nay, all the preachers in Christendom might tell me I ought to do so, but if a prayer over a screw brings about all the results of my toil, I shall prefer the prayer to the trouble.

But, Mr. Rowe says, "a disciple will inevitably imitate the actions and bearing of his master". Is that so? Then, judging by the disciples, what a peculiarly poor sort of creature the master must have been! Mr. Rowe shuts himself up into a very awkward corner. If the disciple is "inevitably" like the Master, the Archbishop of Canterbury with his £15,000 a year, and all the wealthy clerics and laymen of the Church, who live in purple and fine linen while the poor are starving, to say nothing of the Inquisitors, and witch-burners, with all the army of Christian persecutors of ancient and modern times, are like Christ, and he must have been selfish, cruel, and brutal. Or, they are not like him, and are therefore not his disciples, and there are no true Christians, and Christian doctrines are a complete failure.

May I venture to ask Mr. Rowe to take it for granted that I know the New Testament pretty well, and that the passage he quotes from James is familiar to me? He probably also knows that Luther, who had a certain faculty for logic and straightforwardness, rejected the epistle of James, and designated it as an "epistle of straw", because of its flagrant contradiction to the writings of Paul. I am really not responsible for the self-contradictions of the New Testament; and the fact that Paul says: "a man is justified by faith without the deeds of the law" (Rom. iii. 28), and that James says: "What doth it profit, my brethren, though a man say he hath faith, and have not works? can faith save him?" (James ii. 14), is an extremely awkward thing for believers in the Bible, but it does not concern me, who judge Paul and James as I judge Beaconsfield and Gladstone, and trouble not myself at all about the threat that he who does not believe two contradictory statements shall be damned. Mr. Rowe ignores the main point that salvation comes by faith, according to Paul, and that works are only to follow out of gratitude, and are not essential to salvation. The well-known eulogy of charity in 1 Cor. xiii. is not a quarter as practical as the older analysis of charity by Katha Chari, and the plain statement that salvation depends on faith only, inevitably gives faith preeminence. Where was the charity of the dying thief that Jesus took with him to Paradise? Much sounder morality is in the Bhagavat Gita: "He who neglecteth the duties of this life is unfit for this, much less for any higher world".

In paragraph 5 Mr. Rowe complains that I have given no shadow of evidence of the low tone of public morality in every Christian land. I imagined that Mr. Rowe read the daily papers, and knew something of the courts of justice, and of town and country life here and abroad. That Christianity, like every other religion, nominally disapproves of crimes, I freely admit. But I contended that by its easy forgiveness of sins it promotes immorality; that it encourages people to sin by promising immunity from consequences; and that by teaching people that the obedience of a savior will be accepted instead of theirs, it breaks the spring of moral effort. Mr. Rowe has carefully avoided answering this plainly-worded challenge, and falls back on the repetition of texts which can be paralleled and improved on by quotations from pre-Christian moralists, showing that "Christian teachings" are as superfluous in what is good in them as they are mischievous in what is bad.

In paragraph 6 Mr. Rowe asks for evidence that the greater part of the cultivated minority are not Christians. I can hardly suppose that Mr. Rowe is quite ignorant of the mental attitude of the leading men of science towards Christianity. Need I remind him of Huxley, Tyndall, Clifford, in England; of Haeckel, Büchner, Vogt, in Germany; of Bert, Lenormant, in France; or of Galton's famous questions to the hundred English scientific men? I do not see the "peculiar fitness" of the choice of the ignorant to be apostles, unless the gospel is best fitted for the ignorant, as I contend; and if theirs was an "exceptional case" I can hardly be expected to see its "fitness". That Paul frightened Felix speaks more for the superstition of Felix than the skill of Paul. I can quite imagine General Booth frightening the Prince of Wales.

Paragraph 8. I have no objection to men loving their wives—a duty urged on them long before the time of Paul, who advised people to avoid marriage (1 Cor. vii.), so that if his counsel were followed there would be no wives to love—but I contend that the subjection he commanded renders impossible any feeling worthy to be called love between adults. And, after all, does Mr. Rowe really mean that a wife is to look up to and worship her husband with the reverence that the Church gives to its God? If Mr. Rowe thinks that my view that the clergy opposed education is "a fatal mistake", and that Mr.

Gladstone's enthusiastic Christianity is valid against historical documents, I can only refer him to the struggle from the end of the eighteenth century up to 1870. I venture to quote on this head from a pamphlet of my own, on the Church of England as the enemy of the people, in which I give fuller details than I can here: "In 1781, Mr. Raikes, of Gloucester, set up the first Sunday School; and in 1789, Hannah More, horrorstruck at the terrible ignorance she found in country villages she visited, founded several day schools for the instruction of poor children. In her letters she complains—although herself a member of the Church—of the hostility she encountered at the hands of the clergy; and she was actually prosecuted in the Ecclesiastical Court for setting up a school in the village of Wedmore." Dr. Bell's opposition to the schools of Lancaster is historical; he argued that the poor should not be taught writing or ciphering, "for 'there is a risk of elevating, by an indiscriminate education, the minds of those doomed to the drudgery of daily labor above their condition, and thereby rendering them discontented and unhappy in their lot'. Later, pressed on by the determination of the people to get education somehow, Dr. Bell admitted writing and ciphering into his proposed plan for educating the people, and we find him writing to Dr. Barton on March 30th, 1807: 'It cannot be dissembled that thousands, in various parts of the kingdom, are drawn off from the Church by the superior attention paid to education out of the Church' ('Life of Dr. Bell,' by R. Southey, vol. ii., p. 182, ed. 1844). This view had been eagerly pressed on Dr. Bell by Mrs. Sarah Trimmer, a zealous Churchwoman, as early as 1805; she describes Lancaster's plan as 'inimical to the interests of the Established Church', and speaks of Lancaster as 'this Goliath of schismatics', 'engrossing the instruction of the common people' (*Ibid.*, pp., 131, 132). For many years, however, the clergy fought stubbornly in defence of popular ignorance. Archdeacon Daubeny, a typical Churchman, in his charge to the clergy of his archdeaconry in 1807, describes Lancaster's school as 'so wild, so absurd, so anti-Christian an experiment'. And the *Edinburgh Review* above named quotes him as having spoken of Lancaster as the author of 'a deceitful institution', recalling 'the crafty design of the apostate Julian to confound

Christianity'. In the same year the proposal to appoint a Committee of the Privy Council to deal with matters affecting the education of the people was negatived in the House of Lords, not a bishop voting in its favor." As late as 1839, when a Bill was sent up to the House of Lords to enable magistrates to provide schools out of the rates, fifteen bishops out of eighteen voted against it.

I am not concerned to defend the Comtists against the charge of plagiarism, though I can imagine a Comtist retorting that the Christians had stolen their ideal of brotherhood from Buddha and Manu, and had never practised it. If Christianity has abolished slavery, it is odd that the clergy here, and all Christian sects in America, stood in defence of slavery, and that the French and American Freethinkers led the attack against it until popular opinion was converted and credit was to be obtained by preaching freedom. Mr. Rowe will have to rewrite history ere he can persuade the instructed that Christianity has not fought to maintain ignorance and slavery. If this be too great a task, he might at least explain to us how the "fear and trembling" agree with brotherhood.

If it be coldhearted to regard just persons as more useful to society than "the bloodwashed murderer" to whom, with his useless penitence, I made the angels welcome, then cold-hearted I am. But it is a gross perversion of my statement to say that Atheism disdains those who yearn for "moral reformation" and who are seeking to break "the fetters of vice". The bloodwashed murderer who repents after he is deprived of all possibility of committing further crime, and who writes disgusting letters about going to the arms of Jesus *vid* the gallows, is a person for whom I have no respect. It is not moral reformation he is yearning for, but escape from the hell his superstitious fancy dreads. The man who really yearns for moral reformation will feel no comfort in the vicarious righteousness of Christ, for he wants to *be*, not to be *imputed*, righteous; and he will be content manfully to face the consequences of his irrevocable past instead of whining for mercy. And bitter indeed, as he struggles to improve, will be his hatred of the religion which by its soft promises of easy forgiveness lured him into binding round his limbs the chain of vicious habits which can only be broken by long effort and not by any grace of God. Nor did I say a word of courting the society of the already virtuous and leaving the helpless alone. I said that "it is the ninety and nine just persons *who make for progress*", and Mr. Rowe can hardly deny the proposition unless he alleges that crimes help forward the human race. Might it not perhaps be as well if Mr. Rowe was a little more scrupulous in his paraphrases of my arguments? In a written debate, the reader can always turn back, and nothing is gained by misrepresentation.

Mr. Rowe evades my two final paragraphs by calling them "rhetoric", and says he wants fact and argument. But the statement that there are "two chief factors in progress, intellect and character", and that Christianity strikes at intellect by its exaltation of faith and at character by the doctrines I enumerated, is certainly argumentative and ought to be answered, if answer is possible. It does not seem to me—I don't know how it appears to our readers—that the "rhetoric" is chiefly on my side in this debate.

Meanwhile, I make the following further allegations against Christian teachings.

(1) That the teachings of Jesus embodied in Matt. v., 38–42, and Luke vi. 29, 30, would, if carried out, place society at the mercy of every scoundrel, and let thieves go doubly-coated while honest men went bare.

(2) That his teaching in Matt. vi. 25–34, is a direct encouragement to improvidence, and a censure on prudence and forethought.

(3) That his statement in Matt. x. 34–36, is the statement of a narrow-minded fanatic, which has been only too sadly verified in the enmities caused by his religion. The Christian who persecutes and slays may fairly point to this text as his justification.

(4) That his encouragement of celibacy in Matt. xix. 10–12, is foolish and mischievous, and has led to most deplorable results.

(5) That this teaching of Jesus, with the more detailed teaching of Paul on the same subject, in 1 Cor. vii., is answerable for all the evils brought on Christendom by the celibacy of priests, monks, and nuns.

When Mr. Rowe has dealt with these, I will give him some more.

Mr. Rowe's Third Article.

What does Mrs. Besant mean by the "veiled insolence which is the Christian way of dealing with an unbeliever"? If the phrase describes words of mine, they ought to have been specified. If the reference was to some third party, it was irrelevant, and must tend to mar our discussion by the intermixture of foreign matters. No language of the kind quoted will check me in grappling freely with my respected opponent's attack on Christian teachings. Christianity was cradled in free thought. Its Founder engaged in almost daily discussions. It enjoins its votaries "to be ready always to give an answer to every man that asketh you a reason of the hope that is in you" (1st St. Peter, iii. 15). Thereby it encourages honest investigation as the foundation of faith and progress alike. Hence it leads me to subject Mrs. Besant's assaults to the keenest logical scrutiny, however much may be said about "veiled insolence", etc.

It is alleged that I am not sufficiently scrupulous in paraphrasing my opponent's arguments. This is precisely the charge which I desire to advance against Mrs. Besant. What is more, I wish to prove my case, whereas no evidence is furnished against me. It has been stated that I have repudiated the Old Testament and the Thirty-nine Articles of the Church of England; and a good many words, by no means flattering, have been expended on myself as a consequence. With respectful deference, I must express unqualified astonishment. Not only so, but I must emphatically ask Mrs. Besant to mention the sentence or sentences wherein the twofold "repudiation" is contained. Meanwhile, if your readers will refer to my last article, they will discover that I distinctly admit myself bound throughout the present debate by any New Testament appeals to the corroborative authority of the Old Testament in relation to Christian teachings. Also, I represent the Thirty-nine Articles as merely interpretative of the primary records of Christianity, and so distinguished from those records. To do this is not to repudiate the Articles. Certainly it is not to view them as interpreting wrongly. It is only to attach to them their proper degree of importance in comparison with other documents. And yet, because of this, Mrs. Besant actually pourtrays me as making "a significant admission of the indefensibility on the platform of the doctrines which are safely taught from the law-defended pulpit". In such a distortion, on the part of the assailant of Christianity, may be rather discerned "a significant admission", however inferential, of the poverty of fact and feebleness of argument available for her use. It stands more or less on an equality with her constant denunciations of Christianity, and her depreciatory comparisons of it with non-Christian religious systems, minus a particle of proof.

My quotations from St. Luke and the Epistle to Titus, showing that the avowed purpose of Christianity is to provide means for the redemption of man from vice, etc., are very casually noticed. They are met by the remark that the texts only contain "moral truisms current in the world" "before Christianity was dreamed of". This strong statement is unsustained by the slightest evidence. Even were it absolutely demonstrated, it would afford no answer. The issue is not what existed or did not exist before Christianity, but what is the avowed purpose of the latter. So plainly virtuous is the professed aim of Christianity, that Mrs. Besant herself actually concedes that the unbelief which Christianity condemns is assumed by it to be "positively vicious". Further argument on the point is unnecessary. But in order to disparage the comparative importance attached by Christianity to faith and works respectively, we are told that Christianity "threatens one fate for the sceptic and the scoundrel". Where scepticism and evil deeds are alike wilful this is correct, but not otherwise. When alike wilful they inevitably belong to a common category, and merit similar censure. More than once Mrs. Besant has cited Mark xvi., 16, to show that mere unbelief is condemned by the New Testament. The 14th, 17th, and 18th verses of the same chapter correct the mistake, clearly testifying that the condemnation is associated with the rejection of adequate evidence for belief. Unbelief in the face of adequate evidence is unquestionably a wrongful state of mind. What is wrong deserves to be condemned. Hence, as Christianity makes evidence the basis of belief, it is not the case, as Mrs. Besant declares, that Christianity arbitrarily writes on the tombstone of John Stuart Mill: "He that believeth not shall be damned". A thousand times, No. First it must be determined whether the philosopher wilfully rejected adequate evidence. Seemingly Mrs. Besant has wonderful sympathy with John Stuart Mill. Is it not the same "blameless philosopher" who has paid tributes to Christianity which have been sharp thorns in the sides of Atheistic thinkers? When, however, Mrs. Besant, in her rhetorical flights, boldly affirms that the angels welcome Charles Peace while "the devils exult over Mill", her utterances may be dismissed as the creatures of midnight imagination, confusing the calm discussion of principles by profitless personal allusions.

A constant tendency to substitute persons for principles in this debate is betrayed by my opponent. Thus in her fourth paragraph we have numerous personal citations, from the Archbishop of Canterbury of the present, to the witchburners of the past. Our debate has nothing to do with the professors of Christianity, but with its principles. Why does Mrs. Besant repeatedly confuse the issue? When it is shown that the conduct of these classes of men in what is deemed wrong, consorts with Christian teachings, it will be soon enough to drag them into the debate. Otherwise it is simply a waste of time and space. While on this topic, however, I must deal with other illustrations of Mrs. Besant's personal arguments, lest I should seem lacking in courtesy. Her former reference to the low tone of public morality in every Christian land is repeated. But my rejoinder is unnoticed, viz., whether this, if correct, has proceeded from Christian teachings. If it is not the fruit of Christian teachings, how can these teachings be held responsible? In her sixth paragraph Mrs. Besant confesses that Christianity nominally disapproves of crimes, though it is sought to countervail the admission by the allegation that Christianity promotes immorality by its easy forgiveness of sins. When some tangible effort is made to warrant the allegation, I will discuss it. For the present, I press the conceded discountenance of crime by Christianity in the argument. It must follow that immorality is thereby discouraged. Hence, according to my opponent's position Christianity cannot be answerable for the low tone of morality in Christian lands. Whether the lukewarmness of its professors may be held responsible, is an entirely different question. But why has Mrs. Besant refrained from answering the following question in my last article: "How is it, moreover, if Atheism be sublimely more moral than Christianity, that it has allowed this low tone of public morality to continue"? I must again ask for a reply.

Once more, my opponent tries to depict Christianity as rejected by "the greater part of the cultivated minority", and by the leading men of science; roaming over the whole of Europe in order to find nine scientists, living and dead, opposed to Christianity. Professor Tyndall is one. What has Mrs. Besant to say respecting Tyndall's eulogy of "the incomparable life of Christ" in the fifth edition of his "Fragments of Science"? This was mentioned in my last article, but has been disregarded. The phrase involves to some extent discipleship of Christ. But if Tyndall be not a Christian in the fullest sense of the word, both he and Huxley, another of my opponent's witnesses, have at least emphatically repudiated Atheism. Was it inconvenient to Mrs. Besant to name this? And in regard to a third of her scientists, Clifford, now deceased, his violent rush from Ritualism to the extremest Rationalism, involving his dogmatising about hypothetical mind-stuff, an entity outside the range of experience and thereby irrational, deprives his hostility towards Christianity of all weight. Eagerly do I accept my opponent's challenge for an appeal to scientists. Keeping within the range of the nineteenth century, even within the confines of the British Isles, will it be denied that Brewster, Herschel, Faraday, Forbes, Tait, Thomson, Clerke Maxwell, Carpenter, Stokes, Balfour Stewart, Henslow, Lyell, Sedgwick, Flowers, Hamilton, Veitch, Mansel, to mention no others, bore the name of Christian? Further, when scholars of such universal fame as Thirlwall and Whewell have also recently officiated in the Christian Church, are we to be told that the greater part of the cultivated minority are not Christians? For every single scientist of repute who has eschewed Christianity for Atheism, it would be possible to find a dozen who cling firmly to Christian teachings. Once more, therefore, judgment must go against Mrs. Besant.

It was my former contention that Mrs. Besant had misunderstood Christian teachings by representing St. Paul to inculcate a barren faith as required from Christian believers. Her rejoinder again involves a singular omission to notice that Christ's obedience of God's law on man's behalf requires an acknowledgment of sinfulness on man's part, and that such an avowal, coupled with man's shelter behind Christ, through the love of God manifested by Christ, will call forth in him every exertion to comply with his Heavenly Father's commands. To represent me as merely alleging that man is accounted righteous though he is sinful, because somebody else has obeyed God's law, is a most imperfect statement of my position. Did I not abundantly demonstrate that belief in Christ produced an imitation of Christ? Did I not cite a lengthy catalogue of the vices condemned by Christianity? Did I not quote from the Epistle to the Ephesians a portraiture of the virtues enjoined by Christianity? All this is unnoticed. Nay more, in response to my mention of the fruitful charity commended by St. Paul in 1 Cor. xiii., Mrs. Besant seems to think it almost adequate to remark that such Christian charity is not a quarter as practical as that in Katha Chari. We have nothing to do now with outside codes; the issue is whether Christianity commands a barren faith, *i.e.*, faith without works. I read with surprise Mrs. Besant's repetition of the statement in conjunction with 1 Cor. xiii., that in Christianity salvation depends on faith only. Does not St. Paul therein, as quoted before by me, in his comparative estimate of faith, hope, and charity, declare fruitful charity and not faith to be the greatest? Once more, if the appeal be to St. Paul, let me repeat my former citation from St. Paul's Epistle to the Galatians, where he advocates a faith which "*worketh* by love".

Nor can I allow Mrs. Besant so lightly to dismiss St. James' Epistle, which expressly declares that faith is to be shown by works, and that without works faith is dead. This is Christian teaching, and let Mrs. Besant rightly admit it. Her remark that Martin Luther rejected the Epistle of St. James, only serves to bring into greater prominence that the Epistle was in the Canon of Holy Scripture before Luther's days; and that, Martin Luther notwithstanding, it remains there still. So that I am warranted in bringing forward the crushing testimony of St. James against Mrs. Besant's misinterpretation of Christian teaching as inculcating an empty, fruitless faith.

It is unfortunate that my opponent in her study of the New Testament has overlooked such passages as the following, which might be multiplied wholesale: "Let your light so shine before men that *they may see your good works*, and glorify your Father which is in heaven" (Matt. v., 16). A more practical religion than Christianity is, could scarcely be conceived.

We now approach afresh the fourfold way, exemplified in my first article, in which Christian teachings are calculated to promote the welfare of humanity. Seemingly Mrs. Besant's ultimate silence regarding my first argument that Christian teachings strongly encourage the development of mental faculties by every individual, amounts to a surrender on that head. Let the reader note the fact. Moreover her criticisms on the impetus given to the rightful discharge of family duties by Christian teachings, may be rebutted without much difficulty. Omission is again a prominent characteristic. Mrs. Besant persists in refusing to answer whether happy consequences would not follow in this and other lands if husbands would be "wife-loving" according to Christian teachings. Let the reader note this second fact, because my question on the point has been twice put. Mrs. Besant formerly described Christianity as imposing a "degrading position" on wives, in requiring them to be subject to their husbands. My explanation was that this subjection was to co-exist with deep affection, because its pattern was the Church's willing subordination to Christ, its loving and loveable Head. Unable to deny the loving pattern, my opponent simply affirms that such subjection on the part of the wife is incompatible with any feeling worthy to be called love. Is it not possible to love our superior? Millions of Christians, intensely loving Christ, will answer yes. Millions of Englishmen, having bosoms bursting with loyalty towards the Queen, will re-echo the response. Yes, it is possible for wives to love their husbands as the Church loves Christ, and the more so when husbands discharge their duty of "giving honor to the wife as unto the weaker vessel", according to the Christian injunction (1 St. Peter, iii. 7). Mrs. Besant's enquiry whether the wife is to "worship her husband with the same reverence as the Church gives to its God", may be instantly answered in the negative.

Nor is Mrs. Besant more successful in meeting my contention that Christian teachings lead parents to educate their children. If this is not correct, would it not be more pertinent to give the proof rather than try to show that it is a novelty for the clergy to be friends of education? My opponent has displayed a suicidal zeal in regard to this discussion while adducing alleged facts against the clergy. The clergy are only a small fraction of Christians. Christians they were, in the persons of Robert Raikes and Hannah More, Mrs. Besant herself being witness, who founded Sunday Schools, and labored so zealously for day schools in the last century. Assuming for argument's sake the negligence of the clergy a century ago respecting education, that failing no longer exists. Let the reader remember Mr. Gladstone's testimony to the work of the Welsh clergy on behalf of education, given in my last article. In addition, I would now mention that the Church of England, which Mrs. Besant hastens to decry, has spent no less than £27,000,000 upon education during this century. Has Atheism expended the tithe of this amount?

In my first article I labored to establish that Christianity inculcated human brotherhood, with all its happy results on human society, both in bringing together rich and poor and in ameliorating the antagonisms between labor and capital. The major portion of my contention is conceded by silence. Here, again, is a noteworthy circumstance. But it is alleged that Christians have advocated slavery, while Freethinkers have led the attack against it. Softly, Mrs. Besant. Wilberforce and Clarkson, both of them Christians, led the attack on slavery in this country. Christianity inspired them by its inculcation of brotherly love. How would Atheism have guided them? Denying the existence of man's soul as it does, it reduces man to a mere animal. We buy and sell animals, and if man be but the animal which Atheism delineates, we should be entitled to buy and sell human beings too, and thus perpetrate all the horrors of slavery. If, then, Atheists have led the attack on slavery, they have derived no stimulus from Atheism, but once more have illustrated how men can act out in life the very ideal of brotherly love presented by the self-same Christian religion which they disavow.

Once more, see how the brotherly love of Christianity has almost studded our land with hospitals, infirmaries, almshouses, and similar institutions. Free admission is granted to these, without distinction of caste or creed. Christian teachings recommend this—"As we have therefore opportunity, let us do good unto all men" (Gal. vi., 10). Has Atheism built hospitals, infirmaries, almshouses, and the like? If so, where? Does it even teach charity towards all men? If the Freethinkers' Benevolent Fund is to be the test, then its sphere of charity is exceedingly contracted, for even actual Freethinkers who happen not to be members of any organisation have but a slender chance of receiving either the bread or coal tickets distributed by the Committee.

Instead of grappling any further with my illustration of the manner in which the conduct of Jesus Christ before the High Priest and Pontius Pilate "asserted the inherent rights of citizens and subjects", Mrs. Besant prefers to make five new allegations against Christian teachings. Does my respected opponent then yield the point for which I argued? I wish her to answer.

In regard to the first allegation, the verses referred to are couched in parabolic language, which is always exaggerative, and consorted with Eastern modes of speech. Our Savior's life, however, shows that self defence is compatible with Christian teachings, and in these verses He meant to correct the Jewish propensity for revenge and retaliation.

The second passage (Matt. vi., 25–34) does not encourage improvidence, but first asserts the truth that a Heavenly Father presides over the affairs of men; and, secondly, it declares the due order of human interests by ascribing superiority to man's religious welfare.

The third passage (Matt. x., 34–36) is evidently prophetic of the results of Christ's mission. History confirms the prophecy.

The fourth passage (Matt. xix., 10–12) only conditionally encourages celibacy. It leaves each man to his own judgment.

The fifth passage (1 Cor. vii.) conveys no general command on the same subject. In verse 6 St. Paul disavows that he is writing an authoritative command. Moreover, it is clear from verse 26 that his precepts had reference likewise to the exceptional requirements of a "present distress", *i.e.*, prospective persecution. If "priests, monks, and nuns" have wrested the apostle's language from its purpose, in order to bolster up certain types of ecclesiastical discipline and machinery, the responsibility is altogether their own. Christian teachings are not thereby at fault.

Annie Besant's Third Article.

I am afraid that this debate is not likely to be very interesting or very instructive to our readers, if Mr. Rowe adopts the tactics of merely repeating the statements he had previously made, and ignoring the replies I have offered to them, as he does through his last article. I can only again follow him, step by step, regretting the repetitions into which I am forced.

In paragraph 1 Mr. Rowe asks what I referred to as "veiled insolence". The context made my meaning clear. Mr. Rowe bade me examine the Testament "more carefully", asked if I knew certain passages known to every Sunday School child, and absurdly went on to reason as if I was "unaware of them". I have not the slightest objection to the "keenest logical scrutiny".

Paragraph 2. I quoted the statement which Mr. Rowe misrepresented, so that it is hardly accurate to say that "no evidence is furnished". I said that the ninety and nine just persons made for progress: Mr. Rowe twisted this into a statement that Atheism disdained those who were striving to reform themselves. I asked Mr. Rowe in my first article if he repudiated the Old Testament, and I quoted an Article of his Church in support of my contention that good works are worthless without faith. In his reply, Mr. Rowe stated that he was not bound by the Old Testament in this debate, except where the New Testament made specific reference to it (*ante*, pp. 14, 15). If this is not a repudiation of the Old Testament, what is it? Mr. Rowe declined to answer my quotation from the Article, on the ground that it was a "secondary document" and "irrelevant", as not being "an authoritative declaration of Christian teachings". As a matter of fact it is a legally authoritative declaration of them, and a depraving of the Book of Common Prayer is an offence punishable under the Blasphemy Laws.

Paragraph 3. If Mr. Rowe cannot understand the argument that moral teachings common to all religions and current in the world before Christianity cannot be admitted as specifically "Christian" teachings, I fear no words of mine can make it plainer. I refer our readers to the end of the first paragraph of my second article (*ante*, p. 23) and the beginning of my second paragraph. I regret that Mr. Rowe should play on the words "positively vicious". I stated that Christianity assumes that unbelief is positively vicious; Mr. Rowe says: "Mrs. Besant herself actually concedes that the unbelief which Christianity condemns is assumed by it to be 'positively vicious'", as though there were some other unbelief uncondemned by Christianity and not vicious. Christianity assumes *all* unbelief to be vicious; "he that believeth not shall be damned;" not "he that believeth not in the face of adequate evidence", according to Mr. Rowe's gloss. Mark xvi., 14, 17, 18, throw no light on the subject, and so far from miracles being "adequate evidence" Jesus warns his disciples against trusting to "signs and wonders" (Matt. xxiv., 24), and in John xx., 29 he implicitly rebukes Thomas for wanting "adequate evidence" of his resurrection, and pronounces a benediction on those who believe without similar proof. The argument as to Mill leads to a curious dilemma: J. S. Mill is either damned or not damned; if he is damned he rejected adequate evidence for Christianity; if he is not damned, it is because the evidence for Christianity was inadequate; therefore either he is damned, or the evidence for Christianity is inadequate. (Mr. Rowe cannot say that he did not examine Christianity, for he speaks of Mill's "tributes to Christianity"; besides, Mill's works are before the world.)

Paragraph 4. It was not I who substituted "persons for principles". It was Mr. Rowe who put forward the statement that the disciple would "inevitably imitate" the master, and when I compare some of the disciples with the master he objects. Why then have challenged the comparison? I do allege that the conduct of the Inquisitors, witchburners, and persecutors, "consorts with Christian teachings". In the so-called law of Moses the murdering of witches and unbelievers is commanded (Ex. xxii., 18, 20; Deut. xiii.), and Jesus distinctly endorsed the law (Matt. v., 17–19). A similarly bloodthirsty spirit is shown in Luke xix., 27, and in the gloating over the sufferings of those who reject Christ (Matt. x., 14, 15, and many other passages). And what shall be said of the loving spirit towards non-Christians shown in 2 John, 10, 11? I must again repeat that I hold the Christian doctrine of the easy forgiveness of sins and of salvation by faith answerable for the low tone of morality, and that the latter is the fruit of these Christian teachings. Mr. Rowe is good enough to say he will discuss the allegation when some effort is made to warrant it. I beg to refer him to my first article, paragraph 3, and paragraphs 9, 10: to my second article, paragraph 3, and paragraph 6, and await his discussion. I did not notice the question why Atheism allowed the low tone of morality to continue, because we are discussing Christianity, not Atheism. I have no objection, however, to answer this question, with the other in paragraph 11. Atheism so successfully raises the tone of those who accept it that the appearance of an Atheist in the criminal dock—save for defending the right of free speech—is excessively rare: it cannot, of course, raise the tone of the majority who reject it. If Mr. Rowe will turn to the *National Reformer* of November 6th, p. 298, and read the paragraph on the Spencer legacy, he will see why we cannot raise many public institutions: it is a little too much for Christians to make laws which rob us, and then to taunt us with our inability to do things which require large sums of money. But this digression on Mr. Rowe's part seems to imply a certain shortness of arguments in favor of Christianity.

Paragraph 5. I have nothing to say about Professor Tyndall's opinion of Christ. What bearing on Christian teachings has Professor Tyndall's opinion of Christ? He does not apparently admire him enough to believe in him, and if a quotation from an Article of the Church be irrelevant to this discussion, what perfection of irrelevancy must be found in a quotation from Professor Tyndall. And what have Professors Tyndall's and Huxley's "repudiation" of Atheism to do with this debate? It was not "inconvenient" to me to name it, but it would have been absurdly irrelevant. If dogmatising about "an entity outside the range of experience" is "irrational" in Clifford, what becomes of all Mr. Rowe's talk in our previous debate about "God" and "protyle", and other things outside the range of experience? The list of names given would have more weight if I had said that all scientific men of the past and present were non-Christian; as it is, it is surely a little absurd to put Mr. Flowers as a leading man, or to take metaphysicians like Hamilton, Veitch, and Mansel as illustrations. Mr. Rowe is wise to keep within the British Isles, and to go back to Brewster and Faraday, for on the Continent the search for modern eminent Christian scientists would be weary work.

Paragraph 6. I am content to leave as it stands my argument on the barren faith. The condemnation of certain vices and enjoining of certain virtues was not unnoticed by me; I refer Mr. Rowe to my second article paragraph 6. As to 1 Cor. xiii., Paul is not speaking of salvation when he makes charity greater than faith; if my eternal destiny depends on my faith and not on my charity, Paul may praise charity as he will, but faith remains to me the one thing needful.

Paragraph 7. I don't dismiss the Epistle of James; I only say it contradicts Paul's Epistle to the Romans. If Mr. Rowe would reconcile the contradiction for us, something might be gained. Faith may be dead without works, but then it is that dead faith which saves, according to Paul: "We are justified by faith *without the deeds of the law*". Jesus bids his disciples let their good works be seen, in Matt. v., 16. Granted. And in Matt. vi., 1–6, 16–18, he bids them conceal them. It must be a little hard for Christians to discover "the mind of Christ".

Paragraph 8. Mr. Rowe seems to think that I "surrender" a point, where I do not constantly repeat myself. On the contrary, I make my point, and when Mr. Rowe only reiterates what he said before I made it, I leave the question to the judgment of our readers. The consequences of husbands loving their wives according to the Christian teachings would be better than the consequences of their hating their wives; but the consequences of loving equality between husbands and wives would be better than either of the former alternatives. When chattel slavery existed, it was happier for the slave to have a kind master than a cruel one, but the abolition of slavery was better than turning all the bad masters into good ones. So with the wife-slavery inculcated by Christianity. I can't criticise Mr. Rowe's question: "Is it not possible to love our superior?". The naïve masculine assumption of superiority is too delicious. I note that Mr. Rowe says "no" to my question as to husbands and wives; but Paul says "yes" (Eph. v., 23).

Paragraph 9. If Mr. Rowe will look back he will find (p. 12) that I said that the views "of the clergy on education" had changed. To this he answered (p. 21) that "I made a fatal mistake" in so saying, and quoted Mr. Gladstone on the Welsh "clergy". When I proved pp. 27, 28) that the clergy had changed, which is all I originally asserted, Mr. Rowe says that the "clergy are only a small fraction of Christians". How does that disprove my statement about the fraction? I do not know whence Mr. Rowe gets his £27,000,000, and if the figure is correct, I can only marvel how the Church managed to spend it, and yet to leave the people so ignorant until the much-denounced State education came in to save them.

Paragraph 10. So far from conceding the major part of Mr. Rowe's argument, I distinctly traversed each part of it (pp. 12, 13, and p. 28). Wilberforce and Clarkson did not commence the attack on slavery in England, but it was their bitter complaint that "infidel and anarchic France had freed her slaves, while Christian England kept hers in bondage". It is interesting to learn that the Christians who worked for abolition were inspired by Christianity, although the Christian Bible is in favor of slavery and was used as its bulwark, while the Atheists who worked for it were not inspired by Atheism but by the Christianity they rejected. Thus can a Christian reason!

Paragraph 11 I answered above.

Paragraph 12. I did not "grapple" any further with Jesus before Pilate because there was nothing to grapple with. I asked Mr. Rowe how Jesus "asserted the inherent rights of citizens and subjects", and all the answer I was given was a reference to John xviii., 19–23 and 33–38. Not a solitary word is there in these verses in support of Mr. Rowe's contention; if he will explain what he regards as their bearing on the subject, I will "grapple".

Mr. Rowe's answers to my four allegations are very unsatisfactory.

(1) The statements are parabolic and exaggerative (? ex-

aggerated). May be. They are none the less mischievous. Jesus may have meant to "correct" improper propensities, but it seems a pity that he did not choose language less open to misinterpretation. His life, we are told, "shows that self-defence is compatible with Christian teachings". Would Mr. Rowe mind stating to what incidents he refers?

(2) Matt. vi., 25–34 "does not encourage improvidence". So Mr. Rowe says. But it bids us "take no thought" for life, food, drink, raiment, or the morrow. Perhaps Mr. Rowe would kindly say what he would regard as improvidence, which must apparently be taking something less than "no thought".

(3) I quite agree that history confirms the truth of Christ's statement that he came to bring a sword. As this is descriptive of the "results of Christ's mission", what becomes of the beneficial effects of his teachings? We seem to be getting Mr. Rowe's beautiful picture blurred.

(4) Encourages celibacy conditionally! "He that can receive it let him receive it." Jesus, at least, did his best to bring on the world the evils that result from celibacy.

(5) But the argument of 1 Cor. vii., 32–40 is of general application, and the argument based on the caring for the things of the Lord and the world is as valid now as then. I did not allege that either Jesus or Paul imposed celibacy as an imperative duty; I only said their teaching encouraged it, and this Mr. Rowe seems to admit. There was no wresting of the language by priests, monks, and nuns; they thought themselves able to keep celibate "for the kingdom of heaven's sake", and tried to please their master by carrying out his "conditional" injunction.

I submit further to Mr. Rowe the following statements:

(1) That the blessings on hunger, poverty, and weeping in Luke vi., 20, 21, are blessings on the miseries which curse humanity and which every good man should strive to remove. The curses of verses 24 and 25, shew that Jesus is blessing material hunger, poverty, and weeping.

(2) That the words of Jesus in Matt. vii., 13, 14, prove, that if Christianity is true, it is the revelation of the damnation of the majority of human kind; while his declaration in Mark iv., 11, 12, shows that Jesus deliberately concealed his meaning from his fellow-countrymen lest they should understand him and be saved.

(3) That if Matt. vii., 16–20 be true, Christian teachings

as judged by their fruits in Christian practice must be very bad.

(4) That the teaching of Jesus in John vi., 44 and 65, making man's going to him wholly dependent on the divine action, conjoined with the teaching that none can be saved who do not go to him, draws a picture of horrible injustice inflicted on the helpless lost which revolts every feeling of equity and righteousness.

(5) That the doctrine of predestination to life (Rom. viii, 29, 30), involving of necessity the doctrine of predestination to destruction, which is also baldly stated in Rom. ix., 10–22, is a doctrine which must paralyse all human effort, while it paints God as a tyrant wicked and unjust almost beyond imagining.

But I had better stop, for my opponent has only one more article to write, and I shall be rendering his task impossible.

MR. ROWE'S FOURTH ARTICLE.

Rightly has my respected opponent acknowledged that "repetitions" distinguish her attacks on Christian teachings. Not only are the same objections again and again advanced, notwithstanding repeated answers, but it is significant that they are ever renewed with but declining force. Lack of space alone hinders me from presenting several instances in proof. Side by side with this, however, let me place Mrs. Besant's expressed fear that this debate is not likely to be "very interesting or very instructive". Every reader will be able instantly to draw an inference. Where is the room for misgiving, if "the teachings of Christianity" have been successfully assailed? Fortunately, the written words of the present discussion will remain; and I have hopes that they will help to show that "Christian teachings" are sometimes grievously misunderstood in proportion as they are so confidently denounced.

Almost too late comes Mrs. Besant's disavowal of any dislike for the "keenest logical scrutiny". Because I subjected her statements to the very selfsame process, the result is a charge against me of "veiled insolence". What is the foundation? Namely this: I urged my respected opponent to read the New Testament more carefully, and likewise supposed her to be unaware of certain passages. Surely the latter was a kindly explanation, from my standpoint, of her misconception of the nature of Christian teachings, while the former would follow thereupon as an inevitable sequence. A very slight ray of information thus suffices to dispel Mrs. Besant's unwitting delusion. Let me finally dismiss it with the single remark that I decline to imitate her employment of angry phrases. With equal unsuccess is the effort made to show that I have not correctly paraphrased my opponent's arguments. I am declared to have "*twisted*" the closing words of her first article into a statement that Atheism disdained those who were striving to reform themselves. Here is the passage in question: "By all means let the angels have the repentant sinner; but it is the ninety and nine just persons who make for progress". Why, in her last article, when accusing me of *twisting*, has Mrs. Besant furnished the last sentence only of the quoted passage? It is the former and omitted half, loftily leaving the repentant one with Christian angels, upon which I grounded my portraiture of Atheism. Note its emphatic tone: "*By all means* let the angels have the repentant sinner". Does not Atheism in such strong words forsake the repentant one? Does Atheism thereby evince any sympathy for, or proffer the right hand of succor to, the repentant one? Why so eagerly consign the repentant ones to the care of the Christian angels alone, if Atheism is not cold-hearted and does not disdain them?

Having rebutted the allegation of inaccurately paraphrasing Mrs. Besant's arguments, I now substantiate in turn the same charge against her last two articles. They represent me to have repudiated the Old Testament and the Thirty-Nine Articles. Marvellous to relate, Mrs. Besant's pretended demonstration that I have repudiated the Old Testament contains the distinct admission that I have owned myself bound by it where it makes specific reference to the subject of this debate. And this I have done more than once. Could anything be more opposite to "repudiation"? Yet it is in face of such a fact that the question is asked: "If this is not a repudiation of the Old Testament, what is it?". No less astonishing is the pretended evidence that I have "repudiated" the Thirty-

Nine Articles because I have described them as of secondary authority in comparison with the primary records of the New Testament. Mrs. Besant does not deny that the Articles are "secondary" as being interpretative, nor say wherein the "repudiation" of them lies. Had I declared them to interpret the New Testament wrongly, there would have been a pretext for suggesting my "repudiation" of them. This is just what I have not said. When, therefore, Mrs. Besant paraphrases my language as though I had said what I have not said, to what conclusion must the reader be driven?

The readers of this debate will undoubtedly recollect how laboriously Mrs. Besant essayed at the outset to depict Christianity as requiring from its disciples faith without works. Let them now notice the feeble endeavor in her last article to uphold that position. First, my respected opponent writes: "I am content to leave as it stands my argument on the barren faith"; and immediately afterwards proceeds to illustrate that she is not so content by a sort of spasmodic effort to enlarge the contention (*vide* paragraphs 7 and 8). As a preliminary to this matter, I formerly cited Scriptural passages testifying that the professed aim of Christianity is to redeem man from vice. This being true, Christianity must be practical. At first the point was contested; but now the contest has ceased. Have we here, then, another tacit admission of error? Moreover, in order to parry the effect of her former concession that Christianity assumes the unbelief which it condemns to be positively vicious, Mrs. Besant now declares that Christianity condemns all unbelief to be vicious. Assertion, however, is not demonstration. If, as stated in my last article, the 14th, 17th, and 18th verses of the closing chapter of St. Mark do not associate the condemnation of unbelief with its rejection of adequate evidence, it is unfortunate that the absence of such association has not been proved. The verses named imply the testimony of personal witnesses to Christ's resurrection, whose averment was to be confirmed by miracles. Could evidences be more adequate? Does not Mrs. Besant see that the "signs and wonders" against which Christian disciples were cautioned in Matthew xxiv., 24, must have been regarded by Christ as merely cunning delusions; since His Heavenly Father would not be held by Him as ready to bestow genuinely miraculous powers upon "false Christs and false prophets"? Hence, while the last chapter of St. Mark points to miracles as true evidences for Christian teachings in Apostolic times, our Savior did not "warn His disciples against trusting to genuine signs and wonders". Neither is Thomas condemned for "wanting adequate evidence of Christ's resurrection". If he is censured at all, it is for disparaging the concurrent testimony of numerous disciples who had seen the risen Savior (*vide* John xx., 25). Further, there was vouchsafed to him as conclusive evidence a personal sight of the Savior's wounded body. Surely this is, indeed, an association of evidence with faith as its foundation. I am right, therefore, in insisting that Christianity makes evidence the basis of belief, and so am fully warranted in saying afresh that it does not write arbitrarily on the tomb of anyone, whether John Stuart Mill or any other, "He that believeth not shall be damned". Mrs. Besant's logical anthesis regarding the condemnation or innocence of John Stuart Mill does not even possess the merit of cleverness. It leaves out of sight the truism that our Heavenly Father, as man's Creator, must be aware both of the finite capacities of every human mind, and that all evidences will of necessity thereby exercise only a relative influence on finite intellectual faculties.

Returning more directly to the subject whether Christian teachings ally faith and works, Mrs. Besant now disclaims any dismissal of the Epistle of St. James. What was the purpose, then, of her former remark that Martin Luther had designated it an "epistle of straw"? My respected opponent plays fast and loose in the discussion. To quote Martin Luther's observation was not only purposeless but a waste of space, if it was not intended to annihilate St. James·Epistle. On the other hand, if the canonical authority of St. James be recognised, he completely overthrows Mrs. Besant's argument that Christian teachings demand faith regardless of works. It is unavailing to intimate that St. Paul's Epistle to the Romans contradicts that of St. James. Already the assumed contradiction has been dispelled. I now strengthen the refutation by inviting Mrs. Besant to peruse afresh the last thirteen verses, for example, of the twelfth chapter of Romans, wherein it will be found that St. Paul is as earnest a champion of works as St. James. I will not weary the reader by corroborative passages from St. Paul's other Epistles. My former articles contain them. Mrs. Besant does not dispute the quotations: they are only passed over with significant silence. My opponent also concedes that our Savior urged His disciples to perform good works. Then why contend that Christianity inculcates a faith without works? The see-saw alternatives displayed by Mrs. Besant's arguments on the one side, and by her concessions on the other, almost render it difficult to discern what is her actual belief respecting Christian teachings. Did not Christ command his disciples thus: "Love your enemies, bless them that curse you, do good to them that hate you"? (Matt., v., 44.) Did he not further teach: "Whatsoever ye would that men should do unto you even so do unto them"? Did He not make it a fundamental of His teaching that His disciples were to "feed the hungry, clothe the naked, visit the sick", etc.,? (Matt. xxv., 31–44.) Enough is here instanced to unfold the moral grandeur and practical tendency of Christian teachings, to intimate the gain which would ensue to humanity if they were universally practised, and to witness how grave is the misconception which delineates those teachings as exacting a faith fruitless and not exceeding a barren sentiment.

Certain passages are specified from Exodus relative to the destruction of witches and idolaters by my opponent, and it is added that Jesus Christ endorsed them. May I remind Mrs. Besant that such precepts were meant for ancient times, the childhood of the world, when the exercise of force was more appropriate in social government than now? Every human father constantly changes the method of training his children as they advance through the several stages from infancy to approaching maturity of age. A corresponding development appears in Divine Revelation. Nor did Christ ever endorse these Mosaic precepts in any other sense. Moreover His limited reference in the passage instanced by Mrs. Besant (Matt. v., 17–19), is to the sacrificial portion of the Mosaic law alone, which was to be fulfilled in His own sacrifice, as is reasoned out in the Epistle to the Hebrews. My opponent pursuing this line of attack, appears to imagine that harshness of language will give force to her sentences. Only for the sake of the readers of this debate will I consent to repel her ascription of a "bloodthirsty spirit" to Christ. I am sorry to notice that a disputant who can deem it "veiled insolence" when she is thought to be simply unaware that certain passages are in the Bible, can yet be so indifferent regarding the feelings of others. Moreover, will it be believed that in the proof furnished for such irritating terms (Luke xix., 27), the Savior is only uttering a parable, the details being borrowed from Oriental despotism familiar to his hearers, so that His language was obviously figurative and not literal? Further, in the very same chapter, verse 41, the tenderness of Him whom Mrs. Besant caricatures as "bloodthirsty" is touchingly exemplified as He weeps while predicting the coming calamities of Jerusalem. Mrs. Besant is quite reticent about the latter circumstance. With confidence, therefore, do I submit her fairness for the verdict of the reader. Was He who prayed for the soldiers nailing Him to the cross animated by a "bloodthirsty spirit"? (Luke xxiii., 34). Was He "bloodthirsty" who constituted the good Samaritan a model for imitation? Was He "bloodthirsty" who rebuked the disciples desiring to call down fire from heaven upon the Samaritans as they declined to receive Him? (Luke ix., 54–56). Was it a "bloodthirsty spirit" which influenced the same Jesus Christ to direct Peter's forgiveness of an unoffending brother not only seven times, but seventy times seven? (St. Matt. xviii., 22). Whether Mrs. Besant responds to these enquiries or not, Professor Tyndall, one of her cultured minority, answers them with a loud No, as he alludes in his "Fragments of Science" to "the incomparable life of Christ". Even John Stuart Mill, her "blameless philosopher", re-echoes No, as he depicts Jesus Christ to be "probably the greatest moral reformer who ever existed upon earth" (*vide* "Three Essays on Religion", p. 255). Let Renan, too, the French sceptic and philosopher, say whether the accusation of being "bloodthirsty" lies against Jesus Christ. His verdict is as follows: "Jesus remains an inexhaustible principle of moral regeneration for humanity. . . . . Jesus will not be surpassed. . . . . All the ages will proclaim that, among the sons of men there is none born who is greater than Jesus" (*vide* "Renan's Life of Jesus", chap. 28).

From Spinoza, Goethe, and others, I might quote in a similar strain.

But the very mention of these great names reminds me once more how conflicting is Mrs. Besant's method of dealing with them. Her first article pourtrayed "the highly cultivated minority" as dissenting from Christianity. Her second article searched all Europe for nine names living and dead as representing this cultivated minority, Professor Tyndall being one. But after being confronted with twice nine scientists from these islands alone as adherents to Christianity, coupled with the quotation of Tyndall's eulogy of Christ, my opponent actually turns round in her last article upon her own witness Tyndall, and enquires: "What bearing on Christian teachings has Professor Tyndall's opinion of Christ?" Now that "incomparable life" either harmonised with or differed from the teachings which fell from Christ's lips. If it differed from them, Christ would become a contradictory character, and his life therefore no longer "incomparable". Evidently Tyndall has not discerned the contradiction, so that in his judgment the teachings of Christ must accord with his "incomparable life". Moreover, I might have strengthened my list of Christian scientists by the addition of such names as Owen, Davy, Lyell, and others. Even Darwin is at least free from Atheism according to the authoritative declaration of his attitude, taken from his "Life and Letters", by the French translator.

Very little is now alleged by Mrs. Besant in support of her original objections to my fourfold illustration of the guidance afforded by Christian teachings for humanity in this life. There is virtually nothing in Mrs. Besant's last article denying that husbands are enjoined to love their wives, and fathers to train their children, by Christianity; or to impugn my primal argument that Christian teachings inculcate the idea of human brotherhood, and check the tyranny of political rulers. As a last desperate expedient my opponent declares that the Christian Bible is in favor of slavery. Is it fair to make this accusation without assigning the proof, seeing that I shall have no further opportunity of examining the proof if subsequently adduced? I have shown that St. Paul repudiated the principle of slavery amongst Christians in the Epistle to Philemon. Christian teachings have led to its overthrow in every nation where men have learned to love their neighbors as themselves. Christian brotherhood is the inevitable death-knell of slavery. More; I have proved that Atheism lays the strongest foundation for slavery; and it is remarkable that Mrs. Besant has not ventured to examine the argument. So completely is the idea of human brotherhood due to Christianity, that Max Müller informs us that "the very word humanity was unknown before Christianity".

Mrs. Besant's criticisms of my answers to the five allegations against Christian teachings contained in her second article may be briefly dismissed.

1. Christ's constant arguments with the Pharisees, the Herodians, and the Sadducees afforded repeated examples of self-defence.

2. "Take no thought" may be better translated from the original Greek as "be not over-anxious". Human exertion is not hereby excluded, and thus improvidence is not encouraged.

3. Christ's mission resulted in the use of the sword, because believers were soon subjected to renewed persecutions by unbelievers. Hence the "beautiful picture" is spoiled by those outside the Christian pale, on whom the responsibility rests.

4. Mrs. Besant here makes an assertion against Christ without a shadow of proof. Nay, it is in the very face of Christ's quoted words which commence with a proviso, and so establish that he encouraged celibacy conditionally.

5. Here we have another bold assertion without evidence, that the argument, 1 Cor. vii., 32–40, is of general application. I have already specifically proved the contrary.

Five new allegations are now introduced in my opponent's last article. I answer as follows:—

1. A reference to Matthew v., 3 and 6 verses, will indicate that Christ was referring to spiritual poverty, and hunger after righteousness.

2. Nothing in St. Matthew's words represents that the majority do not wilfully choose the wrong path. If the choice be wilful, condemnation is deserved. The words in St. Mark are clearly leavened with the customary exaggeration of Eastern speech. Taken side by side with the Sermon on the Mount and other teachings, we see that Jesus Christ did not deliberately conceal his meaning even

from the poorest, for to the poor the Gospel was preached (Matt. xi., 5).

3. Throughout this debate I have shown that humanity would immensely benefit if Christian teachings were truly put into practice.

4. My opponent must first explain what is meant by going to Jesus Christ ere we can discuss the soundness of her inference.

5. In Romans viii., 29, we find that predestination is not absolute, but based on foreknowledge, whereby it is perceptibly implied that the Divine arrangements do not exclude human free will: but as the results of the exercise of this free-will are discerned beforehand so the Divine arrangements proceed accordingly. Hence human effort is not paralysed but encouraged, and my opponent's strong language is again shown to be unwarrantable.

In conclusion let me invite the reader to study afresh the teachings of Christianity. If Christian teachings are not calculated to promote the welfare of humanity in this life, how is it that the most civilised nations of the earth are Christian to-day? Christian brotherhood is not only compatible with, but it is the incentive to, the foremost human progress. When Christians have been intolerant, or unjust, or obstructive of advancement, they have contravened their religious profession. And yet after all, where shall we find to-day the foremost philanthropists; the chief founders of hospitals, and of schools; the ablest scientists, the boldest explorers? They are Christians. Their names are almost legion. What has Atheism, as the ambitious substitute for Christianity, to bestow on mankind which Christian teachings cannot and do not yield? Atheism reduces man to the level of the beasts of the field by denying the existence of his soul; whereas Christianity dignifies man as the child of God, and correspondingly reveals to him his consequent immortality. Atheism fosters selfishness, ignoring any higher being than human self; whereas Christianity unveils a Heavenly Father whose only-begotten Son yielded His life for human sake, so that we too might be stimulated thereby to suffer for the welfare of others. And is not this willingness to suffer for others the very mainspring of patriotism, and the instrument for procuring civil and religious liberty? Christian teaching bids us to be Christ-like, to sympathise with and to succor the suffering ones as Christ did; to feed the hungry, to cheer the bereaved, to be brave for truth, to assert the voice of conscience in fearless discussion, as did the Master. Mr. Frederic Harrison, one of our leading Positivists, speaking at Manchester on October 30th, paid a noble tribute to the "patience, human love, surrender of will and ambition" which are to be discerned within the pale of Christianity. He deplored the absence of such virtues amongst the Positivists, although Positivism claims superiority over Christianity. The fact is noteworthy. How is the deadness of Positivism to be explained, while Christianity is admittedly full of pulsating morality? The answer is that the "incomparable life of Christ" is at once the standard and the inspiration of Christians. My last words in this debate shall be a portraiture of Jesus Christ, taken from Lecky's "History of European Morals", vol. ii., p. 9:

"It was reserved for Christianity to present to the world an ideal character which, through all the changes of eighteen centuries, has inspired the hearts of men with an impassioned love, and has shown itself capable of acting on all ages, nations, temperaments, and conditions; has not only been the highest pattern of virtue, but the highest incentive to its practice; and has exercised so deep an influence that it may be truly said that the simple record of three years of active life has done more to regenerate mankind than all the disquisitions of philosophers and all the exhortations of moralists."

Annie Besant's Fourth Article.

Mr. Rowe appears to identify dogmatic statements and proofs, but I am quite content to rest my case on the arguments advanced with the—as I venture to think—insufficient replies given. Paragraphs 1, 2, 3 may be dismissed, the reader being left to form his judgment on the merits of the opposing views. I have neither fear nor misgiving as to what that judgment will be. I admit that I could have wished that Mr. Rowe had thought it right to deal with the extraordinary language quoted by me from the 11th and 13th Articles of the Church of England, instead of quarrelling with the Articles as "secondary". They certainly form a part of the authoritative "teachings of Christianity" in this country, and they ought to have been defended if defence were possible.

Paragraph 4. It is perfectly true that I essayed to prove that Christianity made salvation dependent on faith, not on works, and I think I succeeded in my essay. I do not think my statement that "I am content to leave as it stands my argument on the barren faith" is exactly a "feeble endeavor . . . . to uphold that position". On the contrary, it is the expression of my satisfaction in the impregnability of the position, as evidenced by Mr. Rowe's incapacity to touch it. A military engineer who sees his fortification uninjured by the enemy's attacks, can hardly be supposed to think it is giving way if he placidly says: "I can leave that part of the works alone". My paragraphs 7 and 8 do not enlarge the contention; they merely answer points raised by Mr. Rowe in the paper to which mine was a reply. I explained before to Mr. Rowe what I thought of his Scriptural passages, and there is no "tacit confession of error" in not explaining over again. I am afraid that Mr. Rowe must look on our readers as fools when he writes:

> "In order to parry the effect of her former concession that Christianity assumes the unbelief which it condemns to be positively vicious, Mrs. Besant now declares that Christianity condemns all unbelief to be vicious."

The disingenuous assumption that I conceded that "the unbelief" condemned by Christianity was positively vicious, while some other unspecified unbelief may be non-vicious, was fully exposed in paragraph 3 of my last paper. There is not the slightest difference between my first and my second statements. I stated that Christianity damns men for unbelief, and regards unbelief as vice. It is one of the many crimes of Christianity that it metes out the same punishment to the "unrepentant" scoundrel and the "blameless philosopher" of sceptical opinions. By no writhings and twistings can Mr. Rowe escape from the cleft stick of the sweeping anathema: "He that believeth not shall be damned". It is to his credit that his conscience revolts from it, but it is a pity that he is not sufficiently frank to say plainly that he rejects the bigoted curse. Without unbelief no progress is possible; without unbelief we should remain wrapped in every superstition of the past. The unreasoning credulity which is the price of heaven is one of the worst enemies of humanity, and it is only by unbelief that Europe has risen out of the darkness of the Middle Ages, learning to despise the faith that accepts, and to honor the scepticism which demands proof as a preliminary to belief. The "signs and wonders", says Mr. Rowe, "must have been regarded by Christ as merely delusions; since his heavenly Father would not be held by him as ready to bestow genuinely miraculous powers upon 'false Christs and false prophets'". I do not know what Christ thought about "his heavenly Father", but if he did not regard him as likely to bestow genuinely miraculous powers on deceivers he knew very little about him. (I am assuming, for the sake of the argument that the Bible is reliable.) In Ezekiel xiv., 9, we read: "If the prophet be deceived when he hath spoken a thing, I the Lord have deceived that prophet"; it was Christ's "heavenly Father" who sent out "a lying spirit" to deceive Ahab to his destruction (1 Kings, xxii., 19–23); when the false prophet gives a sign or a wonder and it comes to pass, "the Lord your God proveth you" (Deut. xiii., 1–3). What can be the test of the genuine sign save its coming to pass?

Paragraph 5. My reason for quoting Martin Luther's remark about the epistle of James was to show that the flagrant contradiction between the teaching of Paul and that of James had been recognised by a sincere Christian. Mr. Rowe utterly fails to reconcile them, though he says loftily: "the assumed contradiction has been dispelled". As I have already pointed out to Mr. Rowe, those who believe that their fate for eternity is settled in this life, will necessarily lay most stress on the one thing which determines that eternal fate. Now the one thing that determines it is faith without works; not to labor the point again, the salvation of the dying thief proves that good works are not necessary to salvation. I have before said that Christianity inculcates the performance of ordinary moral duties *after* salvation has been secured by faith only; but my contention is, and Mr. Rowe has never ventured to face it, that the exaltation of faith above works as the key of salvation inevitably results in indifference to right conduct, while the easy washing away of sins in the blood of Jesus encourages people to do wrong, so royal a road being made for escape from the penalties of wrong-doing.

Paragraph 6. I deny that precepts commanding the murder of witches and idolators can ever have been useful to the most uncivilised community. A father may vary his method of training his children as they pass through the various stages of childhood and youth, but no father, save a savage, teaches his children to commit brutal crimes at any stage of their development. These precepts retarded, they did not advance, the civilisation of the race, and our own barbarous laws against witchcraft, which were put actively in force up to 1712—in which year five witches were hanged at Northampton—were admittedly based on the Mosaic code. The shocking persecutions of dissenters and heretics — which have stained every section of the Christian church since Constantine donned the imperial purple and became the first Christian ruler—were carried on in obedience to the Mosaic law endorsed by Christ. Mr. Rowe says that Christ's "limited reference"—where is the limitation?—was "to the sacrificial portion of the Mosaic law alone". This is a most convenient assumption, but no word of Christ's warrants it. Mr. Rowe objects to the words "bloodthirsty spirit" as applied to Christ and quotes some instances showing his "tenderness". But how do these avail, save as showing that he was a very contradictory character? How is the "tenderness" compatible with the description of him, "in flaming fire taking vengeance on them that know not God" (2 Thes. i., 8)? or with the torturing of his enemies with fire and brimstone for ever in his presence (Rev. xiv., 10, 11)? or with his "vesture dipped in blood", his "sharp sword" to "smite the nations", his "rod of iron" (Rev. xix., 13–21)? or his declaration: "I will tread them in mine anger, and trample them in my fury; and their blood shall be sprinkled upon my garments and I will stain all my raiment" (Is. lxiii., 3)? Or let Mr. Rowe read Deut. xxxii., 21–42, and then remember that the Jahveh who thus describes himself is the same of whom Jesus said, "I and my Father are one".

Paragraphs 7 and 8. It is hardly necessary for me to say that I utterly disagree with Professor Tyndall's opinion that the life of Christ is "incomparable". So far from Paul repudiating the principle of slavery in his epistle to Philemon, he admitted it by sending back the runaway slave, while he deliberately endorsed it in his directions to slaves in the epistles to the Ephesians and Colossians. The statement that Atheism lays a foundation for slavery is preposterous, but as we are not discussing Atheism I pass it over. While as to Max Müller's statement that the "word humanity was unknown before Christianity", I don't know about the word, but the thing was certainly known; for there were Buddhist hospitals in Ceylon—to take but a single instance—some hundreds of years before Christ was born; in Mencius we have—*pace* Max Müller—"Humanity is the heart of man; justice the path of man". "Charity . . . . is found where, from compassion for the miserable and the poor, who have none to help them, a man erects resting-places for wanderers, and drinking fountains, or provides food, raiment, medicine, for the needy" (Katha Chari).

Of the first set of answers to my five allegations, I pause a moment on 3, 4, and 5. (3). The use of the sword was by Christians against dissenters and heretics; does Mr. Rowe pretend that any Church has ever persecuted and murdered as the Christian Church has done? (4) The "proviso" of Christ is, "he that can receive it, let him receive it". (5) Mr. Rowe has proved nothing of the kind; I pointed out that Paul's argument is based on the way in which married and unmarried respectively regard the things of the world and those of the Lord. Mr. Rowe does not tell us why the argument is now invalid.

With reference to the second five allegations:

(1) I thought I should have prevented Mr. Rowe from giving the usual cant answer about spiritual poverty and hunger after righteousness by drawing his attention to verses 24 and 25 of Luke vi.; according to Mr. Rowe we must read these: "woe unto you that are rich in spirit"; "woe unto you that are full of righteousness"!

(2) Mr. Rowe apparently accepts the damnation of the majority with the cheerful view, "Serve them right". Mark is "exaggerated", a favorite word of Mr. Rowe's when he cannot otherwise explain away some indefensible statement. One cannot but wish that Jesus had been born in the West, and then he would perhaps have said what he meant.

(3) It seems to me that through this debate, Mr. Rowe has conspicuously failed to show "that humanity would immensely benefit, if Christian teachings were truly put

into practice", and most certainly his general assertion connot invalidate historical facts.

(4) Is a mere evasion of an insuperable difficulty.

(5) If God foreknows everything, how can the human will be free?

I notice that Mr. Rowe repeats his statements about hospitals, etc., but he has carefully avoided all reference to the Christian legal robbery to which I drew his attention. One sentence of his, however, I heartily endorse, and that is the one in which he invites the reader "to study afresh the teachings of Christianity". The more they are studied the better, for the more they are known the more will be understood their imperfections, their crudities, their follies. As Mr. Rowe is fond of quotations, I present him in conclusion with one from W. K. Clifford's essay on "The Unseen Universe".

"These sickly dreams of hysterical women and half-starved men, what have they to do with the sturdy strength of a wide-eyed hero who fears no foe with pen or club? This sleepless vengeance of fire upon them that have not seen and have not believed, what has it to do with the gentle patience of the investigator . . . . that will ask only consideration and not belief for anything that has not with infinite pains been solidly established? That which you keep in your hearts, my brothers, is the slender remnant of a system which has made its red mark on history, and still lives to threaten mankind. The grotesque forms of its intellectual belief have survived the discredit of its moral teaching. Of this what the kings could bear with, the nations have cut down; and what the nations left the right heart of man by man revolts against day by day. You have stretched out your hands to save the dregs of the sifted sediment of a residuum. Take heed lest you have given soil and shelter to the seed of that awful plague which has destroyed two civilisations, and but barely failed to slay such promise of good as is now struggling to live among men."

NATIONAL SECULAR SOCIETY'S TRACTS. No. 10.

THE FRUITS OF CHRISTIANITY

BY

ANNIE BESANT,

VICE-PRESIDENT OF THE NATIONAL SECULAR SOCIETY.

LONDON:

PUBLISHED FOR THE NATIONAL SECULAR SOCIETY BY THE

FREETHOUGHT PUBLISHING COMPANY,

63, FLEET STREET, E.C.

PRICE TWOPENCE.

LONDON:
PRINTED BY ANNIE BESANT AND CHARLES BRADLAUGH,
63, FLEET STREET, E.C.

THE FRUITS OF CHRISTIANITY

"BEWARE of false prophets, which come to you in sheep's clothing, but inwardly they are ravening wolves. Ye shall know them by their fruits. Do men gather grapes of thorns, or figs of thistles? Even so every good tree bringeth forth good fruit; but a corrupt tree bringeth forth evil fruit. A good tree cannot bring forth evil fruit, neither can a corrupt tree bring forth good fruit. Every tree that bringeth not forth good fruit is [should be] hewn down, and cast into the fire. Wherefore, by their fruits ye shall know them." Such was the sensible test which Jesus of Nazareth is said (Matt. vii., 15-20) to have given to his followers, that they might apply it to those who pretended to a divine mission, and thus have an infallible criterion whereby they might discern the reality or falsehood of the claim. It cannot be unwise or unfair to apply to Christianity the test of Christ, and so discover whether or no it is a message from a good and loving God, designed for the regeneration of man.

History shall be our guide to pluck for us the fruits which are to prove the goodness or the badness of the tree planted, we are told, more than eighteen centuries ago.

Three hundred years after the supposed death of the alleged founder of Christianity, a candidate for the imperial throne was converted to the faith, and became, with Christian help, sole ruler of the Roman empire. He was the buttress of his new religion; he was present at the Council of Nicæa, that settled the relative positions of the persons of the Christian Trinity; he passed laws to put down Paganism; he confiscated the property of heretics for the benefit of the orthodox; he bought converts by the thousand with gold; he poured wealth into the Church's lap, and the treasurers of public money lavished it, by his command, on the Christian bishops; all that a man and an emperor could do to strengthen a religion Constantine did for Christianity. The fruits it bore in him were clearly marked; he put off his baptism till the close of his life, so that he might sin in safety; he murdered his son; he murdered his wife; he was a cruel tyrant as emperor, and a profligate as man.

During these centuries, down to the time of the Reformation, the Greek and Roman Churches are, practically, our only representatives of Christianity, and it is their fruits which we must gather.

Nor must the admirers of "primitive Christianity" think themselves unfairly used, or speak of these Churches as corruptors of the purity of earlier times. If the writings ascribed to Paul, Peter, and Jude be claimed as belonging to the first century, the morality of Christians must, even then, have been of a very dubious character. *See* such passages as 1 Cor. v. 1. In the second century, Mosheim complains that if a person who has "no clear and distinct ideas of virtue and vice" is "a bad guide in morals," then that "title belongs indisputably to many of the Fathers," and that Christians forged writings, and committed numerous pious frauds to advance their religion. In the third century, the same writer describes the "luxury and voluptuousness" of the Christian bishops, and the similar vices of the priesthood, while in the fourth, he says, sadly, that "the Church was contaminated with shoals of profligate Christians, and that the virtuous few were, in a manner, oppressed and overwhelmed with the superior numbers of the wicked and licentious." Christianity clearly did not succeed in inducing a high standard of public morality.

Indeed, even as early as the beginning of the fifth century, Salvian, a presbyter of Marseilles, draws a black picture of his co-religionists. "Who is there," he asks, "who is not rolling in the mire of fornication? And what more? What I am about to state is grave and mournful. The very Church of God, what does it but provoke him to anger? With the exception of a very few, who fly from vice, what is almost every Christian congregation but a sink of vices? For you will find in the church scarcely one who is not either a drunkard, or a glutton, or an adulterer, or a fornicator, or a ravisher, or a robber, or a manslayer, and, what is worse than all, almost all these without limit. I put it now to the consciences of all Christian people, whether it be not so that you will barely find one who is not addicted to some of the vices and crimes I have mentioned; or, rather, who is it that is not guilty of all? Truly, you will more easily find the man who is guilty of all, than one who is guilty of none. . . . Into this shameful dissoluteness of manners is nearly the entire ecclesiastical mass so sunk, that, throughout the Christian community, it has come to be regarded as a species of sanctity if one is a little less vicious than others." (Miall's "Memoirs of Early Christianity," pp. 366, 367).

Persecution is the bitter fruit which first attracts our notice. As soon as Christianity mounted the throne, penal laws against heretics were enacted. The first stake was raised in Spain, and the first burned heretic shows darkly red in the fourth century after Christ. All meetings of the unorthodox were proscribed by Theodosius (A.D. 380-394), buildings used for their meetings became forfeit to the Emperor, and heretics were declared incapable of making wills or of receiving any advantage from the wills of others (*see* Gibbon's "Decline and Fall," vol. iii., pp. 412, 413). Death and confiscation of property were the legal penalties of Paganism, even in those early days.

In the fifth century, Hypatia, the beautiful philosopher, was seized and pulled from her chariot as she drove towards her lecture-room, was dragged into the great church of Alexandria, stripped naked, struck down, and her body cut to pieces with oyster-shells, and then burned. Her crime was that she was drawing the youth of Alexandria back to the old Pagan gods, and the monks, the army of the Christian bishop Cyril, murdered her in obedience to God's command in Ex. xxii. 20. As time went on, and conversions came in but slowly, persecution was called more vigorously to the aid of the Christian cause. Mosheim relates how Charlemagne converted the Saxons by sending armies among them, doing with fire and sword what the bishops and monks had failed to do, because they made their effort "without the aid of violence or threats" (*see* Mosheim's "Ecclesiastical History," p. 170). In the following century the Saxons were sufficiently advanced to produce some heretics, and Godeschalcus, a monk, was flogged in a council of bishops, A.D. 849, until he burned his own writings.

The Eastern branch of the Christian tree was as stained by human blood as was the Western. In Armenia, by order of the Empress Theodora, 100,000 people belonging to the Paulician heresy were seized, their property confiscated, and they themselves tortured to death.

In the tenth century the Normans, Poles, Russians, Danes and Norwegians, all embraced Christianity: the Normans, because conversion was the price demanded for a large cession of land; the Poles, because their Duke enforced penal laws against Paganism; the Danes, because conversion was imposed as a condition of peace after decisive defeat; the Norwegians, for the same reason.

The Crusades, whether against the Mahommedans or heretics, are all among the fruits of Christianity. Hallam, in his "Europe during the Middle Ages," draws the sad picture of the first crusade: "We should be warranted by contemporary writers in stating the loss of the Christians alone during this period at nearly a million; but at the least computation, it must have exceeded half that number" (p. 30). In 1099 Jerusalem was taken: a *Te Deum* resounded from the Holy City, and then the soldiers of Christ rose from their knees and went through the streets, slaying pitilessly men, women, and children. In the next century Bézières rivalled Jerusalem; it was a city of the Albigenses, and Pope Innocent III. had called for a crusade against the heretics, which "was prosecuted with every atrocious barbarity which superstition, the mother of crimes, could inspire. Languedoc, a country, for that age, flourishing and civilized, was laid waste by these desolators; her cities burned; her inhabitants swept away by fire and the sword;" in the storming of Bézières and the accompanying massacre, 60,000 persons perished, not one human being escaping. "Kill them all!" was the order given to the army; "kill them all! God will know his own" (Hallam, p. 25). These butchers carried out God's commands as recorded in Deut. xiii. 12-16. It is to this same Pope Innocent III. that we owe the establishment of the "Holy Inquisition," whose powers were committed into the hands of the Dominicans by Gregory IX. in 1223. It was only the fuller organization of the penal laws against heretics dating from the time of Constantine. St. Peter Martyr seems to have the honour of introducing burning at the stake as the special punishment of heresy: since God would burn heretics in hell for ever, it was meet that his children should burn them on this side the grave.

In Spain the Holy Office worked hard; established by Ferdinand and Isabella, A.D. 1480, during the following year it burned nearly 3000 persons in the province of Andalusia alone, and otherwise punished another 17,000; 31,912 persons were burned alive by it in Spain during the 236 years of its fullest power; in addition to these it heavily punished 291,450 human beings. In one year 950 persons were burned alive in Ciudad Real. The last woman burned in Spain was an unfortunate creature accused of making a contract with the devil; she suffered at Seville, on November 7, 1781, only ninety-six years ago. In 1492, the Jews were driven out of Spain, under penalty of death if they returned; the Spanish clergy preached against them in the open squares; all help was denied them; they died like sheep as they struggled along the roads out of Spain. In 1502, the Moors were the victims; they, too, were driven out of the land of their birth, and no less than 3,000,000 harmless, peaceful citizens were thus exiled by Christianity.

In the Netherlands, Alva was a shining light of the Church; he was sent there to extirpate heresy, and right bloodily he worked at his task. He "boasted that, in the five or six years of his administration, he had put to death in cold blood more than 18,000 . . . . we know, from other sources, that in one year more than 8000 were either executed or burned" (Buckle's "History of Civilization," vol. ii. p. 451). The Prince of Orange estimated that, up to the year 1566, 50,000 persons had been put to death in obedience to the edicts (*See Ibid.*, note).

The massacre of St. Bartholomew is another fruit of the Christian tree. At Paris, Aug. 24, 1572, the Huguenots were suddenly attacked, and over 1400 persons were slain, the king, from his palace window, shooting at the flying fugitives. A church bell gave the signal for the massacre, and the cross was the sign of the murderers. Pope Gregory XIII. struck a medal to commemorate the event, and chanted a grand *Te Deum* of gratitude. France has many another blood-stained page to show. The *dragonnades*, under Louis XIV., give us some of the most piteous tales of Christian persecution. Soldiers were let loose on the Huguenot population with permission to do all save actually slay: "Afterwards they fall upon the Protestants (A.D. 1685); and there was no wickedness, though never so horrid, which they did not put in practice, that they might enforce them to change their religion. They bound them as criminals are when they be put to the rack; and in that posture, putting a funnel into their mouths, they poured wine down their throats till its fumes had deprived them of their reason and they had in that condition made them consent to become Catholics. Some they stripped stark naked, and, after they had offered them a thousand indignities, they stuck them with pins from head to foot; they cut them with pen-knives, tore them by the noses with red-hot pincers, and dragged them upon the rooms till they promised to become Roman Catholics, or till the doleful outcries of these poor tormented creatures, calling upon God for mercy, constrained them to let them go. In some places they tied fathers and husbands to the bed-posts, and ravished their wives and daughters before their eyes. . . . From others they pluck off the nails of their hands and toes, which must needs cause an intolerable pain. They burnt the feet of others; they blew up men and women with bellows till they were ready to burst in pieces. If these horrid usages could not prevail upon them to violate their consciences and abandon their religion, they did then imprison them in close and noisome dungeons, in which they exercised all kinds of inhumanities upon them" (Quick's "Synodicon," as quoted in Buckle). Some of the barbarities related by Benoît are too horrible to translate: every foul outrage, especially on women, that a filthy imagination could suggest, was practised on these unhappy Protestants to attract them into the Roman Church.

Single names stand out brightly among the victims of Christianity. Ceccus Asculanus, a physician, was burned in A.D. 1337, at Florence, in consequence of some misunderstood mechanical experiments. John Huss was burned A.D. 1415, and his friend, Jerome, in 1416, for heresy. Savonarola, a monk, was tortured and burned in A.D. 1498, for trying to reform abuses. Giordano Bruno was burned at Rome, A.D. 1600, for scientific heresy; and Vanini had his tongue torn out, and was burned at Toulouse, A.D. 1619, for philosophy and heresy.

Protestant Christianity began to persecute shortly after its birth. Servetus, heretic as to the Trinity, and Gruet, heretic as to Christianity as a whole, were both burned in Switzerland, at the instigation of Calvin; and Gentilis, a Unitarian, was put to death at Berne, A.D. 1566. In England, the Reformation began by impartial burning of both sides, and the "Six Articles" were made the rule of faith. Soon after they were passed, 500 persons were in gaol, and Protestants and Catholics were tied back to back, and dragged to execution on the same hurdles. The Protestants got the upper hand under Edward VI., and a commission was granted to Archbishop Cranmer—just then a Protestant—"to examine and search after all Anabaptists, heretics, or contemners of the book of Common Prayer." Joan Bocher and Van Paris were burned alive, and many others were hanged or beheaded. Under Mary, the Catholics had again a turn, and they then killed Protestants. About 277 persons were burned alive between 1555 and 1558, 55 of whom were women and 4 were children. Under Elizabeth, the Protestants triumphed, and Roman Catholics and Puritans both suffered at the hands of the now established Reformed Episcopal Church. A court of ecclesiastical commission was instituted, and fine and imprisonment fell on all nonconformists. Continued refusal to attend public worship was, in 1593, made punishable with death. Racking, hanging, ripping up, quartering, these were the weapons used to convert the English people to Protestantism. Lingard thus describes the rack: "A large open frame of oak, raised three feet from the ground. The prisoner was laid under it, on his back, on the floor. His wrists and ankles were attached by cords to two rollers at the ends of the frame: these were moved by levers in opposite directions till the body rose to a level with the frame. Questions were then put, and if the answers did not prove satisfactory, the sufferer was stretched more and more till the bones started from their sockets." This was the gentle method in which Protestants converted Catholics under Elizabeth. The last people burned alive in England for heresy were two men, named Legat and Whitman, who suffered A.D. 1611.

In Ireland, Protestantism showed itself worthy of the Christianity of which it was a branch. The penal laws against Catholics are among the most disgraceful pages of history.

When the English altered their creed, the Irish utterly refused to follow their conquerors in their change of religion, and clung with passionate devotion to the faith of their fathers. A fierce effort was made to compel conversion. All priests were expelled the realm under pain of hanging, drawing, and quartering; and to conceal a priest was death. A Papist who refused to attend the reformed public worship was fined, imprisoned, and forbidden, when set free, to go more than five miles away from his house. In 1694, Roman Catholics were forbidden to educate their children abroad; and in 1709, Papists were forbidden to teach either privately or publicly, so that Roman Catholic children were left, perforce, without education. In 1703, it was enacted that any Papist child turning Protestant, should inherit all his father's property, to the exclusion of the rest of the family. No Papist might own land, nor have a lease of more than 31 years. If the heir of a Protestant were a Papist he was passed over, and the heritage went to the nearest Protestant relative. If a Papist cultivated his land so as to make a profit exceeding one third of the rent, he forfeited the farm, and it was given to the Protestant who informed against him. A Papist was not allowed to own a horse worth more than £5, and a Protestant discovering him with a more valuable animal was rewarded by becoming its possessor, on the payment of the £5. These acts were only repealed in 1829, and then, not from regretful shame, but from fear of revolution.

In Scotland, Christianity bore the same fruits. The Cameronians were hunted down in every direction; their religious meetings were broken up by soldiers, and they were mercilessly cut down as they fled. Sharp, the Archbishop of St. Andrew's, instituted an ecclesiastical court, that banished its victims to the most unhealthy settlements. Soldiers were turned loose on the people, and the horrors of the *dragonnades* of Louis were repeated by the troops of Charles II. "The fairest parts of Western Scotland were devastated, houses burned, men tortured, women ravished. In 1670 an Act of Parliament was passed, declaring that whoever preached in the fields without permission should be put to death. Some lawyers were found bold enough to defend innocent men when they were tried for their lives. It was, therefore, determined to silence them also, and in 1674, a great part of the Faculty of Advocates was expelled from Edinburgh. In 1678, by the express command of Government, the Highlanders were brought down from their mountains, and, during three months, were encouraged to slay, plunder, and burn, at their pleasure, the inhabitants of the most populous and industrious parts of Scotland. Eight thousand armed Highlanders, invited by the English Government, and receiving beforehand an indemnity for every excess, were left to work their will upon the towns and villages of Western Scotland. They spared neither age nor sex. They deprived the people of their property; they even stripped them of their clothes, and sent them out naked to die in the fields. Upon many they inflicted the most horrible tortures. Children, torn from their mothers, were foully abused; while both mothers and daughters were subjected to a fate compared to which death would have been a joyful alternative" (Buckle, vol. iii., 144-146). In a note, Buckle quotes from Wodrow's "Church of Scotland:" A woman was "sentenced to be let down into a deep pit, under the house of the dean, full of toads and other vile creatures. Her shrieks thence were heard at a great distance." Two men "were bound together with cords, and hanged up by their thumbs to a tree, there to hang all night." A woman was seized and bound, and "they put lighted matches between her fingers for several hours. The torture and pain made her almost distracted; she lost one of her hands, and in a few days died." Thus did Protestants treat Protestants in Scotland. On the other hand, Roman Catholics met with the same harsh treatment. The Scotch Parliament decreed death against them, as idolaters, it being a "religious obligation to execute them," and John Knox declared that "the people are bound in conscience to put to death the queen, along with all her priests."

In France, the Huguenots, in districts where they were strong, showed themselves active persecutors of the Roman Catholics. They attacked the Catholic processions, interrupted the funerals, and insulted the priests in La Rochelle; they forbade the exercise of the Roman religion, and would not allow the Catholics the use of a single church. In 1619, they forbade all preaching, within the limits of Protestant towns, of any minister commissioned by a bishop, and forbade Protestants to intermarry with Roman Catholics, or to be present at any Catholic ceremony; they seized the goods of the Catholic priests. (*See* Buckle, vol. ii. 56—62).

Protestant Christianity in America showed itself worthy of the root whence it sprang. The Quakers were imprisoned, and were flogged from village to village. The Blue Laws of Connecticut remain as a monument of Christian cruelty among those who had fled from England to obtain liberty of conscience for themselves.

These are but a few of the horrible persecutions which are among the most terrible of the fruits of Christianity, and these spring from trees which have their roots in Holy Writ, and which adorn every garden planted by the Lord.

But Christianity is not only cruel; it also "loves darkness rather than light," because ignorance is the con dition of its authority. It has carried on a long crusade against knowledge, and has delayed, by many a long year, the onward march of the human race. In the earliest days, "not many wise men," "not many learned," were called; the "wisdom of this world" was despised by the new Christians, while, on the other hand, the wise and thoughtful among the Greeks and the Romans treated with contempt the superstition which spread almost exclusively among the ignorant and the enslaved barbarians. Of the second century Mosheim writes: "The number of learned men among the Christians, which was very small in the preceding century, grew considerably in this," but he complains that there was a party in the Church which "were for banishing all argumentation and philosophy from the limits of the Church," and that the defenders of Christianity were mostly "destitute of penetration, learning, order, application, and force." In the third century, the sciences had "lost all their vigour and all their lustre," while in the fourth, which saw some of the leading doctors of the Church, the controversial writings were "negligent of order in their compositions," "seldom define their terms, and pour out their pious, but incoherent ideas, in fortuitous combinations, just as they come uppermost." It was in vain that the emperors, inheriting the Pagan traditions, founded schools and colleges; misled by their Christianity, they placed them under the care of the bishops, and some of these being indolent, and others bitterly averse to "every sort of learning and superstition," it followed that "Greek literature was almost everywhere neglected," and "philosophy fared still worse than literature, for it was entirely banished from all the seminaries which were under the inspection and government of the ecclesiastical order." In the seventh century, "the bishops in general were so illiterate, that few of that body were capable of composing the discourses which they delivered to the people;" and it was not until the Arabians arose and revived learning, that any beams of knowledge broke through the thick black fog of Christianity. In the tenth century their knowledge began to filter into Europe, and Mahommedans taught Christian students the elements of Greek learning. So far had Christianity killed out the old astronomical science that for 1500 years Christianity produced no astronomer; and when Copernicus, on his deathbed, left his book to the world, Christianity hunted down those who dared to follow him. The book was burned, its author being beyond reach of the flames; Galileo was forced to recant by the Inquisition. In Spain, the Moors being expelled, learning died away, Torquemada destroying Hebrew books wherever he could find them, and burning, at Salamanca, 6000 volumes of Oriental literature; 119 learned men were thrown into the dungeons of the Inquisition in Spain—not for teaching heresy, but for teaching science. In France, the Huguenots forbade the study of Greek and of chemistry, and allowed no book to be printed without the sanction of the Church. The Roman Church, in the same country, swept away all books that taught learning of any kind. Buffon, Darigrand, and Garlon met with the same fate as Voltaire, Diderot, and Helvetius. Each new discovery in science was met with the cry of "heresy" or "materialism;" and every step science has made has been won against the fiercest opposition. To-day the hatred is as bitter, though less powerful. Huxley, Darwin, Clifford, Tyndall, Lyell—these men are the *bêtes noires* of Christianity, although public admiration shields them from the fate of their predecessors. All advances in education have been made against Christianity. Robert Owen set the example of infant schools, and the party of secular education forced the Education Act through Parliament in the teeth of Church opposition.

How Christianity has darkened the innocent brightness of the world is known to every student. Roman Catholic Christianity made a miserable life a holy life, but was content to leave it to the "religious" only: Protestant Christianity forced it on all alike. The Swiss Calvinists set the example of austerity, and the French Huguenots quickly followed. They forbade theatres, private theatricals, dancing, gay dresses, conjuring, puppet-shows, &c., making gloom synonymous with piety. In Scotland, the Protestants made the Sunday a misery: good Christians might not visit a friend, bathe, or shave, water vegetables, ride, walk, sit at the house-door. Holidays, amusements, festive gatherings, shows, games, all were unlawful. If people transgressed, they "became unruly sons of the Church, and were liable to be imprisoned, to be fined, or to be whipped, or to be branded with a hot iron, or to do penance before the whole congregation" (Buckle, vol. iii. p. 262). Buckle gives several pages to the manufactured "sins" of Protestant Christianity, and winds up by saying:—"Men in their daily actions, and in their very looks, became troubled.

melancholy, and ascetic. Their countenance soured, and was downcast. Not only their opinions, but their gait, their demeanour, their voice, their general aspect, were influenced by that deadly blight which nipped all that was genial and warm. . . . . Thus it was that the national character of the Scotch was, in the seventeenth century, dwarfed and mutilated."

The limits of this brief tract will not permit me to gather more of the fruits of Christianity; but these suffice, at least, to afford some test of the tree which has borne them all. Black, bitter, and poisonous are these fruits; and I appeal to the words of Christ as a fair criticism of the religion from whence they have sprung—

> "A corrupt tree bringeth forth evil fruit.
> "A good tree cannot bring forth evil fruit."

NATIONAL SECULAR SOCIETY.

OFFICES:

HALL OF SCIENCE, 142, OLD STREET, E.C.

PRESIDENT:

CHARLES BRADLAUGH, 20, Circus Road, St. John's Wood, N.W.

SECRETARY:

ROBERT FORDER, 6, Cambridge Terrace, Islington, N.

PRINCIPLES AND OBJECTS.

The National Secular Society has been formed to maintain the principles and rights of Freethought, and to direct their application to the Secular improvement of this life.

By the principle of Freethought is meant the exercise of the understanding upon relevant facts, and independently of penal or priestly intimidation.

By the rights of Freethought are meant the liberty of free criticism for the security of truth, and the liberty of free publicity for the extension of truth.

Secularism relates to the present existence of man, and to actions the issue of which can be tested by experience.

It declares that the promotion of human improvement and happiness is the highest duty, and that morality is to be tested by utility.

That, in order to promote effectually the improvement and happiness of mankind, every individual of the human family ought to be well placed and well instructed, and that all who are of a suitable age ought to be usefully employed for their own and the general good.

That human improvement and happiness cannot be effectually promoted without civil and religious liberty; and that, therefore, it is the duty of every individual to actively attack all barriers to equal freedom of thought and utterance for all upon political, theological, and social subjects.

A Secularist is one who deduces his moral duties from considerations which pertain to this life, and who, practically recognising the above duties, devotes himself to the promotion of the general good.

The object of the National Secular Society is to disseminate the above principles by every legitimate means in its power.

MEMBERSHIP.

Any person may, in the discretion of the Executive, be admitted a member of this Society, who shall sign a form of Declaration as follows:—

"I am desirous of joining the National Secular Society, in order to extend its principles; and I pledge myself to do my best, if admitted as a member, to co-operate with my fellow-members to attain the objects of this Association."

Name..

Address...

Occupation..

Active or Passive ....

Dated this.............*day of*.....................18.....

This Declaration, signed by the candidate, shall be transmitted to the Secretary, with one shilling for a quarter's subscription; and, if the Executive accept the candidate, a certificate of membership will be issued, the total subscription being four shillings per year. Persons unable to pay this subscription may be enrolled free on satisfying the Executive that they do good Secular work. Affiliated Societies whose members join the National Secular Society shall only pay one-third of the above subscription.

The National Secular Society's Tracts may be obtained from the Secretary, Mr. R. Forder, 6, Cambridge Terrace, Islington, N., or from the Freethought Publishing Company, 63, Fleet Street, E.C. The following Tracts have been issued:—

1. Address to Christians. 1 page.
2. Who was Jesus? 1 page.
3. Secular Morality. 2 pages.
4. The Bible and Woman. 2 pages.
5. Secular Teachings. 2 pages.
6. Secular Work. 2 pages.
7. What is Secularism? 2 pages.
8. Who are the Secularists? 2 pages.
9. Secular Responsibility. 2 pages.

The Fruits of Christianity. 16 pages.

The first 9 may be had in assorted packets of 50 for 4d. post free; or of 100 for 7½d. post free. A specimen packet, post free, 1½d. Any special tract may be had at the same rate.

CHRISTIAN PROGRESS.

BY

ANNIE BESANT.

PRICE TWOPENCE.

LONDON
FREETHOUGHT PUBLISHING COMPANY,
63 FLEET STREET E C.

1890.

LONDON:
PRINTED BY CHARLES BRADLAUGH AND ANNIE BESANT,
63 FLEET STREET, E.C.

CHRISTIAN PROGRESS.

If Christianity be a divine revelation, supernaturally bestowed upon man, it is clear that the "faith once delivered to the saints" must be unchanging, unimprovable, perfect. A revelation from God cannot be improved on by man, and the "deposit" must be handed on from generation to generation, neither increasing nor diminishing in amount. The doctrines taught by Christ and his apostles must be taught by their successors until "the end" come, and English Christians of to-day be one in faith with the whole great Church Catholic from the first to the nineteenth century. I do not intend to say that every form, every custom, every rite, of every Christian church in every century must be identical; the accidents may vary, but the substance must remain the same. On grave points of doctrine, opposing views cannot both be accurate: on weighty matters of faith contradictory opinions cannot both be right. The nature of the Deity worshipped, of the worship acceptable to him, the destiny of the human race—these, at least, must be one in their main outline; the fall of man, God's plan of redemption—these, at least, must be "of faith."

But if there be one fact concerning Christianity more clear in history than another, it is that there has not been one solitary doctrine which has been the unchanging inheritance of the Christian world. Whether God were a Trinity in Unity, or a Unity without distinction of persons, even this fundamental doctrine was doubtful during the first few centuries after Christ. For many a long year the Unitarian and the Trinitarian theories struggled for the mastery, until the latter triumphed and became the "Catholic" doctrine. The Christianities of the first centuries, of the dark ages, of the Reformation period, of the eighteenth century, and of our own time, are not the same; the main characteristics of the creed vary with each new development of civilisation, and the heresy slain in one century rises as the faith of the next. This gradual process of purification and development, necessary before the Christianity of the monks of the Thebaïd could become the Christianity of Farrar and of Stanley, is one which would be wholly reasonable and admirable were Christianity a theory of life slowly elaborated by man during his upward march; but the fact is fatal to Christianity as an order of life revealed by a supreme being; to admit it is to say that the statue given to men as a model, sculptured by God, is capable of being improved and beautified by the chisel of man.

A curious book which has fallen into my hands affords an admirable microcosm of Christianity. The spirit of a creed is revealed more plainly, perhaps, in its songs than in anything else; and the hymns of the Christian churches may be studied as—to use some words in my book's preface—"a kind of ecclesiastical history." The book in question is entitled: "A Collection of Hymns of the Children of God in all Ages, from the Beginning till Now;" it was printed in London in the year 1754, and the hymns are arranged in chronological order. We have (1) Anthems from the Bible; (2) Scripture put into metre; (3) Hymns of the Primitive Church; (4) Hymns of the Ancient Waldenses, and the Bohemian and Moravian Brethren; (5) Hymns of the sixteenth, seventeenth, and eighteenth centuries. I propose to glance at these, and see if they can be said to represent, in any fashion, the Christianity of to-day; or whether, on the contrary, Christianity has not, since then, advanced many a mile on the road towards civilization.

Of the "Anthems from the Bible" little need be said: one is a long extract from the "Song of Solomon," beginning:

"Let him kiss me with the kisses of his mouth,"

and proceeding in a strain to which Mr. Collette's attention should be drawn, as being calculated to excite and deprave the young.

Some of the Scripture hymns are quaint. They are founded on incidents recorded in the Bible; thus, the hymn relating the visit of the shepherds to the infant Jesus, concludes:

"Dearest Jesus! do thou kiss us,
Then we too will gladly tell
To each stranger, see who lies there,
It is ev'n Immanuel."

Matt. xxiii. 37, is thus versified:

"Display thy both wings over
Thy chickens and them cover,
O Jesu, Saviour mild!
If devils would disturb 'em,
Let holy angels curb 'em,
And bid them never touch thy child."

Mark xvi. 18, is translated with a faith that is indeed great:

"Should any pois'nous snake
Disturb you in your preaching,
Bid it the place forsake,
And go ye on with teaching;
Should one that bears you grudge,
Worse fumes than arsenic
Within your body lodge,
It shan't ev'n make you sick."

There is a realism about this verse that shows the robust nature of the ancient Christian belief in the literal truth of the Bible. How degenerate are the Christians of our own day!

The hymns of the primitive church are somewhat useful, as popularising the views of the "Christian Fathers," for they are mostly versifications of the old writings of the church, now so little read. It is strange—in the light of after events—to hear Clement of Alexandria speak of Christians as a "a race pacific," while the Æthiopic church sings of

". . . . the church by Thee combined
The apostolic, *that can't be disjoined.*"

If only the Christians of that day could have glanced into the future, and seen all the sects that can't be united!

In these hymns we also find the revolting coarseness of expression from which modern Christianity has only partially freed herself. Thus we have:

"Thy Blood sweat, dear Saviour,
Rain on me like water;
For all the world over
Nought can bless one better:
O Sweat's dear flood! O holy Blood!"

From this time onwards we have, in metrical form, the most offensive doctrines of Christianity: Redemption by blood, God's wrath to man, man's wicked nature, the substitutionary atonement wrought by Christ—all these doctrines, which modern Christianity is covering decently with fig-leaves, show themselves in their original nakedness and are not ashamed.

> "Man is by nature spoiled throughout, full of corruption,
> And we have all caught the infection,
> Which is that dreadful infatuation,
> An inborn and an universal depravation."

How people, who believed this, could reconcile it to their consciences to bring such horrible baby-monsters of iniquity into the world, is one of the mysteries of the faith; for babies are included in so many words:

> "I do believe, since Adam's fall,
> That mankind are by nature all,
> Both father, mother, and each child,
> Nothing but sin, throughout defiled.
>
> They from the very womb are fraught
> With inclinations bad and naught;
> Belief in God, on t'other side,
> And God's true fear have in them dy'd."

The poor babies, however, have a chance:

> "Of Baptism our belief is this:
> It truly necessary is,
> Since God thereby to sinner's race
> Has thought fit to hold forth his grace.
>
> And hence ev'n little children we
> Baptise in Jesu's death most free;
> Them to the Lord we thus present,
> Who then a child sees with content."

Eternal punishment was, of course, an article of faith:

> "But those who're wicked and profane,
> (And devils, too) go into pain,
> Eternal punishment in hell,
> As scabbed sheep, to bear and feel.
>
> We blame, then, those who teach and vent,
> That whoso into hell is sent,
> Or man or devil, must not so
> Eternal Torment undergo."

The Canon Farrar of that day would have found his pulpit in a prison, not in Westminster Abbey.

A number of the articles of the English Church are next presented to us, clad in verse, and in these we have some of the most objectionable of Christian doctrines. It is difficult to understand why modern and enlightened Christians permit the "forty stripes save one" still to be laid on the backs of their clergy. Among these sixteenth-century hymns are some quaint conceits, such as representing the wound made by the spear in Christ's side as a "post-bag," wherein letters may be dropped addressed to the Father; or again:

> "'I am the door,' said Christ; the spear's sad art
> Now hath unlocked him at the very heart."

Or—

> "The Saviour pressed to death, there ran
> Out of his sacred wounds
> That wine, which glads the heart of man,
> And all his foes confounds."

So near to the time of Luther, we cannot be surprised to find the substitution of Christ for the sinner, and the worthlessness of good works much insisted on:

> "What greater glory could there be
> Than to be cloath'd with God?
> He drew his skin upon my skin,
> His blood upon my blood."

One sings that if he had fed the hungry, and clothed the naked, and reared the orphan, it would have been of no avail, for

> "Nothing was precious in God's sight,
> But God's own precious blood;
> Had he not dy'd, my sentence yet
> In perfect force had stood."

One more gem must be selected before we leave the sixteenth century: it describes Christ's agony in the garden:

> "Like melting wax, rivers of blood
> His very heart sweats from within,
> Thro' the pure strainer of his skin;
> Bubbling all o'er his body stood."

In the seventeenth century we find, here and there, a hymn of higher tone, such as the well-known:

> "When all Thy mercies, O my God."

But the mass still remains coarse, and "breathing out slaughter" in tone. Christ's "wounds" are still the main inspiration:

> "As small birds use a hole to chuse
> In hollow tree for cover,
> When whirlwinds blow, when hail and snow
> O'er man and beast doth hover;

So I to thee, Lord Christ, do flee,
Within thy wounds retired;
When sin and death did stop my breath,
Here I again respired."

Or—

"Thy blood shall of my wedding dress
Be then the only splendour."

Here is a picture of God, as seen by Christ in Gethsemane:

"He saw that face, whose very sight
Cheers angels with its beatific light,
Contracted now into a dreadful frown,

All cloath'd with thunder, big with death,
And showers of hot burning wrath,
Which shortly must be poured down."

And this is "our Father in heaven," whom we are to love, and in whose goodness we are to believe!

Quite different is the following love song, which sung to a good jig—*à la* Sankey—would be really refreshing after the wounds-and-death series.

"What though the world foameth and rageth with fury!
I'll give to my beautiful Jesus the glory!
I roundly declare it; I'll know nothing ever,
But only to kiss my dear crucified Saviour.

My Jesus takes notice of hearts for him pining,
He sweetens their grief while round him they are twining:
All this I've experienc'd, therefore I will hold him,
I'll cling round my Jesus, my arms shall enfold him.

Look yonder, my Jesus comes freely to meet me;
He burneth for love, he will amorously greet me:
O love! what in all the world can better please us?
Who'd not with full purpose of heart cleave to Jesus?"

The love of the singer of this can certainly not be accused of coldness.

The eighteenth-century hymns form nearly one half of our book, and are a collection of all the special favourites of that time; many do not err on the side of brevity, and we find twenty-four, thirty-six, and even more verses in a single hymn. Let us hope that, like some of the Scotch Presbyterians, the pious singers sat during their minstrelsy. The poetry still remains very imperfect, and curious, indeed, must have been the ears who were satisfied with such rhythm (?) as:

"Hence 'tis, that the Lord's own bosom friend,
Who God-word and Lambkin still combined,

All mankind in Atheism so hath comprized,
Who'll not the Son to own be advised
As God and Man."

It may be that those truly Christian souls regarded musical verses as savouring too strongly of the world to be meet for the lips of the godly. Art, poetry, music, all these are of the earth, earthy; and Christians of the sterner sort—who ever remember that it is written of those who love the world that the love of the Father is not in them—are always enemies of the beautiful, and turn away their eyes from beholding the attractive charms of delicate and polished grace.

We find our eighteenth-century friends gloating over the "blood" as ravenously as those of an earlier date. One gentle creature sings:

"I'll live and dwell by this blest flood,
The flowing stream of Jesu's blood."

Living by this river, however, is not enough: the Christian needs more:

"Jesus, the hungry sinner's Feast,
Jesus, the sinner's only good;
This will we only thirst to taste,
The Quintessence of Jesu's blood."

Living beside blood; drinking blood. What next? The Christian answers:

"Let my heart keep swimming
In thy purple gore,
And be hourly feeding
On each wound and sore."

The blood next turns into glue:

"When in his blood I saw him swim,
A small drop I did get;
This glued him to me, me to him,
The first time that we met."

Nor are its uses yet exhausted:

"The Saviour's blood and righteousness
My fin'ry is, my wedding dress."

The blood is also used for washing in:

"And no drop so small
Then did from Him fall
Which can't wash us all."

If money is wanted, the blood

"Fills all the treasuries divine,
And is in heaven still current coin.

The bride, being now washed in, dressed in, and drinking blood, comes to the bridegroom, and embraces him "with pleasure":

"He is so precious in her eye
His blood such joys doth lend her,
She thinks no thing in earth or sky
Can sparkle with such splendor;
Quite melted she gazes, and looks in each wound,
And bows 'fore his bleeding sceptre;
She's glad to embrace him, in blood-grace abound,
Since there she only finds pasture."

The climax is reached in a litany:—

"Thy sweat in thy agony
Bedew our souls and bodies!
The bloody gore from thy body
Wash our feet!
Besweated hair
Wipe them!
The pale lips
Kiss us upon the heart!
O bespittled cheeks!
That the Father may not spit on us!
Mouth, venting moisture,
Let none be spued out by thee!"

After all this, it is scarcely necessary for a Christian to tell us:

"Thy wounds and blood,
My Lord and God,
With these shall be my conversation.
On these shall be my meditation,
Till I come to see
Thee."

Pah! the idea is absolutely sickening; and yet I might print page after page of such extracts. There is scarcely a hymn among the 460 in this second half of the book which is not full of blood. But it is, plainly, only our blindness and hardness of heart which prevents us from enjoying the idea, for:

"How can a sinner hear these words:
Grace, Jesus, Blood, and Wounds,
And not discern that harmony,
Which from each word resounds?"

The harmony is not audible to me, so clearly I have no ear for this kind of music.

What sort of creatures are they who so rejoice in these ghastly charnel-house horrors? Naturally they are worms:

"What are we? little hearts;
In Jesu's blood so pure,
Worms swimming on secure,
Enamour'd with his four nail-prints fair."

Again:

"Hear what thy worms are telling,
See how their veins are swelling.

Again:

"I, little worm so poor,
Quite spoil'd through sin and stained,
Yet by my Lamb's red gore
And bloody sweat regained."

The pitiable state of degradation which this self-abasement produces is seen in the whole mental tone of these hymns. There is in them no manliness, no joyous self-reliance, no hearty courage, only a cringing craven beseeching for mercy:

"O tender mercy, glorious grace,
To save a curs'd and damned race!
The Father gave his only Son,
To bleed and die for slaves undone."

Again:

"We all with deepest shame here blush;
To grace we have no right nor plea,
But this, that thou bestow'st it free;
We're humbled, prostrate in the dust."

The lowest depth of nastiness is reached in a long hymn, from which we offer the two following stanzas as the *ne plus ultra* of repulsiveness:

"Our husband's side-wound is, indeed,
The Queen of all his wounds;
On this the little Pidgeons feed,
Whom cross's air surrounds.
There they fly in and out and sing,
Side's blood is seen on every wing,
The bill that picks the side-hole's floor,
Is red of blood all o'er.

Blest flock in the cross's atmosphere,
You smell of Jesu's grave;
The vapours of his corpse so dear
Are the perfume you have.
It's scent is penetrant and sweet!
When you each other kiss and greet,
This scent discovers that you were
To Jesu's body near."

Is there one Christian congregation which would now sing this disgusting hymn? The very lowest and most ignorant of ranters would loathe it. The general ghastliness of thought is relieved, here and there, by verses which are purely funny, such as:

"Then evermore be
An husband to me,
My king who me bought!
Thy little point make me, thy atom, thy nought."

Or:

"In his chair he seats himself who rules us,
And as soon as kissing's over, schools us.

Or:

"Gentle wounds of Jesus,
So mild and pretty,
There's nothing like you sure in any city,
To suit us babes."

Or:

"Now here the thought comes in my heart,
Might I a babe abide!
And throughout in the baby-cart,
My course determin'd ride."

Or:

"Our God the Lamb
Is still the same;
Whate'er he says,
Most surely comes to pass.
Who of the negroes hears,
Nigh swears,
'A church can ne'er be formed there.'
Speak thou, O Lamb!
Thou wert a curse for Ham."

The following is wholly incomprehensible to me; but perhaps it may be full of pious beauty to some Christian soul:

"Let God Father's Daughter-in-law throbbing
By this sound but touched be,
She awakes, tho' love her breath half stopping,
Out of her deep liturgy,
To the blood and water which once spouted
From that body's temple now saluted;
And lo! his own heart's canal
Blood in the cov'nant cup lets fall.
With what suffrage of celestial voices
Does *efflavit animum*
Turn to bathing in the side's abysses!
Heavenly concert yet be dumb,

Till the corpse's bees have had full measure,
Their rose garden traversing at leisure
With a glad and balmy hum,
Ave! Latus saucium!

Who "God Father's Daughter-in-law" may be, and why she throbs, there is nothing to show. I give it up. Well may these Christians pray, in a litany to Jesus:

"Thy meritorious not knowing things
Bridle our curiosity!
Thy surprising simplicity
Make us loath reasoning!

It needs a simplicity very surprising to sing the above.

Another class of hymns is rather difficult to deal with, being piously indelicate to a remarkable extent. Some of these are quite unprintable in these pages, for they need much faith to purify them, and I fear our readers might not all have sufficient. Some idea of these may be gained from the moderately—*very* moderately—decent ones subjoined. The ruling idea is that of the marriage between Christ and his Church, and no kind of delicacy is felt as to details. It is instructive to note how nearly allied are spirituality and sensuality, and how easily love of God slips into the latter. More refined examples of the same curious fact may be found in books of devotion of the present High Church school. Here the feeling is coarser:

"What an unction the Lamb's wife
Feels within her body,
When God's blood, the sap of life,
With its powers is ready.
Tender shudd'ring of her frame,
Which the mortal members
For full union with the Lamb
Apt and able renders."

"I still perceive his spousal bliss,
Dear hearts! I feel; but how it is,
Now my dear husband me has bless'd,
Cannot in words be well express'd;
He loved me, O! so deep,
I should be still asleep
. . . .
And I already count the days,
To be again so blessed,
So greeted, so embraced."

"Thousand Magd'len kisses, Lamb and Saviour
Take from me, from head to feet all over;
All thy skin, each pore and hair,
Take of my salutes its share."

Any sort of comment on these would be superfluous, and they are gems of purity compared with many in the collection.

The marriage theory laid down in this book is curious and is worth noting. In a long marriage hymn it is explained that, "ere sex did rise," God had chosen all souls to be "his alone," and of them he is "the Lord and husband;" but as this betrothal could only be "in faith" until after death, God divided his bride into two, and sent her forth into the world as male and female; but as all souls are the bride of Christ, the human husbands are only Christ's representatives, and

"Our present proxy-marriages
Are done in Jesu's holy name."

The male sex appears to end at death, and—not being godly—I do not find the language used very attractive: the suggestions conveyed by it are—to the ungodly—simply revolting.

When this book was issued, the compiler asked:

"Should an Historiographer
Arise some future day,
Who all events and men with care
Would in just light display,
And should his theme church matters be
Of the now current century,"
. . .

would he take as a guide such a book as this we have been turning over? If so, thinks our writer,

"He'll find a sav'ry store,
Which he with rapture can imbibe.
If he's a heav'n instructed scribe."

Not being a "heav'n instructed scribe," I cannot say that I find the book very "savory;" but I do find it very instructive. No sect of the present day would condescend to use these hymns. Even Moody and Sankey, nasty as they are in their praises of "the blood," would turn away in disgust from these coarse gloatings over it. The most uneducated Christian would not now venture to sing these amorous canticles to the God whom he worships. The whole tone of the age would make it impossible for any congregation to reprint and use some of these hymns. Christianity, spite of itself, is moulded by the civilisation in the midst of which it lives.

It is useful to glance back and see the progress that has been made, even during the course of one brief century. As science has advanced it has raised the whole tone of society, and, with the society, has raised the Christianity. The thoughtful, pure, intellectual Christianity of a Stanley would, three hundred years ago, have been branded as heresy, and would have been expiated at the stake. To-day, Christians are angry if some of their old beliefs are dragged out of the congenial darkness in which they hide. As education progresses, the same process will be repeated, and some of the coarser doctrines left will also be covered with darkness, and the Christians of fifty years hence will look back at them with the shame and the disgust with which educated Christians of to-day regard these hymns of a century ago. Freethinkers who attack Christian doctrines are only born a century or so too soon, and may fight on fearlessly, knowing that time is on their side.